The Lesser of Two Evils

The Lesser

Eastern European Jewry

Dov Levin

# of Two Evils

Under Soviet Rule, 1939–1941

Translated by Naftali Greenwood
with a Foreword by
Mordechai Altshuler

Philadelphia   Jerusalem 5755 / 1995

The Jewish Publication Society

Library of Congress Cataloging-in Publication Data

Levin, Dov, 1925 Jan. 27–
(Tekufa be' sograim, English)
The lesser of two evils: Eastern European Jewry under Soviet
rule. 1939-1941/ Dov Levin: translated by Naftali Greenwood: with
a foreword by Mordechai Altschuler.
p. cm.
1. Jews — Poland — History — 20th century. 2.Jews — Baltic States —
History — 20th century. 3. Jews Bessarabia (Moldava and Ukraine) —
History — 20th century. 4. Jews — Soviet Union — History. 5. Soviet
Union — History 1939-1945. 6. Europe, Eastern — Ethnic relations.
1. Title
DS135.P6L47613 1995   *95-18725*
943.8'004924 — dc20   *CIP*

In blessed memory

of my dear twin sister, Batya Levin
and my beloved parents,
Tavi-Hirsh Levin and Bluma Levin, née Wigoder
and all members of the extended families,
    including their cousins and other relatives
who were killed by the Germans and Lithuanians
    in Europe during the Great Holocaust.

With honor and love

to my dear children,
Tavi-Yizkor,
Basmat and her husband, Jonathan Porath,
Nitzana and her husband, Nimrod Borosh,
and my grandchildren, Rona and Arnon

*The publication of this book was made possible
through a generous grant from the
NATIONAL FOUNDATION FOR JEWISH CULTURE
through the Joint Cultural Appeal*

Contents

Foreword

The horrors of the Final Solution for European Jewry cast a shadow on the lives of millions of Jews during the short period discussed in this work. For them it was a transitional or interim period, something that would prevail "until further notice." In the overall perspective of the history of Soviet Jewry, however, the significance of these events transcends the period under discussion.

Between the outbreak of World War II (September 1, 1939) and Operation Barbarossa, the German invasion of the Union of Soviet Socialist Republics (USSR) (June 22, 1941), more than two million Jews from the Soviet-annexed territories (eastern Poland, the Baltic countries, Bessarabia, and Northern Bukovina) became, to some extent, "Soviet Jews"—in addition to the more than three million Jews in the USSR proper. The two groups together accounted for one-third of all Jews alive at the time.

The Jews in the annexed territories were fundamentally different from their compatriots in the USSR in their social characteristics, culture, and spiritual lives. While much of Soviet Jewry belonged to the professional intelligentsia and was strongly inclined to dwell in large cities, most Jews in the annexed territories lived in shtetls and small towns, where they engaged in traditional Jewish occupations. While Soviet Jewry was eroding as a result of assimilation (intermarriage and estrangement from Jewish culture and customs), the Jews in the annexed territories thrived on their Jewish heritage, both religious and secular, and were only marginally affected by assimilation. While the Jews of the Soviet Union had no public organizations of their own, those in the annexed territories had their own congregations, political parties, and philanthropic and cultural institutions. While most Soviet Jews learned the Russian language, either voluntarily or by force of circumstances, most Jews in the annexed territories used Yiddish in their daily lives. While many Soviet Jewish youngsters were educated in the Communist youth movement, most of their counterparts in the annexed territories were brought up in Jewish youth movements, especially Zionist ones.

Dov Levin's research on the changes that swept the Jewish communities in the Soviet-annexed territories constitutes a detailed examination of Soviet policy, which aimed to make the annexed Jewish community resemble indigenous Soviet Jewry in a short period of time. It also analyzes the reactions of Jewish individuals and groups to that policy.

The period under discussion was marked by the elimination of pluralistic spiritual and cultural Jewish life in the annexed areas, "yiddishizing" it and emptying it of its national content. However, the existence of a large Jewish population whose primary language was Yiddish fostered hope among authors and artists in the USSR that there would be new opportunities for activity in that language that had not existed in the USSR proper. Thousands of Jewish soldiers, officers, and members of the Soviet establishment who were sent to the annexed territories, particularly the younger ones, encountered a Jewish way of life that they had not known before—and this encounter presumably had a lasting impact.

The annexation was especially distressing for the Zionist movements in the territories. Their activities, like those of other political and public agencies, were banned and many of their prominent activists were interned or exiled to remote areas of the country. The "hard core" of these groups, the youth movements in particular, refused to come to terms with the new realities. Instead, they focused their efforts on two overarching and interrelated goals: continued Zionist activity in the underground and finding ways to emigrate to Palestine, Eretz Yisrael (Land of Israel). The experience they gained during the period under discussion would find subsequent expression in Jewish organizational efforts under Nazi occupation and the operations of the *beriha* (escape) movement around and after the end of World War II.

By liquidating independent Jewish frameworks and arresting, exiling, and deporting the community's intellectual and economic elite, the Soviet regime gave individual Jews far-reaching opportunities to advance their education and become part of the state and Party establishment—on condition that they were prepared to adapt themselves to the new demands. These opportunities, not enjoyed by Jews living in countries that overtly discrimi-

nated against them, were accepted willingly. This fueled the already existing animosities of the surrounding non-Jewish population, which was not
accustomed to seeing Jews in the state and public administration. Thus the
Jews in the annexed territories were trapped between the hammer of local
anomie and the sickle of the Soviet attack on their cultural and spiritual
roots. However, the national manifestations of Jewish historical continuity
could not be eradicated in such a short time. Unsurprisingly, then, the surviving Jewish population in the annexed territories continued to harbor national aspirations in the wake of events that occurred at the end of Stalin's
reign of terror. The first visible indications of the community's revival were
the commemoration of Holocaust victims on the one hand and Jewish song
and dance troupes on the other. This movement gained momentum in the late
1960s and the early 1970s, when large-scale immigration of Jews to Israel
began. Many old-timers among the Soviet Jewish population, and a fortiori
the younger generation, were inspired by the Jewish-Zionist fervor of survivors from the annexed territories.

In the perestroika period and the post-Soviet era, the historical episode
discussed in this study has become a focal point of public debate. The question at hand is the attitude of the surrounding population toward the Jews in
the Holocaust period. Various elements, some contaminated with antisemitic
attitudes (especially in the Baltic countries), have alleged that their compatriots' collaboration in the murder of Jews during—and before—the Nazi occupation was merely a response to the Jews' behavior in the first few years
of the Soviet annexation. This makes the historical research presented here
a matter of current significance.

The study is a detailed analysis of the history of the Jews in the annexed
territories until the German invasion. It opens new vistas with which one
may understand the numerous developments that swept Soviet Jewry during and after the Holocaust. In this respect, the significance of this research transcends the brief period under discussion. This is why two
departments of the Hebrew University of Jerusalem—Holocaust Studies,
and Soviet Studies at the Institute of Contemporary Jewry—made this a
joint effort.

Dov Levin's previous research focused on Jewish fighting in the Baltic
countries during World War II; he gained a reputation as an authority in this
field. In the course of this research, Levin realized that an examination of
the social, community, and spiritual changes that the Jews in the annexed
territories experienced just before Barbarossa would enhance our understanding of events in the following period, that of the Holocaust.

Aware that public recollection of these events is fading, Levin encouraged hundreds of witnesses to reconstruct the history of the period. The resulting material was compared and contrasted with the scanty documentation published in the Soviet Union and elsewhere. By verifying and comparing the testimonies, Levin constructed a magnificent framework that elicited a reliable, comprehensive account of the fate of the more than two million Jews who lived in Eastern Europe until the Nazi occupation. The book carefully examines the rapid changes in the economic and spiritual lives of the Jews in the annexed territories, thus incorporating this little-known chapter into the history of the Jews of Eastern Europe in the Holocaust period.

Besides its considerable academic value, this book will be quite useful to anyone wishing to learn about the fate of the Jews of Eastern Europe during World War II.

Mordechai Altshuler

Preface

On the eve of World War II, Nazi Germany and the Soviet Union entered into a non-aggression agreement known as the Ribbentrop-Molotov Pact for its two signatories, the countries' foreign ministers. Under this accord, Germany attacked Poland on September 1, 1939, and conquered the western section of the country. In the same month, the Soviet Union occupied eastern Poland in September, 1939, annexing some of its regions (Polesie, the Bialystok area, and others) to the Belorussian Soviet Socialist Republic (SSR) and others (Wolhynia and Eastern Galicia) to the Ukrainian SSR. Nine months later, the Soviets took over northeastern Romania and the Baltic countries (Lithuania, Latvia, and Estonia), annexing Northern Bukovina to the Ukrainian SSR and Bessarabia to the Moldavian SSR. The three Baltic countries became "independent" Soviet socialist republics.

This string of annexed territories—from Estonia in the north to Bessarabia in the south—had a total Jewish population of some two million, a collective entity endowed with national consciousness and cultural roots. The majority were local residents; a minority were war refugees from western Poland, who congregated in Lvov, Kowel, Bialystok, and other cities. Both groups were forced to undergo an accelerated sovietization process, which ended abruptly with the German invasion of the Soviet Union on June 22, 1941 (Operation Barbarossa).

Because this transitional period was comparatively short (21 months in Poland, 12 months elsewhere), and especially in view of the Holocaust that followed, it has lost much of its significance for Holocaust survivors. This is reflected in contemporary Jewish historiography, including research and reminiscence publications. In this connection, the following remarks by Prof. Chone Shmeruk are worth quoting:

The events that took place in the Soviet-annexed territories between 1939 and 1941 have yet to be fully disclosed in Holocaust research. At present, we still lack a comprehensive account of the period, based on the copious material that appeared in the Soviet Jewish press and the memoirs of Jews who resided in the annexed territories at the time and later migrated to Israel or Western countries.

In general historiography, research on the annexed territories during the period under discussion has usually been selective and schematic, reflecting the ongoing political conflict and polemics between the Soviet Union and Western countries concerning the annexations. The period has been more strongly emphasized in research by members of national groups who emigrated to the West from the annexed territories, but their extreme political tendencies distort many of the facts they provide, including some relating to the Jews.

The controversy has erupted anew in the same spirit, but with greater force, in the former annexed areas. This is especially the case in the Baltic countries, after they seceded from the Soviet Union in the early 1990s and became autonomous political entities.

This book describes, examines, and summarizes the history of the Jews in the annexed territories from the entry of the Red Army in 1939 until the German invasion in June, 1941. It emphasizes the change in politics, culture, and values that swept the Jewish population during the sovietization process and explores the responses of various elements of the Jewish population to these changes. A distinction is drawn between general conditions that existed throughout the territories and specific ones that prevailed only in certain defined areas. Especially strong emphasis is placed on areas where the research findings may shed light on developments during the Nazi occupation (1941–1944) and on the awakening of Soviet Jewry in the 1960s and 1970s. The material generally is presented in the following geopolitical order: the eastern Polish provinces, the Baltic countries, and the areas of northeastern Romania.

In addition to the problems of obtaining authentic evidence from the period, the nature of the material, coupled with later memoirs and research publications that have appeared over the years, poses problems of its own. I refer specifically to the fact that the material has appeared in more than a dozen languages, including English, German, Ukrainian, Belorussian, Lithuanian, Latvian, Estonian, Moldavian, Yiddish, Polish, Romanian, and, of course, Russian (the official language of the Soviet Union) and Hebrew (used for correspondence, diaries, and so on). An infinitely more complex problem, however, is how to determine the authenticity of the sources and place them in proper perspective. This is particularly evident in Soviet sources published between 1939 and 1941, as well as material that continues to emanate from the Commonwealth of Independent States (CIS) to this very day.

With the Nazi invasion of June, 1941, Soviet rule in the annexed territories disintegrated rapidly, and state and public institutions evacuated at once. Consequently, numerous documents that could have shed light on the Jews' situation and the regime's attitude toward them have been lost. Aggravating this problem is the Soviet tendency to withhold information and whitewash incidents (even years after the fact) that would reflect against the Soviet republics in any way. Specifically, Soviet and CIS institutions have been reluctant to release or publish the few documents salvaged from the period that deal with sensitive ethnic and national issues. The contents of Soviet "Collections of Historical Documents" from that period are limited and were probably meant to support the official line regarding various stages of annexation and sovietization. Still, these Soviet collections, encyclopaedias, and miscellaneous publications (especially during and after the 1970s) may contribute significantly to research because they contain personal and geographical information, including statistical data, even though the material is not always reliable. Similarly, almost all Soviet publications in Yiddish and other languages dealing with the Jews in the annexed territories have been investigated.

Sources published during the Nazi occupation and in Western countries by nationally affiliated immigrants were used with caution because their descriptions of Jews as the objects of forced sovietization are frequently overstated and distorted.

Most of the factual and theoretical material used in this research was culled from documents of the time, including personal diaries and correspondence; reports, memoranda, and minutes of groups and organizations; and items and articles published in the Jewish press throughout the world and in bulletins of the J.T.A. (Jewish Telegraphic Agency). These sources also include the first testimonies recorded between 1939 and 1942 by the Association of Polish Jews in Palestine and other institutions; testimonies of individuals who, in various and sundry ways, reached Palestine from the

Soviet-annexed territories; memorial books of communities in the annexed territories; and most of the memoirs written by people from these areas.

Even though the numerous of volumes of memoirs contain significant, important material, they are undeniably incomplete in several respects. Many of the authors told their stories from a narrow, individual perspective, often relying on emotions and even rumors. Some of the authors were affiliated with the Soviet regime (either for ideological reasons or out of convenience) and preferred to ignore certain details. Others presented a one-sided view of events, regarding the Soviet regime with extreme prejudice and blaming it for almost everything.

Yet another research problem concerns the geographic imbalance of the source material. The history of 300,000 Jews in territories that had previously belonged to Romania (Bessarabia and Northern Bukovina) was documented in no more than 20 memorial books and a dozen articles in the Soviet Jewish press. By contrast, the 250,000 Jews of Soviet Lithuania were mentioned in two daily newspapers and discussed in a long list of historical accounts and memoirs. To resolve this disequilibrium, supplement the information, and elucidate questions that came up during the research, it was necessary to rely on another type of source, namely, testimonies. Of 700 testimonies by Jews in the annexed territories that are available in archives (Yad Vashem, Masu'ah, Moreshet, Lohamei Hagettaot, Beit Lin, the Jabotinsky Institute, and others), some 120 contained material relevant to the present research.

Also included were 55 interviews conducted in previous studies on armed resistance by Jews in the Baltic countries during World War II, as well as questionnaires and interviews devised for the present study. Another 129 interviews with people from the annexed territories were conducted through the Oral History Division of the Institute of Contemporary Jewry. The interviewees included members of the political and government establishment, underground activists, prominent figures in education and culture, and individuals who immigrated to Israel from the Soviet Union in the late 1970s and the 1980s. A few interviews with actors from western Belorussia and Soviet Lithuania were conducted at the Israel Goor Archives and Theater Museum in Jerusalem.

A problem that arises whenever such material is presented in English concerns the spellings of towns and personae. As geographic areas changed hands, and as individuals crossed borders and continents, their names acquired a great many variations. The present book cites place names as they existed before and during the Soviet occupation, with relevant variants in parentheses where helpful. There are two exceptions: the cities of Vilnius and Kaunas, for which the entrenched Jewish usages—Vilna and Kovno—are used throughout.

All stages of the research were planned, prepared, and conducted under the auspices of the Institute of Contemporary Jewry. During the past five years, partial findings have been published in hundreds of articles in Hebrew, Yiddish, English, German, Russian, and Lithuanian. Fifty-six of them, pertaining exclusively to the Jews in the Baltic countries, have been gathered in two collections. One is in Hebrew: *Bein ha-patish ve-ha-magal* [Between the Hammer and the Sickle]. (Jerusalem: Makor, 1983); the other is in English: *Baltic Jewry Under Soviet Rule* (Center for Research and Documentation of East-European Jewry at the Hebrew University of Jerusalem, 1991).

Furthermore, after my complete research findings on all the Eastern European areas were co-published in Hebrew (*Tequfa be-sograyim: 1939–1941* [A Period in Parentheses: 1939–1941] Jerusalem–Tel Aviv, 1989) by the Hebrew University of Jerusalem and the Ghetto Fighters' House, two books on the sovietization of eastern Poland appeared: Jan T. Gross, *Revolution from Abroad—The Soviet Conquest of Poland's Western Ukraine and Western Belorussia* (Princeton University Press: 1988), and Norman Davies and Antony Polonski, Eds., *Jews in Eastern Poland and the USSR, 1939–46* (Macmillan, 1991).

All of this made it possible in the present book (the English version of *Tequfa be-sograyim: 1939–1941*) to offer slightly less details on the Baltic countries and the Polish areas but to provide greater details on northeastern Romania (Bessarabia and Northern Bukovina), which figure much less prominently in the historiography of the time.

It is proper to note here that all stages of my research on the period were planned and carried out under the auspices of the Institute for Contemporary Jewry of the Hebrew University of Jerusalem, with the encouragement of my colleagues and friends Prof. Yehuda Bauer and Prof. Mordechai Altshuler. The latter also devotedly and painstakingly re-read my manuscript and made important comments. Mr. Naftali Greenwood, who translated this study into English, performed his duties with both diligence and patience. I express my gratitude and appreciation to all of them, to the hundreds of persons interviewed, and to everyone who provided me with the information and data with which my research came to fruition.

I also wish to thank the Jewish Memorial Foundation in New York City and the Alexander Silverman Fund, each of which helped to support certain stages of the research on which this book is based.

It is my pleasant duty to note that the Hebrew version of this study conferred two esteemed prizes upon its author shortly after its publication: the Yehoshua A. Gilboa Prize, awarded by Masu'ah in Israel, and the Israel Yefroykin Prize, awarded by the Hebrew University of Jerusalem.

Finally, I express my heartfelt gratitude to The Jewish Publication Society and its Editor-in-Chief, Dr. Ellen Frankel, for having handled the editing and publishing of this book with estimable devotion and professionalism.

Dov Levin
Jerusalem

The Lesser of Two Evils

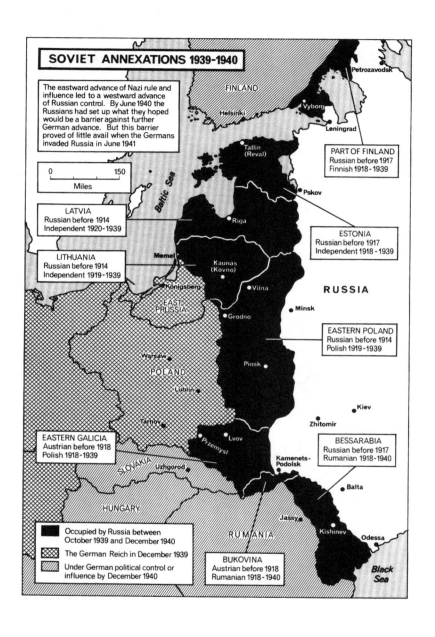

SOVIET ANNEXATIONS 1939-1940

The eastward advance of Nazi rule and
influence led to a westward advance
of Russian control. By June 1940 the
Russians had set up what they hoped
would be a barrier against further
German advance. But this barrier
proved of little avail when the Germans
invaded Russia in June 1941

0   150
Miles

FINLAND

Petrozavodsk

Helsinki

Vyborg

Leningrad

Tallin
(Reval)

PART OF FINLAND
Russian before 1917
Finnish 1918-1939

Pskov

Baltic Sea

LATVIA
Russian before 1914
Independent 1920-1939

Riga

ESTONIA
Russian before 1917
Independent 1918-1939

LITHUANIA
Russian before 1914
Independent 1919-1939

Memel

Kaunas
(Kovno)

Vilna

RUSSIA

Königsberg

EAST
PRUSSIA

Grodno

Minsk

EASTERN POLAND
Russian before 1914
Polish 1919-1939

Warsaw

POLAND

Pinsk

Lublin

Kiev

Zhitomir

Tarnov

EASTERN GALICIA
Austrian before 1918
Polish 1918-1939

Lvov

Przemysl

SLOVAKIA

Uzhgorod

Kamenets-
Podolsk

BESSARABIA
Russian before 1917
Rumanian 1918-1940

Balta

HUNGARY

Jassy

RUMANIA

Kishinev

Odessa

■ Occupied by Russia between
October 1939 and December 1940

▨ The German Reich in December 1939

▧ Under German political control or
influence by December 1940

BUKOVINA
Austrian before 1918
Rumanian 1918-1940

Black
Sea

1

Historical Background

Upon its formation, the Union of Soviet Socialist Republics (USSR) ostensibly recognized the right of every people to self-determination, even if this meant its secession from the union. In practice, however, it vigorously opposed the establishment of independent states between the Baltic and the Black Sea, in areas that had been in the embrace of Czarist Russia. The Soviets' unavailing attempts to impose their own regime in these countries (e.g., the Baltic region, eastern Poland, and Bessarabia in 1918–1920) or to foment Communist revolutions there (Estonia, 1924) left a bitter residue among the neighboring countries to the west and fueled apprehensions of recurrent attempts of this type. This explains why these countries resisted and rejected the relentless Soviet efforts to strengthen relations with them. On the other hand, Western intervention during the civil war, coupled with Poland's dangerous military aggression in 1920, stimulated deeply rooted Soviet suspicions about these countries' policies, especially the fear that they would serve as springboards for yet another breaching of Soviet borders.

These attitudes were articulated clearly in the Western-sponsored negotiations in the late 1930s for the establishment of a diplomatic and military front, with Soviet participation, against the growing bellicosity of Nazi Germany toward the countries of Eastern Europe, especially Poland. Poland forcefully turned down a proposal by Great Britain, France, and the USSR to guarantee the integrity of its borders, believing that the Red Army would invade if Germany ever posed a real threat. Romania and Finland followed suit. The Baltic countries preferred the calculated risk of neutrality over the possibility of a Red Army incursion. Thus the Soviets satisfied many of their claims on the western frontier in the non-aggression treaty that they signed on August 23, 1939, in a surprising turn of events, with their ideological rival, Nazi Germany. A detailed secret protocol attached to this accord demarcated the two sides' spheres of influence in Eastern Europe. Accordingly, the Wehrmacht invaded Poland on September 1, 1939, and overran the western half of the country within two weeks. This blitzkrieg also marked the beginning of World War II.

THE SOVIETIZATION OF EASTERN EUROPE

The sovietization of Eastern Europe took place in three major stages, lasting altogether 21 months (from September 17, 1939, until June 22, 1941). These stages, broken down by description, date, and location, are presented here schematically (see table).

Eastern Poland

On September 17, Red Army units rushed across the Polish border from the east, "to liberate our Ukrainian and Belorussian brethren from their enslavement to the corrupt, degenerate government of Poland." The Soviet press praised the Red Army's "liberation campaign," in stark contrast to its taciturn, disapproving coverage of Germany's occupation of western Poland. After describing the lives of exploitation and humiliation that the Poles had led under the regime of the landowners, the Soviet press noted the establishment of "provisional administrations" that would restore order in the cities and towns.[1] In this context, it was reported that in some localities, local bodies that called themselves "revolutionary committees," and even municipalities, seized the reins of government themselves. Most of these agencies were composed of local Communists and their sympathizers. Even at this early stage, attempts were made to co-opt nonpartisan but pro-Soviet or liberal personalities into the provisional governing institutions, thus broadening them in the eyes of the public.

The Red Army moved in sluggishly. One reason was to circumvent localities and regions that were far from highways and railroads. There were other reasons. In Eastern Galicia, for example, the Wehrmacht entered areas that had been awarded to the Soviets under the secret accord. The German forces pulled back several days later, but not before looting public and

Stages in the Soviet Annexation of Eastern European Areas, September, 1939–June, 1941

	Stage A— Annexation	*Stage B— Integration*	*Stage C— Unification and Consolidation*
1. Eastern Poland * 　Western Belorussia 　　Bialystok District 　　Polesie District 　　Vilna District† 　Western Ukraine 　　Eastern Galicia District 　　Wolhynia District	Sept. 17–Nov. 2, 1939 (6 weeks)	Nov. 3, 1939,–Mar. 24, 1940 (5 months)	Mar. 25, 1940–June 22, 1941 (14 months)
2. Baltic Countries‡ 　Lithuania (incl. Vilna†) 　Latvia 　Estonia	June 15–17, 1940– Aug. 6, 1940 (2 months)	August 7, 1940–Jan. 12, 1941 (5 months)	Jan. 13–June 22, 1941 (5 months)
3. Northeastern Romania* 　Bessarabia 　Northern Bukovina	Jun. 28–Aug. 2, 1940 (6 weeks)	Aug. 3, 1940–Jan. 12, 1941 (5 months)	Jan. 13–June 22, 1941 (5 months)

*After the annexation, these areas were incorporated into existing Soviet republics.
†On October 30, 1939, Vilna and its vicinity were restored to Lithuanian control.
‡Until the annexation, these areas had independent Communist Parties.

private property and savaging the civilian population, especially the Jews. Admittedly, there were also cases in which the Red Army pulled back, allowing the Wehrmacht to enter in its stead. Some of these exchanges included festive changing of guards. These events became increasingly frequent until September 28, when the Soviet-German pact of August 23 was amended to add Lithuania to the Soviet sphere of influence and to grant Germany control of the territory between the Vistula and Bug rivers (the Lublin district and parts of the Warsaw district). For most of its length, the Bug became a natural border between the German and Soviet occupation zones in Poland. The Soviet army had not managed to enter Lublin itself, disappointing the "welcoming committees among leftist circles"[2] that had been organized to greet it. Realizing that the Wehrmacht would be the occupying force, many members of these committees fled to the Soviet zone.

In the meantime, hundreds of thousands of Polish civilians, including many Jews, continued to migrate from one side of Poland to the other. The Soviet Union still allowed nearly free access to and exit from the areas under their control, and in many locations the Red Army authorities even helped people who sought to join it in its retreat. When the borders were stabilized, the Soviets held 196,000 square kilometers of Polish territory, roughly half of the country. Soviet sources at the time estimated the population of this area as more than seven million Ukrainians, more than three million Belorussians, and more than one million Poles. According to this source, the Jewish population also slightly exceeded one million.[3] Other sources reported 1,309,000 Jews, or 9.9 percent of the population.[4]

Less than one month later, the Soviet military and civilian authorities began implementing a plan to integrate the occupied areas into the USSR. Using a carefully thought-out set of measures and devices, they tried to lend the process a spontaneous and democratic facade, as if it had originated in the free will of a majority of the indigenous population. On October 6, the Belorussian and Ukrainian front command announced that elections for "people's assemblies" would be held on October 22. The voters were offered the choice of one list only: the Communist and Nonpartisan Bloc.

According to official publications, the voter turnout was 96.71 percent in western Belorussia (with 90.67 percent favoring this united candidate list) and 92.83 percent (90.93 percent) in the western Ukraine.

The National Assembly of western Belorussia convened in Bialystok on October 28, 1939. Among its 926 deputies were 621 Belorussians, 127 Poles, 72 Jews, 53 Ukrainians, 43 Russians, and 10 others. More than half of the would-be legislators were peasants. In one of the assembly's first decisions, it named a 66-person delegation to set out for Moscow and Minsk, where it would inform the supreme governing institutions that the local population demanded annexation to the Belorussian Soviet Socialist Republic (SSR).

A similar assembly meeting took place in Lvov the following day, with the participation of 1,451 delegates (including 20 or so Jews). The decision was the same: a demand for annexation to the Soviet Ukraine.

On November 1–2, 1939, the Supreme Soviet in Moscow resolved "to honor the request" of the national assemblies of the western Ukraine and western Belorussia. The supreme soviets of the Belorussian and Ukrainian SSRs adopted similar resolutions. These two formal acts completed the first stage of the annexation of eastern Poland, paving the way for the imposition of Soviet law and governance in these areas.

The next step toward annexation was the sealing of the border between eastern Poland and the western, German-occupied section of the country. Although this process had begun as far back as late October, the Soviet authorities now vigorously resisted any German attempt to channel people out of the areas under their control.

On November 29, 1939, the Supreme Soviet in Moscow issued an edict awarding Soviet citizenship to former Polish citizens who had resided in the western Ukraine and Belorussia on the determining day (November 1–2) and to individuals who had reached the USSR under the terms of two agreements: a Soviet-German accord signed on November 16 of that year[5] and a Soviet-Lithuanian accord signed on October 10 in which Vilna and its vicinity were handed over to Lithuania. Similar arrangements were made for the naturalization of persons in the western areas who had not resided there on the determining day.

While the Soviet ukase (decree) did much to rationalize the refugees' legal and civil status, it did nothing to facilitate their economic absorption. This was a grave problem indeed, because hundreds of thousands of refugees from western Poland had flooded Lvov, Bialystok, Kowel (Kovel), Brest (Brest-Litovsk), Rowne (Rovno), Luck (Lutsk), and other localities. In the western Ukraine and Belorussia, the Soviet administration opened registration bureaus where refugees could volunteer for quarrying and factory work in the eastern Ukraine, especially the Donbas area. The first such groups set out in November and December. Although many refugees and others found work in this fashion, others returned by various routes, alienated, homesick, and disillusioned by the absence of suitable conditions.

On December 4, 1939, the Supreme Soviet decided to set new administrative and geographical borders in the annexed areas, using the Soviet model. Thus, six *oblasti* (districts) were constituted in the western Ukraine, two in Wolhynia, four in Eastern Galicia, and five in western Belorussia.

An additional administrative measure was a "passportization" campaign that began in January, 1940. In this operation, residents of eastern Poland, most of whom held Polish identification cards, were to exchange these cards for conventional Soviet internal passports. The first to do so were those who had volunteered for work in Donbas or elsewhere in the Soviet interior.

The practical effect of passportization was to categorize the local and refugee population by its degree of allegiance to the new administration and regime. People whose political and social past made them suspect of disloyalty found restrictive provisions written into their new ID cards. Notable among them was Article 11, which proscribed permanent residence in district capitals or any location within 100 kilometers (approximately 60 miles) of the international frontier.

A similar move was the dismissal of mayors, militia commanders, and factory managers belonging to minority groups, such as Poles and Jews, and their replacement by Ukrainians and Belorussians. This process continued and accelerated. The high-ranking and supervisory echelons of the government and party apparatus, and *a fortiori* the defense system, were staffed largely by officials brought in "from the east," chiefly the Ukraine and Belorussia. By this time, all governmental and public institutions had adopted the conventional Soviet procedures, hierarchy, and formal terminology. Even the hours of work and daily activity had been moved up by two hours to conform with Moscow time.

The nationalization of industry and trade, begun by the military authorities and the provisional civil administration, was now almost fully completed in the fashion spelled out in a resolution by the national assemblies on October 28 and 29, 1939. Petty trade, too, was effectively wiped out by the end of that year. The *zloty* (Polish currency) was abolished by edict in December of that year, and its ruble exchange rate was sharply reduced. This, coupled with the disruption of supply channels, left merchants and artisans starved for goods, raw materials, and, especially, cash.

Replacing the shops and small factories that had been confiscated or shut down by their owners were conventional Soviet outlets —Univermag ("Universal Magazine," a department or general store) or some other form—and craft and service cooperatives known as artels. The new frameworks employed large numbers of artisans and shopkeepers, including former merchants and industrialists. Many of the latter, however, were forced into idleness and socially and politically ostracized. Those who had pledged allegiance to the previous regime—especially army and police officers and activists in civilian parties, including leftist parties such as the PPS (Polish Socialist Party), the Bund (Jewish Socialist Party), and Zionist groups—lived in constant dread. After the relative liberalism of the annexation period, the regime toughened its line toward these elements, who were now castigated, like the formerly wealthy, as "enemies of the people." Widespread, systematic arrests began on the night of February 8, with Poles as the major targets. The detainees and their families were exiled deep into the Soviet interior.

Elections were held throughout eastern Poland in late March, 1940. Their purpose was to ensure full representation of the annexed areas in the bicameral Supreme Soviet in Moscow (the Council of the Union and the Council of Nationalities), and the corresponding institutions in the Ukraine and Belorussia. The election campaign for the governing institutions in Moscow, Kiev, and Minsk was followed by a wave of mass deportations, this time including Jewish, Ukrainian, and Belorussian residents of large and medium-sized cities.

As this was happening, the security agencies took a second look at the hundreds of thousands of refugees and decided that a crackdown was in order. Although quite a few of the refugees had found jobs by this time, and some had even become active in political and public affairs, most were still unemployed in the cities. Few members of this group had exercised the right to acquire Soviet citizenship, given them in the edict of November 29, 1939. The security authorities' grave suspicions about this aggregate (most of whom were Jews) were only part of the problem; in April, 1940, many of the refugees had told special German committees that operated in the major cities of the western Ukraine and Belorussia that they wished to return to their places of residence across the border.

Thus the Soviet internal security service, the Narodny Kommissariat V'nutrennikh Del, People's Commissariat for International Affairs (NKVD), established "refugee rehabilitation committees," in which all the refugees, including those who had already found work, had to sign one of two applications: to accept Soviet citizenship or to return to their places of residence in the German-occupied zone. For various reasons, many if not most of the refugees (including the Jews) chose the second option. The response was swift and harsh. In the second half of June, 1940, dragnet arrests were carried out in locations where refugees had gathered, with special attention given to those who had applied to return to the German-occupied zone. Within a few days, many thousands of refugees were loaded onto trains and exiled to labor camps in Asiatic Russia.

By the autumn of that year, a punitive regime similar to that of the Soviet Union itself had been installed throughout the annexed areas. Its targets were violators of labor discipline (those guilty of tardiness, absenteeism, drunkenness, and so forth). Lengthy queues and a black market became features of daily life, as they had been in the USSR for many years. Nor did the authorities hesitate to launch periodic search-and-seizure operations in the streets, markets, roads, and private homes and institutions, looking for contraband commodities or foreign exchange.

As the schools opened for the 1940/41 academic year—with Ukrainian or Belorussian as the language of instruction—the Russification of the curriculum itself was now felt with greater intensity. There was almost no difference between the curricula taught in these schools and those used in the eastern areas of the Ukrainian and Belorussian SSRs.

Even though the accelerated sovietization maximized the degree of unification of the annexed areas with the eastern Ukraine and eastern Belorussia, the security authorities continued to treat the western population warily. Not until the German invasion of June, 1941, was the old border, that preceding September 17, 1939, totally eradicated. Indeed, the outbreak of the war was preceded by an additional (and final) wave of deportations that included large numbers of "enemies of the people," who, the authorities believed, might represent a security risk in the confrontation between the USSR and Nazi Germany.[6]

The Baltic Countries

By June, 1940, the Soviets had overrun the Baltic countries (with a total population of roughly 6,000,000) and the provinces of northeastern Romania (about 3,500,000), thus exercising all the political/military options given them in the Ribbentrop-Molotov pact.

On Saturday, June 15, 1940, vanguard units of the Red Army marched into the old-new capital of Lithuania, Vilna (Vilnius); the temporary Lithuanian capital in 1920–1939, Kovno (Kaunas); and other localities, followed by lengthy columns of armor and infantry. Some of the invading forces occupied facilities, major public buildings, and strategic locations in and out of the cities; others continued westward, toward the German border. The Chief of the Lithuanian Army General Staff ordered his troops to greet the Red Army as a "friendly" force.

Generally, the Soviet soldiers were indeed greeted with cheers of joy and flowers by masses of civilians, including members of the Communist Party and other leftist organizations.

By this time, two senior Soviet officials—the Deputy People's Commissar for Foreign Affairs, V. G. Dekanozov, and Ambassador N. G. Pozdniakov—had already reached Kovno and were busily assembling the new Lithuanian government behind the scenes. From then on, these two officials were to exercise a decisive influence on the fate of the country. The fate that they had in mind was total sovietization. In Latvia, which along with Estonia was occupied on June 17, this function was discharged by the Deputy Chairman of the Council of People's Commissars and the Deputy People's Commissar for Foreign Affairs, Andrei Vishinsky. The corresponding official in Estonia was Andrei Zhdanov, a member of the Presidium of the Supreme Soviet of the USSR and the Secretary of the Communist Party in the Leningrad area.

The new national government was unveiled in Kovno on June 17. A well-known leftist Lithuanian journalist, Justas Paleckis, was installed as premier and acting president. Within a few days, hundreds of political prisoners, most of them Jews, were released.[7] Many of them, like their counterparts in Latvia and Estonia, went on to fill important if not central positions in the government and party apparatus.

All political parties and organizations, with the exception of the Communist Party and the Komsomol (the Communist Youth Alliance), were dissolved in late June. Most of the newspapers were shut down and replaced, in almost all cases, by Communist Party mouthpieces. Also by late June, a changing of the guard had ensued among senior officials in Lithuania and, to a certain extent, in Latvia and Estonia. Especially affected in this regard were the security, military, and municipal echelons of the internal administration. The Lithuanian Seimas (parliament) was dissolved at this time, and the country's concordat (special treaty) with the Vatican was nullified. The police were reconstituted as a militia. In Latvia, the militia was retained, but a new, semi-military organization called the "Workers' Guard" was established alongside it. The new 10,000-member agency was meant, among other things, to protect factories and facilities. Civilians who had gone overseas were declared absentees and their possessions were expropriated.

The fateful and decisive step toward final annexation was taken on July 5, when elections for the Lithuanian People's Seimas, the Latvian Sejm, and the Estonian Duma were announced and scheduled for July 14. The election rules were published that day in Kovno, Riga, and Tallinn simultaneously, as was the establishment of candidate lists representing the "Labor Alliance," "Laborers' Bloc," and similar groupings. These, in fact, were the only lists allowed. More than half of the 79 candidates "elected" (appointed) in election rallies in Lithuania were Communist Party members, and four of the electees were Jews. In Latvia, all the lists that were presented were disqualified except for one, which was composed of 76 individuals recommended by the Communist Party.

The election experience gained eight months previously in areas of eastern Poland undoubtedly did much to determine the way in which the process was carried out now. In the Baltic countries, however, greater efforts were made to make the process look democratic. This campaign placed special emphasis on the poor and the national minorities. Local residents were showered with good news almost every day: wages were rising, rents were tumbling, and so on. Nevertheless, the security services persisted in arresting leading officials and important activists of parties and organizations that had been dissolved about two weeks before. Nearly all were exiled to the Soviet Union. The authorities hinted that transgressions as minor as failing to vote would be marked in one's ID card, and that the holders of such cards would be declared "enemies of the people," with all that this implied. Consequently, the voter turnout and the votes cast for the unified list approached 100 percent, matching the Soviet norm at the time.

The new legislatures in Kovno, Riga, and Tallinn convened on July 21. Unanimously they resolved to introduce a Soviet regime, nationalize commerce and industry, and send missions to Moscow to demand annexation by the USSR. In early August, the Supreme Soviet acceded to the latter request, officially annexing the three Baltic countries.

Even before this act was ratified, the authorities in Kovno, Riga, and Tallinn issued a series of edicts. Most of the measures were economic, such as the nationalization of banks and large industrial enterprises. The nationalization dragnet in Lithuania included nearly 1,000 factories and their 38,000 employees. A special ministry under acting minister Hayyim Alperovitz was set up to manage the nationalized industries. A Nationalization of Commerce Law turned about 1,600 businesses, buildings, and other assets into state property. Laws restricting land ownership to 30 hectares (75 acres) per farm unit were considered extremely important.

A new Lithuanian constitution turning the People's Seimas into "the Supreme Soviet of the Lithuanian Soviet Socialist Republic" was approved in Lithuania on August 25. The Council of Ministers was replaced by a Council of People's Commissars; almost all of its members were Soviet "experts" brought in from Moscow. The armies of Estonia, Latvia, and Lithuania were integrated into the regulars corps of the Red Army. Another step toward merging the local economy into that of the Soviet Union was taken on September 25, when the ruble was declared legal tender along with the local currencies (litas, latt, and krone).

As socioeconomic sovietization progressed, many changes were introduced in other areas of life. The civil legal code of the RSFSR (Russian Soviet Federated Socialist Republic) was applied in the three Baltic countries. School tuition fees were abolished before the start of the school year in early September, a uniform Soviet-type school system was introduced, and religious education institutions were shut down. Major changes also took place in style of dress, entertainment, and the arts, following the example set by the new elite.

As the transformation continued, there were manifestations of public resistance to the symbols, rituals, "socialist competitions," and myriad public events and festivities with which the new regime constantly embellished itself. Some of the army and police officers who had been dismissed, and members of parties and organizations that had been dissolved, began to take sporadic hostile action.[8] Nevertheless the juggernaut continued to roll. In the autumn of 1940, the struggle against the "church enemy" intensified in all the Baltic countries. For the first time in the history of these countries, official celebration of Christmas was banned.

Elections for the Supreme Soviet of the USSR were held on January 12, 1941. Elected to the Council of the Union were ten delegates (including one Jew) from Lithuania, seven from Latvia, and four from Estonia. Each republic sent 25 deputies to the Council of Nationalities. These elections marked the last official step in the integration of the Baltic republics into the USSR.

It was now time to sovietize the Baltic republics on a more profound level. In March, 1941, each of the Baltic countries set up a People's Commissariat for State Security, Narodny Kommissariat Gossudarstvenoy Bezopast (NKGB), a local arm of the main organization in Moscow. The use of local currencies was banned. *Kolkhozes* (collective farms) were established in Lithuania and Latvia. The Russian language was elevated to the status of the official local tongues; it even became the dominant language in several major institutions where Soviet bureaucrats had pervaded certain echelons. All traditional festivals were abolished; Soviet holidays and memorial days were introduced in their stead.

Regional and national assemblies of the Communist Party became central events in political and public life. The number of Party and Komsomol members began to grow, especially in Latvia and Estonia.

Although the border between the Baltic Soviet republics and the rest of the USSR had not yet been eradicated, residents of the former were allowed to visit the USSR proper for special vocational training or on official business. Missions from the Soviet Union to Vilna, Riga, and Tallinn proliferated. Concurrently, contact with outside countries diminished, as residents feared the consequences of relations with the "capitalist world." Apart from personal letters (which were strictly censored), the population was not allowed to receive mail from abroad. Books, newspapers, and other printed matter were proscribed with special vigor.

Following the Soviet practice, the Baltic borders were sealed on both sides. The only exception was the controlled departure of approximately 100,000 persons of German nationality or ethnicity (Volksdeutsche) between January and May, 1941, as prescribed by the Soviet-German pact in return for the admission of Baltic nationals residing abroad who wished to return. Some of the latter were former volunteers in the Spanish Civil War, who had fled to France. Lithuania allowed non-residents to emigrate; most persons in this category were migrants from Poland who held entrance visas to certain countries, including Palestine.

In the spring of 1941, Soviet relations with Nazi Germany became markedly worse, and the Soviets realized that war with their German partner was inevitable. Lithuania, which shared a 300-kilometer (180-mile) border with the German occupation zone, was an area of great strategic importance. Even though war preparations were undertaken slowly and furtively, the public was aware of them. Some groups, such as the Jews, followed the preparations with grave apprehension; others, such as the Lithuanian, Latvian, Estonian, and even Polish nationalists in the vicinity of Vilna, did so with hopes for change. The national resistance movement among students, soldiers, petty officials, and others gained such momentum that, by the time the war broke out as expected, preparations for a general revolt had already been made. The underground cells were given instructions, including the retribution to be inflicted on collaborators with the Soviet regime—chiefly the Jews.

In late May, 1941, after the Soviet security agencies had uncovered quite a few cells of this type, Moscow decided to apply its painstakingly formulated mass-exile plan to all the annexed areas. The operation was presented in each region as if it were an initiative of the local authorities. Lists of "counterrevolutionary elements" were compiled each day on the district and subdistrict levels. Each entry included the number of household members and the fate that awaited them: imprisonment or exile. The thousands of prisoners who had been incarcerated since the summer of 1940 were included in the exile operation.

The deportations were scheduled to begin on Friday night, June 13–14. The operation was orchestrated by the commissar of the NKGB, Ivan Serov, who had organized the mass arrests and deportations in the western Ukraine.

Many thousands of exiles were shoved into railroad cars. Within a few days they were transported to a collection depot (usually close to the old Soviet border), whence they were hauled to various locations in the USSR, including the Ural Mountains, Central Asia, and the Arkhangelsk area. In all, about 100,000 individuals were deported from the Baltic countries in this operation. Most were Latvians, Lithuanians, Estonians, and Jews; some were Poles, Russians, Belorussians, and members of other groups.

Lithuania and Latvia fell to the Wehrmacht less than a week later. Much of the local armed forces mutinied, and the country was engulfed in chaos and panic. Military resistance was more protracted in other areas, especially in Estonia. In all, only about 25,000 people (mostly Jews) succeeded in retreating from Lithuania in an organized fashion and by their own initiative, including 2,500 Communist Party members and 2,200 members of the Komsomol. About 40,000 people were evacuated from Latvia or fled the country, which was overrun a short time later. Another 65,000 left Estonia. The number of persons who attempted to flee was greater, but some suffered injuries en route or turned around when they encountered battles. By July 1, the Soviet regime in Lithuania and Latvia had ceased to exist. The Germans completed their occupation of Estonia about two months later.

Bessarabia and Northern Bukovina

The Red Army entered Bessarabia and Northern Bukovina on June 28, 1940, on the heels of a sharply worded ultimatum from Moscow to Romania. The takeover was completed within 48 hours. Bessarabia, including the capital of Kishinev, had a population of roughly three million. The population of Northern Bukovina, including the capital of Czernowitz (Chernovtsy), was approximately half a million.

Romanian officials who owned land, factories, or large commercial enterprises—and others, for different reasons—immediately abandoned their homes and fled to central Romania. However, many persons who had been born in these areas but resided elsewhere in the country began to return. The Romanian army retreated hastily. Bitter officers and enlisted men assaulted and abused the locals, especially the Jews. In several localities, Communist Party activists and sympathizers organized provisional "situation committees" to maintain order until the Red Army came in. However, much looting is known to have occurred, especially in the small towns and villages. In Kishinev, a "provisional revolutionary committee" was set up under a leading Communist in Bessarabia, who, along with hundreds of political and other prisoners, had been set free by the mob. The day after the Red Army entered, a "people's assembly" was convened in the presence of the Secretary of the Ukrainian Communist Party, Nikita Khrushchev, in charge of sovietizing the western Ukraine, and the People's Commissar for Defense, Marshal Semyon Timoshenko.

In Czernowitz, *patrools* (combat companies) rushed into action to maintain order and prevent property crimes. Taking over the city hall, post office, and local jail, they released the political prisoners.[9] The first Soviet tanks rattled into the town several hours later. Even though martial law was declared in the city, the mass celebrations continued, reaching their climax with a great military parade on July 3.

Local and regional workers' committees were established in the first half of July by the initiative of the Communist Party, and the demand for annexation by the Soviet Ukraine was voiced in each of their rallies. In neighboring Bessarabia, they demanded unification with the Moldavian Autonomous Soviet Socialist Republic across the Dniester River. The decisions were forwarded to the Supreme Soviet in Moscow, which invited missions from Bessarabia and Northern Bukovina to attend the seventh session of the Supreme Soviet for the purpose of reiterating the request. On August 2, 1940, the Supreme Soviet decided to establish a Moldavian Soviet Socialist Republic embracing most of Bessarabia, and to attach Northern Bukovina and several Bessarabian *oblasti* to the USSR. Northern Bukovina, henceforth to be known as Czernowitz Oblast, thereby gained 365,000 residents.

This rearrangement fragmented the local population, often separating family members. Admittedly, Soviet-Romanian repatriation arrangements (helped by border running) allowed many persons born in Bessarabia and Northern Bukovina, including a large number of Jews, to return. However, many hundreds who had been born there, and who applied for repatriation to the Soviet Embassy in Bucharest and the Romanian authorities, were turned away.[10]

Nationalization began on August 15, about seven weeks after the takeover of Bessarabia and Northern Bukovina and about two weeks after the official Soviet annexation. Affected were banks and savings funds, factories and commercial enterprises, hotels, large residences, absentees' homes, and so on. The nationalization and dispossession campaign had begun as soon as the Red Army moved in. In many instances, actions of this type were taken even before this, accompanied by looting, searches of houses, arrests, and frenetic propaganda against "exploiters" of various kinds, several of whom were tried and exiled to Siberia and elsewhere.

The crusade against property owners and the affluent caused continual dread; even artisans and small-business owners attempted to shed outer indications of their past and find their niche in the proletarization drive. Some kind of official work situation was an imperative for all adults who sought to prove their integration into the new system. Artisans were encouraged to form cooperatives. The nationalized economy generated many jobs in the government retailing and manufacturing systems. Communists and leftist activists who had hoped to claim all important positions in the municipal and district administrations were disappointed: the Soviets imported large numbers of petty officials from various outside localities, especially Soviet Ukraine.

On January 12, 1941, when elections were held for the supreme soviets in the Ukraine and in Moscow, a majority of winning candidates in Northern Bukovina were Ukrainians. Indeed, the Ukrainian influence on all areas of life continued with great intensity throughout the year of Soviet rule in the area, ending only with the German-Romanian occupation in July, 1941.

Ukrainian influence was strong in Bessarabia, also. In the middle of December, 1940, Soviet Ukrainian law was imposed in the new Moldavian republic, including Bessarabia. Convening for the first time on February 10, 1941, the Moldavian Supreme Soviet resolved to replace the Latin alphabet in Bessarabia with Cyrillic characters. In the same session, the Soviet constitution was ratified as the basis of the new republic.

Following the Soviet practice, Bessarabia introduced free education throughout the school system, which grew impressively. One thousand teachers were brought in from the Ukraine, and thousands of local residents were trained for teaching positions.

In Bessarabia, as in the other western areas annexed by the Soviet Union, mass expulsions to Siberia and other distant locations began without warning on the morning of June 14, 1941. Exiled were former activists in parties and various other organizations, and the affluent; family members were similarly deported. According to Soviet sources, a quarter of a million people were evacuated to the USSR from the Moldavian Republic, including its eastern section, when the German-Romanian invasion began. The armies of Nazi Germany occupied Bessarabia a few weeks later.

THE JEWISH POPULATION OF EASTERN EUROPE AT THE
DAWN OF WORLD WAR II

Statistics and Demography

The Jewish communities in the territories annexed by the USSR in 1939–1941 had been there for generations and were entrenched in the local economy. They were recognized as a national minority in all these areas and accounted for 5 to 11 percent of the population. A census in Bessarabia and in Bukovina in 1930 estimated the Jewish population of these areas as 207,000 (7.2 percent) and 93,000 (approximately 11 percent), respectively. According to a 1931 census in Poland, the Jewish population was 1,329,000 (more than 500,000 in Eastern Galicia, nearly 500,000 in western Belorussia, and about 250,000 in Wolhynia)—approximately 10 percent of the population. In a 1923 census, 153,446 residents of Lithuania (7.6 percent) declared themselves Jewish; this proportion rose to 10 percent when Vilna and its surroundings, with 100,000 Jews, were restored to Lithuania in October, 1939. In Latvia, a 1925 census reported 95,000 Jews, 5.2 percent of the population. The combination of a low rate of natural increase and migration of young Jews between the two world wars reduced this proportion to 4.8 percent by 1935. The 4,434 Jews in Estonia in 1934 accounted for only 0.4 percent of the population of this country.

The Jews were only one of many national minorities in these areas. About one-third of the population of Poland (eastern and western provinces alike) was not Polish by nationality. The same was true in Romania; according to the 1930 census, only 72 percent of the 18 million residents of the country were ethnic Romanians. The status of the Jews in all these areas was intimately connected with a larger issue: the existence of national minorities in countries with fanatically nationalistic majorities.

The national identity of the Jews was explicit and pronounced in all these locations. In 1937, 98 percent of the Jews of Lithuania defined themselves as Jewish by nationality. In Poland, where language was a reliable measure of the degree of national identity, 84.3 percent of Jews polled in the 1931 census stated that Hebrew or Yiddish was their mother tongue; only 15.7 percent cited Polish. Jewish national identification was even stronger in the eastern areas. Among the Jews of Vilna, for example, 99.2 percent marked Yiddish as their national language, compared with 55 percent of Jews in Poznan.

Even among the few Jews in Estonia, most of whom were descendants of soldiers discharged from the army of Czar Nicholas II (who reigned between 1894 and 1917), the question of national identity was not in doubt. In February, 1925, 75 percent of the Jews in Estonia affiliated themselves with the Jewish minority and were officially recognized as such.

In the 1930 census in Bukovina, 10.9 percent of the population identified itself as Jewish by religion and 10.8 percent by nationality. Of them, 80 percent stated that Yiddish or Hebrew was their mother tongue. The 1930 census in Bessarabia elicited a similar picture of pronounced national identification. Of the 207,000 residents of Bessarabia who identified themselves as Jewish by religion, only 1 percent concealed their nationality and 2.7 percent asserted that they did not know Yiddish.

Nor were the Jews in these areas inclined to assimilate. Mitigating against assimilation were the backwardness of the non-Jewish society, the rapid growth of the exceedingly religious population, the centrality of Yiddish and Hebrew among the Jews, and the size of the Jewish community. To be sure, several large cities had become focal points of assimilation, and there were isolated instances of this phenomenon in Poland. In general, however, the Jews were ill inclined to adopt the majority culture and language. Jewish intellectuals in the Baltic countries (except for the Courland and Memel areas), Polesie, and Bessarabia, had a penchant for Russian culture and language; those in Bukovina and Eastern Galicia were favorably disposed to German culture. The distinctiveness of "Litvak" and "Galician" Jews was determined by characteristic daily habits, customs, mannerisms, and, especially, a feeling of local affinity.

The Jews in these communities were overwhelmingly urban. Ninety-eight percent of the Jews in Estonia resided in nine cities. Of the 95,000 Jews in Latvia, 93 percent were city dwellers, half of them living in the capital city of Riga. Of the 154,000 Jews in Lithuania in 1923, about 45,000 resided in six cities. The restoration of Lithuanian sovereignty in Vilna further increased the proportion of urbanites among Lithuanian Jews.

The urban preferences of Jews were also conspicuous in the eastern frontier provinces of Poland. The table presented here shows the proportion of Jews in urban areas; the Jewish national average in 1931 was approximately 30 percent.

Percentage of Jews in Selected Urban Areas, 1931

Province	District	Pct. of Jews in urban areas
Eastern Galicia	Stanislawow	34.8
	Lvov	33.2
	Tarnopol	34.7
Wolhynia	—	49.1
Lithuanian-Belorussian areas	Polesie	49.2
	Nowogrodek	42.6
	Bialystok	38.4
	Vilna	29.2

The Jews of Bukovina also congregated in cities. According to the 1930 census, 69,000 of the 93,000 Jews in this area resided in cities and towns, about two-thirds of them in the district capital of Czernowitz, whereas in Bessarabia 99,400 Jews, 48 percent of the Jewish population, resided in 17 cities. If one includes the 100,000 Jews who resided in localities defined as "towns," the proportion of urban dwellers among the Jews of Bessarabia rises to 82 percent. This was so despite the Romanian policy in Bukovina and Bessarabia that favored agrarian social strata at the expense of the urban Jewish element.

The proportion of Jews in the cities had been decreasing in all areas of Poland, Romania, and the Baltic countries between the two world wars. This was caused by a general upturn of village-to-city migration, the ascendency of the local bourgeoisie, the concurrent displacement of Jews who held positions of economic importance, and the low fertility rates of urban Jews. Another factor worth noting is the "Polonization" policy practiced in the eastern provinces of this country in order to reinforce the Polish national group there. Nevertheless, the Jews accounted for more than one-third of the population of numerous cities in the 1930s, as the table shows.

Urban Localities in the Eastern Frontier Provinces of Poland, the Baltic Countries,
Bessarabia, and Bukovina between the Two World Wars

Country	City	Total population	Jewish population	% of Jews*	Census year
Poland	Bialystok	91,101	39,165	43	1931
	Baranowicze (Baranovich)	22,818	9,680	42	1931
	Rowne (Rovno)	40,612	22,737	56	1931
	Pinsk	31,912	20,220	63	1931
	Kowel	27,677	12,842	46	1931
	Grodno	49,669	21,159	43	1931
	Brest (Brisk)	48,385	21,440	44	1931
	Luck	35,556	17,366	49	1931
	Lvov (Lwow)	312,231	99,595	32	1931
	Tarnopol	35,633	13,999	40	1931
	Stanislawow	59,960	20,651	34	1931
Lithuania	Vilna (Vilnius)	195,071	55,006	28	1931
	Kovno (Kaunas)	92,446	25,044	27	1923
	Shavli (Siauliai)	21,387	5,338	24	1923
	Ponovezh (Panevezys)	19,197	6,845	36	1923
Latvia	Riga	385,114	43,672	11	1935
	Liepaja (Libau)	57,113	7,379	13	1935
	Dvinsk (Daugavpils)	44,513	11,106	25	1935
Estonia	Tallinn	137,687	2,203	2	1934
	Tartu	57,500	920	2	1934
Bessarabia	Kishinev	114,196	41,066	36	1930
Bukovina	Czernowitz	112,427	52,592	38	1930

*Figures are rounded to the nearest whole number.

The Economy

The typical Jewish sources of livelihood in all these areas, from Estonia
to Bessarabia, were commerce, industry, and the liberal professions.
The Lithuanian population census of 1923 reported 25,000 Jews in
commerce and credit, 18,000 in industry and crafts, 5,000 in agriculture, 4,000 in liberal professions, and 2,500 in "haulage" (i.e., wagoners).
Thus, about 45 percent of Jewish breadwinners engaged in commerce,
including foreign trade. The proportion of Jews in imports/exports fell
to about one-half just before World War II. In Latvia, roughly 50 percent
of Jewish breadwinners engaged in commerce, 7 percent in the liberal professions, and 27 percent in industry and crafts. The corresponding break-
down in Estonia was 57 percent in commerce, 10 percent in liberal
professions, and 3 percent in other professions (i.e., landlords and religious
functionaries).

The eastern frontier provinces of Poland were economically backward and had no significant heavy industry except for oil facilities in Eastern Galicia and the textile industry in Bialystok. This, coupled with the large number of subsistence farmers, made the Jews seem all the more dominant in commerce. In 1931, one-third of all Jews in Poland (37 percent in Wolhynia and Eastern Galicia) supported themselves in this fashion. Sixty percent of all merchants and traders in Poland were Jewish, including more than 70 percent in the eastern provinces, 80 percent in Wolhynia, and 95 percent in Pinsk.

The share of Jews in agriculture was small: 9 percent in Eastern Galicia, 4.4 percent in Wolhynia. Some of these were peasants who had family farms (as in the Wolhynian village of Ignatowka); others had auxiliary farms that met their household needs.

In the eastern provinces of Poland, there was a very small stratum of Jewish industrialists and factory owners, nearly all of whom were involved in the textile industry in Bialystok. Most breadwinners in this category were small craftsmen in the clothing and food industries. Nearly all such Jews in Poland (98 percent) had very small production units. Throughout these areas the Jewish proletariat was composed of small artisans, not wage-earning laborers. Indeed, these people were often worse off financially than wage-earners; their income was not assured and they were never offered tenure.

However, this occupational structure had not been formed by chance. Few Jews were willing to work on the Sabbath, and the general day of rest on Sunday was disadvantageous for them. In their fierce competition for jobs with non-Jews, Jewish workers faced the obstacles of prejudice and the "revolutionary" label that had been affixed to them, reducing their prospects of finding work in non-Jewish enterprises.

The Jewish tendency to self-employment manifested itself strongly in the liberal professions, especially in the eastern provinces. More than 50 percent of all private physicians in Poland were Jews, including 73 percent in Wolhynia and 58 percent in the Eastern Galician areas of Tarnopol and Stanislawow. In Lvov, 73 percent of the lawyers were Jews, compared with 25 percent in all of Poland. In Bukovina, where anti-Jewish restrictions in higher education were not as daunting, the share of Jews in the liberal professions was especially high: 68 percent of the physicians and 85 percent of the lawyers. Throughout Bukovina, 63 percent of Jewish breadwinners engaged in commerce and credit, 23 percent in crafts and industry, 7 percent in haulage and transportation, and 7 percent in agriculture. In Bessarabia the proportions were 40 percent in commerce and credit, 27 percent in crafts, 20 percent in the liberal professions and services, 10 percent in agriculture, and 3 percent in haulage and transportation.

Despite their education and general aptitude, few Jews were admitted to the civil service (except for teaching positions in Jewish schools in the Baltic countries), and few of those in the armed forces gained promotions in rank.

In general, Polish Jewry was an economically distressed group. In 1935, the National Organization of Free Loan Funds published data indicating that roughly 200,000 Jewish families, accounting for approximately one million persons or one-third of the Jewish population of Poland, required public assistance and relief.

The disintegration of parliamentary democracy, and the ascent of violent antisemitism in the three Baltic countries, Poland, and Romania, aggravated the economic pressure under which the Jewish communities functioned. Because the Jews gravitated to specific economic activities, they were easy targets.

In Bessarabia and Bukovina, the economic harassment of Jews was part of the repressive rule of the areas annexed by Romania after World War I. Anti-Jewish measures included withholding of merchants' import permits, nationalization of enterprises and replacement of Jewish workers with Christians, exorbitant taxation of trade, contraction of credit, and legislation that prescribed ethnic quotas in every business and factory, declared Sunday as a general compulsory day of rest and banned of Jews from the civil service.

Jewish livelihoods were indirectly harmed when competitors belonging to the majority group were given subsidies and relief, including assistance in setting up production cooperatives, cheap government credit, and tax breaks. In 1935, Jews were expelled from Romanian trade unions and professional associations such as the Bar Association and the Organization of Accountants, losing their accreditation and the right to practice their occupations.

The government of Poland behaved similarly in its eastern provinces. Some of its actions were directly discriminatory, such as an edict that outlawed ritual slaughter in districts where the proportion of Jews was less than 3 percent of the population. The Polish government, however, did not content itself with this, instead creating an atmosphere that fomented an economic boycott of Jews.

In his first policy speech in the Sejm on June 4, 1936, the Prime Minister of Poland, S. Skladkowski, asserted that "One must avoid doing offense to anyone in Poland, just as a fair landlord permits no offense to anyone in his home. Economic struggle—*owszem.*" This expression, roughly equivalent to "with pleasure," was widely construed as a go-ahead for discrimination and economic persecution. Although much of this was grass-roots activity—protest vigils in front of Jewish businesses, boycotting of Jewish suppliers and their customers — it also found expression in administrative measures against local authorities meant to drive Jewish peddlers out of markets for "aesthetic" reasons.

In the Baltic countries, Jews were the victims of a government program to elevate the backward peasant class to positions of social and economic influence. Most of the related measures were administrative, such as a toughening of credit terms.

Legal and Political Status

The political and legal status of the Jews in the Baltic countries, Poland, and Romania was anchored in international conventions, as well as in the constitutions of these countries. However, the equality of civil rights promised the Jews in these documents had become dead letters by the time of the Soviet invasion. All these states had also assured the Jews cultural and organizational autonomy, as warranted by their status as a recognized national minority. This promise, too, was not fully kept, and Jewish parliamentarians throughout the areas struggled relentlessly for the promised rights.

In the Paris peace conference at the conclusion of World War I that augured the reconstitution of Europe, the Lithuanian delegation had promised national and cultural autonomy to the Jewish population of the country. In 1922, when Lithuania ratified a new national constitution and gained admission to the League of Nations, the government renounced this commitment. A practical manifestation of autonomy that already existed was the Communities Law, gazetted in March, 1920, which gave the Jewish community legal status and entrusted it with responsibility for personal status. The committees of the *kehillot* (community organizations) were elected democratically, and the kehillot were organized under a Jewish National Council that reported to a Minister for Jewish Affairs. This office was abolished in 1924, leaving only two vestiges of Jewish autonomy on the national level: a chain of 83 "people's banks," headed by the Central Jewish Bank for Mutual Assistance, and a comprehensive Jewish education system. Each local community also had local welfare and religious-service committees (Ezro and Adas Yisroel, respectively). The Jews maintained their representation in the Lithuanian Seimas until the parliament was dissolved on December 17, 1926, marking the end of parliamentary democracy in Lithuania.

In Latvia, Jews were represented in the legislature from its formation in November, 1918, until its dissolution in May, 1934. The eradication of parliamentary democracy also marked the end of most political organizations in the country, including those of the Jews. Jewish cultural autonomy in Latvia had been manifested in a network of state-funded free Jewish schools.

Estonia was the only country in Eastern Europe that honored its commitments to its national minorities with respect to cultural and welfare autonomy. In 1926 it established a 27-member "cultural council" to handle all matters of Jewish education. Because the Estonian Jewish community was so small, it was unable to elect a delegate to the Estonian parliament.

In Poland, in contrast, the government was as opposed to Jewish autonomy as to similar arrangements for any other national minority. Jewish autonomy was based on the Jewish kehillot and school system, but the burden of upkeep in Poland, unlike in Lithuania and Latvia, was foisted exclusively on the Jews. In addition, the kehillot were placed under government controls in order to confine their activities to religion and to entrust the leadership to conservative ultra-Orthodox elements.

Because the Jews' autonomous prerogatives had not been defined in legislation, Polish courts and government ministries did as they pleased. A blatant example was their denial of the right of naturalization, which the Jews and other minorities possessed under the minorities treaty. To reduce the proportion of national minorities in the eastern provinces, the authorities misapplied the naturalization rules, using flawed and deficient administrative lists rather than residency on a given date as the basis for awarding citizenship.

When Jews living in the areas annexed by Romania at the end of World War I, including Bukovina and Bessarabia, applied for naturalization, the Romanian authorities behaved similarly. Romania, like Poland, had endorsed the minorities treaty and promised "full rights to all Jews in the old and new areas who do not hold citizenship of other countries." This public commitment was enshrined in the founding constitution of the state.

Jewish national autonomy in Bessarabia, based on a democratically elected kehilla, did not come into being until 1929. The Jewish communities in Bukovina had been recognized under the Austro-Hungarian Empire. The kehillot in Bessarabia and Bukovina, like those in Poland, were allowed to avail themselves of Jewish resources only. The two areas sent delegates to the parliament in Bucharest, and their activity on the national level led to the establishment of the Jewish Party in May, 1931.

Throughout these areas—the Baltic countries, Poland, and Romania—the majority peoples agreed that Jewish national autonomy must never be realized. Liberal and leftist groups favored assimilation as the solution to the "Jewish problem" in their countries. Nationalist and rightist circles sought to force Jews to emigrate; to promote this goal, they vitiated Jewish political influence and practiced economic harassment.

Beginning in the mid-1930s, when the Nazis took over in Germany, political and physical attacks on the Jews multiplied throughout Eastern Europe. Amendments attached to the new Polish constitution in 1934, along with new election rules, reduced Jewish representation to four deputies in the Sejm and two in the Senate.

Official and public attitudes toward the Jews in Poland took a perceptible turn for the worse in May, 1935, with the death of Marshal Josef Pilsudski, long considered the "decisive factor" in maintaining public order in the country. Pogroms began shortly thereafter: in June, 1935, against the Jews of Grodno; in March, 1936, against the Jews of Przytyk; in May, 1937, in Brest; and in June of that year in Czestochowa. In August, 1937, 350 violent incidents against Jews took place in 80 locations throughout Poland. In most cases, the police stood aside.

Following the example of the Nuremberg Laws that were enacted by Nazi Germany in September, 1935, Polish trade unions began inserting an "Aryans-only" clause in their statutes. The physicians' union took this step in May, 1937; the bar association followed suit. In March, 1938, high-school teachers restricted Jewish membership in their union.

In the 1935/36 school year, conditions for Jewish students in institutions of higher education declined further. Universities introduced separate seating for Jews in lecture halls and assemblies; the Polytechnicum of Lvov was the first institution where the administration and the academic institutions endorsed these "ghetto benches." Enforcement was left to Polish students, who were eager to discharge this duty with their fists. In January, 1937, the University of Vilna was shut down for two weeks after students rioted to prevent the entrance of Jews. In November, 1938, two Jewish students were murdered at the University of Lvov; another was slain in May, 1939, at the Polytechnicum of that city. The University of Warsaw was closed in December, 1938, and January, 1939, because of riots meant to rid the campus of Jews.

In Romania, most of the violent antisemitism was sponsored by right-wing fascist groups that had formed in the 1920s. Their spear carrier was the Iron Guard, an organization that by 1928–1930 had gained government backing and Nazi Party assistance. In 1935, under Nazi inspiration, the National Defense League under A. C. Cuza merged with the National Agrarian

Party under O. Goga, forming a large antisemitic party that espoused "Romania for the Romanians." In December, 1937, this group seized the reins of government in Romania and held them for about six weeks, resulting in a torrent of anti-Jewish regulations, including review of the Romanian citizenship of Jews who dealt with the government as suppliers or clients, and dismissal of Jewish doctors from the government health services.

Even when this government yielded to a personal dictatorship under King Carol II, anti-Jewish discrimination did not wane. In February, 1938, a new constitution prescribed "expulsion from the country of all persons who do not possess citizenship rights." A mass review of individuals' rights was launched; by the time it ended in late 1939, the citizenship of about 37 percent of Jewish citizens had been revoked, with especially high rates of revocation in the areas that Romania had annexed at the end of World War I. By February of that year, all journals and organs in the languages of the minority groups, including Hebrew and Yiddish, had been banned. All political parties, including those that served the Jewish rank and file, were dissolved in March, 1938. Harassment and persecution of Jewish students became so vicious that Jews were effectively barred from all higher education institutions in the country by 1939. In an economic accord that it signed with Germany in March, 1939, Romania undertook to "cleanse" a lengthy list of industries of Jews.

In Lithuania, also, the plight of the Jews worsened in the late 1930s. Jews were subjected to violence, although at a lower degree of intensity and scope than in Romania and Poland. The clauses pertaining to Jewish national autonomy were deleted from the 1938 constitution. Organizations of merchants and artisans campaigned under the slogan of "Lithuania for the Lithuanians" and demanded restrictions on trade by Jews. The government acceded to some of these demands, especially with regard to de facto discrimination in taxation.

Public and Party Activity

The effervescent public and political activity among the Jewish masses in the Baltic countries, Poland, and Romania signaled the decline of the "old," apolitical Jewish world, and reflected the Jews' desire to integrate their largely religious past into the secular present. Nevertheless, this community was somewhat estranged from its immediate surroundings; for example, both the Zionists and the Jewish Communists were inordinately interested in areas outside their own countries. However, none of the Jewish public movements, of whatever point of view, neglected or abandoned the struggle of Jews to fortify their status and exercise their rights in their places of residence. Although there was no shortage of individual Jews who assimilated, no Jewish organization preached assimilation.

The scope of the Jewish parties in these countries transcended that of political parties as narrowly defined. These groups were, in fact, surrogates for political entities, providing their members with an all-embracing environment of cultural, economic, intellectual, and educational activity. Party organizations published their own journals, established their own schools, and guided the activities of trade unions and cooperatives.

As a result of the British moratorium in 1936 on Jewish immigration to Palestine, Zionism lost some of its luster among the Jewish rank and file. This magnified the strength of the Bund, whose goals were associated with Jewish life in the Diaspora countries. The Zionist movements, with the exception of He-haluts (which specialized in vocational training of "pioneers" for settlement in Eretz Yisrael), established autonomous regional frameworks that reported directly to the World Zionist Organization.

Despite the ban on Communist activity in Romania, Poland, and the Baltic countries, the Communist Party continued to exist in the underground. Jews were strongly overrepresented in this movement.

Education

Each Jewish collective discussed in this chapter maintained a ramified network of Yiddish- and Hebrew-language education institutions in the 1936 school year. In Lithuania, the Jewish system comprised 108 schools with an enrollment of 13,600 (80 percent of all Jewish pupils that year), not including 2,000 who attended Jewish classes in Lithuanian schools. A large majority (78 percent) of these institutions were primary schools affiliated with the Tarbut system, which stressed the Hebrew language and Zionism. The other schools were associated with the religious Yavneh organization or with Yiddish-speaking movements that emphasized people's socialism. Along with these was a well-developed Orthodox school system: *heder* and *talmud torah* institutions for boys and famous *yeshivot* such as those of Slobodka, Telz, Ponovezh (Panevezys), and Kelm for teenagers and young adults. Primary schooling in Lithuania was fully funded by government and local authorities; much of the upkeep expense for the 16 Jewish gymnasia (high schools)—14 conducted in Hebrew and two in Yiddish—was borne by the parents.

Restrictions affecting the admission of Jewish students to medical, agricultural, and engineering programs were progressively toughened in the 1930s. Consequently, the number of Jewish students in the University of Kovno fell from 1,050 in 1931 to 350 in 1939. Of the 411 teachers in this university, only six were Jewish.

The Jewish school system in Latvia was composed of 60 primary schools (enrollment of 11,000) and 11 high schools in the 1938/39 school year. Since 1934, when Agudath Israel had taken control of Jewish education in Latvia, the number of Yiddish-language secular schools had decreased significantly and the Hebrew-language secular schools were at a disadvantage. The number of Jews enrolled at the University of Riga decreased by 42 percent between 1934 (764) and 1939 (444).

In Estonia, after protracted discord within the community, the Jews designated Hebrew the language of instruction in the Jewish school system, in which 75 percent of Jewish children in the country were enrolled.

In Poland, the government undertook in its minorities treaty to support Jewish primary schools and assist with their upkeep. However, it never kept its word, instead establishing "bilingual schools"—all studies were to be in Polish with the exception of Hebrew lessons and a bit of religion. These schools did not meet on the Sabbath or Jewish festivals. The number of such schools throughout the country never exceeded 31, and the authorities began closing them down in 1934, transferring pupils to ordinary public schools. In 1930, no government school in Poland went about its work in Yiddish or Hebrew, compared with 1,400 government schools in which the language of instruction was Ukrainian, Belorussian, German, Czech, Lithuanian, or Russian.

Most Jewish educational institutions in Poland were publicly owned and connected with political parties. Agudath Israel supported the Horeb and Beth Jacob systems for boys and girls, respectively; in 1937, the latter system had 818 schools with an enrollment of 109,000, of which 20 percent (schools and enrollments) were concentrated in Eastern Galicia. The Mizrachi movement supported the 134-school, 14,500-student Yavneh system (figures for 1933). Tarbut, identified with the General Zionists, operated 72 kindergartens, 183 primary schools, and 14 post-primary schools, with an enrollment of 45,000 in 1934 and 1935. On the eve of World War II, about 90 percent of these primary schools were concentrated in the two eastern border provinces, from Wolhynia north. The Bund sponsored the Yiddish-language school system TSISHO (*Tsentrale Idishe Shul Organizatsie*—Central Yiddish School Organization) which in 1934–1935 maintained 176 institutions from kindergarten through high school, with an enrollment of 15,500. Among the primary schools in these systems, 314 were located in the eastern districts—Vilna, Bialystok, Pinsk, Nowogrodek (Novogrudek), and so on. The parents were responsible for upkeep. Graduates of the Jewish schools were denied "government rights" (i.e., government matriculation certificates and the possibility of advancing to higher studies in Polish institutions).

The eastern provinces were home to yeshivot whose reputation and influence reverberated far beyond their immediate surroundings, such as Mir, Radon, Grodno, Baranowicze, Brest, Kremenets, Slonim, Kletsk (Klezk), Rowne, Luck, Kobryn, and Korets. The Va'ad Hayeshivos, a central committee in Vilna, administered the affairs of 78 yeshivot, in which 6,000 young men were enrolled.

Romania, too, had undertaken in its minorities treaty to give Romanian citizens associated with all ethnic, religious, and linguistic minorities a fair share of public funds, government budgets, and municipal council moneys for their particular education needs. In practice, the government renounced this commitment, leaving the burden of Jewish education in Bessarabia in the parents' hands. In the 1920/21 school year, the country had 52 Yiddish-language primary schools with an enrollment of 5,757; by the end of the 1930s, few of these had survived. Tarbut, in contrast, maintained its kindergarten–to–high school system until the eve of the Soviet annexation. In the 1939/1940 school year, Tarbut supported 52 institutions (32 primary schools, five high schools, 15 kindergartens) with 5,300 pupils and 250 teachers.

Dozens of Jewish daily newspapers (most in Yiddish) were published in the eastern Polish provinces, Romania, and, especially, the Baltic countries between the two world wars. Their numbers dwindled steadily, however, in part because of official sanctions. As the Red Army moved in, nearly 20 Yiddish-language dailies survived, including four in Vilna alone, in addition to hundreds of journals in Hebrew, Yiddish, and other languages.

As for the masses of Jewish youth for whom Zionism offered no attraction, the following remarks by Jacob Lestschinsky are worth citing:

Jewish youth were profoundly depressed. Not only in Poland and Romania, but also in Lithuania and Latvia, [they] had been deprived of all economic and spiritual opportunities. . . . It should therefore come as no surprise that in the gloomy cellars of Warsaw, Lodz, Bialystok, Pinsk, Kishinev, and Czernowitz, Jewish youngsters aged 15-16 sought redemption in Communist propaganda tracts and spent years in prison.

2

First Reactions

In contrast to the majority peoples in the Soviet-annexed territories, who considered the Red Army invasion of their countries in national and cultural terms, the attitude of the Jewish population was influenced by the substantive and potential dangers the Jews faced when the war broke out. Their concern intensified with the reports of Nazi atrocities in Poland. The Jews in the Romanian provinces and the Baltic countries were also influenced by reports of the Soviet authorities' attitude toward the Jews in Poland, as described by refugees and the press.

EASTERN POLAND

Just before the Soviet occupation, the Jews in eastern Poland had experienced a series of horrors.

When fighting broke out between Poland and Germany on September 1, 1939, parts of Belorussia, Wolhynia, and Eastern Galicia came under German aerial bombardment that lasted until the Red Army marched in on September 17. Because the bombings were aimed at industrial centers, railroad junctions, and important intersections, urban communities suffered the most damage.

Waves of refugees from the western areas of Poland, including thousands of Jews, clogged the transportation routes and aggravated the shortage of commodities. The refugees had been scarred, literally and figuratively, by the horrors of the war, the bombardments, and the Nazis' anti-Jewish atrocities, often experienced first-hand. The Wehrmacht had occupied many localities in the area between the Bug, Narew, Vistula, and San Rivers (staying there until the final disposition of the occupied areas on September 28, 1939), and the Jewish inhabitants had lived through, or fled from, a spate of Nazi terror.

In Eastern Galicia, the German army reached several major towns including Sambor, Strij, Drohobycz, and Borislav (Boryslaw). Wehrmacht troops abused the Jewish population, looting property and causing injuries. In Wolhynia, the Germans held the town of Luboml for some time, terrorizing the Jewish community there. In Belorussia, they overran a string of towns and committed atrocities against the Jews. On Yom Kippur 5700 (September 23, 1939), they entered the town of Kolno, dragging worshipers from the synagogue to a nearby camp and forcing them to clean stables. Before leaving the town, they set the synagogue ablaze. In Sokal, the Nazis tortured the head of the community and the town rabbi, who was forced at the crack of a whip to dance naked as his community looked on. Arson was part of the operation. In Zamosc, the Germans looted and vandalized Jewish homes as soon as they had entered. In Czyzewo, the Germans drafted many Jews to clear away rubble. In Augustow, too, dozens of Jews were rounded up for forced labor; all were shot to death the day before the Red Army came into the town.

As the invading armies from east and west advanced, the Polish governing institutions from the Soviet-Polish border to the banks of the Vistula were wiped out. In this interim state of anarchy, which recurred several times in the areas that the Soviet Union and Germany handed back and forth, violent antisemites and pogrom-mongers were given free rein.

In eastern Galicia, the Ukrainians began to organize pogroms. In other areas, such as Borislav, pogroms were averted only because Red Army soldiers happened on the scene. Ukrainians behaved in this fashion in Wolhynia as well; again, only the arrival of the Red Army prevented plunder and bloodshed. Polish antisemites found this an opportune time to settle scores with the Jews. As vestigial units of the Polish army fled into Romania, they savaged any Jews who happened to be in the way, especially after they discovered that the Soviet forces were closing in from the east. The pretext for this behavior was their association of Jews with the Bolsheviks and their belief that the Jews had "stabbed Poland in the back."

It is worth noting that wherever the Red Army distanced itself from the German forces (under its agreement with Germany), the Soviets helped evacuate Jews and members of other national groups that had reason to fear the Germans. Many Jews were evacuated from several towns in the Lublin area to other localities controlled by the Red Army. The Soviet authorities took similar action on behalf of thousands of Jews in Vilna in October, 1939, when this city was handed over to the Lithuanian army. Many of these Jews (especially workers in the Elektrit factory) were transported to the Belorussian capital of Minsk and other areas in western Belorussia. Quite a few of the evacuees, of course, were affiliated with leftist groups.[1]

Thus the Jews of eastern Poland had good reason to greet the Red Army with relief. A Jew from the Eastern Galician city of Tarnopol described this sensation aptly:

All the Jews in town greeted the Soviet army with satisfaction and relief. In fact, no one understood what was going on. People felt that the period of hiding in shelters was over and that at long last, after two weeks of anarchy, there was some kind of government. As for the consequences of this change, we knew nothing; time would tell. . . . In any case, the bombardments would stop and the Gentile population would spring no surprises on the Jews of Tarnopol.[2]

The diary of a visitor from Palestine who spent the period in Vilna expresses a similar reaction of tremendous release from relentless tension and fear:

The people were relieved of such a sense of melancholy. . . . It is hard to describe the emotion that swept me as I saw in the street, across from our gate, a Russian tank bearing grinning young men with a blazing red star on their berets. As the machines came to a halt, the people crowded around. Somebody shouted, "Long live the Soviet government!" and everyone cheered. . . . You could hardly find a Gentile in that crowd. . . . Many people did not stop and consider what this regime would bring in its wake. Many of our fellow Jews would have to give up life-long habits and indulgences. . . . But who took stock in those days? At a time when the German axe was raised over their necks, everyone greeted the Russians unanimously, as they would the Messiah. . . .[3]

Various accounts attest to the joyous welcome that the Red Army received almost everywhere. When the Jews of Kowel (in Wolhynia) were informed that the Red Army was approaching the town, they "celebrated all night."[4] When the Red Army actually entered Kowel, "the Jews greeted [it] with indescribable enthusiasm."

Shalom Hamiel, in his remarks about Rowne, explained succinctly why the Russians were regarded as "redeemers": "One Jew told me: 'I know who the Bolsheviks are. I know they'll take my property, but they will leave me with my life.' "[5]

As in Eastern Galicia and Wolhynia, the Jewish communities of Belorussia greeted the Soviets with an outpouring of passion and delight. In Baranowicze, "People kissed the soldiers' dusty boots. . . . Children ran to the parks, picked the autumn flowers, and showered the soldiers with them . . . . Red flags were found in the blink of an eye, and the entire city was bedecked in red. . . ."[6] The town of Kobryn was awash in red flags, which local Communists had prepared by removing the white stripe from the two-color Polish flag. The cheering crowd scattered leaflets castigating the fascist Polish regime and lauding the Red Army and its augury of liberation.[7] In Ciechanowice, a band of Jewish Communists erected an "arch of triumph" bedecked with posters bearing general greetings and messages such as "Long Live the Soviet Regime." The Jews of Rozhinoy (Rozana or Ruzhany) treated the day of the Soviet occupation as a religious festival, greeting each other with *mazel tov*.[8]

With this sudden liberation from their desperate circumstances, even Jews who expected an unhappy future under the thumb of the Red Army shared some of their compatriots' good cheer. One such Jew, a well-known Zionist in the town of Slonim, disregarded that day the political and personal ordeal that the Soviet regime had in store for him. "The main thing," he reasoned, "is that we escaped the predatory claws of the Nazi beasts at the very last moment. If so, a Jewish city is about to recite the blessing of deliverance!"[9]

Notably, personal and collective relief was not the only factor that caused this favorable reception of the Red Army. The elders, remembering the Bolsheviks' behavior during their war with Poland in 1920, were pleasantly surprised by the conduct of the soldiers who entered the areas now. Instead of barefoot troops who plundered everything, the USSR now fielded a disciplined army, modestly attired (compared with the Polish army) but equipped with modern technology. Most Polish communities had never seen tanks or other sophisticated machines of war before; these inevitably fostered the impression of a mighty, trustworthy force. Furthermore, the troops had been given explicit orders prohibiting the appropriation of anything from local residents; the army was to tender full payment for any supplies it needed. The Red Army soldiers and officers were polite when conversing with local residents, addressing themselves courteously to questions and requests.

For local Communists, a majority of whom were Jewish, the arrival of the Red Army spelled an end to a perilous underground existence. It was also the fulfillment of a dream: the imposition of Communist rule in their country. Thus the local Communists hastened to find favor in the eyes of the new regime.

The manifestations of relief, however, were accompanied by other assessments. The residents of Strij greeted the Soviet army with mixed emotions: the Poles with loathing, the Ukrainians with a guarded attitude, and the Jews with the sobriety of a community accepting the lesser of two evils. Moshe Kleinboim (Sneh), who spent some time in the Soviet-annexed area, described this ambivalence:

They say the Jews greeted the Red Army with open arms, but that's not what happened. Typically, an aphorism summing up the condition of the Jews when the Soviets arrived was cooked up and circulated instantly, to wit: until now we were condemned to death; now our death sentence has been commuted to life imprisonment. They knew that they'd receive scraps of bread and drops of water, that they wouldn't be able to emigrate, but that they'd be spared the ignominy of Nazi torture and murder. This is how the Jewish masses read the situation.[10]

Other feelings that found expression were socioeconomic and political uncertainty and confusion. As the new regime consolidated itself, these feelings proved to be well founded.

During the preparations for the arrival of the Red Army, and immediately after its advent, young Jews in many locations formed semi-military groupings with names like "People's Militia," "Workers' Guard," and so on. It was the task of these organizations to maintain local security, order, and sound administration. Above all, they were to prevent any disturbances as the Red Army came in. These youngsters often armed themselves with light weapons left behind by the Polish police. In lieu of uniforms, they tied red ribbons to their sleeves. The very fact of armed Jews visibly imposing order made their fellow Jews even more eager to greet the Soviet forces.

THE BALTIC COUNTRIES

Unlike Poland, which had experienced a brutal war in which Jews had been murdered, the Baltic countries were politically stable and militarily calm when the Red Army marched in on June 15–17, 1940. The Jews in these countries, anxious about the growing Nazi menace, were relieved, regarding the arrival of the Red Army above all as a barrier to Nazi influence and all its peril.

Throughout Lithuania, and especially among Lithuanian Jews, a rumor stubbornly circulated that the Red Army had preceded the Wehrmacht into the country by only a few hours, after "Russia's superb espionage apparatus successfully uncovered the Germans' malicious plan."[11] Indeed, Jews, particularly young Jews, were conspicuously present in the masses of onlookers that roared their approval as the Red Army columns approached the cities. They "came out to [the troops], greeting them with cheers and flowers, thanking God, and saying 'better Stalin than Hitler.' "[12] Especially joyous were members of the Communist Party and other leftist organizations, in which the share of Jews, as stated, was relatively large. Non-Jewish Lithuanians in the crowd, many furious about the Soviet invasion and grieving for their lost national independence, noted the Jews' behavior.

Many Jews had been aware of the possibility of a Soviet invasion of Lithuania and regarded it as the lesser of two evils. When the event suddenly and dramatically came to pass, however, it evoked some confusion and apprehension. Meir Kantarowicz, an activist in Section B of the General Zionist Party and a teacher at the Hebrew Gymnasium in Kovno, disclosed his feelings to his students, "voice choking and eyes weeping. Now," he said, "a difficult period has begun for the Jews in general and Zionists in particular." Kantorovitz preferred the advent of the Germans, who killed only bodies, than the Russians, who killed souls.[13]

Although Latvia did not share a border with Germany, the Jewish response to the arrival of the Red Army in this country, also, was essentially favorable. As evidence, the Jews turned out en masse in the streets of the capital and the peripheral cities, profusely kissing the Red Army tank crew members. Some Jews helped to protect Red Army units and thwart acts of resistance and provocation by Latvian military and nationalist organizations such as Aizsargs and Perkonkrust ("Thundercross").[14]

Older Jewish residents, who had strong recollections of the harsh Soviet treatment of Latvia in early 1919, hoped that the USSR would settle for imposing a pro-Soviet regime this time.

The Jews in Estonia did not look forward to a reprise of the period of Soviet rule in 1918–1919. However, alongside the apprehensions of many—especially the affluent and the elderly—the Jews had several good reasons to greet the Red Army with relief and even satisfaction. Nazi influence was growing in this country and had already manifested itself in violent incidents with Estonian Gentiles.

Young Jews with leftist inclinations greeted the Red Army with special alacrity and pronounced delight. These included Socialist-Zionists, members of the pro-Communist Licht association, and Communist Party activists who had operated in the underground until then. One of these, Aaron Gutkin, son of a wealthy industrialist and noted public figure, was the individual who hauled down the Estonian national flag from the top of Pik Herman in Tallinn.[15]

NORTHEASTERN ROMANIA

Apart from the fact that Bessarabia and Northern Bukovina were the last areas of Eastern Europe to be annexed by the Soviet Union in the beginning of World War II, special local circumstances in these provinces affected the way in which local Jews greeted the Red Army.

Many cast their lot with the Soviet Union out of fear that Nazi influence in Romania would grow. Some Jews, including members of Zionist youth movements, shifted their allegiance to the Communist camp at that time.[16] The movement leaders tried to counter these leftist tendencies and even prepared to go into the underground in the event of a Red Army takeover.[17] In general, it may be said that the Soviet invasion of Bessarabia and Northern Bukovina caused the Jews much confusion.

This is not to say that the events themselves took them totally by surprise. As residents of areas that bordered the western Ukraine, they were relatively well informed (by refugees and the press) of developments in the Soviet-annexed areas. For this reason, and evidently in view of memories of Bolshevik rule in Bessarabia in 1918–1919, some Jews—mostly industrialists and landowners, but also some public figures—made last-minute preparations to flee to the interior of Romania. To do this, however, they had to cross the Prut River, and few succeeded. Exacerbating the confusion was the vagueness of the Soviet ultimatum. The Soviet deadline for evacuating Bessarabia of Romanian forces was evidently extended by at least 48 hours before the invasion, but Red Army columns rolled into Kishinev as early as June 29, leaving no time for reasoned decisions.[18]

As the Romanian army retreated, it vented its rage on the civilian population. Special fury was reserved for the Jews, who were accused of pro-Soviet sympathies and provocative attacks on the retreating Romanian troops.[19] Anti-Jewish violence was especially rampant in the Bukovina area. In Czernowitz (Chernovtsy), soldiers opened fire on a crowd of leftist demonstrators, killing one young Jew, just a few hours before the first Soviet tanks entered the city.[20]

Attacks on Jews—beatings, humiliation, looting—became a mass phenomenon in the towns and villages of Northern Bukovina. Many Jewish soldiers en route to their units in the Romanian army were hurled from moving railroad cars. The anti-Jewish brutality of Romanian soldiers continued on Romanian soil (i.e., that controlled by King Carol II).[21] In response, masses of Jewish refugees streamed back to Bessarabia and Northern Bukovina from various parts of Romania. Those affiliated with the left were especially impatient as they waited for the Red Army. Quite a few young Jews, men and women, affixed to their sleeves the red ribbons that identified them as members of "combat companies" that had been established to maintain order and prevent attacks on equipment and property. They helped break into prisons and release political prisoners, including Jews active in the Communist Party. When the Communists in Czernowitz invited Jews to take part in the guard formations that patrolled the city just before the Red Army came in, members of Ha-shomer ha-Tsa'ir (a left-wing Zionist youth movement) responded by issuing a German-language leaflet in honor of the invading forces.[22] Much of the rank and file, such as the "Yiddishists" and, in particular, the socially disadvantaged, were more than pleased at the thought of Soviet rule, displaying their joy with utter sincerity at the festive parades and assemblies that abounded at the time. In some cases, Jews taunted and mocked the retreating Romanian troops.[23]

In Bessarabia, Jews waited with tense anticipation as the Red Army approached. When it arrived, they turned out en masse to witness and greet it. A Jewish officer in the Red Army at the time described the reception in his memoirs:

As we entered Kishinev, we found all the sidewalks on the main street (Alexandrovka) full of Jews. They greeted us with delight, applauded as we passed, and showered us with wreaths of flowers. The Jews of Kishinev observed my face and knew I was Jewish. Whenever I walked down the streets, they approached me and conversed with me in Russian. Almost all the adults knew Russian; so did members of affluent families and the intelligentsia.[24]

The Jewish masses in Bessarabia were indeed gripped with enthusiasm at the sight of the Red Army columns. Not only laborers, artisans, unskilled workers, and the poor, but also the well-to-do, regarded the new rulers as their redeemers.[25] A Zionist and public functionary from the town of Romanovka described the experience in a letter to his relatives:

A great miracle took place, almost like that of Purim. With the help of the Soviet government, we were redeemed from disaster. Dozens of Jews in our town had been on the blacklist drawn up by the Romanian "Hamans," who intended to destroy them. I myself was among those at the top of the blacklist. Thus, thanks to the new Soviet regime, we were saved from certain death.[26]

However hyperbolic this account may sound, it mirrors the feelings of many Jews—that is, that the new regime had saved them from catastrophe.[27] The Jews of Bessarabia, it would seem, had not forgotten the 1903 pogrom in Kishinev.

3

Identification and Integration

The totalitarian nature of the Soviet regime being what it was, the military and civilian authorities in the annexed territories did not content themselves with asserting their legal and administrative pre-eminence. Rather, they required the local populace to accept the system's ideological underpinnings at all times and in all ways, and to take part in its political institutions. For long-term political reasons, the Soviet authorities sought to achieve the political and ideological integration of the majority peoples in each of these areas (Ukrainians, Belorussians, Lithuanians, and so on). Nevertheless, they invested considerable effort, at least at first, to attract members of national minorities that had natural pro-Soviet sympathies at the time: the Latgalians in Latvia, the Russians in Lithuania, the Czechs in eastern Poland, and, particularly, the Jews in all the annexed areas. For the last-mentioned, the authorities even circulated Yiddish-language leaflets in many localities.

The first manifesto that the Soviet government issued, just before the Red Army entered eastern Poland, spoke only of "the sufferings of our Ukrainian and Belorussian brethren." However, several days later, the Jews were included in the sympathy and warmth that semi-official Soviet representatives displayed. These representatives, such as Red Army soldiers and commanders (many of whom were Jewish), repeatedly stressed the equality that the Soviet government offered all peoples and racial groups, thereby implicitly promising that the Jews' sufferings under the previous regime would come to an end.

The Soviet Jewish press expressed few reservations in its coverage of the Jews of Eastern Poland, including them, along with the Ukrainians and the Belorussians, among the peoples that had suffered gravely under the reactionary Polish regime. This regime, they asserted, had continued Czarist policies that degraded all the minorities, including the Jews.

The Jewish community of eastern Poland was virtually leaderless when the Red Army entered the area, and there were no major Jewish institutions to echo the rank-and-file's spontaneous reactions of joy. This was not the case in the Baltic countries, where the Red Army entered without the tumult of war and mass migrations. Here, at first, the day-to-day activities of the Jewish communities' leadership continued almost routinely, and Jewish newspapers rolled off the presses as if nothing out of the ordinary had occurred. Here, as in Poland, large numbers of Jews were grateful to the Soviets, if only because their arrival had spared them the alternative of a Nazi takeover. This feeling manifested itself in the local Jewish press.[1]

In Latvia many Jews remembered the militant rule and, especially, the harsh economic policies applied by the Bolsheviks (Soviets) in early 1919. Some Jews, however, hoped that the Soviet Union would settle this time for a liberal pro-Soviet regime or, at least, an arrangement of the sort made for the People's Republic of Mongolia.[2] Secularist circles—Zionist and non-Zionist—regarded the downfall of the previous regime as marking the end of Agudath Israel (Orthodox) control of the state Jewish education system. The Zionist mouthpiece in Latvia, *Unzer Vort,* congratulated the new government for this accomplishment, asserting that it had "already shown itself to be democratic and progressive compared with the previous oppressive regime, which had consigned the 90,000-strong Jewish community to [the control of] a handful of clerics."[3] When the new Prime Minister of Latvia met with the chief rabbi of the Liepaja (Libau) community, A. B. Nurock, the Jewish public was similarly enthused.

The Jews in the annexed districts of Romania also were relieved and hopeful for a few weeks after the havoc that they had experienced. A revealing manifestation of this feeling is provided in the memoirs of Zvi Yavetz, who had been a gymnasium pupil in Czernowitz at the time. He related that he had come home late at night after attending festivities in honor of the new regime in the center of town: "It was the first time in my life that I was happy to return alone at night without fear of an altercation with some Romanian or Ukrainian on the way."[4]

As in the other annexed areas, the Jews tended, in the first few weeks of the Red Army presence, to interpret almost everything in the most favorable light, to overlook flaws, and to suppress their apprehensions. These tendencies peaked when the first secretary of the Ukrainian Communist Party, N. S. Khrushchev, announced, in a large assembly in Kishinev, that no residents of Bessarabia would be penalized for their past. Similar remarks about the "glowing future" awaiting Bessarabian Jewry, among other population groups, were uttered in early July, 1940, by the Soviet poet Itzik Fefer when he addressed an assembly in Kishinev in Red Army uniform. Although he did not neglect to assail the Bundists and the Zionists, the tone of his speech was moderate and consistent with the "honeymoon" that the other annexed areas were experiencing.

In these Romanian districts, as in the Polish areas and the Baltic countries, there were still some Jewish individuals and groups, including Yiddishists and Zionists, who entertained delusions about the possibility of carrying on under the new regime. The Yiddishists pinned their hopes on the regime's sympathies for Yiddish culture; the Zionists made cautious inquiries with the authorities, expecting some sign of change in their attitude toward Zionism.

The advent of the grinning soldiers, coupled with proclamations and assurances by representatives of the military and civilian administration, evoked expectations in Jewish hearts that were whetted by an influx of Jewish repatriates from the west side of the Prut River (i.e., from the Regat, part of the kingdom of Romania).[5] The Soviet authorities were especially interested in advertising this phenomenon and stressing its human and political significance.[6] In Kiev, the daily newspaper *Der Shtern* published the story of a young Jewish physician who had completed his studies in Bucharest and fled from the Romanian capital. In Bucharest, he had been waylaid by students from the "Iron Guard," an antisemitic fascist organization. Many such academics, as well as other refugees, found high-ranking official positions in their professional fields under the new regime.

JEWS IN SOVIET GOVERNING INSTITUTIONS

In the very first days of the Red Army presence in eastern Poland, parts of Romania, and the Baltic countries—and, in certain cases, even preceding the takeover—Jews were active in setting up the institutions of the new government. They were prominent in guard formations of the militia, bodies known as revolutionary or provisional "committees," and so on. The presence of Jews in these organizations was conspicuous in the towns and cities.

Some participants belonged to Jewish leftist circles; and some were young adults who identified with the Soviet regime despite the lack of a defined ideological background. Most, however, were Communist Party members who, having just emerged from prison or the underground, regarded themselves as natural partners in laying the foundations of the new regime.

In the Soviet military administration it was widely (and correctly) believed at the time that the Jewish minority was one of the most reliable elements in existence at that stage. This was especially true in eastern Poland, where the Soviet authorities had not had time to prepare properly for the new situation in view of the dizzying speed of events in the autumn of 1939. Jews were visible in all agencies of the civil administration as the Soviet regime consolidated itself before the official annexation of the western Ukraine and western Belorussia in November, 1939.

A Jewish Communist who had been released from prison by the outbreak of the war and reached the town of Chelm, which was under Soviet rule at the time (it was subsequently handed over to the Germans), describes the entire town as having been in Jewish hands; the mayor was Jewish, and all the policemen and municipal office holders were Jewish Communists with the exception of "a few Poles."[7] In Zamosc, so many Jews joined the local militia that they accounted for a majority in its ranks. When the Soviets quit the town (after the border between the Soviet and German areas was drawn), scores of Jewish militiamen joined Red Army formations that were retreating to the east.[8]

In Telechany, Pinsk district, the Polish police commander turned the town over to the local Jews before he fled the area:

The local police commander appeared on the portico of the police building with his replacement, Rabbi Glick, the brothers Leibel and Ephraim Klitnik, and other comrades who were known in Telechany to be Communists. The commander announced tersely that they were quitting the town. . . and to ensure the safety of the people and the property, he was handing all weapons in the police station to community representatives headed by Rabbi Glick. Rabbi Glick and the commander shook hands, and Rabbi Glick, speaking Russian, told the crowd that had gathered, "I'm running the town of Telechany from now on. Anyone who disobeys my orders will be punished very severely. I hereby appoint Comrade Leibel Klitnik as the town commander."

Leibel's brother Ephraim was subsequently appointed magistrate and deputy chairman of the municipal council.[9]

The same thing happened in Eastern Galicia. A Jew headed the provisional committee of the town of Strij. In Borislav, well-known Communists who had spent many years in Polish prisons assumed important positions in the municipal administration. According to Jewish sources. Jews accounted for 70 percent of the members of the militia in certain Eastern Galician localities.[10]

Among the localities in Wolhynia in which Jews served as mayors (or, as the function was known then, chairmen of municipal councils) at the time, the most conspicuous were cities in which the Jews were a majority or a plurality, such as Dabrowica (94 percent Jewish according to a 1931 census), Ostrog (61 percent), and Luck (50 percent). In the last-named, the largest city in Wolhynia, the Jewish mayor was quickly replaced by a Ukrainian brought in from "the east"; this process was repeated in many other places. After the National (People's) Assembly elections, the absolute and relative representation of Jews in the militia, too, diminished, as Ukrainians—locals or "imports" from the Eastern Ukraine—took over.

A new Jewish elite of sorts, composed of officials and confidantes of the new establishment, took shape at this time. Its members were people who, until the Red Army takeover, had been marginal players in the arena of Jewish public activity. This new elite replaced, to some extent, the veteran elite that was immobilized, silenced, or eliminated by the circumstances of the war and the new realities. This trend persisted even after Ukrainians and Belorussians dislodged the Jewish functionaries who had established the provisional institutions.

In Lithuania and the other Baltic countries, the advent of the Red Army was rarely coupled with the flight of local administrators, and there was no need to set up provisional governing bodies. Thus the integration of Jews into the various administrative echelons was less spontaneous here. In the main, the authorities availed themselves of Jewish intelligentsia affiliated with pro-Communist circles, such as MOPR (an international organization for political prisoners, also known as "Red Aid"), and the leftist Kultur Lige. Indeed, Dr. Leon Kogan, Minister of Health in the People's Government of Lithuania, and the deputy ministers for trade and industry had been known for many years as sympathizers and active supporters of the Lithuanian Communist Party when this party was in the underground, even though they were officially unaffiliated. The same was true for Victor Mitselmacher, the acting Minister of Health, and Jacob Ziman, who was appointed to the Supreme Court. Another de facto member of the Party, Berl Latvis-Fridman—one of the few attorneys in the Party—was named to the Supreme

Court, so that two members of this august body, which had only 11 members in all, were Jews. In early 1941, the veteran Communist Eliahu Bilevitz was named Minister of Food. Thus at least one Jew, not including deputy ministers, sat in the Lithuanian cabinet (the Council of People's Commissars) throughout most of the period of Soviet rule. These cabinet members and deputy ministers were the first Jews to occupy such positions in 16 years, since Shimshon Rozenboim, an attorney, had been the Minister of Jewish Affairs during the "golden era" of Lithuanian autonomy. A similar situation prevailed in the Lithuanian parliament (the Seimas). At the time, the legislature had four Jewish delegates out of 79, and one of them (Yankl Vinitski) was elected to the Seimas presidium (which eventually became the Supreme Soviet of the Lithuanian SSR).

While almost no Jews had served in the internal security services in independent Lithuania, growing numbers of Jewish policemen were now seen in the public domain—a development that the Jewish rank-and-file greeted with undisguised satisfaction. Jews were appointed to responsible positions in the militia and the NKVD. Nominees for the latter had been Communist Party members during the underground period and had spent many years in prison. Even so, the representation of Jewish functionaries in governmental and public institutions, particularly in the high-visibility echelons, did not exceed the proportion of Jews in the population.

In Latvia, where governmental, municipal, and cooperative systems had been off-limits for Jews, the Jewish presence became conspicuous. For example, one of the best-known physicians in Riga, Dr. M. Yoffe, was named to head the local health administration. V. Blumenthal was appointed to manage the governmental bank. Reuven Arsh served as mayor of Preili. Many Jews joined information and press services. In the army, Jewish soldiers were promoted in rank and appointed as *politruks* (political officers), and Jews were admitted to an officer candidate training facility known as the Riga Infantry School.

The Jews' opportunities to participate in the military and defense system became almost unlimited when a "Workers' Guard" was established on July 2, 1940, as a government auxiliary "in the struggle against counterrevolutionary elements." This organization, operating in Riga and other towns, was constructed along military lines and had 10,000 members, both men and women, some of whom carried light arms and wore special uniforms. Among those joining the ranks of this organization were not only Jewish Communists and members of the Komsomol but also former members of the Bund, Left Po'aley Tsiyon, and Zionist *hakhsharot* (training centers where young Zionists prepared for lives of pioneering in Palestine), affiliated with socialist Zionist movements. The centers of the Workers' Guard also hosted ideological and social activities. Jews constituted a majority of members in certain locations, and activities there were conducted, at least for some time, in Yiddish. Many Jewish members of the Guard, and others with ranking positions in the army, the security system, and the Party, played important roles in the subsequent war against the Nazis, either in the regular army or within other frameworks.

It was clear to the Jews of Estonia that they had to adjust to the new conditions and make the most of the integration opportunities that the new regime offered them. A Jew from Tartu, about 20 years old at the time, who set out to greet the Red Army, described himself and his immediate surroundings in the following words:

From the day the Russians came in, there was a feeling that we could do anything and that antisemitism was gone for good. The first indication of this was the appointment of Jews to government positions—something that had never happened under the previous regime.[11]

Jews were indeed appointed to governmental and public positions. L. Eisenstadt was appointed to a high-ranking position in the Ministry of Finance and edited the major newspaper *Rahva Haal* for some time. A Dr. Markovitz was appointed to manage the Merchant Bank. One Shmotkin served as a senior official in the Ministry of Trade, and a man named Savior was the Commissar of Nationalized Businesses.

Integration into the army and the security system was of special interest to the Jews. Jews with leftist leanings took up important positions: Victor Feigin, who had fought in the Spanish Civil War and was active in the Communist underground in Estonia, was appointed to command the central prison in Tallinn and subsequently served as the security officer of the Council of People's Commissars. Young Jews of lower-class origins were promoted to officer rank in the militia and the security services. Idel Jakobson, born to a well-known Jewish family in Tartu, was appointed head of the NKVD investigations department.

In Bessarabia, the hasty flight of the Romanian officials on June 29–30, 1940, created a gaping void in the local police system and other government services; most of these posts were taken up by local Jews. The new appointees were mainly former political prisoners, Communist activists, and young adults from proletarian families. Jews of similar origins were named to head municipal councils: Izia Morgenstern in the town of Soroka, Krig in Yedintsy, Haym Lipschitz in Britchevo (Briceva), Avraham Wallach in Lipkany, and others. In most cases, however, these individuals and others in key positions did not retain their posts for long;[12] most yielded them to local non-Jews or replacements "imported" from the eastern side of the Dniester. Some of the latter, too, were Jews, and even though few came into contact with their local compatriots, the very presence of these ranking officials evoked national pride.

In Northern Bukovina, a blatant Ukrainization policy, manifested from the very first, kept the Jewish presence in the high and middle governmental echelons to a minimum. In contrast, a relatively large number of Jews—especially doctors, engineers, accountants, economists, lawyers, and the like—were appointed to managerial positions in the administrative and service sectors. A relatively rare instance of the appointment of a Jew to a senior governmental position occurred when Mikhail Doktorovitz, a member of the Czernowitz local council and the principal of Jewish School No. 14, was named to an eight-member delegation invited to Moscow for the seventh session of the Supreme Soviet. It was in this session that the decision to annex Northern Bukovina into the Soviet Union was made.

JEWS IN ELECTED OFFICE

The integration of Jews into local governmental institutions was usually the result of Jewish initiative combined with Soviet acquiescence in principle, sometimes after the fact. In contrast, the participation of Jews as candidates for elected office was a markedly political act and an integral part of a considered, sober internal policy. Such a policy was apparent as early as late October, 1939, when elections for the National Assembly of the western Ukraine in Lvov and of western Belorussia in Bialystok were hastily arranged. Admittedly, some of this was window-dressing. Even as candidates for these institutions were presented to the profuse election assemblies held throughout eastern Poland, it was clear that the number, credentials, and national affiliations of the candidates had been determined in advance by the senior echelons in Moscow (and perhaps also in Kiev and Minsk) that administered the annexation of these areas into the Soviet Union. Even at that early stage, the domestic policy of "outreach" to the majority peoples in these areas, chief among them the Ukrainians and Belorussians, had presumably taken shape. As for the Jews, both groups in the area—the locals and the refugees from Nazi occupation—had already demonstrated their abundant sympathy for the regime. Evidence of this was the enthusiastic reception they gave the arriving Soviets and their full-fledged integration into the provisional government. These factors were reflected in the decisions of central election committees in the western Ukraine and in western Belorussia, which determined, in most if not all cases, how many candidates might run in each locality and what their national affiliations would be.

A typical example of this state of affairs was the election of a Jewish candidate from Kletsk (Kletzk, a town in the Baranowicze district) to the Belorussian National Assembly. After local decision-makers ruled that the representative of this city had to be a Jew, the position was offered to Joseph Frenkl, former principal of the Tarbut school in the town, who had recently been liberated from a Polish concentration camp (Bereza-Kartuska). Because Frenkl had once studied Talmud and Bible, his candidacy was frustrated by the internal security services (the NKVD). The Kletsk memorial book describes the end of the affair:

It was just before election day [for the National Assembly]. From the Baranowicze district they were asking for the candidate's first name and some details about his personality. We were grilled for hours, getting nowhere . . . proposing various names, but each was flawed. The *vostochniks* ("easterners")[13] were livid: how could this be? A town with more than 5,000 Jews couldn't come up with a single one who was fit to be a delegate to the National Assembly? The final meeting was held late one evening. We were warned by telephone from Baranowicze that if we didn't announce the candidate by the approaching deadline, Kletsk might forfeit its right to delegates. Finally the man was found: a young worker in Moshe Elyanik's oil factory, whose name we hadn't heard of thus far . . . and he was approved.[14]

There were also Jewish delegates of a different kind: vostochniks from the veteran Soviet republics. One of these was Grigori Moiseyevich Gershman, secretary of the regional committee in Bialystok at the time. The following excerpt from his memoirs, dictated by himself, tells us much about other Jewish officials who were "imported" to eastern Poland:

I was born in 1904 to the family of a rural shoemaker. In 1915, my father was taken to war, so I had to earn my own living. In 1920 and 1921 I participated in the *otryads* [special units operating against anti-Soviet gangs]. In 1923–1925 I held a high-ranking position in the Komsomol. In

1926–1928 I served in the Red Army. I was appointed to the Central Committee of the Belorussian Communist Party. In 1932–1935 I was drafted for political work in a high-ranking position in the army. In 1936 I worked in the People's Commissariat for Forests and in the People's Commissariat for Heavy Industry. Since September 17, 1939, I have been working in western Belorussia. . . . I have been a member of the Communist Party since 1924. I was cited for excellence at work by the Presidium of the Supreme Soviet.[15]

The Jewish delegates were determined in a similar fashion in the western Ukraine, but their numbers were immeasurably smaller. Many of them came from the Wolhynia area. The Rokitno memorial book describes the bitter fate that befell one of these delegates. In that town a Jewish housewife named Mushka Schuster, a plasterer's wife, was elected to the National Assembly in Lvov. She was not asked if she desired this; nor were her qualifications for the position made clear. The fact that she had a proletarian husband may have sufficed. After the National Assembly was dissolved, she returned to her kitchen and dropped out of sight. When the Germans entered Rokitno in the summer of 1941, they murdered her on the spot.[16]

It should be recalled that in October, 1939, there was no official, recognized public Jewish organization of any kind in eastern Poland that could discuss and determine the Jewish position on issues connected with the changeover of regimes. Notably, however, Jewish functionaries from Eastern Galicia held a secret consultation in Lvov before the elections for the National Assembly of the western Ukraine. In these elections, scheduled for October 22, the population was to express its formal support of the Soviet annexation of the southeastern Polish territories held by the Red Army. This group of functionaries sent an emissary to Polish public leaders in Lvov to ascertain their position in the approaching elections. The Jewish leaders in Eastern Galicia feared that a mass Jewish turnout on election day would be construed as an expression of identification with the new regime and a betrayal of Polish interests. The Poles replied: "There's an order—it's got to be obeyed; after all, there's no choice. . . ." Then they explained their behavior: "These people had no idea whatsoever that there was any room for discussion of disobedience or resistance."[17] This is the only reported instance of an organized Jewish attempt to debate the issues on the agenda at the time; the explanation for this, without doubt, was the very hopelessness of action of this kind under the circumstances.

When the lists of National Assembly candidates in Lvov and Bialystok were completed, it was found that the Jewish representation fell far short of that warranted by their involvement in the election campaign, and their share in the population at large. Of 926 candidates for the Belorussian National Assembly, 72 were Jews—7.7 percent representation in a Jewish community that accounted for approximately 10 percent of the population. In contrast, the number of Poles in this assembly was 127, or 13 percent, roughly commensurate with their share of the population at the time. A delegation of 66 members of the National Assembly in Bialystok, which set out for Moscow to present the Supreme Soviet with its request for annexation, included only two Jews (about 3 percent); these two delegates were not given the floor in Moscow or in Minsk, whereas the Polish representation presented its case in its own national language.[18]

Numerical discrimination against Jewish representation in the Ukrainian National Assembly, which convened at the same time in Lvov, was even more blatant. Of the 1,495 delegates elected to this forum, a mere 20 (1.3 percent) were Jews,[19] even though the Jews constituted about 10 percent of the population. In Lvov, where 30 percent of the population was Jewish, two Jews were elected to the 160-member National Assembly. Not a single Jew was present in a 65-member delegation that set out for Moscow.

It is therefore safe to assert that the National Assembly elections in Bialystok (western Belorussia) and those in Lvov (the western Ukraine) clearly emphasized the Jews' negligible role in the political leadership, including high-visibility institutions. This marked the recurrence of a phenomenon that had manifested itself in lower levels of government because of vigorous action to emphasize implementation of Belorussian and Ukrainian language, culture, and values. The Jews in the Ukraine were to pay heavily for these policies, which were evidently instituted for domestic political reasons.

With the approach of elections for the People's Seimas in Lithuania, an important player in the Jewish scene went into action: the Bureau for Minority Affairs, a section of the Central Committee of the Lithuanian Communist Party. As early as July 3, 1940, the Bureau, headed by former teacher and journalist G. Ziman (Zimanas), took the initiative of convening a broad consultation of representatives of pro-Communist Jewish institutions and agencies. The four Jewish candidates for the People's Sejm—Yankl Vinitski, Berl Latvis-Fridman, Itzik Dembo, and Noah Matskevitz—were almost unknown to the Jewish public. Moreover, they accounted for a mere 5 percent of the candidates, even though one-tenth of Lithuania's population was Jewish. However, there is no doubt that the very inclusion of Jewish candidates strengthened the Jewish masses' commitment to the election process and increased their willingness to vote.

The Jewish press appealed emotionally to the community of small merchants, shopkeepers, and artisans, stressing national themes:

The present elections are doubly significant for us Jews. For us, the new regime not only signals the socialist liberation of oppressed social strata, but also the national liberation of all the Jews in Lithuania, with no exception whatsoever. . . . [Therefore,] there isn't a Jew who cares how many Jews get into the Sejm, for everyone knows that this makes no difference—every delegate in the new Sejm, from whatever national group, will devote equal concern to members of all national groups equally.[20]

In Latvia, too, Jewish Communists, newly surfaced from the underground, took part in the People's Sejm elections (which were supposed to decide on annexation to the Soviet Union). Two examples were K. Berkovitz, a member of the Central Committee, and G. Leibovitz, a member of the Riga Municipal Committee. One of the most active figures in the election campaign was the well-known leftist Max Shatz-Anin, whose civil rights and license to practice law, both revoked after the fascist coup in 1934, had recently been restored. Another member of this group was Dr. Michael Yaffe, the only candidate representing the Latvian Workers' Bloc under which the Communist lists had coalesced. Among the Jewish groups that rushed to the side of the new regime and declared their support of the Latvian Workers' Bloc was the Progressive Jewish Teachers' Association. In is interesting that assemblies meant for the Jewish population were held exclusively in Yiddish.

Left Po'aley Tsiyon pre-empted the Jewish Teachers' Association.[21] Several days before the elections—at the peak of the intensive propaganda campaign—the daily *Kamf,* a Communist Party organ that had just begun publishing, published a manifesto signed by the Socialist Zionists that urged their comrades, sympathizers, and all Jews in Latvia, "to participate in the Sejm elections on July 14–15, and to cast their ballots for the only list that assures peace, well-being, and equality for all citizens of the country—the Latvian Workers' Bloc." Explaining their position, the authors of the manifesto asserted that "the fate of the Jewish masses has always been bound up with that of people's proletarian democracy."

The day after the election returns were published, the Jews' underrepresentation in the Latvian Sejm (1.2 percent compared with 4.5 percent of the population) was more blatantly evident than ever.

In neighboring Estonia, not a single Jew was elected to this supreme governing institution, perhaps because the Jewish community there was miniscule (0.4 percent). In all the Soviet-annexed areas (with the exceptions of

Bessarabia and Northern Bukovina, where elections of this type were not held), the Jews' share in these superordinate elected institutions was substantially smaller than their share of the population.

Because the National Assemblies elected in the autumn of 1939 in the western Ukraine and western Belorussia were ad hoc institutions that were dissolved after they had discharged their duties, the Jewish residents of these areas were allowed, in the spring of 1940, to elect their delegates to the Supreme Soviets of the Ukrainian and Belorussian SSRs. Elections for these councils in Kiev and Minsk were scheduled for March 24, 1940, as were elections for the Supreme Soviet of the USSR.

The press, including the Jewish dailies with their ubiquitous photographs and curriculum vitae of Jewish candidates, made it clear even a month before the elections that the Jews' representation among the candidates was not commensurate with their share of the population.[22] It also transpired that many if not most of the Jewish candidates were vostochniks—Soviet functionaries from the eastern region of Belorussia.

In all, 12 of the 202 candidates from western Belorussia elected to the supreme soviet in Minsk were Jewish[23]—6 percent representation of a Jewish population that accounted for more than 10 percent of the population of these provinces.[24] The Jews of western Ukraine were even more gravely underrepresented (as had happened in the National Assembly in Lvov). Of 80 delegates from this area who were elected to the Ukrainian Supreme Soviet in Kiev, only one was Jewish: Meir Springer, the offspring of a poor family who had also been elected to the Ukrainian National Assembly. His electoral district for the Ukrainian supreme soviet was the Kowel area.

In this area, too, an attempt was made to run a Jewish candidate for the Supreme Soviet in Moscow. From some reason, the authorities sought a non-partisan candidate who would appeal to the sympathies of the public at large, and they fixed their sights on Asher Frankfurt, former principal of the Tarbut Gymnasium and now principal of the Yiddish Gymnasium in Kowel. The NKVD summoned Frankfurt to its offices one night and (as it transpired the next day) subjected him to a respectful and even a sympathetic interrogation. The NKVD summons recurred several nights in a row, and on one of these occasions he was told explicitly that he was to be a candidate for the Supreme Soviet. He argued that he was a Zionist (albeit a non-active one) and hence unsuited to the position offered; they disregarded this. He then pleaded illness (a heart condition) but was assured transportation in a special railway car and an apartment for himself and his family in Moscow. In one of the last of these nighttime sessions, he was told that his candidacy had been approved by the Party Secretary in the Ukraine, Nikita S. Khrushchev. After this he began to receive invitations to election assemblies. However, the longest tenured of the political prisoners—the local Communists—came out sharply against him in a gathering of the liberal professionals' cell of the Party, vigorously protesting the candidacy of a person with a Zionist background. These protestations evidently had their effect; Frankfurt was ordered to report to the Party secretariat, where he was informed that his candidacy had been rescinded in view of the state of his health. After the Nazi invasion on June 22, 1941, the authorities offered to evacuate Frankfurt to the Soviet heartland on the special train reserved for Party and government officials. He turned this down and perished with the rest of the Jews of Kowel.[25]

A total of 55 persons from the western Ukraine and western Belorussia were elected to the Supreme Soviet in Moscow: 43 (27 and 16, respectively) to the Council of the Union chamber of the Soviet, and 12 (six from each region) to the second chamber, the Council of Nationalities. None of them was Jewish. Once the election returns became known, the festive atmosphere that had accompanied the election campaign vanished. A wave of arrests and mass deportations of Jews ensued, especially among the refugees.

The election campaign for the Supreme Soviet in Moscow (the Council of the Union and the Council of Nationalities) was different in substance and momentum in the areas annexed to the Soviet Union in the second stage: Lithuania, Latvia, Estonia, Bessarabia, and Northern Bukovina. The elections in these areas were held on January 12, 1941. Again, none of the candidates for the Union Council was Jewish; of the 100 candidates representing Lithuania, Latvia, Estonia, and Bessarabia (25 from each area) for the National Council only one, Itzik Meskup ("Adomas"), was a Jew. His selection may have been related to the fact that he was the Second Secretary of the Central Committee of the Lithuanian Communist Party at the time.

Most of the campaign propaganda appeared in the two local Jewish dailies, *Der Emes* and *Vilner Emes;* its publication was at the initiative of the newspapers.

In the outlying cities and smaller towns, the major arena for informational and propaganda operations aimed at the Jews was the Jewish school system, which was, in fact, the only recognized Jewish institution that might be used as a cultural and social center for the Jewish population.

Elections for local governing institutions in the western Ukraine and western Belorussia were held on December 15, 1940, about 15 months after the Red Army had entered these areas. As before, because the Belorussification and Ukrainization policies were already in full swing, the Jewish electorate was perceptibly underrepresented. Among 476 members of the municipal council in Lvov, for example, 252 were Ukrainians, 121 were Poles, 76 were Jews, and 27 were of other nationalities.[26] Thus the representation of Jews in the Lvov council was 18 percent, compared with their 30 percent share of the population.

Several of the Jewish members of the Lvov municipal council were not local residents. It may be presumed that some had achieved their positions by virtue of reputations they had acquired on the Jewish public scene as artists and cultural figures. Jacob Zaykin, for example, was dispatched from the Soviet Ukraine to serve as the administrative director of the government Jewish theater in Lvov. He was affiliated with the Communist Youth Organization, had studied in Kiev and Moscow, was a lecturer in history, and had worked in the Academy of Sciences. In his campaign appearances, Zaykin stressed that his appearance as a candidate representing a district regarded before the war as a Jewish ghetto in Lvov was no coincidence. This, in effect, underscored the change for the better in the Jews' political circumstances relative to the Polish period. In one of these assemblies, he asked the following rhetorical question: "Who would have permitted himself to address an election assembly in prewar Poland in Yiddish, a language that all the new voters understand?"[27]

A standout among the candidates for the Lvov council was Ida Kaminska, a well-known stage actress and the artistic director of the governmental Jewish theater in the town. She was summoned to the Party's municipal committee, where she was informed that the Party and the people appreciated her artistic endeavors and therefore decided to present her candidacy for the municipal council as a member of the Communist and "unaffiliated list." Other Jewish candidates for the Lvov council were Pearl Urich, a successful actress and a refugee from Poland; Sophia Okrant, a woman with a "rich proletarian past"; Professor Jacob Parnass, a biochemist; Professor Kutscher of the Soviet Institute for Trade; and the Yiddish poetess Rachel Korn.[28]

Another Jewish notable elected to a local municipal council (this time in the Eastern Galician town of Borislav) was Dr. Yehiel Deutschmeister. The Soviet-Jewish press described him effusively:

The proletarians of Drohobycz and Borislav are well acquainted with Dr. Deutschmeister. They remember him from the dreary, difficult days, hard times long past. [Deutschmeister is] a talented man who was active in the trade union and delivered speeches in workers' assemblies. He is the son of a tailor. . . . In his youth he peddled cigarettes and matches in the town streets. He peregrinated on foot until he reached the University of Zagreb, Yugoslavia, where he studied medicine. . . . He was very well received by the oil industry workers. The Polish police had often subjected him to body searches . . . . He is now a candidate for the Borislav town council.[29]

Indeed, this account contains all the credentials deemed vital for public office at the time: proletarian origins, revolutionary activity, and concern for the proletariat.

The authorities and the leaders of the institutions that ran the election campaign rarely referred to the Jews as a national minority or as a specific segment of the population. The Jewish press treated the theme more gingerly than they had in previous elections. Only on election day, December 15, 1940, did the daily newspaper *Oktyabr* run a front-page article entitled "Paragraph 123," devoted to the Jews of the Soviet Union in general and those of western Belorussia in particular. The theme of the article was the assurance of the Jews' national rights under the Soviet constitution, with special emphasis on the aforementioned paragraph.

Two days after the elections, the same paper rhapsodized about the voting behavior of Jews of conspicuous "people's" origins.[30]

INSIDE THE COMMUNIST PARTY APPARATUS

Although the Polish Communist Party, with its heavy Jewish representation, had been dissolved in 1938, many former members continued to regard themselves as full-fledged Communists. For them, the arrival of the Red Army in eastern Poland marked the honorable end of a life of extreme hardship in the underground. Practically speaking, nearly all of these individuals helped to consolidate the new regime in their areas of residence; most were appointed to key positions. It is no wonder that the public regarded these persons (and other Communists who, for some reason, were not named to important positions) as representatives of the new regime, if not its very embodiment. Their status in the public arena soared. However, the major institutions of the Ukrainian and Belorussian civil administration and Communist Party received them with less exuberance. These institutions had dispatched their own people to the annexed localities and relied chiefly upon them, either by appointing them to high-ranking Party and administrative positions or by placing them on the lists of candidates for elected office. The "outsiders" established a regime of high-handed power by virtue of authority given them in Moscow, Kiev, and Minsk, and their instructions hindered veteran Communists who sought official admission to the Party. All of this sowed frustration and disillusionment among local Party members.

Even though the victims rarely spoke out at length about this sensitive topic, the matter could not be concealed for long. The plight of the Jewish Communists, including former prisoners who had just reached the Soviet-controlled areas from the Nazi-occupied zone, was especially grave. Below are excerpts from the personal account of a man who had breached the walls of Lublin prison at the beginning of the war and had somehow reached the Wolhynian town of Luboml with his comrades:

All the offices had already been taken up by Ukrainians, including a large number of nationalists and fascists. . . . They demanded sleeping arrangements, food, and the possibility of further travel. We introduced ourselves as Communists who had just been liberated from Polish prisons, penniless and literally crippled, who were therefore requesting the Soviet government's assistance. Hearing this, they replied that Communists never "abandon" the field of struggle; we should have stayed where we were and fought the Germans in the underground just as we had struggled against Poland. Thus we should not aggrandize ourselves for having been political prisoners, since the Soviets themselves, after all, were liable to throw us back whence we came as advance forces in the German[-occupied] area of Poland. This plunged us into so terrible a state of despair that a few of us . . . geared up then and there, beginning that very day to head back toward the Bug [River].[31]

Other Jews who had held high positions in the former Polish Communist Party now arrived, some straight from jail, from Warsaw and other areas in western Poland; most of these congregated in Bialystok. Their fate was equally harsh and bitter.

The problem of practical arrangements for these refugee Communists was entrusted to committees of MOPR. These committees were an integral part of the establishment; the relevant Soviet institutions used them to monitor this particular group and every individual associated with it (i.e., "everyone for whom orders to be cautious, wary, and suspicious had gone out"). This is not to imply that the veteran Communist activists, including those from the West, were altogether neutralized. Even though their official reinstatement in the Party progressed slowly and with virtually no tangible results, many of them found various positions in the new regime, albeit in marginal ranks. One of the few leading Jewish Communists who regained most of his prior status in the Party, and who gained admission to the Belorussian Communist Party, was Dovid Richter. However, once the newspaper *Bialystoker Shtern* was established, he, too, was assigned the duties of a mere deputy editor, subordinate to a Soviet Jew named Beinish Shulman.

In no few instances, Jewish Communists (especially those who arrived from western Poland) were accused of ideological deviations, including Trotskyism. One person so accused was the author and historian Berl Mark, who reached Bialystok as a refugee. Only after extensive pleading by veteran comrades who served him as "character witnesses" was the charge retracted.[32] In Lvov, author Jacob Shudrich was accused of Trotskyist leanings. He fought the charges furiously, asserting his fealty to the official Party line time and again. An investigative committee of writers was set up; it cleared Shudrich of the accusation following an investigation that had brought him to the verge of collapse.[33]

It hardly mattered whether the accusations were pertinent or whether they were trumped-up charges made against the background of the Ukrainization and Belorussification policies. The purge of Jewish Communists seemed to have become an accepted phenomenon, especially in the western Ukraine.[34] So serious was the situation that some Jewish Communists who had reached the area from western Poland chose not to disclose their previous political affiliations.[35]

The problem of reinstating veteran pre-war Communists was exceedingly difficult and complicated. In this regard, the plight of the refugee Jewish Communists, who had no acquaintances in their new localities, was especially grave. In view of the great stringency built into the reinstatement procedures, progress was very slow; only a relative handful passed the candidacy process and obtained Party cards.

Nevertheless, many Jews (and non-Jews) made strenuous efforts to gain admission to the Party ranks, some for reasons of ideological identification and others in view of the benefits of affiliation with the ruling party—prestige, personal convenience, and the sense of having "made it" in economic and social terms.

In contrast to the hurdles that the Party placed in the path of persons seeking admission—newcomers and veterans alike—the Komsomol and the Pioneer (Communist Party children's organization) branches opened their doors to teenagers and children. Membership in these organizations became highly acceptable, and Jewish youth thronged to them. This was especially so in the towns and the outlying cities, where youth movements had played a paramount social function. All were welcome, even those who had previously belonged to Zionist, religious, or Bundist movements or parties. In this case the authorities' attitude was the opposite of that taken toward Party membership; they were eager to channel the cream of youth—talented, politically aware teenagers, along with outstanding workers and pupils—to the Komsomol.

The Pioneers also attracted relatively large numbers of Jews. This was because a large majority of Jewish schoolchildren, unlike those of other national groups, attended municipal schools in which Pioneer chapters began to operate. The predisposition to join youth movements, which had spread among Jewish households in the 1930s, may have further boosted the Jewish presence in the Pioneers. Thousands of Jewish children and teenagers enrolled in markedly political frameworks and spent the next year and more imbibing Communist indoctrination.

In contrast to eastern Poland, where the Communist Party had not existed when the Red Army arrived, and the Romanian provinces, where the local Communist Party was co-opted by its Moldavian and Ukrainian equivalents, the Communist parties in the Baltic countries were able to maintain relative institutional autonomy even after Soviet annexation. The largest of the three Baltic groupings was the Communist Party of Lithuania (CPL); its membership upon surfacing from the underground was approximately 2,000, nearly half of whom were Jewish. Jews accounted for a similar, but not a larger, share of the 1,000 members of the Komsomol and the 6,000 members of MOPR. Notably, too, the veteran Communist leader Itzik Meskup ("Adomas") retained, de facto, the highest-ranking position in the party— First Secretary of the Central Committee—as the new regime became consolidated during its first few weeks in Lithuania.

Addressing the fifth CPL convention (the first since the Party's emergence from the underground) in Kovno on February 4–9, 1941, Party Secretary-General A. Snieckus sharply criticized municipal Party organizations, such as those in Vilna and Kovno, that failed to bolster the Party's active core by co-opting members of the national groups that formed majorities in those localities (i.e., Lithuanians and Poles). In due course, his prescription became Party policy. By January 1, 1941, the share of Jews in the CPL plunged to 15.2 percent (479 individuals). Even this, however, exceeded the proportion of Jews in the population (10 percent).

The Party's attitude was that the proletariat would provide the cadres but the veterans would provide the administrative leaders. For this reason, Jews were still well represented in the middle and higher echelons, including the senior leadership. In early 1941, five of the 21 members of the Central Committee (24 percent of the total) were Jews.[36] The reduced numerical representation of the Jews in the Party was not matched by any degradation of their status, especially with regard to the veterans. The latter continued to maintain close relations with former comrades from the prison and underground period, and members of these two groups visited each other in private capacities. Several non-Jewish Communist leaders even had Jewish wives.

A standout among the Jews who had climbed to the top of the Communist apparatus was G. Ziman (Zimanas), editor of the Party organ *Tiesa* (Truth). In Jewish public opinion, he was regarded as a very important authoritative figure, if not the only one, in the making of Party decisions affecting the Jews.[37]

Jews were given major positions in the Lithuanian Komsomol. On January 1, 1941, as the new regime became consolidated, the Komsomol had 1,755 Jewish members (23.8 percent). The proportion of Jewish members was even higher in the major cities. In Vilna, for example, 46 of the 65 Komsomol members in the polling committees for the Supreme Soviet were Jews.[38]

Now, as during the period of the previous regime in Lithuania, MOPR provided the Communist Party with important assistance. The fact that Jews accounted for much (if not most) of the MOPR membership in many locations had a strong effect on the nature of the activity. Much cultural activity, for example, was conducted in Yiddish. It should be noted that the new regime fondly recalled the Jews' support of MOPR under the previous regime and did them no harm, even when they belonged to the "capitalist and employers" class.

RELATIONS BETWEEN THE JEWISH MINORITY AND THE
AUTHORITIES AND LOCAL PEOPLES

The indigenous peoples of the area regarded the Soviet regime as an enemy, and the Red Army as an intruder who had come to stamp out Baltic independence and conspire to dismember Poland from the east. In the eyes of these peoples, the Soviet annexation was both a political and a social disaster. The Jews, in contrast—although they were loyal citizens of their respective countries—hardly shared these sentiments. Their alternative was a regime of Nazi terror; the Soviet occupation was decidedly the lesser of two evils. The nature of relations between the Jews and the local non-Jewish peoples was determined by these utterly contradictory basic attitudes. There was, however, a "third party" in these relations: the Soviet establishment and its attitude toward the Jews and the national groups in the areas under its control.

The principle of equality among all population groups was one of the conceptual building blocks of the Soviet regime. In this light, the commander of the Soviet force that entered the Wolhynian town of Beresteczko in September, 1939, proclaimed from the very start that "we don't distinguish between man and man. Everyone's equal; there's no difference between a Pole, a Russian, a Jew, a Ukrainian, and anyone else."

The Soviet regime publicized its position regarding the desired "fraternity of peoples" in the area. In late March, 1940, *Pravda* ran an article about a conference of women in Lvov, during which Polish women heckled a speaker who had dared to deliver her remarks in Yiddish. "The Polish women," the Moscow newspaper reported, "were given an object lesson in the realities of equality of people's rights in Soviet Russia. Following the Yiddish speech, which had been translated, the other speakers, too, orated in the local vernacular."

The Soviets also made their official stance on the issue of fraternity of peoples very clear to the other peoples in the area. Authorized Party spokesmen ruled out antisemitism unequivocally and gave this point special emphasis in the election campaign for local institutions, the Supreme Soviet, and the National Council in Moscow. The October 26, 1939, edition of the J.T.A. *Bulletin* reported that the Soviet authorities had disseminated in the western Ukraine 30,000 flyers in Ukrainian, asserting that the Jews were fully privileged as a people. In a Supreme Soviet election assembly in Vilna, G. Ziman (Zimanas), secretary of the Minorities Bureau of the CPL Central Committee, proclaimed:

The day the Red Army soldiers came to us, antisemitism took a death-blow. All the antisemites have felt it. Some antisemites have given up their incitement; some are still running wild. But all the antisemites will get what they deserve. . . . Of all governments in the world, only the Soviet government is wholly untainted by antisemitism. Stalin said that antisemitism deserves the death sentence. The Communist Party will never allow antisemitism, since everyone knows that antisemitism is counterrevolutionary.

One of the new regime's fiercest attacks on antisemitism was published in the CPL organ *Cinia;* the Yiddish-language daily *Unzer Vort* rushed to translate it for publication in one of its last issues.[39] Just before the elections for the people's parliament, the demand to eradicate antisemitism became one of the Party's major slogans in its campaign among the Jews. The masthead of the election-day issue of the newspaper *Kamf* featured a giant headline: "For Equality and the End of Antisemitism." Max Shatz-Anin, a much sought-after speaker at mass election assemblies in Jewish neighborhoods, said in his last speech before the election, "For the sake of exterminating antisemitism, it's worth propagandizing widely. But if this doesn't help, vigorous measures should be taken to extirpate antisemitism, just as it has already been extirpated in the Soviet Union."

The Soviet regime backed its demonstrative stand against antisemitism with action along two parallel paths: namely, official emphasis on phenomena that could be construed as expressing the fraternity of peoples along with a crackdown against manifestations of blatant antisemitism. In October, 1939, in the Eastern Galician town of Zaleszczyki, would-be vandals of Jewish property were jailed. In June, 1940, a Soviet court ordered the execution of four Polish rioters who had participated in the murder of Jews in Gironda before the advent of the Red Army, and sentenced seven rioters to six to eight years in prison.[40] In December, 1940, groups of Ukrainian peasants who had attempted to assault Jews in the town of Strij were jailed. In September, 1940, the authorities acted to disprove rumors that Jews had murdered priests in Kishinev and Bendery (Bessarabia). The residents were ordered to turn out and observe the churches, still standing intact, and the priests who had ostensibly been murdered, still alive. Concurrently, persons suspected of spreading these rumors were jailed.[41] When rumors about the kidnapping of a priest by Jews spread in Ponevezh (Panevezys), Lithuania, reinforcements were rushed in to prevent pogroms. In Eastern Galicia, use of the pejorative *zhid* was banned upon penalty of three months' imprisonment. The locals' argument—that this word was accepted and not necessarily derogatory in Polish—was dismissed.[42]

Nevertheless, the Soviet apparatus did not come out squarely against antisemitism; in fact, antisemitism and chauvinism usually were mentioned in the same breath. In an assembly of propagandists before the Supreme Soviet elections, Grigori Gershman, First Secretary of the Party committee in the Bialystok area, proclaimed, "Antisemitism must be stamped out, but the struggle against antisemitism should be combined with a struggle against Jewish chauvinism. Jewish nationalists should not harbor the delusion that the Red Army has liberated the Jews only. It has liberated all the peoples in western Belorussia."[43] Thus, in the Soviet view, there were two sides to the struggle against nationalism. Evidence of this, from a high-ranking source, surfaced in remarks by P. Ponomarenko, Secretary of the Belorussian Communist Party, on February 12, 1940. Wishing to emphasize the change in the Jews' circumstances under Soviet rule, Ponomarenko stressed the hardship that had characterized Jewish life under the Polish regime. At the same time, he asserted that "counterrevolutionary" parties such as the Bund and Left Po'aley Tsiyon, together with the nationalist bourgeoisie, had helped the "colonizers" succeed in their schemes to drive wedges in the workers' class of the miscellaneous national groups.[44]

Antisemitism and chauvinism became routine clichés in the sociopolitical lexicon of activists in the new regime. "Chauvinism" referred not only to the Lithuanian nationalists' attitude toward the Poles, but also to the Jews, whose attitude toward all Gentile peoples was somewhat negative. There were also spontaneous reprisals by Jews against their non-Jewish assailants. In the western Belorussian city of Volkovisk, the retreating Poles staged a pogrom against the local Jews, slaughtering seven. When the Red Army came into town, a 70-year-old shoemaker named Leibush Menaker seized a rifle, "went to the apartment of the rabid antisemite and pogrom organizer Shimonsky, arrested him, and turned him over to the Soviet authorities."[45] The local postman of the same town was identified as having participated in pogroms in Lida; he, too, was handed over to the Soviet authorities.

Nationalist antagonisms also surfaced within the Komsomol. The Komsomol's Yiddish-language journal, *Shtraln,* printed an article with the headline "Stamp Out Chauvinism in All Its Manifestations."[46] The journal's editor, Aaron Garon, noted that some young Jews were making no effort whatsoever to achieve rapprochement with the Lithuanians.

Oddly enough, the invading Soviet regime was at times one of the few agencies that created common ground between the local peoples and the Jews, since both were cringing under the socioeconomic regimen that the Soviets imposed in the annexed territories. The Jewish masses suffered from the economic decrees no less than other peoples in the area, and Jews, like others, had been swept up and exiled to Siberia. This led to spontaneous, grass-roots manifestations of fraternity of peoples even without Soviet "guidance." In the Wolhynian town of Rozyszcze, for example, Jews helped free from NKVD detention a Pole who had treated the Jews respectfully. In Maryampol (Marijampole), Lithuania, elderly Jews wept as the Lithuanian president, A. Smetona, passed through the town while fleeing from the Soviets.[47] Close relations between Jewish and non-Jewish political prisoners in Soviet jails were known to exist. On balance, however, these cases were few and far between; they must be treated as exceptions in the shaky relations between the Jews and their non-Jewish neighbors.

To be sure, the Soviet authorities were aware of local peoples' sensitivities to what they considered the excessive cultivation of the Jewish minority. The official line was therefore moderated by a vigorous policy meant to prevent offense to the Jews, coupled with an ardent desire to avoid the impression of a Jewish takeover. Two manifestations of this cautious policy were the appointment of Jews to high-visibility positions and the admission of Jews to Party membership.

This was especially evident in Eastern Galicia, where an exceedingly rigid Ukrainization policy was being pursued in any case. Poles and Jews had been relegated to positions of marginal importance in Eastern Galicia, as they were in Wolhynia and Northern Bukovina. In the Moldavian SSR and the Bialystok area, Jewish delegates were seriously underrepresented in major institutions.[48] Even so, nationalistic elements among the majority peoples identified the Jews as agents of the despised regime. The Jews' perceptible sense of relief upon the arrival of the Soviets, and their penetration of governmental positions previously denied them, were construed as proof of identification with the new government. Labeling of the Soviet administration as a "Jewish regime" became widespread when Jewish militiamen helped NKVD agents send local Poles into exile. Nor is it difficult to guess what Lithuanian peasants felt at the sight of "Jewish young men and women visiting the villages to wage pro-kolkhoz propaganda and to teach the peasants the basics of farm labor."[49] Landlords and estate owners must have harbored much bitterness when forced to greet, with strained politeness, young Jews who came to confiscate their property.[50] In several cases, Jews were involved in desecration of Christian religious artifacts. In Volozhyn, for example, a Jew who was told to prepare the market square for the erection of a statue of Stalin detonated a large cross that stood in the way. In Wiszniew, a town in western Belorussia, Jewish Communists took down the flags of the local church, affixed red flags to the flagpoles, and paraded with them across town to the market square. In Zolkiew, militiamen, some of them Jews, expropriated a monastery in order to house refugees from western Poland. The local Poles declared that the day would come when they would avenge themselves on the Jews for this "defilement."[51]

Since the avenue of pogroms had been closed, hatred was channeled into other paths. Government officials in Lithuania attacked Jews in the guise of anti-bourgeois or anti-Zionist diatribes.[52] In the Eastern Galician town of Tarnopol, militiamen attempted to incite market-day visitors to boycott Jewish businesses. When Jewish women protested and threatened to file grievances against the militiamen, they replaced the expletive *zhid* with the term "bourgeois elements." In Lithuania, too, the expression "Communist Jews," used not so long ago, metamorphosed into "bourgeois Jews."

In most cases, the locals had to keep their enmity to themselves. However, the authorities could not thwart a string of explicit and implicit threats of the "your-day-will-yet-come" variety. Many of these threats were embedded in political slogans connected with the struggle against the Soviet regime. When votes in the town of David-Gorodok were counted after the Belorussian National Assembly elections, ballot slips were discovered with messages such as "Down with the Soviet regime," "Death to Bolsheviks and Jews," and so on. A leaflet dated March 19, 1941, issued by the Lithuanian Activist Front, stated: "The hour of Lithuania's liberation is close at hand. . . . Local uprisings must be started in the enslaved cities, towns, and villages of Lithuania, or, to put it more precisely, all power must be seized the moment the war begins. Local Communists and other traitors of Lithuania must be arrested at once. . . . (A traitor will be pardoned only if he proves beyond doubt that he has killed at least one Jew.) . . . Inform the Jews right now that their fate is sealed, so that those among them who can leave Lithuania today will do so. . . . When the right moment comes, seize their property, making sure that nothing is lost."[53]

Indeed, when the Soviet regime was expelled and the constraints on carrying out the threats were removed, the locals were first to strike at the Jews. When the Red Army forces pulled out of Vilna on October 28, 1939, handing the city to the Lithuanians after a brief rule of six weeks, a wild week-long pogrom erupted during which two Jews were killed and approximately 200 were injured. On the night of June 25–26, 1941, several days after the Soviets left Lithuania, Lithuanians massacred 1,200 Jewish children, women, and men in Slobodka, a suburb of Kovno.[54]

The day that Nazi Germany's armed forces began to march into the Soviet Union signaled the beginning of the mass murder of Jews throughout Eastern Galicia by local Ukrainians. Nor did the repressed hatred overlook Jews who had been deported to the USSR. Jewish soldiers in the Polish armed forces, for example, experienced it in the bitter complaints of their Polish counterparts: "These zhids greeted the Red Army enthusiastically."

4

The Economy and Society

NATIONALIZATION AND EXPROPRIATIONS

One of the first substantial measures taken by the new regime was the application of a basic socialist tenet: state ownership of production factors. In practical terms, this meant the expropriation and nationalization of capital, industrial plants and commercial establishments, and real estate. The first Jews to be dispossessed summarily of their economic and social status were the affluent types known in their community as *gevirim,* a weighted term combining praise, awe, and resentment. Examples were the owners of the spinneries in Bialystok, oil wells in the Drohobycz area (Eastern Galicia), large wholesale firms in Rowne, lumber mills in Pinsk, grain brokerages in Kishinev, banks in Riga, and estates in Bukovina. Indirectly harmed were small business owners, artisans, and shopkeepers, who had been keeping themselves going thus far with the help of public funds and mutual-assistance societies, which were nationalized at once along with other banking institutions.

In Poland and, to a certain extent, in Romania, the great nationalization campaigns took place in the immediate footsteps of the incoming Red Army, long before the appropriate nationalization laws had been gazetted. They were often accompanied by searches of homes and detention of property owners, who were ordered to turn over not only keys and cash registers but also documents, safes, and even personal items of value. Nationalization and confiscations were backed up by discrediting, defaming, and threatening people who had acquired wealth and were now alleged to have done so at the expense of the masses. Some of the wealthy were placed on trial; several were sentenced to death.[1]

The second stage—carried out after conditions had stabilized and the new regime had been consolidated—consisted of systematic action to reorganize factories and integrate them into the state economy. Again, these measures were taken in the absence of policies concerning the nationalized properties and the fate of the owners. The latter were usually treated in one of two ways:

1. *Absolute dispossession.* Owners were ousted from their factories and their identity cards were marked with Paragraph 11 or 39, which restricted their freedom of movement and right to change domicile. Most individuals in this category had difficulty finding work; some were even imprisoned and exiled, at times with the help of the security forces and local Communists.

2. *Dispossession coupled with demotion.* Factory owners remained in their plants as job foremen. This usually happened in small factories and in enterprises where the owner's professional qualifications were needed. In the small Wolhynian town of Zofjowka, for example, 20 tannery owners were allowed to stay in business because the authorities had a special interest in their products. The testimonies of merchants and factory owners of the time indicate that treatment was inconsistent even within one area, such as eastern Poland. Official attitudes evidently differed from place to place and, at times, even from instance to instance. It seems that the local party and security agencies made the relevant decisions in accordance with their views. Purely economic considerations (e.g., availability of materials, the need to make use of experts) affected the decisions as well, of course.

One of the functionaries who reached Slonim (western Belorussia) just after the Red Army occupation, in order to set up a civil administration in the town, was a Jew named Matvey Kolotov (Motl Kolotnitsky). At the very first assembly, he proudly noted his proletarian lineage; he was a wagoner's assistant. He established a headquarters in the former district administration building and ran his operations from there. The building that had once housed the Polish Savings Fund became home to a branch of Gosbank (the Soviet government bank), where Kolotov replaced the Polish clerks with "Jewish boys and girls, with a few Russian clerks thrown in." Several newly appointed Gosbank officials were former executives of the Jewish Commercial Bank and the local Jewish People's Bank. These two institutions and all their employees had been transferred to the new Gosbank branch.

Because work at the seven lumber mills in the town had been suspended by the owners, Kolotov summoned the former owners (all of them Jews) and harangued: "You've caused work to stop and thereby made 1,000 laborers idle, just when we, your liberators, have come to save you. Therefore, I give you two options: to resume work as before—we'll buy up everything you produce—or to turn your factories over to the workers. I want an answer within 24 hours!" When the former owners asked about their own fate, Kolotov replied: "You'll be employed as experts at the normal rate of remuneration. After all, even Lenin ordered us to exploit the talents of the bourgeoisie until the proletariat can assume the leadership itself." The factory owners, consulting among themselves, decided to forfeit the mills voluntarily. They were allowed to continue working, and their status as job foremen guaranteed them a relatively high monthly wage from the state exchequer. Their former employees elected nearly all of them to the union locals (works committees), and some were even given the honor of waving the Red flag at mass rallies or demonstrations.

The honeymoon, however, lasted only a month. Just before the People's Assembly elections in Bialystok, swarms of NKVD agents arrived and began investigating "bourgeois" elements and former public figures. Quite a few Soviet officials also reached the area; most of these, known as "leather jackets," were appointed to run the local plants. It was not long before all the former mill owners had been dismissed.[2]

A knitwear shop in the town of Zheludok (Lida subdistrict) was nationalized in another stage of the process. Soviet officials entered the shop, calculated the value of the inventory, loaded everything onto a truck, paid the shop owner the 50,000 rubles they thought he deserved, and drove away. About a week later, the merchant was summoned to the civil authorities and ordered to pay an "income tax" of 150,000 rubles. His explanations and entreaties were disregarded; he was forced to pay up in full, forfeiting savings that had taken many years to accrue. Yet he was a happy man, for he had not been arrested nor had his family been sent to Siberia, as had happened to others in similar cases.[3] Once these matters became widely known, additional merchants relinquished their businesses voluntarily.

In the Baltic countries and Romania, the refugees and media provided detailed information on the nationalization process in eastern Poland and the hardships imposed on former business owners. The central authorities in Moscow, too, followed the nationalization process in Poland, and for this reason, among other things, the nationalization of factories in the Baltic countries and the annexed areas of Romania proceeded relatively quietly.

For one thing, owners had been prepared, at least psychologically, as soon as the Red Army came in. The following account from Lithuania illustrates this state of affairs:

At first, the owners and employees of the businesses, factories, and plants were given to understand that they would all keep their positions and that nothing would change. A week later, however, the owners were displaced and allowed to wander through their plants like ghosts. After another week, the authorities asked them not to come in anymore, since they no longer needed them and would get along without them. The dispossession was carried out slowly, delicately, and quietly, with neither shouting nor commotion.[4]

The high proportion of Jews in ranking industrial positions explains this community's great vulnerability to the nationalization process. Chief among the victims were Jewish industrialists in major industrial cities such as Bialystok and Lvov. Quite a few Jewish industrialists also were dispossessed in smaller cities (especially with respect to flour mills, tanneries, and so on) and in medium-sized cities such as Pinsk, the capital of Polesie. Nationalization in this town affected 42 lumber mills, 37 linen factories, 25 asphalt plants, four plywood factories, three tanneries, one match factory, one turpentine plant, and 27 flour mills. In the town of Lida, the Soviets took over 38 industrial plants, nearly all—or, in any case, the largest of them—Jewish-owned. They included a rubber products plant that employed 1,000 workers in three shifts and factories that manufactured chemical products, nails, cast iron, edible oils, beer, lumber, flour, printing, and other commodities.

The process recurred with at least as much vigor in the Baltic countries and the Romanian districts after their annexation. In Lithuania, for example, no group of industrialists and merchants was more egregiously victimized by nationalization than the Jews.

For economic and other reasons, many factories were aggregated into production and marketing groups called "trusts" (a term adopted by the Soviets) in order to build appropriate conglomerates for each industry. All the Jewish printing shops in Vilna, for example (with that owned by the famous company The Widow and Brothers Rom at their forefront) were merged into a single enterprise called "Government Printer No. 1". Smaller enterprises, too, were undoubtedly unified within new frameworks.

The nationalization of commerce was immeasurably more complex than that of banks and industrial enterprises, chiefly because commercial businesses were so numerous and dispersed. The government of Soviet Lithuania decided to dispatch commissars to every private business, merchandise warehouse, restaurant, hotel, and so on, covering any enterprise that had an annual turnover of 150,000 litas or more (one litas was worth about ten dollars at the time). Without these commissars' consent, the owners were forbidden to carry out any business transaction and had to hand over the keys to their establishments. In special cases, they might be allowed temporarily to manage the newly nationalized enterprises.

In all, 1,593 businesses with a total annual turnover (1939) of 500 million litas were nationalized in Lithuania in the autumn of 1940.[5] Approximately half of them belonged to the following industries: clothing 374, metals 163, food 148, and haberdashery 123. The owners' national affiliations were as follows: Jews 1,327, Lithuanians 147, Germans 28, and "mixed" 65. Nationalized businesses previously owned by Jews were located in all parts of Lithuania. At least 83 percent of all businesses nationalized in Lithuania, and virtually all of those confiscated in the eastern districts and especially in the Vilna area, had belonged to Jews. This gave rise to a pervasive feeling among the Jewish public that Jews were the main victims of nationalization.

The nationalization decree did not spell out what agent was authorized to determine the annual turnover of a business, nor did it define the determining year. The authorities initially based these assignments on income tax assessments, but because this process was frequently complicated and protracted, especially in outlying towns, the decision to nationalize businesses was handed over to the local branch of the Communist Party or the trade union. This led to arbitrary decisions often based on ignorance, hostility, and vengeance. Indeed, the tentacles of nationalization occasionally reached businesses whose turnover did not reach one half or even one third of the determining sum.[6] Nationalization was even more blatantly arbitrary in Estonia, where the number of businesses harmed far exceeded the 6 percent defined as "large enterprises."

Even though the nationalization laws exempted small businesses, and even though there was never an official decree ordering these establishments to close their doors, the regime did not tolerate private commercial initiative on any scale. This de facto policy had the effect of depriving hundreds of thousands of Jews (shopkeepers, market-stall owners, peddlers, artisans, and so on) of their source of livelihood. Red Army soldiers, who had been given three months' salary in advance, and the many Soviet officials who followed in their tracks bought up everything they saw irrespective of its price. In response, the locals, too, began to snap up merchandise indiscriminately. Shopkeepers, afraid of being accused of speculation, withheld nothing. As the shops and warehouses were emptied, a grave shortage of basic commodities, such as footwear, clothing, and kitchen implements, occurred. In some localities, even the purchase of bread required lengthy queuing. Thus quite a few merchants and shopkeepers found themselves with "bags of money" and no merchandise, explaining that the goods "got lost". The situation was aggravated by the vast difference in exchange rates between the local currency and the ruble. (In Northern Bukovina, the value of the lei [the local currency] plunged by a factor of 40!). Moreover, restrictions on withdrawal of currency from banks and savings funds resulted in a moratorium on the relief funds (dollars and pounds sterling) that many Jews had been receiving from overseas. Numerous Jewish families were reduced to dire poverty.

Nationalization sometimes happened precipitously. In Czernowitz, for example, several large grocery stores located on main streets were left in private hands for some time. Not only were the shop owners spared immediate losses in the nationalization process, they even made a tidy profit selling liquor to the Soviet officials who were in charge of the municipality. These shops' turn came about six months later (in December, 1940): one morning, without forewarning, the owners found the doors padlocked and sealed.[7]

In other cases, shopkeepers and peddlers who had struggled to keep their businesses going under the new circumstances were forced to liquidate under the weight of the new taxes. Sovietization virtually wiped out the class of salesman, which had accounted for much Jewish commerce. Many of these salesmen, members of a rather poorly regarded group in the Jewish community, now sought alternative employment. Those who stayed in the trade became employees of governmental services and often encountered former employers in their new workplaces—this time as their equals.

The nationalization of houses and apartments, which usually took place in the second stage, was marked by unclarity and lack of explicit criteria. Local functionaries had broad discretion that they could exercise arbitrarily. The main victims were the Jews, who were the most urbanized population group. In principle, the property (including the homes) of anyone who had ever employed wage labor was liable to nationalization. In Lithuania, approximately 14,000 residences were nationalized. The housing nationalization law was first implemented in major cities and industrial centers, meaning that again the Jews bore the brunt of the action. Not only were landlords dispossessed of their property and regular income; in many cases they were ordered to leave their own homes and relocate to different cities. In extreme cases, this was done brutally and on 24 hours' notice. In Poland and Romania, synagogues and yeshivot were expropriated for use as warehouses, social clubs, restaurants, and the like.

At first glance, the nationalization of land (any farmstead larger than 30 hectares) had less of an impact on the Jewish population; the proportion of Jews engaging in agriculture did not exceed 6 percent in any of the annexed areas. However, the proportion of landowners who lost real estate and agricultural properties in this stage of nationalization was many times greater. The major (perhaps the decisive) reason for this was a provision of the nationalization law restricting land ownership (within permissible quotas) to those who worked the land themselves and derived their livelihood therefrom. Many of the Jewish landholders in Eastern Galicia, southeastern Lithuania, Northern Bukovina, and elsewhere employed wage laborers for this purpose, treating agriculture as something of a side income.[8] Few Jewish farmers succeeded in evading the wrath of this decree; those who did generally promised henceforth to treat agriculture as their sole occupation. A letter to the editor of the Jewish daily *Folksblat* describes one such instance in southern Lithuania:

We, Jewish peasants from Simnas, are pleased to inform you that the lands that had been taken from us were restored to all of us today. We are elated, since all of us were strongly connected to the land, literally with our bodies and souls. We are willing to give up the most precious of our possessions, homes and shops, if only our lands are restored to us.[9]

There were also cases—relatively few—in which indigent Jews received parcels of land and basic equipment to start up a farmstead. Jewish families who joined the kolkhozes that came into being in the annexed areas were also granted land and farm equipment.

In Bessarabia, where the proportion of Jews who made their living from agriculture was relatively high, only a few were allowed to continue farming after the nationalization and agrarian reform. The parcels they were allowed to keep for their livelihood were constrained by family size. A household head who received a piece of land, or who was allowed to stay on his land (or part of it), had to prove that he and his family indeed performed the labor themselves, without the benefit of wage labor. Harvest activity, too, was strictly inspected. Nevertheless, some Jewish families in various parts of Bessarabia continued to work their own farmsteads; others remained in agriculture as members of cooperatives.[10]

Many Jews found positions planning and implementing the nationalization policy, either as "trustees" of the regime or as experts. The latter, as previously stated, included former owners of plants or businesses. Some of the non-Jewish experts (Poles in the western Ukraine and western Belorussia, for example) were reluctant to fill the positions offered them for national or political reasons; in some areas this gave Jewish officials access to prominent economic positions (at least at first) at a rate far exceeding their share of the population.

In the Baltic countries, however, many non-Jewish economists agreed to work for the nationalization apparatus. Even so, the number of Jews in key positions there was relatively high,[11] especially on the staff of the government commissars who nationalized large and medium-sized enterprises and businesses. The following figures attest to the national origins of the commissars in 337 of the 460 enterprises nationalized in the first stage (July-August, 1940): Lithuanians 153 (45 percent), Jews 107 (32 percent), Poles 40 (12 percent), and Russians 37 (11 percent).[12] According to these figures, a Jew was much more likely, in proportional terms, to be an industrial commissar than a blue-collar laborer.

LABOR MARKET

Since the masses had come to expect the socialist regime not only to solve their unemployment problems but also to bestow progress and palpable benefits on all proletarians, job-seekers began to flood the major cities and industrial centers from the first. The Jews joined these throngs in ample numbers—especially unemployed young adults in the smaller cities, who regarded this migration as an opportunity to fulfill dreams of personal advancement. Some of these individuals fulfilled these hopes in one form or another, but most found the job search in the large urban centers a problematic and protracted process.

In terms of their standing in the labor market and their work attitudes, the Jewish community was composed of three groups:

1. Workers, clerks, teachers, and other wage-earners, along with members of the liberal professions, who had previously been employed in private or public enterprises. All of these stayed on the job.

2. Breadwinners or family members who had previously been idle (especially in Poland), along with individuals who had been dismissed from their positions and left without a source of livelihood because of the political and economic transformation that had taken place. Insofar as they became job-seekers, their situation was no different than that of new employees. In the provinces of eastern Poland, their numbers grew with each passing day, especially when refugees from the German-occupied zone

began to pour in. Persons in this situation eventually accounted for a majority of working-age Jews.

3. Members, or membership candidates, in the Communist Party and the Komsomol; MOPR or trade union activists; and liberated political prisoners. Because these were relatively few, they were in special demand for key positions and situations entailing responsibility in the Party, government and public administration, and the various security agencies.

In the dynamic that had ensued (i.e., the eradication of existing labor structures and the construction of new ones), even tenured ("continuing") workers were occasionally left jobless and had to queue at the trade union offices or labor exchanges. The lives of the "continuers," as a class, did not change in any fundamental way, although members of this group did harbor expectations of substantial advancement. However, the majority of "new" employees, especially those middle-aged or older, faced a transformation of their lives with respect to work. For them, the quest for work was a fateful necessity. Not only did they need employment for their economic and psychological well-being; they also regarded the attainment of an official position, even a part-time job in a factory, as an admission ticket to the laborers' class, the preferred place to be in the nascent socialist society.

The most desperate job-hunters were persons who had reason to fear because of their previous political or social positions. For them, a job would both confirm their rehabilitation and provide an "insurance policy."

Most "workers in demand" were placed in key positions—from government and Party leadership down to nationalized shops—at the very onset of the annexation. Even though they regarded themselves as fulfilling a mission or task on behalf of the new regime, they indubitably were affected by personal motives, such as the desire to advance to a higher, more respectable, or more interesting position, or at least one better suited to their capabilities and education. In view of the relentless demand for reliable people to staff the new and overhauled apparatuses, workers in demand enjoyed a measure of occupational mobility, mostly in the direction of higher ranking and more important positions. Most of these persons were placed in planning and administrative positions on the local and district levels, factory management (chiefly apparel, leather, lumber, food, and printing), management of retail and service enterprises, and leadership of trade unions. Others were assigned to manage special departments (for routine security and the like) and divisions of the bureaucracy.

Lubcz, a town in the Baranowicze district, illustrates this phenomenon. Not only was the chairman of the local soviet Jewish; so were the managers of all the retail shops, without exception. The same was true for a local winery and canned food factory, the district office, the chief accounting division of the local tax office, and a footwear cooperative. Moreover, a majority of the 200 Soviet clerks who were brought in to fill positions of responsibility were Jews.[13]

In the middle of August, 1940, 51 percent of the employees of the Lithuanian Ministry of Industry were Jewish; most occupied positions in the senior and middle echelons. Jewish workers (including quite a few former contractors) were conspicuously represented in the central offices of the "trusts," the new economic development companies, and even the long-established companies of these types that swallowed up the nationalized private enterprises. Thus, for example, of 1,000 or so employees in the branches of the cooperatives affiliated with the Lietukis retail chain, at least 226 were Jewish.

The economic development companies and other employers eventually took on quite a few new (i.e., not continuing) workers as well. This was a consequence of the new method of administrative management, which spawned a ramified bureaucracy composed of hundreds of frameworks and innumerable sub-frameworks that multiplied with each passing day in almost every town from Estonia to Bessarabia. Thousands of bookkeepers, cashiers, lawyers, and members of related occupations were hired to meet all these needs. As time passed, new occupations were created, such as norm-setters, planners, and so on. Demand for Russian-speaking workers mounted.

All workers, both continuing and new ones, had to fill out long, detailed questionnaires concerning their social origins, relatives overseas, and, of course, political party affiliations and public activity. To the extent possible, those filling out the questionnaires attempted to stress the presence of proletarians and artisans in their families, and to conceal the fact that any of their parents or siblings had been merchants, shopkeepers, or owners of property or factories.

One way or the other, ostensibly sworn enemies of the workers class and the regime sometimes "infiltrated" workplaces, sometimes by exploiting personal connections.[14] As a rule, however, job-seekers of this kind did not easily succeed in finding work in their places of residence. For example, Boris Bernstein, a former commercial bank manager and well-known Zionist functionary in Kovno, pounded the streets until he found a menial job, to which he clung until he was exiled. When Rabbi Benzion Kagan of Braynsk, son-in-law of the town rabbi, applied to the local labor exchange for work, the bureau director told him that the matter could be arranged only if the rabbi declared himself to be an atheist. After complaints and appeals to the top Party echelons, Rabbi Kagan was assigned a petty bookkeeping position and was even excused from work on the Sabbath and Jewish festivals.[15] In Przemysl (Eastern Galicia), Jews who had held positions in the Polish government apparatus were dismissed from the municipal administration. In the Lvov and Stanislawow districts, former Jewish estate holders and relatives were hard-pressed to obtain work of any kind.

Because former property owners and persons forced into idleness for political or other reasons were threatened with the withholding of food-ration vouchers and the inscription of one of the two restrictive paragraphs (11 or 39) on their ID cards, many of them made strenuous efforts to find work of some kind. However, to obtain a governmental or public position, as previously stated, one had to fill out a detailed questionnaire, risking the label of "hostile" or "unreliable." Therefore, former political-party functionaries, landlords, merchants, and shopkeepers preferred menial, hard physical labor, and became teamsters, railroad depot porters, lumberjacks, and so on. These jobs offered a shroud of anonymity, sparing their holders humiliation, denigration, and other unpleasantness.

An especially difficult fate awaited the masses of Jews, most middle-aged or older, who had earned their daily bread from petty trade, peddling, brokerage, and similar "hand-to-mouth" vocations. Religious functionaries and former employees of Jewish public institutions shut down by the new regime found themselves in similar straits. Since these people had been turned into unskilled workers, their fate was sometimes many times more bitter than that of the dispossessed bourgeoisie, who still had savings and could offer the Soviet economy their skills and expertise. Thus it became a common sight to find a middle-aged Jew, formerly a member of the elite in Jewish society, wearing a "Russian shirt" and boots, leaning over a table in some burgeoning bureaucracy, working as a petty clerk. Only a few small merchants remained in this field as wage earners in government retail shops and similar establishments. Many were assigned to unskilled labor such as building roads and bridges, cleaning sidewalks, and shoveling snow. Some became seasonal farm laborers. A few drew on inventories they had cached away, selling them on the black market. Memorial books and testimonies of various kinds offer information on this phenomenon as it occurred in several communities in Wolhynia (western Ukraine).[16]

Another relatively large segment of the Jewish community that met with grave difficulties in adjusting to the changing times were members of the liberal professions, especially lawyers. Attorneys who expressed willingness to practice their profession were put through a series of supplementary training courses, to which the authorities admitted only candidates of "proletarian descent" and those found to be ideologically or otherwise pure.

In Czernowitz, for example, lawyers who wished to join the professional cooperative bureaus (an integral part of the judicial system) had to appear before a special committee from Kiev that convened in a public auditorium. Each attorney was told to present his life history to the committee members, who asked the audience if they knew the individual and what they thought of him. For the onlookers' "convenience," a list of lawyers summoned to appear before the committee, with the dates of their appearances, was posted on the auditorium door. On more than one occasion, people who bore a grudge against a certain lawyer, for having lost a lawsuit or for being caused some other ostensible harm, showed up in order to denounce him. In other cases, people in the audience accused a lawyer of antipathy toward the "workers' cause." The victimized candidates were hauled to the "people's court"; some were sentenced to years in prison or exile. This procedure drummed many lawyers out of the profession. Dr. Aryeh Schmeltzer, for example—one of the most important Zionist leaders in Czernowitz—preferred to work as a bookkeeper. Many members of the large community of Jewish lawyers in Northern Bukovina, who had toiled under crippling limitations under the Romanian regime, drew similar conclusions. Ranking jurists and those with commercial and fiscal experience were co-opted into the governmental banking and financial system, which was growing rapidly in scale and activity in view of the all-embracing nature of the Soviet economy. The lawyers' professional and social status underwent a "devaluation" in this period, as the practice of law, an occupation of high social status before the war, now lost most of its substance and prestige.

The plight of physicians was less severe. The change of regime did not harm the substance of their profession, although it did affect the way in which they were employed. Many Jewish physicians were hired by the state medical service, marking a breakthrough of sorts relative to their pre-war condition, when they had virtually been barred from state and public medical institutions. Although they found that the Soviet system left no room for private practice, some continued to receive private patients, knowing that Soviet citizens often preferred the ministrations of a private physician despite the comprehensive government health insurance that they carried. Needless to say, they went about this with circumspection and thereby improved their standard of living considerably.

Quite a few doctors were commonly known as public figures who had taken part in the activities of community and Communist Party institutions that had been discredited as opponents of the new regime; these physicians met with difficulty in finding work. A well-known physician in Baranowicze, Dr. Nahumovsky, "was utterly depressed, since as a Zionist he was not allowed to do any responsible work even though he was a well-known physician of long standing. . . . His property was confiscated, his private hospital was turned over to the government, and he was sent to work elsewhere. Even there his situation was unstable, since he was a candidate for exile to Siberia."[17]

The situation of engineers resembled that of most physicians. They found work in all areas of industry and administration, including some that had previously barred Jews. They, too, had the feeling that the obstacles the previous regime had placed in the paths of Jewish engineers had now been swept aside.

The major problems facing members of the liberal professions were, in great part, typical of all workers: acquiescence to the nearly total proscription of self-employment in the Soviet economy and to the need to adjust to the new conditions. Even though physicians and engineers earned more than others, it was hard for them to get by on official wages alone.

Many members of the liberal professions found work as teachers, especially in the annexed Polish and Romanian provinces. Droves of teachers had left these areas, and the new regime was making energetic efforts to develop the education system in every town and village. Thus hundreds of young Jews, some lacking higher education, passed courses of several weeks' duration and were sent to work at all levels in the school system.

Members of the middle class, now struggling to survive on their meager savings, also applied en masse for teaching jobs. When the authorities set up a four-classroom school in the village of Pepeny (in the Balti/Beltsy district of Bessarabia) on the estate of a Romanian landowner, a Jewish shopkeeper who had previous teaching experience was appointed as the principal and teacher of two classes. His son, a recent graduate of a Hebrew high school, was hired to teach the other two classes. The estate owner's coachman became the school custodian.

In other areas, such as Eastern Galicia, Jews sought work in traditional fields. In Kolomyja, Jewish experts continued to run the clothmaking trade under the Soviets. In the Kusow vicinity, Jewish artisans who had made rugs continued to do so after having formed cooperatives. In the Strij area, many

Jews worked as tanners. In Borislav and Drohobycz, hundreds of Jews continued to work in the oil fields and refineries even after the Jewish owners had been dispossessed and their property nationalized. Some of the remaining employees were expert drillers, several of whom were cited in the local press as "outstanding workers."

There was a large congregation of Jewish railroad workers in the Stanislawow area in 1939–1941. This unusual situation had its roots in the period of Austrian rule prior to World War I. The Poles had fired nearly all of the Jewish workers in the 1920s, but many of them reclaimed their positions under sovietization. In several localities in Wolhynia and Belorussia, Jews with no railroad experience now found work in this industry.

A conspicuous example of continuity was the baking industry in Lvov, which had been dominated by Jews until the war. The bakeries were nationalized in late 1939, aggregated into a single municipal enterprise, and converted into branches of this municipal enterprise for baked goods. Every branch was given a production quota and had to deliver its output to government shops, each of which would sell the bread in a different part of town. A local Ukrainian was appointed to head this enterprise in 1940; he was replaced sometime later by a Ukrainian Soviet. Apart from this largely representative position, however, all the work—management, planning, and direct labor at the ovens—remained in Jewish hands. Former bakery owners were hired to work alongside the wage laborers who had been there before September, 1939; the former owners, now wage earners, served as work foremen, among other functions.

In Wolhynia, Polesie, and other areas of western Belorussia and Lithuania, many Jews continued working in the lumber and forestry industry. Now, however, they held governmental inspection and management positions that formerly had been reserved for Poles and Lithuanians, when Jews were employed as lumber haulers, forest watchmen, and other duties that did not require appreciable skill.

"Traditional" Jewish industries such as apparel, footwear, food, furs, printing, and hairdressing were also noted for very high employment continuity in all the annexed areas. One may therefore state that rather than fully exploiting the new opportunities that sovietization offered them, most Jews continued plying their traditional trades.

To increase output and enhance pride and interest in the workplace, the authorities often encouraged "socialist competition" (*sotsgevet* in Yiddish) between factories and institutions. Outstanding performers were given cash prizes and vacations at resorts in the Caucasus, Crimea, and so on. Such cases, of course, were lavishly covered by the press.[18] This method of competition and prizes was adopted in commercial establishments, in which Jews were rather strongly represented.[19]

Alongside the advantages of a governmental workplace for its employees, new and old alike, there were many constraints and obligations. It was standard Soviet practice to pin each worker to his or her workplace; any intent to quit or relocate required a special permit. These regulations were significantly toughened during the sovietization period. Second, any serious departure from standard operating and maintenance instructions could result in an accusation of sabotage of the Soviet economy; the same was true of infractions of discipline such as insubordination, tardiness, absenteeism, and drunkenness. Drunkenness (and the absenteeism it caused) was rife among non-Jewish workers and not unknown among the Jews. One of the "sins" of Jewish workers was absenteeism on the Sabbath and, especially, on Jewish festivals.[20] Notably, however, these were exceptional cases. Only a privileged minority could behave with impunity. The large majority of workers, especially the new ones, dreaded the loss of their jobs and strived to obey all orders with extreme stringency and devotion. This was evinced strikingly the day that the German-Soviet war broke out; unlike many of their non-Jewish colleagues, the Jews reported for work that day and the next, even though the enemy was hot on their heels.

NEW PATTERNS OF LIVELIHOOD

Despite the booming labor market, especially in the second stage of sovietization (the integration stage), many Jews still struggled to find suitable work in their former occupations. In several localities, such as Vilna, Lvov, and Kowel, unemployment had been a plague even under the previous Polish regime, and it worsened with the arrival of refugees from the war in Poland.

It is not surprising that one of the major expectations of the Jews in these areas was the alleviation, if not the elimination, of unemployment. Here and there, the authorities continued to fight unemployment in conventional ways such as make-work and even expansion of projects. Concurrently, in the annexed areas of Poland and Romania, they encouraged the unemployed to volunteer for work in Soviet industrial centers, chiefly in the Donbas area and other parts of the Ukraine.[21] Many thousands responded to this call for practical and ideological reasons; they included Jewish artisans, young adults, and refugees. Upon reaching Donbas and other destinations in the Soviet

Ukraine, however, the volunteers met with a reality very different from that described by the authorities. The problem was partially reflected in the Soviet press at the time. A series of articles lauding the contribution of Soviet policy to the eradication of unemployment contained reverberations of the misadventures with which the Jews in the Soviet Ukraine had met.

In December, 1939, *Der Shtern* published a letter signed by Jews from the western Ukraine, thanking Comrade Stalin "for having saved [them] from the economic distress and unemployment" that had prevailed before the war in Poland. The Soviet press abounded with notices of this kind and descriptions of the good life in workplaces in the Soviet interior, especially in the first few months of 1940. Although the initiative behind these notices had presumably been taken by official agencies, it seems likely that, at least in the initial period, these pieces reflected some degree of genuine, sincere identification of certain Jewish groups with the policies of the new regime.

The articles on the situation of Jewish workers in the USSR ceased publication after March, 1940, but those that had previously appeared highlight the difficulties that beset these workers in their adjustment to hard physical labor, occupational unsuitability, housing problems, harsh climate, and wages that did not always ensure a reasonable standard of living. Indeed, gloomy letters began to arrive from the Ukraine, and within a short time, in the spring of 1940, a stream of returning volunteers ensued.

The artisans, too, had to adjust to the new system. Most of them had either worked alone or had employed a few workers whose material conditions were no worse than their own. In both cases, the authorities offered a constructive solution within the conventional cooperative framework of the USSR—the *artels*. This "artelization" was an integral part of Soviet socioeconomic policy, which sought to turn previously self-employed artisans into wage laborers. The transition was made gradually but steadily, as the authorities pressured the artisans by choking the supply of raw materials for private activity and imposing heavy taxes. Although this policy forced even small artisans to join artels, some Jewish artisans maintained their private businesses, despite the heavy official pressure, until the German invasion in June, 1941.

All members of artels, laborers alongside former owners, enjoyed equal privileges, including equal shares of net income. The artels were organized by industry or by a group of related industries, such as sewing, hatmaking, and shoemaking; haulage and portering; framemaking and glassmaking; and so on. Since few non-Jews were engaged as artisans in the towns and cities, quite a few artels were Jewish through and through. Among them were 30 artels in Luck (in Wolhynia), especially those devoted to women's tailoring, shoemaking, furs, and so on. In the service artels, such as hairdressing and laundering, a decisive majority of members were Jewish.

A member of the hairdressing artel in Brestowice (Bialystok district) wrote the following to his son in Chicago:

> You ask what an artel is? —Everyone brings his working tools to the artel, and everyone works in the same building. They point to a certain building that they want, and city hall arranges for them to get it. They choose a manager, whose job it is to provide the workers with the tools they need. Fifty-five percent of the income is set aside to provide all the equipment for the hairdressing shop. The other 45 percent is given to the workers. There is a treasurer, because records are kept for each and every worker. There are several artels in Brestowice.[22]

Leadership in the small artels was usually exercised by local Jews. In the large ones, however (especially in the areas in Poland and Romania), functionaries were brought in from the east. Some of these, too, were Jews.

One of the first artels set up in Lithuania was of wagoners and haulers in Kovno; nearly 80 percent of its 130 members were Jews. The membership included former owners of hauling companies and their employees. In addition to horses and wagons, the artel owned a smithy, a harness shop, a wagon repair shop, and 20 hectares of pasture for the horses. It also obtained a plot for the construction of stables. On average, the members earned 600–800 rubles per month. Over time, artisan artels also began to organize in smaller cities and towns that had not had them.

It goes without saying that self-employed artisans, owners of small factories, and other middle-class elements were strongly attracted to the flourishing, affluent artels. The artels, however, were cautiously selective when it came to admitting new members. Thus, for example, the porters' artel in Kovno obstructed the admission of 23 Jewish porters who had formed a work group and wished to join. At first the artel employed them under a subcontracting arrangement; only later did it agree to hire them on the basis of a daily wage, and even then only the youngest and healthiest of them.

There were also cases of refusal to permit the establishment of an artel. This happened to the butchers in Kovno, after they had come together and pooled their resources. The reason for the refusal was that "the USSR doesn't have a butchers' artel." With great difficulty the would-be artel members recouped their money. There were even cases in which artels interested in augmenting their membership placed newspaper advertisements to this effect. The authorities usually took a favorable view of the growth of the artel network, since it was regarded as good for production and a solution for individuals or very small factories to which the nationalization law did not apply, but whose chances of survival on their own were poor.[23]

In view of the structure of the Soviet economy and the occupational composition of the Jewish population, the establishment of the artels was hardly a solution for the masses of Jewish and non-Jewish middle-class breadwinners who had been dispossessed of their sources of livelihood. The Soviet leaders were aware of the problem; when they carried out the annexation, they spoke sympathetically, declaring that "the Communist Party will not fight against the small shopkeepers; it will even help them become a productive element."[24] This message was directed with special vigor at youth.

Here and there, Jews were allowed to undergo vocational retraining in general programs and in accordance with economic and technical needs. In early 1940, the authorities in the cities of the former Polish provinces, and especially in western Belorussia, offered special courses for bookkeepers, industrial laboratory workers, medical laboratory workers, and the like. Notably, these courses were suitable for persons with little formal education, making them appropriate for yeshiva students, former religious functionaries and public servants, and salespeople of various kinds. By the time of the German invasion, many members of these groups had managed to find work in the vocations they had acquired in this fashion. On balance, however, this was a marginal solution only.

One of the adult (ages 17–45) job-training programs established by official initiative was a series of courses in construction trades (building, plastering, carpentry, metalwork, plumbing, and so on). This activity began in the spring of 1941 in Vilna, with about 50 students including "small shopkeepers, bookkeepers, chronic unemployed, and refugees who had not been allowed to work during the tenure of Smetona (the former president of Lithuania)."[25] During their studies, each participant was given a stipend of 150 rubles per month. Graduates in the Baltic areas (including transport and factory [F.Z.O.] apprentices), unlike those in the Polish districts, were unable to benefit from their studies because of the Soviet-German war that broke out that summer.

In view of the scanty official interest and the inefficiency of the minimal measures taken to reform the bankrupt middle class systematically and constructively, the weaker elements within this class were reduced to indigence. Unlike in the former Polish provinces, where petty trade was eradicated by the end of 1940, small shopkeepers in the Baltic countries were allowed to stay in business until the termination of Soviet rule.

Accepted livelihoods at the time included private tutoring (mainly in the Russian language), bookkeeping and accounting, religious studies, and the like. Women of various ages provided child care in others' homes and toiled as cooks and domestics. Men found occasional work as night watchmen, newspaper peddlers, distributors of leaflets, and so on. Especially sad was the plight of former business owners who, for reasons of age or state of health, were unfit for any other trade and whose meager savings ran out or depreciated; these had to call on local relatives or those in other countries for assistance.[26]

Since the authorities were unable to develop efficient services in all locations, it became very difficult to meet simple needs such as the repair of shoes, clothing, a broken tool, or a cracked window. Thus the public again called on the veteran artisans—shoemakers, tailors, metalworkers, glaziers (a large majority of whom were Jews)—who therefore continued to play an important role in certain areas, such as Eastern Galicia. However, there was no doubt that the days of traditional Jewish artisanship were numbered, and its practitioners would have to adjust to the new conditions.

As the authorities toughened the political and cultural aspects of their domestic policy, so did they take an appreciably harder line on economic agents, such as small shopkeepers, who had not yet been integrated into the governmental and public economic system. Private trade was now allowed only with a permit issued by the municipal department of trade or the district executive committee. "Artisans and manufacturers who sell their wares ready-made" (i.e., who had not yet joined cooperative frameworks), were grouped with other self-employed breadwinners under the income tax law and ordered to register within two weeks. Wagoners, taxi owners, landlords, religious functionaries—indeed, anyone with various sources of income, including artisans, shopkeepers, and small industrialists—were ordered to declare their total income retroactively. In this manner the circle of the legally self-employed progressively narrowed. These successive edicts were sorely distressing to the persons affected, but in view of the dramatic events taking place next door (expulsions to Siberia and the outbreak of the war), the degree of damage they actually caused cannot be gauged.

STANDARD AND QUALITY OF LIVING

Although jobs with governmental or public employers were in demand for the social and political security that they offered, the main goal was a livelihood. The jobs available did not always pass this test. In the western Ukraine and in western Belorussia, wages were paid in zlotys until the end of 1939, as if the Poles were still in charge. Even though wages were increased, especially in the lower salary brackets, prices of certain commodities outpaced them rapidly. In this sense, no improvement occurred even after salaries were paid in rubles at the accepted Soviet exchange rates. In western Belorussia, most wage-earners earned 150–600 rubles per month.[27] Workers in artels, government factories, and public institutions earned 250–400 rubles per month; physicians, engineers, and teachers brought home 350–500 rubles. Many active manufacturing plants allowed employees to increase their wages by surpassing the fixed production quotas. The administrative and service workers, among whom the Jews were heavily represented, were unable to benefit from this practice.

The average monthly wage in Eastern Galicia was about 300 rubles. Typical monthly wages in Eastern Galicia were 200 rubles for artel cashiers, 250 for production workers, 250–300 for teachers, 350 for school principals, 300–450 for physicians, 700 for chief bookkeepers in artels, and 750 for managers of factory production units.[28] At the time, a kilogram of bread cost one ruble, a kilogram of sugar 2.5 rubles, and a kilogram of meat between 7–18 rubles (depending on the cut of meat, the extent of koshering treatment, and so on). Prices of apparel and footwear were relatively high; for example, a pair of shoes in Eastern Galicia cost 50–80 rubles. Because most Jews were in the middle-income range, the community as a whole was economically hard-pressed. Furthermore, quite a few commodities were not available at the official prices. Those who had been in dire economic straits even before the war broke out were especially affected. The Jewish population in Wolhynia was better off; most of this community had avoided economic hardship before the war and was now integrated into the new economic system with relative success.

An indication of the hardship emerges in letters written by parents in Brestowice to their son in Chicago. These parents were experienced in sending letters overseas (another excerpt of the father's correspondence is quoted on page 270), and they were aware of the censorship being practiced):

August 28, 1940
Why should I sadden you? . . . After all, you can't do anything to help us but sigh. It is very hard to observe how long one has to queue, and there's no sugar [this was originally stated in Hebrew, evidently to outwit the censor]. But people have to live under these conditions. There's no fruit at all. . . . Everything froze because of the terrible winter [i.e., the general hard-

ships]. . . . The harvest was burned and all the rest went for the comrades [the authorities].

September 22, 1940
We are satisfied with the Soviet regime, which liberated us from Polish enslavement. . . . I'm writing you for the third time—we're not lacking anything. . . . You ask what the youngsters are doing. Some of them moved to larger cities. . . . Some are in Brestowice working as street engineers [i.e., they are unemployed]. . . . A few are taking evening courses. . . . You ask what about the shops? Imagine that I'm a free man now, with neither bills nor concerns. . . . There's a shop here where you can get just about nothing. . . .

October 21, 1940
In the meantime, we ought to be satisfied that we still have something to eat. . . . We bake black bread [*shvartse bondes*] for Shabbat, and the same for the festivals. As for white hallot [Sabbath bread], we shouldn't say a thing. . . . For now, how do you like hearing that our aunt was evicted from her flat and moved in with Yankl. You can imagine how crowded it is. . . . She stays with me, too. . . . In a few words, she now feels the war palpably and tangibly . . . but she's not the only one; there are many like her. . . . Regards from Elka. . . . Things are very bad for her; she has nothing to live on. Prices are sky-high [here the censor deleted a lengthy passage]. . . . I am greatly saddened to hear that our rabbi has such serious troubles. Everyone with God in his heart is helping him. . . . We are helping him, too, as best we can. . . . In many homes they weigh each bit of bread before eating it. . . . You ask whether we are baking bread? There are government bakeries in town.

November 11, 1940
All of us have jobs. I work as a military barber [i.e., in the barbers' artel that served military personnel]. . . . Yankl is a clerk in a flour mill: he receives the wheat and ships out the flour. We earn 250 rubles per month. . . . Michal, Yankl's daughter, works as an assistant bookkeeper and earns 150 rubles per month. So we're getting along, in today's terms.

May 5, 1941
I'm still working for the army. How good it is that I have a vocation, and how sad is the plight of those who don't or who aren't working. Many of the small shopkeepers have gone over to farming. Some went into town and became laborers. . . . In your last letter, you asked how we get by on our salaries. . . . We get by somehow, since if you can't make do you have to tighten your belt. As for your question about the prices we pay for goods and foodstuffs, I can't say [an allusion to censorship constraints]. With money you can get anything in town. The cost of things isn't as high as you might imagine. Don't be sorry that I'm not writing much. . . . Understand me and everything will be clear to you. . . . None of us is suffering from privation. . . . It's much healthier to keep this letter short. . . . [29]

The economic woes of the Jews in the annexed Baltic countries were less grim. Although this was chiefly owing to the relatively short duration of Soviet rule, the Jews' previous affluence helped. It is also worth noting here that economic (and general) sovietization was milder in the Baltic countries than in the Polish and the Romanian provinces. It comes as no surprise that not only Soviet soldiers and officials but also Jewish refugees arriving from Soviet-ruled Polish areas constantly marveled at the plentitude in the Baltic countries as opposed to the privation in their places of origin.

The shopping spree perpetrated by the Soviet officials, who yearned for nearly everything, created shortages of certain goods and caused prices to skyrocket. In time, the average wage in industrial, service, and white-collar jobs reached 300–400 rubles per month,[30] ranging from 150 at the lowest level (washroom attendants) to 1,300 at the highest (trust managers).[31] Those in the middle and lower ranges had to adjust to lower standards of living as rising prices overtook their wages. The monthly wage of a police clerk, for example, was above the median at 600 rubles but sufficed only for the purchase of one suit. These conditions, coupled with the steady depreciation of the currency and the fear of imminent shortages such as those chronic in the Soviet Union,[32] caused many Jewish families, including some that were far from affluent, to join the shopping and hoarding panic. Products suited to the new realities, such as leather jackets, boots, breeches, corduroy vests, and bicycles, were in great demand. Also eagerly sought were suits of English wool, radios, cameras, and even gold coins. Since these had long since vanished from the shelves of the nationalized stores, and since trading in gold was forbidden in any case, customers had to avail themselves of middlemen on the "gray" or black market. On the other hand, in some instances people with low or irregular income (or whose bank accounts had been blocked or expropriated) were forced to sell furniture, books, and other personal effects to make ends meet.

With the exception of high-ranking government and Party officials, most individuals suffered a perceptible decrease in their standard of living. A young Jew who visited his aunt in the Belorussian town of Amdur noted that the refreshments were scanty. His aunt apologized: "That's right, today there's nothing to serve a guest, since the Bolsheviks have destroyed everything. Can one buy or sell anything today? If it weren't for our milch cow, we'd be many times worse off; we'd literally be starving to death."[33]

One of the most grievous problems in urban areas, which, for this reason, beset the Jews in particular, was the housing shortage. Even before the Red Army came in, vacant apartments and rooms were in short supply in the large cities. Moreover, rent was relatively high (about half the wages of a middle-level wage earner). The situation grew worse when rooms were expropriated for Soviet officials and army officers and when the small and large cities absorbed a massive influx from the outlying towns.

As stated previously, landlords who had been defined as rich or as "enemies of the people" suffered greatly. Many of those who had not been evicted from their homes or expelled from their cities of residence were forced to accept boarders. At times, the boarders took over the entire residence and harassed the owners in all sorts of ways. To avoid such unpleasantness, owners of large and even medium-sized dwellings hastily took in relatives or tenants whom they knew. Others swapped their dwellings for smaller accommodations.

One cannot deny, however, that many Jews derived many direct and indirect advantages from the new regime. For one thing, Jewish youth gained access to extensive opportunities for study. For another, the new regimen was highly beneficial to wage earners in certain industries. "It was a good year for us," one leather worker attested with reference to this period. "Until now we got by on seasonal work only. When the Bolsheviks came in, there was work all the time and plenty of money—plenty of everything."[34]

In families with sons and daughters of working age, standards of living rose in accordance with the employment that they were able to find. In some cases, people who had never dreamed of a resort vacation were sent on a summer holiday to the Crimea or the Caucasus.[35]

It therefore comes as no surprise that the working class and other rank-and-file harbored genuine sympathy for the new regime—at least in the first stages of sovietization—along with gratitude and expectations of further economic improvement. Most of the artisans, too, suffered no detriment; indeed, some found themselves better off than before, at least in the sense of being assured not only a monthly salary, albeit low, but also social benefits such as subsidized rent, low-cost electricity and water, free education for their children, and, at times, merchandise in special stores reserved for members of artels. Especially talented and expeditious artisans climbed the social ladder by virtue of their proletarian origins, becoming experts in their trades or going over to better paying vocations. The conditions of seasonal workers, such as those in construction and other trades, who had previously been idled by any crisis, improved markedly.

A new phenomenon of surprising magnitude took shape in the Jewish community at the time: women accepting jobs outside the home. In the period 1939–1941, many Jewish women found positions in administration, teaching, governmental supply and sales systems, and artels and small factories. The material distress of many families was greatly alleviated by the second breadwinner. Still, many households, especially in social groups that had not succeeded in adjusting to the new realities, could not make ends meet. When they attempted to cope by turning to the black or gray markets, they risked a clash with the authorities.

The Jewish community underwent far-reaching socioeconomic changes during the sovietization of Eastern Europe. The self-employed class was eradicated, most of its members becoming wage earners. The upper classes and, to some extent, the middle classes were dispossessed of their belongings. The Jews were expelled from their positions in traditional economic sectors such as banking, industry, and trade, the last-named having been a pillar of the Jewish economy. In this sense, the Jews' losses and suffering exceeded those of non-Jews immeasurably.

Most Jews held one of two views toward the economic and social uncertainties. Some came to terms with the new realities and tried to adjust to the changes and the new economic circumstances, believing that the difficulties were temporary and would perhaps pass as the regime settled in and the Soviet economy improved. Others did not acquiesce in the loss of their property and social status, and secretly hoped that the political constellation that had taken shape in Eastern Europe was not final. Be this as it may, the Nazi invasion in June, 1941, put all these hopes and illusions to rest.

5

Education and Research Institutions

ADOPTION OF NEW PATTERNS

In view of the great indoctrinational importance of the educational system, and with a new school year approaching, the newly constituted local authorities overhauled the educational system in the annexed areas with perceptible haste and revolutionary fervor. This affected the Jews immediately, since half the members of the system (students, teachers, parents, and families) were Jewish. For the Jews, education was an exceedingly important issue and frequently the subject of fierce discussion. In the Baltic countries (especially Lithuania and Estonia), it was one of the Jews' major assets; educational achievement had been a source of pride for Jews ever since the autonomy period.

In the former Polish and Romanian areas, the first steps in the rehabilitation of the educational system were dictated in part by the need to compensate the local population for past discrimination, including the dominance of Polish and Romanian as languages of instruction. Although these changes were meant above all to benefit Ukrainians, Belorussians, and Moldavians, they also affected the Jews, because the Soviet constitution assured them, like all national minorities in the Soviet Union, the right to study in their own "mother tongue." True, official zeal for educational reform was not as intense with respect to the Jews as it was for other minorities. Furthermore, the continued existence of Jewish schools under the new realities met with objective difficulties, one of which was the content of Jewish education.

Some Jewish schools in these areas were "Hebrew" (Zionist) or Orthodox; as such, they were ideologically unacceptable to the new regime.[1] Admittedly, hundreds of Jewish educational institutions on various levels had been established in the Soviet Union in the 1920s and 1930s, with Yiddish as the language of instruction. By 1939, however, the Yiddish educational system in the eastern Ukraine, eastern Belorussia, and other localities was in the midst, if not near the end, of a steady decline.[2] Enrollments were dropping and the curricula were being drained of their national content and connections with Hebrew sources and Jewish culture and tradition.

The affiliations of the Jewish institutions presented another obstacle in the sovietization of Jewish education in the annexed areas. Unlike most of the other minorities' schools (Polish, Lithuanian, Romanian, and so on), which were governmental and controlled centrally by administrative edicts, the Jewish schools were connected with various public organizations: some Zionist (e.g., Tarbut), some Orthodox, (e.g., Yavneh or Safa Berura), and some Yiddishist (such as TSISHO, *Tsentrale Idishe Shul Organizatsie* [Central Yiddish School Organization]). Under the new circumstances, these were doomed to elimination.

A new Yiddish-language educational system was put together by establishing new governmental Jewish schools and "governmentalizing" some of the existing Jewish schools. Both types of institutions, following the standard Soviet practice, would use Yiddish as the language of instruction if the parents demanded this. It is noteworthy that casual preparations for setting up these new schools began shortly after the Red Army arrived; perhaps more important, this happened just before the election campaign for the National Assembly of the Baltic legislatures, which were meant to confirm the Soviet annexation of these areas. Parents were ostensibly entitled to choose the language of instruction (with the exception of Hebrew, which was not allowed). In fact, however, their range of discretion was limited from the outset; at the very most they might express a wish that their children study in Yiddish or some other foreign language such as Polish or Russian. Furthermore, certain educational officials—especially those brought in from the Soviet Union— regularly advised parents (off the record) that "the healthy instinct of parents who keep their children's future in mind would guide them to select Russian as the language of instruction."[3] Underlying this recommendation was the presumption that the parents would eventually wish to send their children to Soviet universities or other institutions of higher education, almost all of which were Russophone. However, local educational functionaries, including Jewish Communist activists, were usually interested in opening Yiddish-language schools and did their best to promote this goal.

There is no way of gauging the impact of these efforts on Jewish parents, but it is a fact that a large majority of this public, including the parents of pupils in the former Polish schools, voted for Yiddish as the language of instruction. The Jewish schools that came into being at this stage reflected this desire. In Bialystok, for example, 15 such institutions were established: three primary schools (up to fifth grade), three high schools (up to tenth grade), and nine "incomplete" high schools (up to seventh grade). At first, there was a Jewish district inspector of education for the Yiddish schools. In other localities such as Pinsk, parents who had enrolled their children in the former Polish school—and, evidently, teachers too—resisted the changeover to instruction in Yiddish. According to the Jewish press at the time, it was pressure by the students, wishing to study in their mother tongue, that tipped the scales in favor of Yiddish. The municipal education department took their side.[4] Moreover, the 270 students in the local Hebrew gymnasium changed over to Yiddish at the time.

Various Soviet statistics on Jewish and other schools in western Belorussia suggest that fewer than 4 percent of schools in this region were Jewish. It is therefore self-evident that at the time the Soviet educational system was established, the proportion of schools using Yiddish was lower than the share of Jews in the population (approximately 10 percent). To some extent, this was because some of the "Hebrew" schools had been shut down by that time, especially in small localities where other Jewish schools existed. In Zhetl (Dyatlovo in Russian), for example, the Tarbut school became a Belorussian institution, whereas the Yiddish school continued to exist in the new Soviet format. Very few of the relatively small localities were allowed to sustain more than one Jewish school, and even this was true only at first. An example is the town of Nesvizh (Nieswiez), where, for a certain period of time, the former Tarbut school (adapted to the Soviet Yiddish model, of course) coexisted with a Jewish school affiliated with the TSISHO system. Enrollment in the latter school, roughly 100 when the changeover was made, ballooned to 600 afterward; the former Tarbut school eventually became Russian.

There were also localities in which Jewish schools merged. In Baranowicze, the Yiddish-language Sholem Aleichem High School merged with two religious girls' schools, Beit Jacob and Yesod Torah, in the new building of one of the religious institutions. In Kletsk, three schools (Tarbut, Yavneh, and Talmud Torah) merged into a new school with an enrollment of 300 pupils in grades one through seven. The new institution was called the Jewish Incomplete High School *(Di Nisht Fule Yidishe Mitl'shul)*.

A similar reorganization of Jewish education took place in the western Ukraine and especially in Wolhynia, where until 1939 most Jewish children had attended schools affiliated with the Hebrew Tarbut system (71 of the 89 Jewish education institutions from kindergarten through gymnasium, including the Yavneh and TSISHO schools, were affiliated with Tarbut). Of 44 Jewish primary schools in Wolhynia during the period of Polish rule, only 26 continued to operate in Yiddish under the Soviet regime. In 18 localities in this province, Jewish education was eliminated altogether. The changes in Wolhynia on the post-primary level were less radical (unless the yeshivas are taken into account): of seven Jewish high schools that had existed under Polish rule, six survived under the Soviets—using Yiddish as the language of instruction, of course. The total Jewish enrollment of the Yiddish-language schools in Wolhynia in the 1939/40 school year was roughly 8,000, slightly more than half of the mid-1930s enrollment.[5]

Numerous testimonies suggest that parents and teachers initially attempted to cross swords with Soviet officials in defense of Hebrew. Jewish officials, infected with the attitude of the *Yevsektsia* (the Jewish section of the Communist Party), often contended that Hebrew was a "reactionary" language, unfit for use; non-Jewish officials usually argued that it was ancient and obsolete. In one exceptional case, the commissar for education in the town of Ludmir permitted the use of Hebrew in the classroom until November 15, 1939, when he ordered religious studies to cease at once and the local Tarbut committee to dissolve. The schools in Ludmir went over to Yiddish.

A network of Yiddish-language government schools also was established in Eastern Galicia. In this area, Hebrew (secular) and Yiddish education had been poorly developed under Polish rule. At times, principals and teachers were allowed to keep their positions, provided they accepted the educational tenets of the new regime and were capable of teaching in Yiddish. An example was the Hebrew gymnasium of Lvov, where most of the teachers, including the Hebrew-language teacher and the principal, Dr. S. Eigel, kept their jobs. A Jewish major named Hazan was brought in from the Soviet Union to serve as the pedagogical principal. In localities that had not had Jewish schools before the war, the initiative to commence studies in Yiddish was sometimes taken by Jewish parents or local officials after it became known that the Soviet authorities were amenable to this, at least in principle. In several instances, this initiative was taken by Jewish Communists who were sensitive to the cause of Jewish education and exerted their influence to meet the needs of the Jewish population.

As in western Belorussia, the authorities sponsored parent consultations and assemblies in order to determine the nature of the schools and solicit the parents' views on education in Yiddish. A similar process took place in the western Ukraine.

In Lvov, the Jewish institutions included one bilingual school, two teachers' colleges, and two vocational schools. In Stanislawow, the authorities sent questionnaires to the parents of all pupils who had attended the local Hebrew school, asking them to indicate the language in which they wished their children to study. Some parents marked Ukrainian, others Yiddish. Eventually, in the fall of 1939, two Yiddish-language schools were founded in this city. In Tarnopol, the parents vacillated about whether to send their children to a Jewish school at all. They eventually favored a Yiddish-language institution, believing that "it would be good for the children to learn together and be educated by Jewish teachers."[6] In Kolomyja, the Mizrachi and Agudath Israel schools were shut down and replaced by eight Yiddish-language schools, including a "complete" high school (up to tenth grade). A Yiddish-language high school was opened in Przemysl. The authorities had planned to do the same in Strij but dropped the idea when they had difficulty finding suitable teachers.

With the help of figures culled from various sources—Soviet, Jewish, contemporary, and later—we may estimate the number of Yiddish schools in Eastern Galicia at approximately 20 in Lvov, 14 in the vicinity of Lvov, 20 in Tarnopol, and 15 in the Stanislawow area—a total of 69 institutions. The figures suggest that in the 1939/40 school year, the first under Soviet rule, Yiddish-language schools with Jewish enrollments outnumbered the "national" public Jewish schools that had been active before the war. This may be a manifestation of the contraction of traditional schooling or of the withdrawal of Jewish children from Polish schools. Perhaps, too, Jewish enrollments had actually increased.

The table presented here shows comparative data on the educational system in the western Ukraine. The figures appeared in an article entitled "Zeks Chadoshim" (Six Months), published in the Soviet newspaper *Der Shtern* on March 24, 1940. The data show that the number of Jewish schools multiplied by a factor of 4.5. Although one may doubt their accuracy for the period of Polish rule (since Wolhynia alone had more than twice as many Jewish schools as the number shown), the number 103 is reasonable. In Eastern Galicia, as stated, there were 69, and Wolhynia had 34. The number of pupils may be estimated at 45,000.[7]

The turnabout in official Soviet attitudes toward instruction in Yiddish became evident in the western Ukraine as early as February, 1940 (i.e., in the middle of the first school year). Several schools that formally remained

Education System in the Western Ukraine, by National
Affiliation of School and Regime

Schools	Under Polish Rule	Under Soviet Rule (Jan. 1, 1940)
Polish	4,907	984
Ukrainian	371	5,536
Jewish	23	103
Other (*)	142	377
Total	5,443	7,000

*This line did not appear in the original article; it is included here to
bring the numbers up to the total.
†Total enrollment: 1,150,000.

"Yiddish" began to teach general subjects in Ukrainian. In many cases Yiddish, the sole language of instruction, was replaced by Ukrainian and Russian, first in the higher grades and later in the lower ones. This trend gathered strength the 1940/41 school year, both in western Belorussia and in the western Ukraine.

The table shown here summarizes a similar development in western Belorussia:[8] Two trends stand out against the general increase in the number of schools: the steady decrease in the proportion of Jewish schools (and, to a certain extent, of Belorussian schools) and substantial growth of the share

Schools in Western Belorussia in the 1939-1941 School Years, by Language of Instruction

| Language | No. of Schools (% of Total): 1939/40 School Year | | | 1940/41 School Year | |
	Feb. 14, 1940	May 1, 1940	Sept. 12, 1940	Dec. 15, 1940	May 23, 1941
Belorussian	4,048 (79.8)		4,278 (75.9)	4,224 (74.6)	4,400 (74.2)
Polish	538 (10.7)		932 (16.5)	930 (16.5)	875 (14.7)
Yiddish	197* (3.9)	170	150 (2.7)	150 (2.6)	134 (2.3)
Russian	175 (3.5)		173 (3.1)	229 (4.2)	401 (6.7)
Lithuanian	56				79
	} 113 (2.1)		110 (1.8)	116 (2.1)	} 120 (2.1)
Ukrainian	57				41
Total	5,071 (100.0)	5,633	5,643 (100.0)	5,665 (100.0)	5,930 (100.0)

Source: Soviet press (see n. 8)
*Jewish enrollment: approximately 55,000.

of Polish and Russian schools. There is no doubt that the latter trend was caused largely by the conversion to Russian-language instruction by 63 Jewish schools, out of the 197 that had existed in the beginning of the 1939/40 school year. The Tarbut school in Nesvizh is only one example. (One reason for the choice of Russian rather than Yiddish was the Hebraphiles' contempt of Yiddish as a language of instruction and study.) This transition gathered momentum as the 1940/41 school year approached. Thus, for example, parents of youngsters enrolled in the Jewish high school in Kletsk decided to ask the Education Commissariat in Minsk to change the language of instruction in this school to Russian. Similar decisions were taken in other schools (usually institutions formerly affiliated with Tarbut and, to a lesser extent, TSISHO). The rationale was chiefly instrumental, i.e., the graduates would thus have reasonable prospects of admission into Russophone institutions of higher education. In any case, this rationale was evidently more convincing now than at the stage of annexation, when expectations were still usually optimistic and the parents had not yet recognized the Soviet realities for what they were. In the initial stages of sovietization, for example, Jewish parents did not know that the higher- and vocational-education systems did not offer Yiddish-language programs. When they eventually realized this, they began to transfer their children to Russian, Ukrainian, and Belorussian schools. Even though this process was undoubtedly furthered by educational policies favoring Ukrainization and Belorussification, it definitely mirrors the general, relentless contraction of Jewish education in the Soviet Union, which, as stated, became evident in the mid-1930s. Be this as it may, about 50,000 Jewish pupils still studied in Yiddish in western Belorussia at the end of the 1940/41 school year, compared with 55,000 the previous year.

Since the Jews in Eastern Galicia were more closely affiliated with Polish or German culture than with Ukrainian, it comes as no surprise that they rejected the Ukrainian tongue in general, and especially as a language of instruction. Jewish parents preferred Yiddish-language schools, where, in most cases, the previous teachers had retained their jobs. The choice of Yiddish schools may even have been intended to express covert wishes for a national identity. The very existence of these schools may have given the Jews some satisfaction, since the fact of having their own schools consolidated their status as equal to that of any other national group. The parents may also have hoped to find a bit of traditional Jewish atmosphere there, even though it was clear from the very start that classes would meet on the Sabbath and

Jewish festivals, and that the curriculum would exclude Jewish history, Bible studies, and anything similar.

By the time the sovietization of education in the former Romanian provinces and the Baltic countries began, the former Polish districts had completed their first school year under the Soviet system. The preparations for the next school year (1940/41), marked by a further contraction of the number of Jewish schools, were in full swing. Thus the Jewish educators and the rank-and-file in the Romanian and Baltic areas knew what they were facing.

In Lithuania, the first preparations for dismantling the traditional Jewish educational frameworks were made under the supervision of the minorities section of the Central Committee of the Communist Party of Lithuania (CPL), headed at the time by Genrik (Jacob) Ziman (Zimanas), a former teacher. Ziman took this opportunity to draw up a pungent reckoning with Zionism:

We are not fighting Hebrew, for if Hebrew were the language of the masses, we would be the first to consent to [its use]. Therefore, what matters is not the language . . . but rather the sociopolitical factor. The path taken thus far has been wrong because Hebrew has become a way to make every man a Zionist and lead him to Palestine.[9]

In the second half of July and early August, assemblies took place in the cities and towns, in which, one after another, decisions were made to go over to instruction in Yiddish.

The teachers were appointed and assigned to classes so that veteran pedagogues—those with the greatest influence—would be separated from their former pupils. Principals were treated similarly. Party members and sympathizers were regularly appointed to the position of principal; former Yiddish teachers were given second preference. Pupils, too, were usually placed in classes with a minimum of homogeneity and a maximum of dispersion. Where six Jewish high schools had existed in Kovno, for example, only two remained. Each, however, had a larger enrollment than before. More than 20 other Jewish institutions of learning continued to operate in this city, including the ORT vocational high school, now known as Government Vocational School No. 4. Its enrollment of approximately 200 now ballooned to 500, including many students from the peripheral towns.

In Ponevezh (Panevezys), the Hebrew gymnasium and Yavneh gymnasium were replaced by High School No. 3. Instead of the three Jewish kindergartens that had existed before the annexation (affiliated with Yiddisher Bildungs Gezelshaft, Tarbut, and Yavneh), there were now two, with a combined enrollment of 160 children. In Telz, newly established Yiddish-language schools replaced the Yavneh gymnasium for girls, and the public primary schools for boys and girls were merged into a single institution with an enrollment of 260. In Svencionys (Svencian in Polish) a Jewish pre-gymnasium came into being. In several locations, such as Maryampol, Key-dan, and Rasein (Marijampole, Kedainiai, and Raseiniai in Lithuanian, respectively) the Hebrew gymnasiums were shut down but no Yiddish high schools were established in their place, either because of low potential enrollment or because the authorities took exception.

In all of Lithuania, according to semi-official data (see table), there were 160 public primary schools in which Yiddish was the language of instruction; their enrollment was 15,000. There were also 10 high schools with 4,500 students. The number of teachers in these schools was roughly 500. Even these incomplete data[10] suffice to show that the number of Jewish public schools in Vilna, relative to the size of the city's Jewish population (about 55,000 at the time), was smaller than in Kovno (which had a Jewish population of about 35,000). Hence, many Jews in Vilna sent their children to non-Jewish public schools.

In Soviet Latvia, the authorities found the time to organize a teachers' course in the summer of 1940. All the former Jewish schools (Hebrew, religious, and Yiddish, governmental and private) were shut down. Some, including three high schools and at least ten elementary schools in Riga, were reopened along Soviet lines. One of these (No. 92) had an enrollment of 590 students in 16 classes with 23 teachers. Riga also had a Yiddish evening school for adults, with an enrollment of 812 (ages 16–40) in 18 classes. Dvinsk (Daugavpils in Latvian) had one complete high school, three incomplete high schools, one vocational high school, and three public primary schools. In all, the number of Jewish schools in Latvia in 1940/41 may be

Jewish Schools in Lithuania, 1940/41, by Locality and Type

Type of School	Number	Locality				
		Vilna	Kovno	Shavli	Ponevezh	Other
Kindergarten	13*	4	7	1	1	Unknown
Public primary	160	18	13	3	2	124
Secondary	10	4	2	1	1	2
Vocational	4	2	1	1	—	—
Adult evening	14	4	3	1	—	6

*Minimum; there may have been a greater number.

estimated at 40 (including ten high schools), compared with 62 under the previous regime.

In Estonia, there were two Yiddish-language schools in 1940/41, one in Tartu and the other in Tallinn. In the latter institution, the principal and the entire faculty kept their jobs, with the exception of two non-Jewish teachers. When the Hebrew classes were abolished in this school, the students were reassigned to Yiddish classes. Although the Jewish leftist club Licht had been disbanded, active members continued to take an interest in the Yiddish schools and help to sustain them.

In Bessarabia, official data indicate that 1,833 primary schools were established in the reorganization: 1,183 Moldavian, 400 Russian, 227 Ukrainian, and 23 "other."[11] There is no doubt that the last-named category included 11 Jewish schools (compared with 37 Hebrew schools that had existed in the 1938/39 school year), with an enrollment of 4,803.[12] Even though Hebrew was used in a large majority of the Jewish schools at the time, the teaching of this language was abolished almost automatically in the new schools. Jewish parents in Bessarabia, however, were not always eager to have their children continue their studies in Yiddish, reasoning that if they could not study in Hebrew as before, the vernacular (Moldavian or Russian) was preferable and more useful. It is a fact that the number of Jewish education settings in Bessarabia dropped perceptibly, especially in the peripheral towns. In Bessarabia, as in the western Ukraine, few principals kept their jobs. The practice was to "import" teachers from across the Dniester, chiefly from the Ukraine.

In Northern Bukovina, almost no Jewish schools, Hebrew or Yiddish, remained in the period immediately preceding World War II. Nevertheless, the Jewish daily *Der Shtern* reported on October 1, 1940, that there were 12 schools of this type in the 1940/41 school year, all, of course, using the Soviet model. Czernowitz itself had two complete high schools, one of which (No. 26) had an enrollment of 1,500. There were also two incomplete high schools in Czernowitz. In all of Northern Bukovina there were 630 schools at the time, most using the Ukrainian language.

Even though the data for Jewish schools in the Soviet-annexed areas are sketchy during 1939–1941, their total number can be estimated at 535 and their enrollment at 143,000. These figures are itemized in the present table and do not include kindergartens, schools for adults, and so on. Including them, the total number of Jewish schools in the annexed territories undoubtedly reached at least 575, and their enrollment at over 143,000.

Jewish Schools and Enrollment in the Annexed Areas During the 1939/40 and 1940/41 School Years

Area	No. of Schools	Enrollment
Polish districts (1939/40)	300	100,000
Western Ukraine	103	45,000
Western Belorussia	197*	55,000
Baltic countries (1940/41)	212	30,000
Lithuania	170*	19,500
Latvia	40	10,000
Estonia	2	500
Romanian districts (1940/41)	23	13,000
Bessarabia	11	6,000
Northern Bukovina	12	7,000
GRAND TOTAL	535	143,000

*Because most schools were in small localities, their enrollments were relatively small.

CURRICULA AND TEACHING METHODS

Although the introduction of Yiddish as the language of instruction usually was the most conspicuous change made in the Jewish schools (especially the former Hebrew institutions), it was only one change among many. The cessation of studies on the Sabbath and Jewish festivals was eliminated at once—a decree that caused a serious jolt. The next step was a consequence of the alignment of local curricula with the Jewish-Soviet model. This measure, less dramatic and actually rather quiet, was the elimination of Jewish history, Bible studies, and anything else connected with Jewish studies. The only subjects that distinguished Jewish schools from others were Yiddish language and literature.

The new curriculum, modeled largely on that used in Kiev and Minsk, included teaching and analyzing the growth and development of Yiddish literature, especially in the past 100 years. The major authors listed in the official course program were:

1. Those who had written before the Revolution and were recognized in the Soviet Union as revolutionaries, or whose works had included personae or plots connected with the Revolution, such as Morris Vinchevsky, David Altstadt, and Shlomo Spektor. The classics, too, were taught: Mendele Mocher Seforim, Sholem Aleichem, and I. L. Peretz. Selected for emphasis among their copious works were sections describing the

hardships faced by the Jewish masses and stressing the class conflict and the fraternity of peoples.[13]

2. Soviet Yiddish-language authors such as Dovid Bergelson, Itzik Fefer, Peretz Markish, and Dovid Hofstein. However, it was forbidden to teach or even mention Jewish authors who had been imprisoned and disgraced during the great purges.

Thus, apart from the Yiddish aspect—the study of the language and its literature and the teaching of all practical and technical subjects in this language—there was no difference between the Jewish schools and those using Ukrainian, Belorussian, Lithuanian, Moldavian, and so on. Moreover, while students in the latter institutions were taught the history of their peoples and lands in their geography lessons, Jewish history was outlawed.

Since most of the Yiddish-language textbooks used in the annexed areas before sovietization had been locked up or consigned to destruction,[14] the new schools greeted their students with no scholastic material on hand. Textbooks widely used in the Jewish schools in the USSR were one possible and immediate solution. These, however, these did not reach the schools in the annexed areas in time or in sufficient quantities.[15] Consequently, the schools in the former Polish districts suffered from chronic shortages. A grave lack of textbooks was also evident in Latvia, and the situation was especially serious in Bessarabia and Northern Bukovina. In one school, there was reportedly one book for every 20 students.[16]

For the 1940/41 school year, Yiddish-language publishers—especially the new publishing house established in Lvov (a branch of the Ukrainian State Publishing House for National Minorities in Kiev)—were asked to accept orders for the Jewish schools in the Romanian provinces and the Baltic countries that had been annexed to the Soviet Union. The *Der Emes* publishing house in Moscow applied itself to this task with special vigor, undertaking to expedite the publication of more than 50 titles in mathematics, geography, and history. (The last two were especially important because of political requirements and the doctrinaire interpretation of human affairs that they had to carry.) Texts and commentaries from Russian-language textbooks by politically acceptable authors were thus translated into Yiddish.

The Libhober fun Visn (Lovers of Knowledge) society of Kovno, which was still allowed to exist by virtue of its leftist coloration, also undertook to help prepare the largest possible quantity of textbooks, based on models provided by the Kiev-Lvov publisher. Working around the clock, the society succeeded in preparing 15 textbooks (a total of 76,000 copies) for the 1940/41 school year.[17] In view of the great demand, however, only half of the quantities ordered by schools in Latvia and Lithuania reached these areas. In Latvia, systematic activity by local educational authorities, orchestrated by the "Jewish section" (Yidsektor) of the Party publishing house, alleviated the textbook crisis somewhat.

Alongside the changes in the content of study and the politicization of all areas of school activity (as discussed in greater detail below), innovations began to appear in the institutional structure of the schools, methods of teaching, types of incentives for improving achievement and discipline, supervision and in-service training for teachers, enhancement of parent involvement in school life and in their children's education, scholastic aids, and so on. The intent was to mimic the standard Soviet model in almost all respects. Admittedly, several of these innovations had already made inroads in Jewish schools; now, however, they were given high priority.

A major example of a device that became very popular was the activity group. In Jewish High School No. 12 in Vilna, for example, the following groups were active: biology, literature, drama, geography, politics, *apikorsus* (anti-religion), MOPR, and sports. The last was especially favored. The anti-religion group heard lectures and held discussions from various points of view: historical-materialistic, political, psychological, and so on. Members of this group urged non-member students to attend school on Jewish festivals.[18] In High School No. 12 in Kovno, approximately 400 students out of the 600 enrolled took part in the groups. Other groups held activities for the public at large, focusing on members' parents and relatives.

The high schools and other institutions placed much emphasis on the development of students' "wall newspapers," which were supervised by the school administration and Komsomol cell. Most information in these media concerned major events, festivals, and Soviet memorial days such as May Day, Lenin Day, International Women's Day, Red Army Day, and Stalin Constitution Day. The schools went to great lengths to prepare for commemorative festivities connected with the October Revolution.

Each institution, by the initiative and with the encouragement of its Komsomol cell and administration, set up class committees and a student council. These took action to toughen discipline and improve scholastic achievements. Troublemakers and slackers were subjected to denunciations, disgrace, and pressure; outstanding students were lauded and showered with praise in assemblies and through the local press. The conventional way of stimulating high achievement was the *sotsgevet,* "socialist competitions" arranged between comparable schools or different classes within one school.

Although schools for adults had existed previously, their number grew immeasurably in the period of Soviet rule. The principals of Jewish schools were urged to apprise parents and working youth of the importance of adult education.[19] The Jewish public responded energetically. In Riga, for example, nearly 1,000 Jews (out of approximately 40,000 in the city) enrolled.

Although adult students were urged upon registration to mark their preferred language of instruction, not all the adult Jewish students in Vilna were placed in Yiddish-speaking classes, as the data from the end of the 1941 school year indicate (see table).[20]

The Poles behaved similarly. In part, this may have been due to the minorities' preference for the vernacular (Russian or Lithuanian) for reasons of utility, as manifested in Vilna and elsewhere when children were registered for the regular schools.

One of the vigorous official measures applied in an attempt to treat the cultural backwardness and political lassitude of the local population was instruction in basic literacy skills. In Lvov, a comprehensive anti-illiteracy campaign was launched. Most of the courses, which were offered in Ukrainian, Polish, and Yiddish, were held in workplaces; some were given at the expense of work hours. In Kovno, the first basic literacy course was sponsored by the porters' artel. No official data were published on the proportion of Jews among these students, but the information in the table below permits one to deduce an estimate.

In higher education, the circumstances of Jews took a marked turn for the better. Jewish youth took full advantage of the fact that studies were free and that all institutions of higher education were accessible, with no discrimination whatsoever. Accordingly, they thronged the universities and the academies of music, arts, and so on.

Classes and Enrollments in Evening Schools in Vilna in 1941, by National Group and Language of Instruction

Nationality	Enrollment	(%)	Language of Instruction	Classes	(%)
Polish	3,551	(60)	Polish	84	(33)
Jewish *	1,642	(28)	Yiddish	23	(9)
Lithuanian	516	(8)	Lithuanian	74	(30)
Russian	218	(4)	Russian	69	(28)
Total	5,927	(100)	Total	250	(100)

*Language of instruction was Yiddish.

Illiteracy in Vilna, 1941 (Partial Data)

	No. of Illiterate Students	(%)	No. of Classes Required
Poles	6,550	(77)	168
Jews	1,462	(16)	36
Lithuanians	350	(4)	8
Russians	247	(3)	6
Total	8,609	(100)	218

Jewish refugees from western Poland met with some difficulties when they sought admission to these institutions, since Soviet citizenship was a prerequisite. Others—former Zionist or Bundist activists, and the like—were turned away because of "bourgeois origins" or previous "anti-Soviet" activity. However, the overwhelming majority of Jewish youth enrolled, believing themselves equal to any other group. Jewish students at the University of Vilna were allowed to take examinations in Marxism-Leninism, a compulsory subject, in Yiddish. This university established a Yiddish studies faculty in October, 1940, chaired by Noah Prylucki; 35 students enrolled that year. YIVO (Yidisher Visenshaftlikher Institut)—the Institute for Jewish Research—which had merged with the Academy of Sciences in Vilna that year, served as an efficient workshop and abundant source of material on these subjects.[21]

Now, as before, Jewish students were more strongly attracted to academic disciplines (the humanities, medicine, and engineering) than to the colleges that trained manpower for heavy industry, transportation, and so on.

SOCIOPOLITICAL FUNCTIONS

An article in the Jewish newspaper in Minsk, written by the principal of Jewish High School No. 12 in Brest (western Belorussia), contained the following assertion:

One of the major tasks that the schools faced in 1939/40 school year was how to eradicate the influence of the chauvinist educational doctrines that used to prevail. . . . stressing [instead] the anti-religious and internationalist education of youth.[22]

The author of the article went on to describe groups that were active in the schools of the time: the Komsomol, the Pioneers, the Red Cross (first aid), *Ossovyakhim* (defense against aerial and chemical warfare), and MOPR.

The Pioneers functioned as the official political framework for children in primary schools (ages 10–15); the Komsomol filled this role in the high schools (age 15 and over). However, formal difficulties and stringent admission rules excluded many applicants from the Komsomol. Of roughly 300 students enrolled in the high school in Shavli (Siauliai in Lithuanian), for example, the Komsomol accepted only 35. In High School No. 12 in Kovno, with an enrollment of 600, only 10 were Komsomol members at the beginning of the school year. Pioneer membership in the schools was immeasurably larger. The Pioneer induction ceremony and public initiation, usually celebrated with impressive pomp, were high points of school life.

Theoretically, one joined the Pioneers and the Komsomol out of inner conviction, and not by coercion or duress. What really happened was totally different; many felt themselves forced to join in the wake of various pressures, including threats.[23] Within the organizations, however, the appropriate educational atmosphere prevailed. The group counselors usually were outstanding students who exuded a sense of mission and purpose. An article describing the Jewish schools in the Lvov area lauded the counselors' responsibility, devotion, and love for their charges, adding, "They are effective auxiliaries for the principal and teaching staff in their educational work."[24] Komsomol members were highly influential in their schools; teachers and even the administration often had to accept their views or, at least, take them into account.[25] Their impact on the activities of the activity groups, the organizing of "socialist competitions," and the preparation for festive social events was decisive. Nor did they refrain from straightforward propagandizing among the students and their families. Finally, they recruited students for special campaigns meant to "strengthen the regime," such as harvest work.

An inseparable part of the schools' political and social function was the systematic and comprehensive cultivation of relations with the Jewish public. Parent assemblies were devoted to discussion of current political and ideological issues that the establishment considered vitally important, such as the changeover to Yiddish and declaring Sunday as the day of rest.

Evening entertainment events ("concerts and meetings," as they were called) were held for the Jewish public under the auspices of the schools and kindergartens; the response was favorable if not enthusiastic. In the major cities, Jewish journalists, authors, and actors played important roles in school festivities. In the peripheral towns, the Jewish schools, including their principals and teachers, were the most important, if not the only, mediators for the integration of the local Jewish population into festive and official events.

One method that was intended to create closer relations between schools and productive society was the institution of patronage or adoption *(shef-tum)*, in which a school system took a manufacturing enterprise under its wing. Because most of the workers in these factories were not Jewish, the "adoption" ceremonies and the artistic performances that followed them were held alternately in Yiddish and the local vernacular.

FRICTION AND MANIFESTATIONS OF PROTEST

On top of the shortages of scholastic tools and the difficulties connected with the introduction of Yiddish as the language of instruction, the school system faced problems in the changeover from an essentially religious-national curriculum to a Yiddish-Soviet one. Although some of these problems were brought to public attention in teachers' assemblies and press reports, others were concealed from all but a handful of individuals, either because people were afraid to discuss them publicly or because the authorities swept them under the rug.

At the very beginning of the school year, a vigorous campaign was conducted among the students' parents to switch the day of rest in Jewish schools to Sunday. As in the previous struggle over language of instruction, the schools and kindergartens summoned the parents to assemblies, held discussions, and made decisions. One of the recurrent trends of reasoning in these assemblies, variously phrased, was that "We're fed up with hiding behind a religious wall that drove a wedge between Jew and Gentile. Just as we object to antisemitism, so must we resist the doctrine of divinely mandated Jewish separatism."[26] Other arguments used to sway the parents included, "This way, you'll be together with your children at least once a week" and "How can you let parents and children have different days of rest?". At the end of the debate, the collective would decide, unanimously or by an overwhelming majority, in favor of aligning Jewish children's day of rest with that of Soviet children—that is, Sunday. Other decisions were taken at these gatherings, and each (including one congratulating "the mighty Red Army and the liberator of peoples, Comrade Stalin") was adopted in the same spirit.

Formally, mass resolutions of this type provided legal and even "democratic" backing for this far-reaching reform of the Jewish students' traditional day of rest. However, parents and students, including those who were not religious in the accepted sense of the word, were not inclined to take this decree lying down. The Ukrainian high school in Kostopol, Wolhynia, in which the Jews were a majority in the higher grades, is an example of this response. In November, 1939, the school was ordered to change its five-day week, with Friday as a day of rest, to a six-day week, with Sunday as the sabbath. According to rumors that reached the area, the Muslim residents of the central Asian reaches of the USSR had been given the consideration of enjoying Friday as the day of rest. Consequently, the Jewish students in the higher grades absented themselves en masse from the Saturday classes. Summoned to the *komsorg* (the official responsible for the Komsomol), they were told delicately but firmly that their absence was tantamount to a strike, an action that the Soviet Union could not permit, and that their parents would pay the price for their actions. The students took the hint and backed down.

Against this background, constant tension and covert struggle developed between some students (silently supported by their veteran teachers) and the school authorities. Sometimes, overt clashes broke out. Even though students were not officially required to write on the Sabbath, they were pressured in various ways to abandon this traditional proscription. Students from the former religious schools were especially consistent in their opposition to writing on the holy day, but others shared their objections, influenced either by their parents or by their own convictions. However, only one instance of organized activity for the prevention of studies on the Sabbath is known: the Torah Dissemination Committee in Telz, Lithuania, urged parents to fight the introduction of Sabbath classes for their children.[27]

Despite official efforts to counteract these manifestations of protest, students continued to absent themselves from school on the Sabbath and Jewish festivals, especially on the High Holidays and Passover. In the Wolhynian town of Rokitno, for example, students decided to boycott the Jewish school on Yom Kippur. However, fearing that their parents would be punished, they compromised by reporting without their books and without food, making study impossible.[28]

In one class in Jewish School No. 26 in Czernowitz, a test was scheduled for Yom Kippur. When the request of several students to be tested orally was turned down, these students, who had never set foot in a synagogue in their lives, attended Kol Nidre services "in protest." At Passover time, several ninth-grade students in High School No. 11 in Kovno, along with their teacher, brought matsot from home and consumed them ostentatiously.[29] These manifestations were often motivated by national concerns and a wish to resist the new norms; evidence of this is the fact that many of the "heroes" had not been noted for their observance of the commandments. The national motive was especially conspicuous in student activities at Hanukka time.[30]

Students at the former Tarbut school in the western Belorussian town of Ludmir organized clandestinely for the study of Bible, rabbinical homiletics, and Jewish history. Furthermore, they would "doodle and engrave Hatiqva, Tehezaqna (the Jewish Socialists' anthem), and so on, on every wall and blackboard." In Kovno, several groups of students in the Hebrew gymnasium congregated around their former Hebrew literature teacher, M. Kantarowicz, who lectured them on Zionism. This kind of activity recurred in many other localities.

Other forms of protest included jokes and wisecracks against the regime, even in the teacher's presence. The paramount protests consisted of the inscription of Zionist graffiti on walls and the wearing of Betar shirts in class. In Tartu, Estonia, some students continued to wear the blue and white cap that had been standard in the former Jewish school.

In early October, 1939, one of the students wrote the following in his diary:

We'll demonstrate: not to persuade the state to change its attitude—that doesn't stand much of a chance—but simply a spiritual demonstration, so that we and the teachers will feel this tragic transition, carried out against our will. . . . We'll speak Hebrew and answer only in Hebrew to teachers who call on us in Yiddish. If they try to outsmart us at the expense of Zionism, we'll respond even to the extent of walking out of the classroom."[31]

At the sight of former teachers who had forsworn the national values that they had preached only yesterday, students would look for appropriate opportunities to assail them in public. Numerous incidents took place against this background.

In Jewish Public School No. 26 in Czernowitz, a student named Moshe Braytner (a member of Ha-no'ar ha-Tsiyoni) refused to join the Komsomol because "he was a Zionist and would not relinquish his fervent wish to be a *haluts* (pioneer) on a commune in Palestine." His behavior caused the school administration great embarrassment; the students admired it to no end.

A huge poster (the letters of which were assembled from pasted-together Jewish National Fund [JNF] stamps) was unveiled in the Jewish government school in Shavli for Tu bi-Shvat, 5701, Arbor Day on the Jewish calendar (February 12, 1941).

One of the most common forms of activity among the former students of national schools was "book rescue." The books being rescued were Hebrew books that belonged to libraries of schools and public institutions and were condemned to being put in mothballs or destroyed. In Lahwa, a town in western Belorussia, such books were spirited out of the former Yavneh school "in the dead of night, at risk of life and limb, and were concealed in secret places." Students of the former Tarbut school in Nesvizh clandestinely hauled these kinds of books to a synagogue and inserted them among the religious books. The writings of Bialik, Tchernichowsky, Ahad Ha'am, and others "would go from hand to hand."

Students of the former Hebrew gymnasium in Kovno obtained the key to a room in which all the Hebrew books had been gathered. After drawing up a list and renting a wagon, they entered the room and hauled away "valuable books on Zionist and historical subjects." This done, they erased the gymnasium imprint in each book and distributed the volumes among private homes. Similarly organized activities were carried out by students in the Jewish schools of Ludwipol, Vilna, Shavli, and other localities.[32]

School administrators were not interested in inflating the matter into a scandal and settled instead for investigations, admonitions, and occasional threats. Several suspected students were placed under surveillance, and the conventional method of pairing problematic students with "reliable" buddies, ostensibly to help them with their homework, was extended to those whose "problematics" were political.

In general, the introduction of Yiddish in the former Hebrew schools, and Sunday as the day of rest in Jewish schools of every stripe, was carried out with rousing success. Much of this should undoubtedly be credited to the attitude of a large majority of Jewish teachers, including the Hebrew teachers, who accepted the decree as a necessary evil. Presumably, too, most of them maintained silent allegiance to the Hebrew school but feared the loss of their jobs and livelihoods.

A former teacher in the Hebrew gymnasium of Shavli describes the Jewish teachers' state of mind in those days:

All the Hebrew teachers, myself included, accepted the Soviet decree and became government teachers in the Yiddish gymnasium. A few days later, we heard David Ben-Gurion reproach us harshly and bitterly over Radio Palestine. We heard our disgrace and were ashamed of our cowardice. But even had we stood our ground, we would not have done the cause of Hebrew education the slightest good—the Soviet authorities would have dismissed us without the slightest hesitation.[33]

As the persons responsible for a vital and sensitive segment of the sovietization process, the teachers came under official scrutiny, surveillance, and great suspicion. To prove their allegiance, they were frequently put to difficult, humiliating tests. A former teacher in the school in Rokitno, known as an Orthodox Jew who regularly led the High Holiday services, was imprisoned and then forced to denounce Orthodoxy and Zionism to his erstwhile students. On Yom Kippur 5700 (October 12, 1940), he was ordered to bring a sandwich to class and eat it while his students, who had reported to school with neither books nor food, looked on.[34] Teachers in the Jewish school in Slonim were ordered to teach on Rosh Hashana and Yom Kippur, even though only four or five children attended each school that day. The municipal education committee in Slonim then reprimanded the Jewish teachers for the Jewish children's absences on the Sabbath and Jewish festivals, accusing them of negligence in the dissemination of anti-religious propaganda among the parents.

The principals of many schools in the former Romanian and Polish provinces were Jews who had been brought in from the Ukraine and Soviet Belorussia. These principals, who exercised great power, made sure that the curriculum was taught in full. Veteran teachers, who were sometimes ordered to report on the contents of their lessons and even conversations with their colleagues, suffered greatly at their hands. Nor were the parents oblivious to the teachers' behavior. As time passed, some students mended relations with their veteran teachers, either having learned the lesson that one should not judge others without standing in their shoes, or because they had found that some teachers had actually remained true to the supreme values that they had preached. The anger that they had felt for teachers who had disgraced themselves slowly yielded to a kind of pity. The few teachers who had resigned or were expelled from the profession for their adherence to national principles were held in special esteem. Some students, such as Komsomol activists in the Reali Gymnasium (science-oriented high school) in Kovno, had the audacity to criticize their former teachers in public, warning them not to delude themselves that by going over to Yiddish they would stay on as educators in the gymnasium, continuing to "poison their students' minds." To thwart such a possibility, they suggested that the reactionary teachers be dismissed from their jobs at the gymnasium. The warning was repeated by higher authorities as well.

The 1940/41 school year ended in the shadow of the German-Soviet war. In the middle of June, 1941, about one week before the war, several teachers and students, along with their families, were deported deep into the Soviet interior. On Sunday, June 22, 1941, when students came to school to obtain the results of their final exams, the Red Army was fiercely resisting the advancing Nazi forces on the western border of the annexed areas, and cities were being subjected to aerial bombardment. Since these areas were already integral parts of the Soviet Union, the fate of the short-lived educational system there is connected with the steady contraction of Jewish education in the USSR in general. The question is whether the Jewish educational system in the annexed areas should be viewed as the continuation of a generations-old tradition (admittedly in Soviet garb), or as a short-lived phenomenon, doomed from the start to be a fleeting episode, in view of the Soviet attitude toward the Yiddish language as a provisional medium for the imparting of Soviet values.

Indeed, certain developments in the former Polish provinces strongly suggest that, as early as the 1939/40 school year, the authorities regarded the Jewish educational system as temporary. The intention to downscale Yiddish education became fully evident at the start of the second school year. In Lvov, for example, Jacob Rappoport, principal of the Yiddish high school in 1939/40, was dismissed and replaced by a principal who had arrived from the Soviet Ukraine; the institute itself became Ukrainian.

One of the reasons for abolishing Yiddish as the language of instruction, as the Soviets pointed out, was that there were no institutions of higher education in that language. Officials stressed the importance of ensuring educational continuity and sparing the children unnecessary difficulties. They also alleged that the Jews themselves were abandoning Yiddish-language schools for general ones. The conspicuous and relentless decline of the Jewish schools in western Belorussia and especially the western Ukraine, was largely inspired by the local Soviet leadership, but it was reinforced by Jewish parents' tendency to prefer Russian schools. It also may be stated that the Jews were willing to integrate into the Yiddish-language educational system as long as the regime legitimized and ardently supported it. However, the lack of national spirit in the curriculum, the difficulties of Yiddish, the shortages of teachers and books, and, finally, the official assaults on the Yiddish schools, led to growing disaffection among the Jewish public, including circles that had initially sided with the Yiddish program. For these reasons, the rapid decline of the Jewish schools in these areas was predictable.

In Bessarabia, Jewish teachers and exponents of Yiddish culture were terrified at the end of the 1940/41 school year by recurrent rumors of an official intention to wipe out Jewish education. "If the school year began in major tones, it ended in minor tones—very sad ones. Who knows what's going to happen next year?"[35]

In Soviet Lithuania, Jewish education seemed to be holding its own; there were almost no indications of real infringements, at least on the surface. However, Jewish educators were exceedingly anxious from the very start, mainly in view of what they knew of the fate of Jewish education in the USSR.

The apprehensions and stubborn rumors concerning the imminent downfall of Jewish education were not officially confirmed by any authorized Soviet agency. On the contrary; with summer vacation on the horizon, a teachers' college in Pinsk and an in-service course in Vilna, serving hundreds of teachers in the Jewish educational system, were about to open. Just before the end of the school year, dozens of Jewish public primary schools were officially informed that they were to be upgraded to the status of incomplete high schools. None of this, however, totally dispelled the fears. All it may have suggested was that, insofar as there were plans to eliminate Jewish education in the annexed areas, they were evidently meant for the long term.

INSTITUTIONS OF YIDDISH CULTURE

As the Jewish educational system in the Soviet Union shrank drastically in the late 1930s, so did the institutions of Yiddish studies and scholarship. In 1936 the Institute of Jewish Culture, part of the Ukrainian Institute of Science, was shut down.[36] The institute had employed nearly 100 people in its bibliographic center, work and study rooms, laboratories, archives, and other facilities. It was replaced by an institute called the Bureau for the Study of Soviet-Jewish Literature, Language, and Folklore *(Kabinet far Yidisher Sovetisher Literatur, Shprakh, un Folklor ba der Ukraynisher Visenshaft-Akademie),* which its few staff members called "the death of Jewish-Soviet culture."[37]

In Minsk, an institution for Jewish literature and folklore *(Sektor fun Yidishe Literatur un Folklor ba der Visenshaft Akademie fun Vaysrusland)* still operated as part of the Belorussian Academy of Science. This policy (i.e., shutting down most of the institutions while allowing a few to remain open) was in effect when the Red Army entered Vilna. The Lithuanian capital was the world center of Yiddish culture. Since 1925 it had been home to YIVO, with its rich archives (about 200,000 items), 40,000-volume library, museum, and bibliographic center.

Even though most of the founders of YIVO were "ultra-Yiddishists," including exponents of the Bund, Left Po'aley Tsiyon, the Folkists, and the Territorialists, the institute's leadership under Dr. Max Weinreich attempted to maintain a purely scientific ambiance. Thus YIVO distanced itself, to the extent possible, from the partisan entanglements and political polemics that convulsed the Jewish community. Notwithstanding this, Jewish Communists, led by Yiddish culture activists in the USSR, expressed growing objections to the institute and its administration.[38]

The occupation of Vilna by the Red Army on September 19, 1939, left its imprint on YIVO. Only two members of the administration remained: the well-known author and philologist Zalman Rejzen, who also edited the progressive daily newspaper *Tog*, and advocate Joseph Tshernikhov, a Territorialist leader who had achieved fame for, among other things, having defended Communists in Polish courts. These two struggled desperately to sustain the institute under the conditions of the new regime.[39] Soon, however, they too became victims; they were arrested and exiled to the Soviet Union, where they perished. A similar fate befell dozens of other Jewish public figures in Vilna, including Bund leaders Anna Rosental and Jacob Zhelznikov, who were also important members of the Friends of YIVO Society in that city. Two other members of the YIVO board in Vilna miraculously survived. Zelig Kalmanovitch, editor-in-chief of the monthly journal *YIVO Bleter*, was detained in neighboring Latvia; the director of YIVO, Dr. Max Weinreich, was in Copenhagen en route to a scholarly conference. Weinreich never saw his home town again.

In the 40 days of Soviet rule in Vilna (after which the city was restored to Lithuanian control), YIVO continued to exist by force of inertia. The eight-month interim period of autonomous Lithuanian rule in Vilna earned it a brief respite and even a modest efflorescence.

Among those who succeeded in reaching Vilna from Poland were the well-known philologist and scholar of Yiddish culture Noah Prylucki, a mainstay of YIVO in Warsaw, and others previously affiliated with this institution. Most resumed their scholarly activity in Vilna, with or without the patronage of YIVO. Several of them joined the YIVO board. The American Jewish Joint Distribution Committee provided YIVO with substantial aid for its continued operation, with the help of its Vilna agent, Isaac Gitterman, and several well-known Lithuanian Jews who raised funds for YIVO and its publications.

When the Soviet Union annexed Lithuania in the summer of 1940, all the institutes of Hebrew and Yiddish education and culture were either shut down or metamorphosed into new frameworks. YIVO was not spared. In the initial stage, lasting from the middle of August, 1940, until the end of the year, the institute underwent "purification and reorganization." The Jews of Vilna were apprised of the nature and substance of this process in the characteristic phraseology of the time:

At long last, YIVO too has been extricated from the swamp! . . . The caprices of the YIVO administration, in which a handful of Bundists and Zionists combined to dig in and turn this lair into a nest of personal privilege and careerism on the one hand, and struggle against the Communist Party and its sympathizers on the other . . . with the help of the people's government, YIVO has finally become what it was supposed to be all along. Henceforth it will serve no one but its true owners: the Jewish masses who had built it lovingly and devotedly."[40]

The labors of purifying and reorganizing YIVO were entrusted to Comrade Moshe Lerer, the institute's "curator" (i.e., commissar). Since Lerer had spent many years as the YIVO archivist, one of his responsibilities was the handling of revolutionary literature in its various shades. Zelig Kalmanovitch was one of the first victims of the purge, which also embraced literary and archive material, with special emphasis on publications critical of the Soviet Union.

Only in the final stages of the nationalization of YIVO, in late October, did anyone realize that the institution had been an academic research center. As for the university-level teaching of Yiddish, a solution previously dismissed was resurrected: the establishment of a chair in the local university. Noah Prylucki was installed as its head. On October 1, 1940, Prylucki also was named the docent of the new chair in Yiddish language and culture, an integral part of the philology department in the Faculty of the Humanities at the University of Vilna.

Even the nationalized YIVO was somewhat exceptional in view of the centralistic model conventionally used in the USSR. After the decision to keep it alive had been made, YIVO was expected to merge into a broader governmental system. Indeed, in January, 1941, when the Academy of Sciences of the Lithuanian SSR was established in Vilna, the "Jewish Scientific Institute" became part of the academy and was renamed the Institute for Jewish Culture *(Institut far Yidisher Kultur),* corresponding to the Institute for Polish Culture and three Lithuanian institutes—linguistics, history, and ethnography. To give the new institute a markedly academic caliber, and to ensure a maximum of coordination with the Chair in Yiddish Language at the university, Noah Prylucki was appointed on January 7, 1941, to head this body. Hirsh Osherowitz, brought in from Kovno, was named the scientific secretary. Shortly afterward, Osherowitz yielded his position to Leib Vershbovitz of Kovno, who was an attorney, a Folkist confidant, and a contributing editor to the Folkists' daily newspaper *Folksblat.*

In response to interest expressed by pro-Soviet Yiddishist groups in New York, such as IKUF *(Idisher Kultur Ferband),* to the fate of YIVO, Prylucki described the situation in a letter dated February 27, 1941:

What used to be YIVO has become governmental, and at present it is an organic part of the Academy of Sciences of the Lithuanian SSR, now being organized. In a few more weeks, we shall be able to begin work on the operating plans that were set forth: to bring in certified scholars from other centers, to publish a journal, and to issue two series of monographs: one strongly scholarly and the other scholarly but geared for the masses. The budget will be covered by the state. The Institute has been flooded with material of late: nearly 20,000 books and many thousands of important documents. We are always in close contact with Jewish institutes of science and culture in Moscow, Kiev, Minsk, Odessa, Lemberg (Lvov), and elsewhere. We are pleased to note that their attitude toward us is very friendly.[41]

Much of Vilna Jewry had a rather different perception of the institute that YIVO had become. Various assessments of its quality elicited questions about its future size and its very existence. Admittedly, many Jews were deeply concerned about the future prospects of other cultural institutions— the Jewish theater, the school system, publishing houses, the press, and so on. However, there is good reason to state that in the matter of the scholarly institutes for Yiddish culture, as in other respects, the Lithuanian SSR was a conspicuous exception compared with areas such as western Belorussia and the western Ukraine—let alone the erstwhile Romanian provinces or Latvia and Estonia, where no such institutions were established at all.

6

Cultural Life

Hardly any Jews in the annexed areas harbored delusions about the Soviet attitude toward religion. Indeed, rejection of religion, which the regime, following Marx, labeled "the opium of the masses," was one of the best-known characteristics of Soviet thought. Many adults had experienced this policy first-hand in the years immediately following the Revolution in October, 1917, when they were refugees in Russia. Even so, many Jews, especially in Yiddishist circles, persisted in hoping that Jewish culture might survive and even expand under the new circumstances, along the accepted Soviet lines of "Socialist content and national form." Much of the Zionist camp, for which Yiddish culture was a medium of activity and part of daily existence, shared these hopes to some extent. Since the new realities spelled the end of Hebrew culture, these Zionists regarded Yiddish culture as the lesser of two evils. In this sense there was hardly any real difference between Folkists, Bundists, and Zionists. Even the Jewish Communists expected Jewish culture to flourish. Only later did many of them realize that it was the general intent of the Party to limit Jewish cultural activity to propaganda and information purposes only.

Yiddish lovers overseas took great interest in Jewish culture in the annexed areas. These included known pro-Soviet groups such as IKUF in America. Indeed, the cause of Jewish culture could be used to generate pro-Soviet publicity and prove that the Jews lacked no opportunities under Soviet rule. The Soviet authorities used the existence of Jewish cultural institutions and frameworks to control and indoctrinate the Jewish intelligentsia in the annexed territories—just as official Jewish cultural activity in the USSR itself was rapidly declining. This also explains the massive out-flux of Yiddish authors, playwrights, and cultural "apparatchiks" to the an-nexed areas. Ostensibly doing the state's bidding by helping to integrate their colleagues into Soviet culture, they were also seeking a legitimate channel for their creativity and a milieu in which they might become active once again.

The large numbers of Jewish literary and theatrical artists and journalists who had congregated in the annexed areas undoubtedly contributed to the cultural activity there. Cities such as Bialystok, Lvov, Vilna, and, to a cer-tain extent, Kishinev became centers of a vitiated Jewish culture, as had hap-pened previously in Warsaw, Lodz, and Bucharest.

This activity, more than any other aspect of Jewish life, left behind a rel-atively rich residue of authentic material, subsequently augmented in nu-merous memoirs by authors, journalists, and artists.

THE PRESS — PRESSED INTO SERVICE

At the time that the Red Army marched into the western Ukraine and Be-lorussia, there were three Jewish daily newspapers in the USSR: *Der Shtern* in Kiev, the capital of the Ukraine; *Oktyabr* in Minsk, the capital of Be-lorussia (both founded in 1925); and *Birobidzhaner Shtern* (est. 1930), in the autonomous Jewish district of Birobidzhan. There were also several literary journals (*Sovetish* in Moscow, *Sovetish Literatur* in Kiev, *Der Shtern* in Minsk, and *Forpost* in Birobidzhan) and a children's newspaper named *Zay Greyt* in Kiev.

Like the other Soviet newspapers, the Jewish ones, especially *Der Shtern* and *Oktyabr,* extensively covered what they called the liberation of the west-ern Ukraine and Belorussia and the various stages of the annexation. How-ever, these newspapers, pressed into the service of the regime in both content and form, could hardly satisfy the reading habits of masses of Jews who, for decades, had been accustomed to diverse, lively print media. Thus the Jews in the annexed areas, especially those in journalistic and literary circles, ea-gerly waited for the military and civilian authorities to allow the existing journals to reappear or new ones to be published, even if forced into the ac-cepted Soviet mold.

The authorities, however, were in no hurry to satisfy the Jewish readers' wishes, instead making sure that local Ukrainian or Belorussian newspapers appeared first. In Vilna, where the Poles and Jews constituted a majority, the first publication allowed to appear (in September, 1939, when this city was still designated for inclusion in western Belorussia) was a Belorussian-language civilian newspaper—although it lasted only a few weeks. None of the four Yiddish-language dailies in Vilna reappeared, including the *Vilner Tog,* edited by the generally pro-Soviet author and philologist Zalman Rejzin.

On the day that the Red Army entered the city, *Vilner Tog* had come forth with a massive headline, "Jewish Vilna Receives Red Army Festively," followed by articles exuding the same spirit. Vendors distributed thousands of copies of this issue, and as typesetters and printers geared up for a second edition, Soviet military police burst into the press facility, confiscated all copies of the newspaper, and halted publication. The official rationale came later: "Private individuals just don't publish newspapers in the Soviet Union."[1] After Vilna was handed over to Lithuania and the latter was annexed by the USSR, the Jews of Vilna were given a newspaper to read: a local Soviet-Jewish one. It, too, was short-lived.

Even though the Polish territory annexed by the Soviets in 1939 had a Jewish population of 1,500,000 (including refugees), only one Jewish newspaper, *Bialystoker Shtern,* was allowed to circulate in October of that year. *Bialystoker Shtern* proclaimed itself to be the mouthpiece of the municipal and district committees of the Communist Party of Belorussia and the municipal and district executive committees. However, since Bialystok was the urban hub of western Belorussia, where many thousands of Jewish refugees (including some 50 authors and journalists) had settled, the paper actually became the medium of all Jews in eastern Poland. Even so, its regular format was restricted to four pages and its press run to no more than 6,000 copies. Technically, it was a continuation of the newspaper *Unzer Lebn,* which had appeared in Bialystok since 1918 under the editorship of Pesah Kaplan.

The governing institutions in Minsk asked a local Jewish author, Zelig Akselrod, to set up the new publication, even though Akselrod was not a Party member. Just before he reached Bialystok in October, 1939, Akselrod sought out and located the Jewish Communist functionary Hersh Smolar,[2] who had just been released from a Polish prison in Brest, and asked him to join him as founder and manager of the newspaper.

The first managing editor was I. Teveliev of Minsk. In early February, 1940, he was replaced by a former press operator from Minsk, Beinish Shulman. "The man was conversant in literary affairs, had once studied in yeshiva, was well versed in Jewish and Soviet literature, and knew how to value a Jewish word. He had the great virtue of knowing how to navigate the Soviet labyrinth."[3] B. L. Gontman became the official managing editor in early October, 1940, and held this position until June 22, 1941, when the war with Germany broke out and the newspaper was published for the last time.

For some reason (perhaps its editors' status), *Bialystoker Shtern* practiced a unique spelling policy for most of its 20 months of existence. Although it spelled Hebrew words in the Soviet-prescribed fashion, it printed the final Hebrew letters in their traditional form almost to the very end of its existence. Only in Issue 191 (out of about 200 issues) did it complete the word *Shtern* in its banner with the regular *nun* (n) rather than the final character. Its format was revised significantly at least three times, each revision reducing the size further. The frequency of publication decreased similarly.[4] Apart from exceptional cases (e.g., pre-election periods or Soviet Press Day, May 5), the paper was only four pages long. The last edition appeared on June 22, 1941, the day the war with Germany erupted; the secretary of the editorial board and the deputy editor pasted a copy "on building walls in the deserted streets of Bialystok."[5]

In keeping with Soviet journalistic norms, *Bialystoker Shtern* bulged with official material that had to be printed, such as telegrams from TASS (the Soviet news agency), lead articles, various edicts, and sundry notices from Party institutions. In fact, this newspaper (like the other Soviet Jewish newspapers) was packed with material translated from Russian, Belorussian, Ukrainian, and the like. Entire pages were devoted to Soviet memorial days and events (such as Red Army Day and the anniversary of Lenin's death), administrative and economic affairs, and, of course, the frequent election campaigns in the region. This alone forced original Jewish material into a marginal role.

Specifically Jewish themes were discussed during and between election campaigns in a section labeled "Help for the Propagandist and Informationist"; the material printed included anti-Judaism polemics, especially when Jewish festivals were at hand. Information on saliently Jewish themes also appeared occasionally in special sections such as "Jewish Cultural News," "Events in Birobidzhan," and "In the Institutions of Jewish Education." The general problems of Jewish education were covered, and there was a special insert for children. The papers reported now and then on changes in Jewish life in various communities in western Belorussia. The editorial board accompanied such reportage with a general remark absolving itself of guilt of "separatism" or "nationalist/chauvinist leanings."

The managing editors, imported from the Soviet Union, were undoubtedly aware of the great risk that they and the newspaper would face if they imprudently handled subjects that might be construed as nationalist. Wherever the Jewish national issue was mentioned, it was based on quotations from unimpeachable sources of authority, ranging from Lenin and Stalin to Ponomarenko (secretary-general of the Belorussian Communist Party). The secretary of the editorial board describes the prevalent state of mind:

Not everyone knew how limited our possibilities were and how suspicious they [the Soviet authorities] were of every manifestation of autonomy. After we printed a conversation with a Jewish laborer who was identified as "a former Bundist," we received a reprimand from Minsk itself for having undermined the status of *Bialystoker Shtern,* since one was allowed to mention the Bund only as a fascist organization.[6]

Bialystoker Shtern took every opportunity to attack the Bund, devoting more energy to this than to assaults on Left Po'aley Tsiyon and the other Zionist organizations.

The newspaper hardly ever mentioned Jews outside the Soviet Union and, like other Soviet newspapers at the time, had little to say about any aspect of world developments; a trickle of information appeared on the margins of the newspaper and was credited to TASS. *Bialystoker Shtern* was conspicuously averse to report on sensitive topics such as the forebears of Communist ideology, Jewish nationalism, Soviet relations with Nazi Germany, and religious affairs. The editorial board was exceedingly cautious in its treatment of the Jewish writers from Poland who had gathered in Bialystok. Naturally, they were interested in publishing their writings in the only Jewish newspaper in the area, which would give them the status of contributors to Soviet newspapers, with all that implied, including enhanced social stature and higher remuneration. A few, to be sure, succeeded: I. Yonasewitz, Y. Akrutny, M. Knapheys, B. Heller, S. Zhirman, and D. Mitzmacher. Books by the last four authors, published by the Soviet government publishing house, were favorably reviewed by *Bialystoker Shtern.* Other contributors included the poets Peretz Markish (of Moscow) and Shmerl Kaczerginsky (of Vilna), critic M. Popes, and Pesah Binetsky.

The *Bialystoker Shtern* editorial board was a forum and meeting place for the Jewish intelligentsia. Even the rank-and-file occasionally turned to it for information and advice. The board, for its part, sponsored encounters with the readership, even after the paper became a weekly. In its letters to the editor's column, readers lauded the practices of the new regime, Soviet life, and so on. Letters expressing the joy and satisfaction of Jews who had volunteered for labor in the industrial centers of the Soviet Ukraine were prominently displayed. As *Bialystoker Shtern* continued to grow smaller, however, many Yiddish readers became disillusioned and shifted their allegiance to the daily *Oktyabr,* which was originally from Minsk.

As stated, *Bialystoker Shtern,* virtually the only Jewish newspaper in eastern Poland,[7] was published until June, 1941. A few issues reached Wolhynia and Eastern Galicia, where a Jewish population of approximately 600,000 was without a local newspaper in its own language. The two Jewish dailies in Eastern Galicia, the Polish-language *Chwila* and the Yiddish-language *Der Morgen* (*Togblat*), had ceased publication during the German siege. Immediately after the Red Army entered Lvov, the authorities allowed two daily newspapers in Ukrainian and Polish to resume publication but saw no need to replace the Yiddish-language *Der Morgen* with another Jewish newspaper.[8]

On June 1, 1941, about three weeks before the German invasion, a Jewish daily named *Der Royter Shtern* made its debut in Lvov. The editor was one Hershfeld; his deputy was Gordon or Gadon.[9] Very little is known about this newspaper. The fact that it was about to publish a special edition marking the anniversary of Soviet rule in Northern Bukovina and Bessarabia suggests that its function was to cover Jewish affairs in all the areas annexed to the Ukrainian SSR. For this purpose, the author and journalist Tania Fuks, a refugee from Lodz, was sent to Czernowitz on June 10 to gather information on developments in education. By June 28, 1941, however, *Der Royter Shtern* was no longer in existence and Czernowitz had fallen to the enemy.

In the Baltic countries, unlike eastern Poland, where the hostilities had destroyed the local press, about ten Jewish newspapers continued to appear for some time after the Soviet takeover in June, 1940. Chronologically, the eradication of the Jewish press may be divided into three periods: (1) June–August, 1940, the transition period; (2) August, 1940–February, 1941, during which one Jewish newspaper reappeared and another one made its debut: *Folksblat* in Kovno (which became *Emes* in December, 1940, and *Der Emes* shortly thereafter) and *Vilner Emes* in Vilna; and (3) February–June, 1941, when only *Der Emes* survived.[10]

Among the local newspapers, the most enthusiastic in its reception of the Red Army and the establishment of the people's government in Lithuania was *Folksblat,* which, for all practical purposes, had been taken over by the Communists sometime before.[11]

As early as June 28, the Minister of the Interior had ordered the closure of several newspapers, including the daily *Dos Vort* (the organ of the Zionist Socialist [Z S] Party and the working Eretz Yisrael [Palestine] bloc) for "disloyalty to the new order, chauvinism, reactionary leanings, and anti-Soviet propaganda." Many were surprised to find that *Di Idishe Shtime,* the organ of the General Zionists, was allowed to continued publishing for the moment, and that its editor, R. Rubinstein, head of the Zionist Center in Lithuania, was allowed to continue in his official capacity (with an overseer from the new regime looking over his shoulder). This anomalous situation did not last long. In the middle of July, Rubinstein's 20-year tenure as editor was terminated for good. About five days later he was arrested; later he was exiled to Vorkuta. The editor of *Dos Vort,* Ephraim Greenberg, was arrested also. Pinhas Lamdansky, a leftist engineer, replaced Rubinstein as the editor of *Di Idishe Shtime* and its afternoon edition, *Hayntike Nays.*

Unlike *Folksblat,* which had the audacity to put out the first-ever Saturday edition in the history of the Lithuanian Jewish press, and which quickly adopted the phonetic Soviet-Yiddish spelling, these two Zionist newspapers—*Di Idishe Shtime* and *Hayntike Nays*—continued to appear only on weekdays and made no conspicuous external changes, continuing to use Hebrew words and mention details from the Hebrew calendar. In contrast, the contents of *Di Idishe Shtime* underwent great change. By July 14, most of the material was concerned with the elections for the People's Sejm. *Di Idishe Shtime* evidently obtained the slogans, some of the articles, and various other items from the Jewish section of Agitprop (the "agitation and propaganda" agency). Two weeks after the elections, and even later, *Di Idishe Shtime* and *Hayntike Nays* were still being exploited in the efforts to replace Hebrew with Yiddish as the language of instruction in Jewish schools. On August 1, the readers of *Di Idishe Shtime* were informed that they had received the paper's last issue; the next day, just before the Soviet Union made its annexation of Lithuania official, the only Jewish daily to appear in Kovno was *Folksblat,* which had adopted the format of *Di Idishe Shtime.* The vendors of the revamped *Folksblat* were instructed to distribute it to all subscribers of *Di Idishe Shtime* and *Hayntike Nays;* the agents of the defunct papers had provided them with subscriber lists for this purpose.

The Jewish press in Vilna met a similar fate. Although the *Vilner Kuryer* (Courier) had been shut down in early July, the Zionist *Vilner Togblat,* headed by the venerable Dr. Jacob Wygodsky, was still allowed to appear. Wygodsky's virtues, in addition to his personal popularity among the Jewish masses, included his sympathy for the Soviet Union and its vigorous stance against antisemitism. In an editorial, Wygodsky, while reiterating his pro-Soviet views, remarked that Soviet censorship had thwarted the publication of two books and a series of articles that he had written on the Soviet Union.[12] This editorial seems to have been the political swan song of the veteran Jewish leader. Although his name as editor remained on the masthead of the newspaper for another six weeks, he was replaced in early July by leftist author Dovid Umru of Kovno. He continued, however, to be identified as the publisher.

On August 20, 1940, *Vilner Togblat* was shut down for good and replaced the next day by *Vilner Emes*. Thus, for the next half-year or so, there were only two Yiddish-language newspapers in Lithuania: *Vilner Emes* in Vilna and *Folksblat* (subsequently *Der Emes*) in Kovno.

Dovid Umru edited every issue of *Vilner Emes* during its seven months of existence. Apart from general news and articles reprinted from the Soviet press, much space was devoted to local affairs of Vilna and the vicinity. The secretary of the editorial board, Shlomo Beilis, the writers, and most people involved in the newspaper were from Vilna. They included poets from the Yung Vilne group—Abraham Sutzkever, Hirsh Glik, Chaim Grade, Leizer Wolf, Leah Rudnitsky, Shmerl Kaczerginsky, and Shalom Zhirman. One of the contributing editors of *Vilner Emes* was Berl Mark of Bialystok, who focused on Jewish affairs in the western reaches of Belorussia and the Ukraine.

Jewish cultural issues and events in Vilna, such as YIVO activities and the establishment of a chair for Yiddish language and literature at the University of Vilna, were covered extensively. Full pages were devoted to the theater and to education, in cooperation with the directors and cast of the local Jewish theater and the teachers and principals of Yiddish-language public and high schools. Although *Vilner Emes* devoted much space to Soviet Jewish literature, it also acted vigorously to cultivate local literary talent. While stressing the fraternity of the four major national groups (Lithuanians, Belorussians, Jews, and Poles) in Vilna, the newspaper did not flinch from mentioning the threats to the physical security of the Jews of Vilna, which persisted under the new regime. The method used was indirect: comparison of the pogroms under the previous regime with the repression of "hooliganism" under the present one.

A few weeks before the elections for the Supreme Soviet in Moscow (January 12, 1940), editor Dovid Umru was summoned to the propaganda department of the Lithuanian Communist Party, where he was told that the Party had decided to shut down the newspaper.[13] *Vilner Emes* breathed its last on March 13, 1940. The next day, the readers of *Der Emes* of Kovno were informed that their newspaper had merged with *Vilner Emes* as "a conspicuous and positive step toward the coordination of journalistic activity. Henceforth, the best talents of the two papers will be concentrated in one, which will be able to discharge its Bolshevist duties properly." To placate the Jews of Vilna, who had been accustomed to a selection of Yiddish newspapers, *Der Emes* promised, among other things, to be "no less Vilna than Kovno" in terms of the information and the topics treated. This promise was indeed kept, to some extent.

In late 1940, the supreme institutions of the Lithuanian Communist Party resolved the disposition of *Folksblat* once and for all by turning it into a Party Central Committee organ called *Emes* (subsequently *Der Emes*). *Emes,* edited by Yoisef (Yosl) Schochat, made its debut on December 7, 1940. Like *Folksblat* in its last metamorphosis (since August, 1940), it, too, appeared on the Sabbath; its day of rest was usually Monday. On February 7, 1941, the newspaper adopted Soviet-Yiddish spelling for all purposes, including advertisements, but continued to use Hebraisms rather freely (albeit using Soviet orthography).[14] Thus the names of places and streets (e.g., *Fayerlesher Gas* instead of *Ugniagesiu Street* in Kovno, and *Breite Gas* instead of *Didzioji Street* in Vilna) were largely preserved in their conventional Yiddish forms, eschewing the Lithuanian equivalents. Furthermore, the tendency to Russify the vocabulary was not yet perceptible in this newspaper; an outstanding employee, for example, was called a *shlogler* (record-setter), not an *udarnik.*

After *Vilner Emes* was shut down and *Der Emes* became the exclusive Yiddish-language organ of the Lithuanian Communist Party Central Committee, the editorial board was expanded and financial and technical assistance increased. However, it was not long before this newspaper, too, was scaled down.[15]

Even though the official editorship was entrusted to an editorial committee from the outset, Yosl Shochat was firmly in control. Former *Folksblat* staffers (including the assistant editor, Moshe Gluch) were prominent among the members of the editorial board, which also included several former staffers of *Di Idishe Shtime.* The paper devoted most of its space to general issues, but there was also room for reports, accounts, and information that touched directly or indirectly upon Jewish life in the Soviet Union and, in particular, in Lithuania, with emphasis on the sovietization of the latter. In addition to *spetskorespondentn* (special writers), who focused mainly on developments in the large cities, some 40 contributing editors reported from time to time on Jewish public events throughout the country. The labor front and the productivization of the Jews were of special concern to *Der Emes*. Initially its reportage dealt only with the accomplishments of individual factories, emphasizing outstanding workers and members of management. As time passed, however, the newspaper began to print critical remarks about workers and even turned its wrath on members of works committees and boards of directors.

Der Emes diversified its presentation by running "commercials" (for nationalized factories, artels, cinemas, and theaters) and family notices. The last were almost totally devoid of traditional Hebrew terms and expressions. Instead of *mazel tov,* for example, the ads used expressions such as "Best wishes upon the birth of the little pioneer." Gradually, the content of the "Looking for Relatives" notices changed. Fewer advertisers were searching for loved ones among the Polish refugees; more frequently, they were attempting to locate relatives in the Soviet Union with whom contact had been lost during World War I.

An unmistakable change took place in the attitude of *Der Emes* toward the circumstances of Jews outside the Soviet Union. Reportage on the fate of the Jews under Nazi rule in Poland and elsewhere was conspicuous in its sparsity. Lithuanian Jewry itself, as a national collective, was rarely mentioned, with the exception of comparisons of the plight of the Jews under the previous regime with the security and serenity that Soviet rule had brought them. The newspaper also repeatedly explained the chauvinist menace of emphasizing Jewish particularism and solidarity.

Members of the editorial board, led by Yosl Shochat (a leading CPL functionary), occasionally dabbled in matters that far transcended ordinary journalistic work. For example, the board sent informational material about I. L. Peretz to more than 150 Jewish schools in Lithuania, and the paper sponsored assemblies and concerts for teachers, pupils, and parents in Kovno. One of the last events of this type was a ceremony in which *Der Emes* extended its patronage to a Jewish kindergarten in Kovno.

The last edition of *Der Emes* appeared on June 22, 1941, as indicated by the secretary of the editorial board, Hirsh Osherowitz.[16] Later, most of the newspaper staff perished, some in Lithuanian pogroms against Jews as the Soviet forces withdrew, others murdered by the Nazis. Only those who succeeded in fleeing into the Soviet interior survived.

In addition to the daily press, the Lithuanian Jewish weekly *Shtraln,* founded before the Soviet occupation, appeared rather regularly in 1940–1941. This journal, usually 24 pages long, was edited by Isaac Karlin and published under the auspices of the central committee of the Komsomol in Lithuania. Its graphic presentation (replete with photographs) and its contents improved after Lithuania became a Soviet socialist republic, and one may use *Shtraln* to estimate the proportion of Jews in the Lithuanian Komsomol movement and the problems that they encountered there. *Shtraln* also printed literary works (usually poems) by local artists and those in the other Soviet-annexed areas, along with those of Soviet Jewish writers.

In Latvia, the Zionist organ *Unzer Vort* was allowed to continue publishing after the elections for the local Sejm. This publication did much to shape a sympathetic consensus and attitude toward the new regime in the Jewish "street." In contrast, the daily *Haynt,* an Agudath Israel organ, was shut down quickly[17] and replaced on July 1, 1940, by a daily called the *Kamf* (Struggle), edited by H. Margolis. Although the *Kamf* was purportedly meant to voice the views of the municipal committee of the Communist Party in Riga, it actually addressed itself to all Jews in Latvia. The editorial in the newspaper's first edition spelled out its substance and goals:

We shall focus on the tremendous constructive role played by the mighty So-viet Union in the liberation of all oppressed classes and enslaved peo-ples. . . . We shall struggle against all the forces that have thus far distorted the free and multidimensional development of the Jewish masses, econom-ically, politically, and culturally. . . . We shall expose the false game that Zionists of all stripes are playing in the autonomous state, aspiring to sow political confusion among the Jewish masses and distract them from their true problems. . . . We shall fight the careerist assimilationism that aims to drive a wedge between the young generation and the masses of our peo-ple. . . . We shall demand that the state do everything possible to assist the productivization of middleman and parasitical elements.

During the election campaign for the People's Sejm, and for several months thereafter, *Kamf* continued to use standard Yiddish spelling and He-brew words in their original form. From the very start it published an evening edition twice a week,[18] including Saturdays (but not Mondays). Be-ginning on July 13, each Saturday edition included a special youth supple-ment, in which Hebrew names were occasionally rendered in the Yiddishist (phonetic) spelling conventionally used in the Soviet Union. The paper also published several issues of a children's supplement called *Yunger Kemfer.* During the Sejm election campaign, *Kamf* ran numerous features and arti-cles condemning antisemitism (quite a few were translated from the local non-Jewish press).[19] The veteran leftist Jewish functionary, attorney Max Shatz-Anin, was a standout among the authors of the propaganda and expository pieces that appeared in the paper.[20]

The last edition of *Kamf* appeared on January 12, 1941—the day on which elections for the Supreme Soviet were held. There had been 168 editions in all, including 157 in 1940.

In October, 1940, the publishers of *Kamf* began publishing a journal in Latvia on Jewish political and literary affairs.[21] The new journal, initially a monthly, was called *Ufboi* and was edited by H. Leibovitz. The first three editions had a circulation of 3,000 and were 76, 78, and 99 pages long, respectively. From the outset, *Ufboi* used Yiddishist spelling. In February, 1941, after *Kamf* had ceased publication, *Ufboi* metamorphosed into a biweekly organ of the Latvian Communist Party. H. Margolis took over as editor, the deputy editor (for technical matters) was B. Schneid, and the proofreader was the author Mark Razumni. The journal then expanded its format and increased its circulation, first to 5,000 copies and, by April, to 6,000. Twelve editions of *Ufboi* appeared in the journal's nine months of existence; the last came out in June, 1941.

It is worth noting here that Yiddish readers in Northern Bukovina and Bessarabia had no local newspapers; they had to "make do" with the Jewish press in the Ukraine and other parts of the USSR.[22]

A summary of Jewish periodicals published in the Soviet-annexed areas in Eastern Europe in 1939–1941 is found in the table shown here.

LITERATURE AND LITTERATEURS

Jewish leftists—Communists in particular—were strongly optimistic about the Soviet attitude toward Yiddish literature. Their view was shared by many Yiddish-language authors in the Baltic countries, eastern Poland, and northeastern Romania, who nevertheless objected to the Soviet system on political and ideological grounds.

It is therefore no surprise that Jewish artists in various disciplines (literature, theater, and so forth) streamed from western Poland into the Soviet-occupied area not only to escape Nazi occupation but also to enjoy the general and creative opportunities which, they assumed, awaited them in the Soviet zone.[23]

Jewish writers in the eastern Polish provinces congregated chiefly in Lvov, Vilna, and Bialystok. Their initial actions focused almost exclusively on attempts to meet basic needs such as food and shelter, and to locate relatives who had dispersed when the war broke out. An estimated 40 refugee authors reached Bialystok, far outnumbering their indigenous Jewish colleagues.[24]

The first address of most of the refugee writers in Bialystok was a shelter established by the new regime, known as *Dom Pisatelya* (Writers' House), at 42 Sienkiewicz Street. Apart from the Soviet-Polish author Bronievska and perhaps one or two others, the authors who settled there were all Jews who had fled from the Nazi-occupied areas. One of them related:

Zisha Bagish, a Jewish poet from Romania, was named commissar of the Jewish authors. He set up shop in a special bureau in the municipality of Bialystok and took charge of matters pertaining to the Jewish writers. Every new writer who arrived had to report to Bagish and fill out a questionnaire about his origin, his parents' occupation, the newspapers and journals he'd worked for, whether he had belonged to any political party in Poland, and so on. This questionnaire, of course, was forwarded to the appropriate addresses, thus terrifying authors who had committed bourgeois sins at some time in the past. After filling out this questionnaire, they got a voucher for free lunch in a restaurant.[25]

After lunch, the inhabitants of the shelter had "to scrounge around for another lunch."[26] Occasionally they were also given vouchers for other commodities, redeemable at special shops or at the Writers' House. Each refugee author also received a modest sum of money (200–600 rubles). In all, the plight of the refugees was grave indeed; many were forced to take on sundry jobs to survive. The poet M. Knapheys is a case in point. Knapheys, incarcerated in Polish prisons for his Communist sympathies, spent part of that winter shoveling snow in the streets of Bialystok, suffering frostbite on two fingers.

In due course, Zisha Bagish was deposed and replaced by Dovid Sfard, the former secretary of the leftist writers' circle in Poland, who now held the additional position of deputy secretary of the local writers' association. Intimately familiar with the community of Jewish writers in Poland, Sfard moderated literary affairs for those arriving from the Nazi-occupied area. The organizational secretary of the Jewish section of the association was Rivka Drayer.

Because the Bialystok Writers' Association was affiliated with the Belorussian Writers Association in Minsk, the headquarters in Minsk had the right to approve or reject membership applications. Representatives of the main organization visited Bialystok for this purpose. Dovid Sfard describes the atmosphere:

The Lesser of Two Evils   128

Jewish Periodicals in the Soviet-annexed Areas, 1939–1941

Area	Jewish Population (incl. refugees)	Publication	Duration of Existence (Approximate)	Number of Editions	
Western Belorussia	700,000	Bialystoker Shtern*	20 months	200	Daily and weekly. Other periodicals that reached the area: Der Shtern from Kiev, Oktyabr from Minsk
Western Ukraine	750,000	Der Arbeter,* Royter Shtern	3 weeks	20 (?)	Daily Other periodicals that the area: Der Shtern from Kiev, Oktyabr from Minsk
Northern Bukovina	100,000	Der Arbeter*			Other periodicals that Reached the area: Der Shtern from Kiev
Bessarabia	200,000	Besaraber Shtern*			Other periodicals that Reached the area: Der Shtern from Kiev
Lithuania	250,000	Vilner Togblat†	2 months		Daily
		Di Idishe Shtime†	6 weeks		Daily, with evening edition
		Folksblat†	6 months		Daily
		Vilner Emes*	7 months	176	Daily
		Der Emes†	6 months	166	Daily
		Shtraln†	12 months	43	Weekly

(*continued*)

Area	Jewish Population (incl. refugees)	Publication	Duration of Existence (Approximate)	Number of Editions	
Latvia	100,000	*Unzer Vort*† *Kamf** *Ufboi**	1 month 6 months 9 months	168 12	Daily Daily with evening edition Monthly and biweekly Other periodicals that reached the area: *Kamf* from Riga
Estonia	4,500	—	—	—	—

*Published after the Soviet occupation.
†Predated the Soviet occupation.

Those were days of judgment. All the writers shuffled around, anxious and profoundly concerned. . . . Before this, or perhaps after it, the Belorussian Writers' Association held a general assembly in Minsk, in which Berl Mark was instructed to introduce the writers of prose, and I, the writers of poetry. . . . Our two lectures were typeset. . . . Months passed and the lectures were not published. . . . We now experienced our Belorussian colleagues' state of mind and apprehension, for the association had never, thus far, accepted so large a group of writers in one go, let alone writers from a capitalist country. Thus, even the Party's recommendation, even its command, would not suffice to admit [us]. That's because the four-letter office [the NKVD] was liable to send them a letter, out of the blue, bearing one tough question: Why did you admit so many spies at once? You might pay for that question with several years in prison, or with your life. So they continued to look for a pretext, an excuse, or support of some kind for their proposal to publish the lectures.[27]

Several Jewish Communist writers found jobs at *Bialystoker Shtern*. Non-Communists were given administrative jobs, sometimes as managers of nationalized residences. Several of them refused to accept these positions because they were ordered to spy on the tenants.

Finger-pointing began to proliferate, sometimes behind closed doors, sometimes in public. In a literary gathering in Bialystok, attended, among others, by poet Itzik Fefer of Moscow, one of the Warsaw writers began to gesture in the direction of several of his Polish colleagues, saying "This one's a Zionist," "This one's a Bundist," and so on. Fefer's response was quick and to the point. Silencing the name-caller with his own medicine, Fefer explained that "*this* one didn't care what went on in Poland."[28] Even though his response made waves,[29] the defamation never ceased altogether. Refugee writers in Bialystok joked about colleagues from Warsaw and Lodz who had rushed to "paint themselves red" and churn out enthusiastic reportage and features in the local newspaper, "as if their forefathers had been Communists from time immemorial."

In Lvov, unlike Bialystok, the most prominent personalities were local authors born in Eastern Galicia. Some of them had resided there before the war; others had lived in Warsaw or elsewhere in western Poland and returned to their indigenous milieu when the fighting began. About 40 authors fit these definitions.[30]

In autumn of 1939, a writers' association with Ukrainian, Polish, and Jewish sections was established in the western Ukraine. In 1940, its membership was composed of 50 Ukrainians, 90 Poles, and 34 Jews.[31] A key figure among Jewish writers in Lvov was Alter Kacyzne, a playwright, essayist, narrator, and poet. Kacyzne, who in 1935 had edited a pro-Communist journal in Warsaw, was one of the most prominent figures in Yiddish literature and culture in Poland. He had reached Lvov as a refugee from Warsaw, and was favorably received by the Soviet authorities. He was given two important duties: artistic consultancy to the governmental Jewish theater in Lvov and directorship of the "Jewish Hour" on Lvov radio. Many observers, judging the opportunities available to Jewish refugees in the world of art by the official attitude toward Kacyzne, adduced that the Jews faced no obstacles whatsoever. However, key positions in the Lvov writers' circle were contested by locals who were ideologically identified with the Soviet regime, such as Dovid Kenigsberg, Jacob Shudrich, and Sonya Friedman. Indeed, Kenigsberg was chosen as head of the Jewish section of the writers' association, and Rachel Korn was elected to the local soviet in Lvov.

In Lvov, the admission of Jewish writers to the association also met with difficulties. For example, when Shmuel Jacob Imber's application came up for discussion, Dovid Kenigsberg stood up and reminded Imber that he had expressed himself in a fashion disloyal to the Soviet Union in an article he had penned long before. . . . Imber's admission to the association was suspended until a special committee could examine the matter. The committee, composed of good friends of the candidate (Jews and Poles), investigated his works with agonizing slowness.[32] The association also took exception to the candidacy of poet Moshe Shimmel, because before September, 1939, "bourgeois organs" such as *Haynt* and *Nasz Przeglad* had published his poetry. Shimmel, in one of his first subsequent efforts, responded with "self-criticism": "The Soviet regime opened my poet's eyes for me."[33] He was not believed; he was given a job as cashier in one of the town's cinemas and for some time was on the verge of starvation.

Under the circumstances that developed after the transitional stage, however, some writers were able to continue plying their craft, adjusting themselves to the Soviet organizational frameworks and patterns of artistic endeavor.

The government often attempted to indoctrinate writers with its values, and it often did so with the same routine, superficial attitude that it took toward other population groups. One method used was compulsory organized study of Soviet Communist Party history, based on a standard text. This was called the "Short Course."

One of the lecturers who taught these courses to writers in Bialystok was Party secretary Grigori Gershman. Author Moshe Grosman described his impression of the encounter in his memoirs:

He told us about Marxism, Leninism, Stalinism, as if talking to a group of uninitiated kids in a youth movement, that is to say, in an elementary, primitive manner, while his tone of voice was that of a professor or scholar disclosing the novelties of his innovation. Such rhetoric, poured into the ears of writers and journalists who themselves had published their views on sociopolitical problems and were well-versed in the methods and intentions of the Socialist and Communist movement, was nauseating indeed. So the audience sat there with hunched shoulders and bent heads. . . . But Gershman, the former shoemaker and today secretary of the party of the Belorussian Republic, wasted little time on theoretical matters and went over to more concrete problems: You must know that all the destructive elements in Poland, such as the Endeks [Endecja or N.D.—National Democrats, a reactionary and antisemitic Polish party], hasids, Fascists, Zionists, Bundists, and spies, must be annihilated! Ripped out by the roots! Bolsheviks cannot coexist with all these spies! When he uttered Stalin's name, all of us stood up and applauded, as was the custom.[34]

Not surprisingly, the audience grumbled here and there, although no one dared speak his mind. Grosman, who described this assembly, heard his neighbor, the author Shlomo Sheinberg, whisper *sotto voce:* "They're treating us like little children, packing us in like all the little kids under one *tallis* on Simchas Torah." No less typical, was Sheinberg's response when he was given the floor. After repeating his simile of the children gathered under the prayer shawl, each kissing the Torah scroll, he presented a different conclusion: "Indeed, we all kiss the new Torah and pledge it our allegiance. We are ready to pledge our souls for the new and enlightened ideal, crowned with the brilliance of the great Stalin. . . . " At the end of the assembly, the secretary of the association informed Sheinberg that he had been hired to proofread the Belorussian railway employees' newspaper. Then Sheinberg informed Grosman that his only son had been lying ill without warm food for about two weeks. "Don't judge a man until you stand in his shoes," he advised.

At first, no one knew exactly what attitude the Soviet authorities would take toward the general question of Jewish culture. Especially vague were the conditions and the basis under which Jewish literary endeavors would be allowed to resume. As for Hebrew, there were no illusions. If anyone had hoped that Hebrew would be recognized as a medium of current artistic activity, these hopes expired quickly. Refugee writers who had not belonged to the leftist camp in Poland were also profoundly uncertain and anxious. It quickly transpired, however, that the authorities might permit literary activity in Yiddish, provided that it follow the formula of "national in form and socialist in content." The literary and artistic genre of the time was known as "socialist realism," and it was this standard against which every work and its creator was judged. Another problem was how Soviet values would be integrated into the previous cultural tradition, since the transition from the Polish period to Soviet rule entailed a change of basic perspectives in all areas of life.

The first group to accept this challenge were the poets. Swept away by the initial general euphoria, they spared no effort to turn out paeans of thanksgiving and joy, comparing the bleak and terrible past with the glittering present.[35] As time passed, the local Jewish press (in Bialystok, Kovno, Vilna, Riga, Minsk, and Kiev) accommodated a growing deluge of poems by authors from the new areas. Although the themes varied, the dominant ones focused on glorifying and lauding the socialist homeland, the Red Army, the righteous regime, the leader Stalin, and so on.

As soon as the new realities were stabilized, more or less, it was the prose authors' turn to gear up for action. Some of them had been allowed to reside in the large cities; they developed appropriate relations with cultural institutions and newspaper editorial boards. Several members of this group even managed to have their works published in the local and Soviet Jewish press. The major themes were description and condemnation of the gloomy past under the previous regime; self-congratulation for the privilege of living under the socialist superpower's patronage and taking part in its upbuilding and defense; descriptions of the equality, social justice, and fraternity of peoples that prevailed in the USSR; and praise for the leaders of the state, the Red Army, and the Party, under whose tutelage these tenets had been realized. In one form or another, these motifs were evident in the works of most of the authors who were allowed to work and publish their works overtly. In this respect, authors and poets who had previously belonged to the leftist or pro-Soviet camp were hardly distinguishable from those who had eschewed or even opposed the prevailing line. Most of them quickly made peace with the fashionable clichés of Soviet literature of the time. The difference was that those who had belonged to or sympathized with the Left before 1939 did this out of identification and fervor; the others complied under duress or for lack of choice. For the latter, the new system was a necessary evil.

Jewish writers in Lvov, having no access to a local forum such as *Bialystoker Shtern,* had to seek out media in Kiev (the daily *Der Shtern* and the monthly *Sovetish Literatur*).

Works by authors in the annexed areas, like the general and Jewish press and the writings of veteran Soviet Jewish authors, made little substantive reference to the events of the war and the sufferings of the Jews under the Nazi occupation.[36] This lacuna was evidently caused by the Soviets' tepid policies toward Nazi Germany at the time, with the Ribbentrop-Molotov pact in effect.

Many writers, including well-known veterans, found it difficult to publish their works. Even in Bialystok, where a Jewish newspaper had existed since late 1939, few authors found their way into print. Most of those who succeeded had status and connections; however, *Bialystoker Shtern* was too small to accommodate even them. Thus they turned to the two Minsk newspapers, *Oktyabr* and *Shtern.* Some went farther afield, publishing in the Jewish journals of Lithuania. A few poets in Lvov found their publishing opportunities in Kiev (the monthly journals *Shtern* and *Sovetish Literatur*). A few went as far as *Shtraln* in Kovno and *Ufboi* in Riga. Once they appeared in the local press, several works by Jewish poets in the annexed areas were reprinted in various Yiddish-language journals overseas (e.g., *Idishe Kultur*).

One cannot gauge the extent to which the status and connections of refugee Jewish writers and poets in Bialystok were stronger and more deeply rooted than those in Lvov. Nor can one estimate the degree to which the cultural establishment in Minsk was more considerate than that of Kiev. Still, it is a fact that the board of the monthly journal *Shtern* in Minsk eventually co-opted two Bialystok-based authors (Binem Heller and Dovid Richter). Furthermore, all the authors and poets in the annexed areas who managed to publish books in Moscow and Minsk in 1940 were from Bialystok (B. Heller, M. Knapheys, Y. Emiot, J. Rubinstein, L. Wahl, S. Zhirman, and M. Burstein). Notably, too, nearly all of these books were printed in editions of 3,000 copies, compared with only 1,500 for books by important Soviet authors such as Peretz Markish in 1938. The turn of the Lvov authors came in 1941: books by I. Ashendorf, Nachum Bomze, Rachel Korn, and Yerahmiel Green were published in Kiev that year (actually, in the first six months, before the war broke out).

It was generally believed in major institutions of Yiddish literature and culture in Moscow and elsewhere that writers from the "western areas" should be integrated into general Soviet artistic frameworks and encouraged to create prolifically. The board of the Jewish-owned *Der Emes* publishing house, in a special meeting in Moscow, discussed various plans for 1941 and decided "to devote appropriate space in these plans for works by Jewish authors from the western Ukraine and western Belorussia."[37] At the same meeting, the board weighed a proposal to launch, that very year, a series of publications containing the finest Yiddish literature in the USSR. This series, entitled *25 yor Sovetish Yidishe literatur* (25 Years of Soviet Yiddish Literature), would include a volume devoted to young authors from the new areas.

The Ukrainian publishing house for national minorities, part of the Young Writers' Bureau in Kiev, took special interest in young authors from the annexed areas. With the assistance of this agency, the first works of young Jews and members of other national groups were appraised favorably by experts. Another forum that made its debut in 1940 was the literary anthology *On-hoyb* (Beginning), with works by 21 previously unpublished authors.

In view of their special status and important role in he indoctrination process, Jewish writers, more than any other segment of the Jewish population in the annexed areas (with the possible exceptions of theater people and journalists), were allowed to mingle intensively with well-known Soviet Jewish personalities in the cultural world. This interaction, which began just after the Red Army entered the annexed areas, manifested itself in visits by ranking personalities in the Jewish literary circles of Minsk, Kiev, and Moscow. Full-fledged delegations came in their wake. The most impressive of these, in terms of size and composition, was a mission from Moscow that set out on February 14, 1940, to meet with Jewish authors in Bialystok. The mission was composed of eleven authors, the manager of the *Der Emes* publishing house in Moscow, and the secretary of the Jewish section of the Belorussian Writers' Association. The pretext for the visit was the upcoming elections for the supreme governing institutions in the former provinces of eastern Poland. The mission stopped over in the Belorussian capital of Minsk for the laudable purpose of hearing the Secretary-General of the Communist Party, P. Ponomarenko, ask them "to take part actively in preparations for the election of deputies to the supreme soviets of the USSR and the Belorussian Soviet Socialist Republic."[38]

In official encounters with their colleagues (in Bialystok, Lvov, Kovno, and elsewhere), the visiting Soviet authors set an exceedingly officious, cautious tone. The locals, especially those who did most of the speaking for them, quickly followed suit, striving to prove in every possible way that they had adjusted to the new realities. In a party held in Bialystok on the 15th anniversary of the founding of the literary journal *Shtern* in Minsk, author and critic H. Smolar, speaking for all local authors, proclaimed, "We already feel that we are *Shtern*'s partners in action and that we are duty-bound to collaborate in its future development."[39] In keeping with the custom at such events, several local authors then recited their works.

A number of authors in the annexed areas, chiefly in western Belorussia and the western Ukraine, gained the privilege of performing for an audience of Soviet Jews when small groups of Bialystok and Lvov authors were invited to visit their Soviet colleagues. During their stay, several visiting authors from the western Ukraine signed book-publishing contracts with *Der Emes* publishing house,[40] and were allowed to spend several weeks at a "rest home" near Moscow. S. Mikhoels, the director of the Jewish theater in the Soviet capital, invited his guests to a performance of *Masoys Benyomin hashlishi* (Journeys of Benjamin the Third), with himself in the role of Sender'l.

In January, 1941, a national committee chaired by the secretary of the Soviet Writers' Association, A. Padeyev, was established in Moscow to orchestrate festivities all over the USSR for the 90th anniversary of the birth of I. L. Peretz. The committee members included A. Kacyzne, Y. Perla, and the theatrical director Ida Kaminska (from Lvov), and M. Broderzon, J. Rubinstein, and the theatrical director A. Morawsky (from Bialystok). The committee secretariat also invited the local writers' associations in Riga, Kovno, Vilna, and Czernowitz to take part.

Evening literary events for the public *(sheferishe oventn)*, at which authors recited excerpts from their works, were popular venues for encounters between Yiddish-language litterateurs and the general public or, as happened on occasion, their Soviet colleagues. In Lvov, such events were held on the premises of the local writers' association, which had Polish, Ukrainian, and Jewish members. Special evening events were devoted to Jewish literature, with lecturers such as Alter Kacyzne, Rachel Korn, and Hirsh Weber. Author Tania Fuks describes these affairs as the "honeymoons" of the Jewish writers in Lvov. In Brest, local Jewish authors performed at a Yiddish reading fest devoted to the 15th anniversary of the newspaper *Oktyabr*. These literary events served as one of the first tests of the political and ideological fitness and literary quality of the authors and their works, as judged by the criteria of the time. Jewish theaters in Bialystok, Lvov, Vilna, Riga, and other cities occasionally held literary parties in honor of various cultural personalities.

Another officially sanctioned way for getting to know literary works was the local radio, which occasionally offered Yiddish-language programming[41] about classic Jewish authors such as Sholem Aleichem and I. L. Peretz. On other occasions, Jewish authors recited excerpts from their works for Jewish students and workers.

When the Red Army occupied Lithuania in June, 1941, it found several dozen Yiddish-language authors there, including members of the Yung Vilne (Young Vilna) group such as Abraham Sutzkever, Chaim Grade, and Shmerl Kaczerginsky.

Even though progressive Lithuanian authors and their Jewish colleagues had been on good terms under the previous regime, much time passed before the government institutions and authorities responsible for literary and cultural affairs in Soviet Lithuania established direct relations of any kind with the Jewish literary community. However, they manifested a positive regard for Jewish literature in various ways. For example, they recommended the naming of streets after Jewish authors and artists[42] and staged national activities for the 90th anniversary of the birth of I. L. Peretz. Jewish literature was given respectable coverage on "Thirty Minutes of Yiddish," a program broadcast three to five times each week on the government radio station in Vilna. Yiddish authors in Vilna received several times more "air time" on this program than did their Kovno counterparts.

As time passed, the general writers' association of Soviet Lithuania admitted ten of the 30 recognized Yiddish-language authors whose works had been published in one form or another under Soviet terms. However, they were accepted only as individual members, and they engaged in hardly any activity under the association's auspices.

Some works by the Vilna authors contained current motifs and manifestations of sympathy for the regime.

By March, 1941, as noted, *Der Emes* of Kovno was the only daily Yiddish literary forum left in Soviet Lithuania. Several Yiddish-language Jewish authors had received regular positions on its editorial board; others worked for the Jewish theater, in teaching, in various governmental public institutions, and so on. None of them made a living solely by creative writing. The board of *Der Emes* also recruited artists for its intensive public activities, such as gala conferences and mass assemblies for parents.

With the approach of elections for the Supreme Soviet of the USSR in Moscow, the *Der Emes* board announced a literary contest in order to encourage the creativity of local Yiddish-language authors. The weekly magazine *Shtraln* followed with a similar announcement, offering two prizes; however, the German-Soviet war broke out before the deadline for submissions.

A special event in Yiddish literary activity in Soviet Lithuania was the appearance of the 216-page *Bleter 1940,* a journal on literature and the arts published under the auspices of the association of Jewish authors and artists in Lithuania.[43] Most of the 24 contributing authors and poets had resided in Lithuania, Latvia, Poland, or Vilna before the war.[44]

Bleter 1940 was the first of only two book-length Yiddish-language collections of works by local authors and poets to appear in Soviet Lithuania in 1940–1941. Admittedly, there were plans to publish Yiddish books in 1941–1942, after the government publishing house in Lithuania set up a Jewish section (under Yankl Yosade). These plans reached the stage of initial inquiries about the publication of a monthly journal of literature, criticism, bibliography, and sociopolitical problems; it had even been given a name, *Sovetishe Bleter.* The war put an end to all these plans; of all the promised publications, only a thin volume of poems by Hirsh Osherowitz got as far as the page make-up stage.[45]

In Latvia, so few Yiddish-language authors and poets were allowed to publish their works under Soviet rule that their works could not fill up the two local forums—the daily *Kamf* and the journal *Ufboi.* For example, twelve of the 21 articles and literary works in the third edition of *Ufboi* (January, 1941) were written by veteran authors from the USSR.

In Bessarabia and the western Ukraine, the authorities allowed no Jewish daily or other local journal to be published, thus depriving local Jewish litterateurs (estimated at 50 in number) of any opportunity to publish their works in the area. The 200,000 Jews of Bessarabia, left without any medium in their own language, received *Der Shtern* from Kiev; the authors among them were advised "to write in Moldavian or publish in the Soviet Yiddish press."[46] Only a few, mainly those who had proved that they had adjusted to the conventional Soviet line without deviation, succeeded in publishing in Soviet-Jewish forums outside of Bessarabia; this happened only on rare occasions.[47] To make a living, some authors accepted teaching positions in Jewish schools.

The most noteworthy opportunities for expression of local Yiddish culture, amid this scanty environment, were the Yiddish broadcasts that Radio Kishinev introduced at the very beginning of the Russian occupation.[48] This medium, something of a novelty for the Jewish public, created the illusion of the existence of Yiddish culture.[49] Jewish authors were also allowed to perform at the various "meetings," literary assemblies, concerts, and other mass encounters that were common at the time and held under official auspices—especially just before elections and Soviet festivals, but also on weekdays in workplaces.

Two other settings for Jewish cultural activity were clubs and libraries, especially those that had belonged to the leftist-Yiddishist Kultur Lige and survived in the new format.

Jewish authors in Northern Bukovina also met with many difficulties—even in the city of Czernowitz, an important center of Yiddish culture.[50] Even the lucky few who were recognized as progressive authors were ordered to choose "deserving" themes and adopt the terminology and style of socialist realism. Their tutors were veteran Soviet Jewish authors who visited the area occasionally.

The plight of Russian- and Ukrainian-language authors with regard to publishing opportunities was not as grave. However, very few of them were Jewish.[51] Poems by Klara Blum of Czernowitz, who wrote in German, were published in Russian translation by the government publishing house Goslitizdat.[52] Her translated anthology included several works with Jewish biographical motifs, such as "The Mother and the Ghetto in Czernowitz," which, noted *Literaturnaya Gazeta,* articulated "the poetess's antipathy toward anyone who persecutes and offends her people."

Further manifestations of Yiddish creative endeavor came to light in the special literary events held that year, mostly in Czernowitz. Performances by Soviet Jewish authors such as David Hofstein and Itzik Fefer drew large audiences. Here, too, streets were named for great Jewish authors whom the Soviet authorities favored at the time, such as Sholem Aleichem.

The foregoing suggests that many of the Jewish litterateurs' optimistic expectations of reasonable creative and publishing opportunities were dashed. Although these authors were held in high esteem, the fact remains that only a few of the 150–200 Jewish authors and poets who resided in these areas were able to support themselves by their writing. Furthermore, the literary outpouring at the time, as measured in numbers of volumes, was rather feeble, as the table on page 140 shows.

One factor limiting the publication of Yiddish literature in the annexed areas was the situation of Jewish publishers in the USSR and, more important, their organizational and managerial talents. Most Yiddish-language Soviet

Yiddish-language Books by Authors in the Annexed Areas, Published in the USSR in 1940–1941

Year of appearance	Western Belorussia	Western Ukraine	Lithuania	Latvia	Estonia	Bessarabia	Northern Bukovina
1940	7	—	1	—	—	—	—
1941	3	4	1	—	—	—	—
Total	10	4	2	—	—	—	—

publishing took place in the three republics in which a large majority of Jews resided: in the RSFSR, at the *Der Emes* publishing house (named for the major daily newspaper that existed until 1938) in Moscow; in the Ukraine, at the Yiddish section of the government publishing house for national minorities in Kiev; and in Belorussia, at the Jewish section of the government publishing house in Minsk.

The three publishers, especially those in Moscow and Kiev, maintained a division of labor of sorts, or at least a measure of coordination. The Kiev facility, for example, published mainly textbooks and children's books, whereas *Der Emes* concentrated on fine literature. The Kiev and Minsk publishers also turned out books and pamphlets of regional importance, local propaganda, and translations from Ukrainian and Belorussian.

The annexations in 1939 and 1940 increased the Yiddish reading clientele by many thousands. Because these publishers could not meet the tremendous demand with their existing inventory, they began to reprint old books and publish new ones, including some by Yiddish-language authors in the annexed areas.[53] The number of Yiddish publications in the USSR grew from 339 in 1939 to 359 in 1940, including an increase from 152 to 169 in Kiev. The Kiev publishing house opened a branch in Lvov, which published 44 Yiddish titles in 1940. Circulation of the veteran Soviet literary monthlies began to soar. *Sovetish Literatur* in Kiev, for example, expanded its print run from 1,850 in 1939 to 2,500 in early 1940, and to 3,000 for the edition of November–December 1940. Circulation of the Moscow almanac *Sovetish* grew from 1,500 copies in early 1939 to 3,000 a short time later.

Even as the veteran Soviet publishers contended with grave technical and administrative shortcomings, shortages of raw materials, and other problems, the annexed areas offered numerous well equipped (nationalized) publishing houses whose managers were eager to take on the printing of various Yiddish-language publications. In response to an article on this subject in

Der Emes of Kovno, L. Strongin, director of the government publishing house in Moscow, wrote the following:

We believe that the activity of a Yiddish-language publishing house may be organized in any new Soviet republic that has a large Jewish population with literary and cultural talents. Of course, this would be undertaken in close coordination with the existing publishing houses. . . . Another possibility is a division of labor and specialization in particular fields. For example, since Lithuania has an considerable polygraphic basis in Yiddish, the publishing house in Lithuania may put out many of the textbooks and much of the children's literature as well as translations of selected Soviet literature, in addition to local publications.[54]

Nevertheless, in 1939–1941 no Yiddish-language books were published in western Belorussia or the western Ukraine, except for Minsk and Lvov. Local enterprises in Vilna and Kovno published several titles (mostly textbooks); in these cities the veteran experienced *Libhober fun Vissen* ("Lovers of Knowledge") society was an important participant, at least at first.[55] In 1940, the *Kamf* publishing house in Riga published a series of Soviet propaganda books translated from Russian. Nearly all the independent initiatives of these publishers had come to an end by the time the Germans invaded in June, 1941.

The order to purge books that were contrary to official views and inclinations, including all Hebrew books, did not spare the lending libraries and reading halls. At first, all libraries were shut down for inventory. Books found to be "unfit" to read—Hebrew ones above all—were removed and placed in storage; books in Yiddish and Polish were subjected to a selective "weeding." Next, the separate Jewish libraries were shut down; any books deemed fit to read were transferred to the general government libraries. When the latter also received Soviet books in Yiddish, reading in public libraries came under total control. The Jewish community library in Lvov became a Jewish branch of the government library at the Ukrainian Academy of Sciences and was used largely for research.

The "purification" of the great Sholem Aleichem Library in Bialystok was carried out by three well-known Communist authors from Poland, under the watchful eye of a special expert brought in from Minsk. Since she did not understand Yiddish, somebody had to describe the content of each book and await her decision. Author Moshe Grosman, allowed to enter the library to locate old publications of his, described the purge in his memoirs:

The works of Russian and Polish classicists were not banned as a matter of principle. When it came to Jewish authors, however, they began to argue about whether Chaim Nachman Bialik could be considered a Jewish classicist. The case against Shalom Asch was open and shut, since he was a prominent pro-Fascist. . . . They bargained about Itzik Manger. Another question that came up was how to treat Peretz. . . . It was up to the inspector from Minsk, and she ruled: Peretz is a classicist, his *belles lettres* were OK, his journalistic writings were out. As for Bialik—as she was told, he'd lived in Russia at the time of the Revolution, but because he moved away, there was no doubt that he had to be banned along with the others.[56]

Thus thousands upon thousands of Jewish books were purged and delivered to Soyuzutil (a trash-recycling agency).

In Vilna, a renowned center for books on Judaism, three of the eight Jewish municipal libraries, containing 80,000 of the original 230,000 volumes, remained open to the public. The Mefitsei Haskala Library, with 55,000 volumes (in Hebrew, Polish, and Yiddish) and 2,000 subscribers, formerly the property of the kehilla, was nationalized on November 1, 1940, and given to the municipal culture department, after which it was called People's Library No. 5. The famous Strashun Library became People's Library No. 4; after it was nationalized, it acquired an additional 1,600 readers, bringing the figure to over 4,000 (100 on daily average). The children's library that formerly belonged to the Z.B.K. (Zentraler Bildungs Komitet [Central Education Committee], which administered the Yiddish secular schools) became the Public Governmental Children's Library. The great Abraham Mapu Hebrew Library in Kovno was locked up as soon as the Red Army entered the city. Its Hebrew books were hauled off to storage; its few Yiddish books were taken elsewhere.[57]

In the peripheral cities and small towns, all libraries that had belonged to "reactionary organizations" were closed temporarily, meaning for whatever time it took to overhaul the administration and inspect all the books for their political leanings. Since this was a complicated process, the reopenings were delayed in many localities, to the displeasure of the press.

The Jewish libraries in Bessarabia, especially those belonging to the leftist-Yiddishist Kultur Lige, continued to exist under the Soviet regime, usually combined with other libraries[58] and only after painstaking inspection. In several localities, Hebrew books were burned or hurled into the mud. Many individuals with personal libraries rushed their books into hiding.[59] In Kishinev and other large cities, Yiddish books brought in from the Soviet Union were available at low cost, but nowhere in Bessarabia was even one

Yiddish title published throughout the sovietization period.[60] The omission even included election propaganda.

Despite these developments, the Jewish writers in the annexed areas were optimistic about the future of Yiddish literature, because the authorities favored its continued existence and the conditions for further creative endeavor were relatively auspicious. However, authors were seriously encumbered by difficulties in adjusting to Soviet realities. Furthermore, the Yiddish education system in the western Ukraine and western Belorussia was scaled down drastically in the 1940/41 school year, an ill omen for growth prospects of the potential Yiddish readership. Indeed, many question marks accompanied Jewish writers in their work. Thus, believing in and hoping for the future of Jewish culture in the USSR on the one hand, and bedeviled with doubts on the other, Jewish writers were hurled into the maelstrom of the war. A few managed to flee into the Soviet Union; others shared the fate of their brethren in the area overrun by the Nazis.[61]

THE THEATER

Unlike Jewish education and the Jewish press in the Soviet Union, which had been deteriorating rapidly and perceptibly since the late 1930s, Jewish activity in the theater continued to blossom, to some degree with official encouragement. At the time that the Red Army entered eastern Poland, Jewish governmental theaters were active in ten Soviet locations including Moscow, Kiev, Kharkov, Minsk, Birobidzhan, Odessa, Zhitomir, and Baku. The Jewish governmental theater (Goset) in Moscow sponsored *Di Moskver Melukhishe Idishe Teatrale Shul* (Moscow Government School for Jewish Theater), managed by Solomon Mikhoels.

Authorities in the western Ukraine and western Belorussia were favorably inclined toward (or at least tolerant of) Jewish activity in the theater from the moment the new regime took over. Some of this may be understood in the context of the special role of the theater in Soviet society as an instrument of indoctrination. However, there were also local factors, such as Jewish theatrical tradition and activity in the cities and towns of eastern Poland. Another factor was the tremendous wave of refugees, which brought at least 50 of the finest Jewish thespians from Poland to the annexed areas (nearly all congregating in Bialystok and Lvov).

In November, 1939, a Jewish governmental theater (Idisher Melukhisher Dramatisher Teater) was established in Lvov, and the refugee actors who had found shelter in the town rushed to join. The star of the troupe was Ida Kaminska, who had left Warsaw several days after it had fallen to the Germans. Her first stop was Bialystok, where the Soviet authorities invited her to set up a Jewish theater. However, citing family reasons, she moved on to Lvov,[62] where she was warmly received. There it was proposed that she set up a Jewish governmental theater with full official support. Indeed, the Jewish theater was placed in "Category A," as were the Ukrainian and Polish theaters in Lvov.

Ida Kaminska was named general manager of the theater. Its first administrative director was the actor Gershon Roth. The famous playwright Alter Kacyzne was the artistic advisor. The playwrights Israel Ashendorf, Yerahmiel Green, and Leibush Dreykurs gravitated to the theater and collaborated with it.

The theater management was overhauled in the spring of 1940, the Soviet authorities explaining to Ida Kaminska that her position should be held by somebody "from the other side" (i.e., from the Soviet side of the border). Even after stepping down as general manager, Ida Kaminska continued to direct it in the artistic sense. Her status in the theater remained unchallenged and central until June, 1941. Such was her reputation that the Soviets maneuvered her onto the town council of Lvov in December, 1940, using her for public and political purposes.

The cast of actors grew in the middle of 1940 when a group from Dniepropetrovsk, where the local Yiddish theater there had shut down, joined the Lvov troupe. This expansion was beneficial in several ways: the Lvov theater could now work on several plays simultaneously and offer richer programs. The repertoire placed conspicuous emphasis on the Jewish classicists, who described the shtetl and the common folk. The number of Soviet plays was still small. When the Lvov theater staged Peretz Markish's *The Ovadis Family,* the press went out of its way to stress this first exposure of the local Jews to Soviet realities: "This work will teach the Jewish population about the life of a Jewish family on a collective in Birobidzhan. . . . By means of this work, the Jews of the western Ukraine have seen for the first time healthy Jews such as these, young Jews clutching weapons, something that can happen only under Soviet rule."[63]

Just before the war broke out, the theater in Lvov rehearsed Peretz Markish's *Kol Nidre,* which depicts Jewish life in Poland before September, 1939, the danger of German occupation, and the Jews' jubilation upon the arrival of the Red Army.[64] It is noteworthy that this theater had performed 11 of the 17 plays in its repertoire for Polish Jewish audiences before the war. While emphasizing this evidence of continuity, however, one should also note the innovations made in the Jewish theater at this time. Aside from the adjustment of contents to Soviet realities, a major change took place in the public status of the theater. The Soviet authorities stressed the fact that the Jews of the western Ukraine had never before merited a governmental theater of their own; this novelty would surely augur a genuine blossoming of Jewish theater. The Soviet sources describe the generous governmental support that the theater and its actors received, absolving the management of the need to ensure the theater's existence and permitting the actors to devote all their energies to creative art.

The Jewish theater of Tarnopol, was elevated to municipal/governmental status. By performing in all the towns in the vicinity, it played an important role in the larger field of culture.[65]

A drama group in Przemysl performed *Uriel Acosta* by Karl Gutchkov and *Platon Kretchet* by Alexander Kornyetchuk. A Jewish troupe in Drohobycz performed *Uriel Acosta*. The town of Kolomyja had a Yiddish dramatic group. A Yiddish-speaking Jewish artistic group took first place in the "Municipal Olympics" in the town of Buczacz. Jewish schools had drama groups that performed for pupils and parents, especially in the 1939/40 school year.

The "Jewish Hour" radio broadcasts in Lvov played an important role in disseminating theater art in Yiddish. Indeed, Eastern Galicia became a hotbed of Jewish theater activity in 1939–1941.

The Jewish theater was consolidated in Bialystok, too, relying on the superb stage skills of Jewish refugees who had reached this city from Warsaw, Lodz, and other localities in western Poland. In late 1939, Bialystok hosted a general conference of refugee actors, by the initiative of the authorities. A short time later, a Jewish governmental theater (Bialystoker Idisher Melukhisher Dramteater) opened in the town, under the leadership of the well-known Warsaw actor Abraham Morawski and with a cast that included members of the Jewish governmental theater in Baku. Its inaugural performance was Peretz Markish's *The Ovadis Family,* directed by Morawski, followed by two selections from the classic repertoire of Soviet Jewish theater: *Der blutiker shpas* (It's Hard to Be a Jew) by Sholem Aleichem and *Hershele Ostropoler* (Hershele of Ostropoli) by Gershenson, directed by Jacob Mindlen, a young Jewish director from the USSR who succeeded Morawski. The last performance, advertised as the artistic climax of this institution, was supposed to be the dramatic poem "Shpanier" (Spaniards) by M. Lermontov (translated by Aaron

Kushnirov), about Spanish Jewry during the Inquisition. This production never reached the stage. In June, 1941, the entire troupe, with more than 70 members, set out for a performance tour in eastern Belorussia. While it was in Mogilev, the Germans invaded. The actors were evacuated to the Saratov area along the Volga River, whence most of them were dispersed in Central Asia.

Another theater group was founded in Bialystok in late 1939: a Yiddish-language satirical forum called "The Miniature Governmental Jewish Theater." Its manager was Moshe Broderzon; the participants included members of the "Ararat" theater of Warsaw, headed by Dzhigan and Shumacher. A Jew from Minsk named Shuster was appointed the authorities' inspector for the group. Following conventional practice in theaters of this type, the Miniature Theater addressed itself to the conditions of Soviet life at the time, for which reason its efforts were frequently banned by the censor. By last-minute improvisation and embedding of clever allusions in the script, the actors from Warsaw and Lodz often outsmarted the censors, making the offerings of the Miniature Theater far from pleasing to those responsible for political hygiene. The Miniature Theater also was criticized for its repertoire, especially for "clinging to the shmaltz of yesteryear."

The outbreak of the Soviet-German war caught the Miniature Theater on a visit to Odessa. The actors were sent on to Kharkov, whence they broke into small groups and drifted through Central Asia.

Traveling Jewish theaters came into being in Grodno and Pinsk. In the cities and towns of western Belorussia, numerous Jewish drama troupes and circles operated under the auspices of local agencies for the performing arts.

Jewish theatrical activity in Vilna was diverse and rather good. For one thing, the Jewish population in the area had had a rich tradition in this field; for another, the masses of refugees from Poland who reached Vilna included quite a few theater people. The first play to be performed by the government-sponsored Jewish theater in Vilna was *Hirsh Lekert,* written by Soviet-Jewish playwright A. Kushnirov and directed by N. Eliashiv. The main protagonist of the play, a shoemaker named Hirsh Lekert, had been executed in the first decade of the twentieth century for having attempted to assassinate the Russian governor. The local Jewish community recalled the incident and generally regarded Lekert as a hero, and the play was well received by the audience.

The next offering was the musical comedy *Der gericht geyt* (The Trial is Under Way), by the Soviet Jewish playwright Y. Dobrushin. Its central characters, former householders who engage in speculation behind a facade of piety and scholarliness, are ultimately placed on trial. In another presentation, which attracted large audiences, Leib Shriftzetser portrayed Hershele of Ostropoli and succeeded in giving him a familiar local visage. The well-known Vilna comedian Motke Chabad excelled in similar performances.

With the approach of the May Day festivities in 1941, the theater was officially declared the "Jewish Governmental Dramatic Theater of Vilna." To mark the event, a festive debut performance was staged of the Soviet play *Platon Kretchet* by Alexander Kornyetchuk, winner of the Stalin Prize. Although the managers of the Vilna theater, Dovid Umru and Chaim Grade, planned a rich repertoire for their enterprise, their only successful production was *200,000,* alternately titled *Amkho* (Common folk), directed by Henrik Sharo and starring Morris Lampe as Shimale Soroker. It made its debut on June 21, 1941. After the performance, the management and cast attended an official reception at the Italia Café and then partied at the famous Welfke's Restaurant until dawn. Just then, the Nazi armies crossed the border and the war began.

An alternative to the Jewish Governmental Theater in Vilna under Soviet rule (1940–1941) was the Maydim puppet theater, founded in 1933 by a group of young thespians.

Close on the heels of the Red Army as it reached Lithuania, the drama section of Iteg (Idishe Teater Gezelshaft, a theatrical association in which Communist influence had been considerable even before the occupation) performed the Soviet play *Di fayern fun laykht-turem* (Lights of the Lighthouse) by O. Karasiev in Kovno and several peripheral cities. This play, rehearsed and readied before the Red Army takeover, was meant to "warn" and instruct all honest citizens of the USSR—especially those living in the border areas—to beware of the saboteurs and spies who were conniving to destroy the Soviet Union.[66]

In Kovno, practical efforts to establish a governmental Jewish theater were combined with the production of Peretz Markish's *Moltzayt* (The Feast). The reasons why this work was preferred over several Sholem Aleichem opuses (which nevertheless had many advocates) were mostly political and ideological. The manager of the theater admitted as much: "Indeed, we wanted our first play to carry the name of a Soviet author and a theme connected with the civil war and the pogroms; we intended to keep Sholem Aleichem in reserve for the second or third performance."[67]

The premier performance was staged with great festivity on March 8, 1941; the large celebrity audience honored it with lengthy ovations. In all,

Moltzayt was performed 18 times in more than two months and was attended by 7,000 persons.

The debut of *Stempenyu* (based on Sholem Aleichem's writings) on June 11, 1941, was the last performance by this theater. Its fate had been sealed a month earlier, when the authorities decided to merge it with the Jewish theater in Vilna.[68] In any case, the Germans invaded less than two weeks later.

Unlike its counterparts in the western Ukraine, western Belorussia, and Lithuania, the Jewish governmental theater in Latvia relied mainly on local actors (veterans of the Jewish stage in Riga), reinforced by a few "young actors from workers' studios." Soviet Jewish actors subsequently joined the troupe. It took the manager-designate, Hertz Leybovitz, two or three months to ready the new institution *(Idisher Teater LSSR)* for its debut. The theater finally opened on October 1, 1940, with preliminary festivities and a performance of *Hirsh Lekert,* written by the Soviet-Jewish playwright A. Kushnirov and directed by Y. Tsisser. This was immediately followed by another work by a Soviet playwright, Dovid Bergelson's *Der toyber* (The Deaf Man). By the end of 1940, the Riga Jewish theater had performed three more plays: two by Soviet Jewish authors and *Massoys Benyomin ha-shlishi* (Travels of Benjamin the Third) by Mendele Mocher Sforim.

In the first three months of 1941, the repertoire shifted to non-Jewish playwrights; in the spring and summer of that year, Jewish playwrights were again preferred. These plays (*The Ovadis Family, Zvey kunyleml* (Two Eccentrics) and *Di gas fun freyd* (The Street of Joy) were the ones chosen for a performing tour to the Latgala province in the east and the Courland area shortly before the war broke out.

The last performance of the Jewish theater in Riga was another Soviet Jewish offering: *Ziamke Kopatch* by M. Daniel. The hero is a shoemaker's apprentice who displays notable valor in the civil war. The role was played by a Jewish actress from Birobidzhan, L. Yanovskaya.

The Jewish Governmental Theater in Riga hosted additional Jewish cultural activities, including a literary fest marking the centenary of the birth of Abraham Goldfaden and a solemn convocation for the 23rd anniversary of the founding of the Red Army. The actors and musicians of the theater were joined in these events by Jewish soloists from the governmental opera and 90 members of the *Yevakans* troupe (the Jewish choral ensemble). Most of the works in these events were Jewish, and a majority of them were performed in Yiddish.

In Kishinev, a governmental Jewish theater was up and running several months after the Soviet occupation. In time, it became the central Jewish theater in the Moldavian SSR *(Der Yidisher Teater fun der Moldavisher SSR)*. Before this, this city did not have a permanent Jewish theater; it was created by the authorities, which also placed a 1,500-seat auditorium at its disposal. A Soviet Jew from Odessa named Abelov was appointed its general manager; the artistic director was Jacob Sternberg, a well-known Romanian Jewish author and playwright. The literary advisor was Mottl Saktzier. Its cast, originally composed of 20 local actors, was reinforced by several performers from the Government Jewish Theater of Baku, which had been dissolved a short time earlier.

For its debut, the Kishinev Jewish theater eschewed works by Soviet Jewish authors in favor of *Kishefmachern* (The Witch) by Abraham Goldfaden, the patriarch of Jewish theater and a revered personality among Romanian Jews. The performance evoked such interest that it was attended by high-ranking officials in the Jewish theater in Moscow (Goset). In the spring and summer of 1941, the theater in Kishinev performed the following: *Hershele Ostropoler* by M. Gershenson; *Shleimke* by I. Gordon; *Di Kreutzer sonata* by Leo Tolstoy (reworked by I. Gordon); *200,000* by Sholem Aleichem; and *Ziamke Kopatch* by M. Daniel. Early in the summer of 1941, the authorities ordered the theater to relocate to Beltsy, but the move never took place.

In Czernowitz, a traveling Jewish theater was established in late 1940 with well-known actors such as A. Tempner, Willa Paster, and Sidi Tal. In its four years of existence it managed to stage seven performances, including *Tevye der milkhiker* (Tevye the Milkman), *Fisher* (Fisherman) by L. Kobrin, and *Di Kreutzer sonata* by Leo Tolstoy.[69] The Jewish theater in Kiev visited the Northern Bukovina town of Khutin, presenting, among other dramas, *Zvey kunyleml*.

The foregoing information, supported by additional sources, indicates that more than 100 plays were performed on stage by Jewish theatrical companies (including dramatic groups of suitable quality) in the annexed areas in 1939–1941. Assuming that each play was presented ten times on average (including performing tours to other localities), the number of Yiddish-language theatrical performances in these areas during the period under discussion exceeded one thousand!

Aside from the eight local theaters that performed only in Yiddish, traveling theaters, drama groups, and autonomous performing-arts groups staged Jewish and other plays in the annexed areas. The eight theaters were arrayed as follows:

Western Belorussia: a dramatic theater and miniature theater in Bialystok

The western Ukraine: a dramatic theater in Lvov

Lithuania: two dramatic theaters (Vilna and Kovno) and the Maydim puppet theater in Vilna

Latvia: a dramatic theater in Riga

Bessarabia (Moldavia): a dramatic theater in Kishinev.

This activity was most conspicuous in Eastern Galicia, especially Lvov. The Jewish theater there performed 18 plays (i.e., a new play almost every month). The Jewish theater in Bialystok put on 12 in the same period of time. The Jewish theater in Riga was especially prodigious, putting on 11 plays in 11 months plus two performing tours in peripheral towns.

Notably, six of the seven permanent theaters chose works by Soviet playwrights for their debut performances; only the Kishinev theater had the audacity to make its debut with a work by a Jewish playwright (Abraham Goldfaden). In contrast, the majority of theatrical companies that predated the permanent theaters chose to premier with works by Sholem Aleichem and I. L. Peretz. The dramatic groups behaved similarly.

Among the 52 plays performed in 1939–1941, it is noteworthy that more than two-thirds (36) were by Jewish playwrights and were performed in most localities. Only 13 of the 36 were by Soviet Jews, chiefly I. Dobrushin, P. Markish, M. Daniel, and L. Reznik.

Because Sholem Aleichem was strongly favored in the USSR at the time, his plays were chosen most frequently in numerical terms (seven of the 36) and in number of localities (17 of 55). Works by Goldfaden and, to a certain extent, I. L. Peretz, L. Kobrin, and others enjoyed similar popularity. The Soviet Jewish playwrights in greatest demand were Peretz Markish, M. Gershenson, M. Daniel, and I. Dobrushin.

The relatively small proportion of Soviet plays (five of 16), even among those by non-Jewish authors, is an indication of the extent of the autonomy enjoyed by the Jewish theater at the time.

Summing up, the Jewish minority in the annexed areas was given relatively ample opportunity to develop Jewish theater in the period under discussion. This period of time, with its unique conditions, indeed witnessed a flourishing of Jewish theater in terms of scale, quantity, and—no less—Jewish content.

7

Religious Life

The eastern provinces of Poland, the Baltic countries, and Bessarabia and Bukovina were home to a Jewish population of which a large majority maintained an Orthodox way of life and adhered strictly to the Commandments. Official Soviet ideology, in contrast, categorically rejected all religions, Judaism included. One may hardly wonder, then, that the Soviet takeover of these areas elicited grave apprehensions in Orthodox circles.[1] Indeed, the authorities began to subject the Jewish religion and its adherents to contempt in all media, especially before festivals and holidays, and persisted in doing so until the Nazi invasion. The verbal onslaught reached its climax with the approach of the High Holidays and Sukkot in the autumn of 1940.[2]

The propaganda campaign breached the confines of the daily press. For example, the local committee of the Lithuanian Communist Party in Vilkomir (Ukmerge in Lithuanian) saw fit to hold a conference on the meaning of the Jewish religious festivals on the eve of Yom Kippur. The main speaker was Hayyim Shochat, principal of the Jewish high school. Shochat "proved," citing examples from Jewish history, that the clerics and plutocrats had succeeded in molding the festivals' content to suit their sectarian interests.[3] In the summer of 1940, five lectures in Yiddish on anti-religious themes were delivered in the Kletsk district of western Belorussia, at the initiative of the Communist Party, for an audience of 2,000.[4]

Rabbis and religious functionaries also came under attack. The anti-religious journal *Bezbozhnik* reserved special vitriol for the hasidic rebbes—

those "remnants of the most reactionary forces among the Jews. . . . As one uproots weeds, so must hasidism be uprooted."[5]

Even as they sponsored and sanctioned these campaigns, the authorities asserted that religion belonged to the domain of citizens' personal affairs. On June 29, a mass rally on "the separation of church and state" in Kovno gave vent to the following assertion:

> Our aim is to achieve true freedom of thought. No one has the right to interfere with the piety of the pious, but neither has anyone the right to force nonbelievers to study religion, to marry under the ritual canopy. Civil registration should be instituted at once.[6]

Indeed, this attitude had informed the Soviet regime ever since it overran the eastern provinces of Poland nine months earlier.

One consequence of this position was the liquidation of the organizational framework of Orthodox life, the *kehilla* (Jewish community organization). In Poland, the status of the kehilla, its rabbis, and its religious judges had been secured in law; the kehilla was a recognized legal framework that provided the Jewish population with general civil services such as the registration of births, marriage and divorce, and the handling of problems of personal status. The formal status of the clerics who had previously handled such problems (as well as Jewish burial, upkeep of cemeteries, and related matters) was altogether unclear in the initial period of Soviet rule. The Orthodox public was forced to concern itself with the question of the upkeep and operation of religious institutions such as ritual baths, yeshivot (Talmudic academies for teenage and adult men), and schools for young boys.

The picture came into focus quickly. As the kehilla was paralyzed and its offices closed, the rabbinical institutions were dispersed and their official services terminated. Rabbi Dr. David Kahana described the situation in Lvov:

> In October, 1939, the Soviet authorities summoned Abraham Kupfershtein, a religious leader in the community, and presented him with a decree stating that there was no more room for an Orthodox kehilla. They ordered him to hand over the office keys, minutes of meetings, and the archive files. . . . When the kehilla was dismantled, so was the rabbinate. Birth and marriage records were confiscated from the rabbinate employees and taken to the general municipal registration office, which handled all registration from then on.[7]

The process recurred throughout the Soviet-occupied provinces of Poland. Moreover, the changeover from separate Jewish registration to general registration was completed with alacrity, because any birth or change in personal status required the official, recognized authorization of the government registration office.

In Czernowitz, the elected board of the kehilla was dispersed and replaced with an appointed committee of government-sanctioned individuals whose status was conspicuously unclear.[8] In Bessarabia the kehillot were liquidated either because they failed to gain the recognition of the Soviet authorities (as in Khutin[9] or because the kehilla leaders hastily divested themselves of the community's assets and sought to dismantle the institution on their own. By eliminating the kehilla as an organizational framework, the authorities made sure that all services connected with religious practice and observance of the Commandments would be provided on a volunteer basis; as such, they would no longer enjoy official sanction, let alone material assistance.

Below are excerpts from a diary kept by the rabbi of the kehilla of Bendery (Bessarabia), including details on the demise of this institution:

The former head of the kehilla, Mr. B., visited me today and said they wanted to liquidate the kehilla's property (i.e., the Hebrew Gymnasium building—one of the most opulent in town), the *talmud torah* building, and the convalescent center on the outskirts of town. He wanted to hand the matter over to the provisional municipality, the body they call the municipal executive committee.

From tomorrow on, there will no longer be any kosher meat because there's no more kosher slaughtering in town. The talmud torah and the gymnasium have been shut down, too. All the kehilla has left, then, is the cemetery, and he asked me whether I would like to take responsibility for the burial society, managing it and being responsible vis-à-vis the government, because not a single member of the former kehilla wants to take part in this work. I've got no other source of livelihood at the moment. . . . I had no choice but to agree, and thus I've become the director and bookkeeper of the burial society. I've been left with the two workers who cleanse the bodies, and the cemetery caretaker. . . . According to the Cemeteries Law they are municipal property, but they've allowed us to take care of them under my responsibility and I agreed. Mr. Shmeltz, the former chairman of the burial society, has agreed to work with me as a member of the committee. This pleases me.[10]

Even though religious practice was ostensibly relegated to the personal domain, and despite the Soviets' declared espousal of separation of religion and state, observant Jews were not permitted to be observant. Sometimes this affront was caused by the socioeconomic changes that the Soviets had introduced. Thus, for example, the general day of rest (Saturday or Sunday) was abolished and replaced with an adjustable "day off." This was first of all an impediment to family life, since a husband, wife, and children could not always arrange the same day of rest. Even when Sunday was declared everyone's day of rest in late 1939, the authorities did not recognize the Jewish Sabbath, let alone the festivals, as sabbatical days. The effect of this was to discriminate against observant vis-à-vis non-observant Jews. The latter desisted from work on Sundays as before, while masses of Orthodox breadwinners were forced to desecrate the Sabbath because most had become state or municipal employees after trade and industry had been nationalized. In the city of Vileyka (western Belorussia), for example, A. Ziskind was placed on trial for not reporting to work on the Sabbath. Convicted of negligence, sabotage, and subversion against the regime, he was sentenced to exile in Siberia, where his traces vanished.

The cooperative system (the artels) also continued to work on the Sabbath and Jewish festivals. It should be borne in mind that the organized workplace provided not only a livelihood but salient proof of membership in the "proletariat," as opposed to the classes of "parasites," "speculators," and miscellaneous "enemies of the people." It is no wonder that few Jewish breadwinners were able to withstand the harsh temptation to sacrifice the sanctity of the Sabbath for a job in an organized framework.

Many Jews, including some not necessarily observant, found it quite difficult to leave home on the Sabbath. A few were able to find jobs that circumvented this desecration. Watchmen's positions, for example, were prized by the Orthodox. The rabbi of Bendery describes the blossoming of this industry:

Many of "our people" (the Orthodox) chose the occupation of night watchman. A guard is paid like an unskilled worker, and every budget includes a salaried position for one. We have no way of knowing why in the time of the Romans, large shops up and down the main street made do with two guards, while nowadays every shop and institution needs a night watchman. . . . "Guardsmanship" has become the occupation of Sabbath-observant Jews, because they don't have to desecrate the Sabbath to do it. Even our Reb Berl Abelman has become a guard in the office located in his home. Each and every night he steps into his office, turns on the lights in what used to be his dining room, and buries his head in some profound Talmudic issue. In this fashion he "safeguards" government property.[11]

Rabbi S. Kahana of Lvov describes one way in which Jews attempted to safeguard the Sabbath from desecration. Some of the artels were staffed only by Jews; when most of the employees were Orthodox, the authorities allowed them to choose a day other than Sunday as the weekly day of rest. Of course, they selected Saturday, the Jewish Sabbath.

Rabbi Kahana added:

On major festivals the problem was more serious. In Lvov a spontaneous organization of religious Jews could be sensed. The word was passed from mouth to ear: "If you're absent or late for work one day, nothing terrible will happen."[12]

Jews employed in a mattress workshop in Riga contrived to avoid working on festivals by declaring these occasions as days of general renovations in the plant.[13]

A Jewish mother from the town of Brestowice (near Bialystok) articulated the sense of impotence and anger about this state of duress in a letter written to her son in America:

People are celebrating Sukkot as I write this letter. It's the first festival on which we didn't go to *shul*. Mishke worked on Rosh Hashana, and I cry every day. . . . On Yom Kippur we didn't fast. Mishke begged and begged until they let him spend half the day in shul. The children went to school that day. . . . In a few words, the mood was just as you can imagine. I, even I, milked the cow. Our world is upside down. They say God gives hell first and then heaven; with us it's the opposite—first we had heaven, and now we're immersed in genuine hell.[14]

Testimonies from the Baltic countries point to a totally different picture, one not detrimental to the right of worship. In Lithuania, all the synagogues were left intact until the Nazi invasion ended the period of Soviet rule. In Czernowitz, "all the synagogues [were open] and full of worshipers." Why were some synagogues in these areas allowed to operate normally? Perhaps local officials permitted this because higher authorities had issued no instructions to the contrary. An American Jewish weekly offered the following explanation:

Many of the Jews of Lithuania, who have become white-collar workers, plant managers, and administrative functionaries, still adhere to their custom of attending synagogue on the Sabbath and festivals. Admittedly, they do this almost secretly, but they do it. True, the Jewish Communists propagandize against them, but the Russian Communists take no interest in this whatsoever. It isn't considered counterrevolutionary as it used to be.[15]

This persistence is confirmed in notes taken by Rabbi E. Petchenik while traveling through Eastern Galicia in late 1940:

> I . . . attended a conference of rabbis who had to make a ruling about persons who had to work on Rosh Hashana and Yom Kippur and nevertheless wished to attend services. The ruling was: they should wake up at midnight, recite the service, and complete their prayers by the time they had to go to work in the morning; after their day's work they should immediately return to the synagogue for Ne'ila [the concluding service at sunset]. . . . Indeed, at Kol Nidre, when people did not need to be at work, the synagogue was so crowded that the neighboring yards and streets were virtually under siege. . . . The Jews thronged the streets and shook hands, even if they did not know each other, pronouncing New Year's greetings from the bottoms of their hearts.[16]

Most peddlers and petty shopkeepers who were allowed to keep their businesses (after commerce and industry had been nationalized) continued to rest on the Sabbath. Some local authorities, especially those of small towns, intervened in this matter.[17]

The liquidation of the kehilla magnified the importance of the synagogue, even though the economic base of this institution was seriously compromised. The synagogue became the rendezvous of Orthodox Jews, thus permitting the continuation of religious services, including public worship.

On the whole, the Soviet regime neither banned public worship nor forbade the existence of synagogues. Nevertheless, synagogues and worshipers frequently came under attack. One manifestation of this was the imposition of heavy taxes based on inconsistent or vague criteria, with the decision often made by the local authorities. Sometimes they based the tax on the floor space of the synagogue. In other cases, in order to tax rabbis who insisted on keeping up their religious functions, the floor space of the rabbi's own home was the tax base.[18] The tax bills handed to the rabbis were between 1,000 and 5,000 rubles per year[19]—large sums under the circumstances. Concurrently the rabbis were placed under heavy pressure, including threats and persuasion, to yield their synagogue duties. Rabbi Yehezkel Levin of Lvov, for example, was offered important public and scholarly positions if he agreed to quit the rabbinate. Upon refusing, he was first summoned to the NKVD offices and interrogated at length; finally the Levin family was forced to relocate to a small town near Lvov.[20] The Great Synagogue in Lvov was given a tax bill of 100,000 rubles. Since the congregation was unable to marshall this sum, the synagogue was closed. Synagogues elsewhere, including several in Eastern Galicia (Tarnopol, Strij, Kolomyja, and Nodvorna) were shut down under similar circumstances. In the western Ukrainian town of Drohobycz, "all the synagogues. . .other than the Central Synagogue [were shut down]. . . ."[21]

In the Bessarabian town of Yedintsy (Edineti), synagogues and yeshiva study halls were expropriated and turned into warehouses and barracks. In Beltsy, they were put to use as factories. The Great Synagogue of Britchevo (Briceva) was turned into a "cultural center." Synagogues in Northern Bukovina were handed over to artels. Two of the five synagogues in Vertuzhany (Vertujeni) were seized and reopened as high schools. In Bendery, in addition to four synagogues shut down by the authorities, the worshipers themselves locked up another two. The explanation given in one of these cases was that "they should not be accused of being Zionists and haters of the people." In the second case, that of the "synagogue of the butchers," "the secretary of the municipality asked the former lay director of the synagogue to bring him a letter signed by the worshipers in which they offer the building to the municipality, which would like to establish a cultural center there."[22] The author of this testimony (the town rabbi) added: "He'll produce such a letter too, knowing the worshipers will be too scared, suspicious, and apprehensive to sign!" It was no wonder, the rabbi concluded, that "the lay managers of almost all the synagogues that are still open have resigned; only old men who have nothing to fear take this burden on themselves."

Similar cases of arbitrary seizure and expropriation of synagogues and community institutions, evidently by local initiative, took place in western Belorussia. In Nesvizh, a shoemakers' cooperative set up shop in the former kehilla building, a carpenters' cooperative in a Talmud Torah, and a used furniture warehouse in the *shtibl,* a small prayer facility that was part of a larger synagogue known as the Kalteshul ("cold synagogue"). The Markshul ("market synagogue") was turned into a dance club; when worshipers mustered the courage to protest this, the authorities told them that "this is what your Jewish youngsters want. . . ."[23]

In Janow, near Pinsk, large expropriated synagogues were used as stables and warehouses. In Zheludok, the authorities turned a synagogue into a dance club for Red Army soldiers and left the local church alone. A song-and-dance troupe took over the Mir Yeshiva building; the 6,000-volume yeshiva library was hauled away for shredding. The Volozhin Yeshiva became a restaurant. In Kletsk, the yeshiva study hall was turned into a merchandise warehouse; the main building became a municipal lounge. In Vileyka, the authorities appropriated the synagogues by using a tried-and-true trick: "The NKVD contacted the Jews of Vileyka and asked them to sign a petition affirming that they do not object to the closure of the synagogues. Obviously, anyone who worked in a governmental position was afraid to turn down the request."[24]

It is evident that the authorities' attitude toward synagogues was not uniform. In most localities, synagogues were left intact and the cost of their upkeep, including stiff taxes, handed to the congregations. Authorities in other locations, especially in western Belorussia and Bessarabia, expropriated synagogue buildings, locked out the worshipers, and turned the devotional buildings into warehouses or clubs.

Was the Jews' inclination to take part in public worship influenced by the attitude of the regime? Again, the picture is not uniform. Several sources mention successive prayer quorums and synagogues filled to overflowing, especially on the Sabbath and festivals, and even on weekdays. In some localities, the synagogue underwent a revival of sorts:

> When one entered the *beit midrash* [a synagogue also used for study] in Sokoli in the morning or evening, one could not perceive that one was under Bolshevik rule. . . . The beit midrash was filled with worshippers reciting the public service, *minyan* after *minyan* [prayer quorum]. . . . In the evening, groups of Jews sat around each table, engrossed in religious study. At one of the tables, the rabbi taught a page of Talmud with his study group; at another sat a rebbe, teaching a chapter of Mishna. . . . Behind the heater and between the benches sat simple Jews, conversing on matters of the most exalted kind and retelling tales of old times.[25]

However, even if the number of worshipers had not diminished, their composition had changed: the young among them were dwindling.

In many cases, the pressure had results other than or contrary to those intended; sometimes it spurred the religious public to intensify its organizational efforts. Perhaps, too, the elimination of the other community institutions caused the public functionaries to gravitate to the synagogue, which they made the focus of national and religious activity.

Synagogues played an important role in the organizing of relief for the thousands of Jewish refugees from western Poland. The public activists who congregated in the synagogues arranged food, money, and housing for the refugees and even tried to find them work. After June, 1940, when thousands of refugees were exiled into the Soviet interior, the synagogues were bases for the mailing of parcels to the exiles—food (especially packages of matzoh for Passover), clothing, and religious needs. The synagogues also became headquarters for extensive mutual-aid activity. Official freeloan funds had ceased to exist; institutions such as Linath Tsedek (accommodations for the poor), and nuptial funds had been dissolved. All of their functions went over to the unofficial care of Jews on an individual basis, and those who did the most in this regard were the hard-core activist groups that used the synagogues as their base. Jewish orphanages and geriatric homes had been merged into the general welfare system and served a mixed population, making it necessary at times to provide for individuals for whom the general institutions were unsuitable—especially the Orthodox.

In Eastern Galicia the authorities issued no regulations against kosher slaughtering. In Bessarabia, in contrast, the authorities prohibited the ritual slaughter of livestock but allowed slaughtering of poultry to continue. When the kehilla in Yedintsy was abolished, Rabbi Yeshayahu (Issaya) Elkis assumed responsibility for the slaughtering of poultry and allowed it to take place in his home. This activity was heavily taxed. In Czernowitz, the capital of Northern Bukovina, the community paid the rabbi a salary to continue ritual slaughter.

Ritual slaughter in Latvia was banned in the autumn of 1940. The Jews appealed the decision, but to no avail. In fact, however, ritual slaughter continued, if only on a small scale. Elsewhere the Orthodox public solved the problem pragmatically, taking advantage of various possibilities.

Lvov had several separate kosher abattoirs when the Red Army entered, which continued to function for a few weeks. By the end of 1939, however, they had been shut down; the Jewish slaughterers were hired by the governmental services to supply meat to the population at large. Here, too, a way to provide kosher meat was found. Each employee in the government abattoirs had a personal rubber stamp that he used to mark the meat he had prepared. The Jewish slaughterers simply continued to observe the ritual laws, including the secret excision of the forbidden part of the femoral area, and marked this kosher meat for identification in the butcher shops. The butchers' Jewish employees completed the subterfuge by referring Jewish customers to these cuts.[26]

Conditions in smaller localities were easier; meat was supplied by cooperatives that often had a large share of Jewish employees. The Jewish population knew that the meat provided by these cooperatives was kosher.

One of the first tests of the Soviet authorities' attitude toward religion came about on Passover, 1940, the first Passover under the new regime. The

Jewish population geared up to secure its supply of matsa, focusing its efforts in two directions: (1) obtaining official consent for supplying matsa through the governmental frameworks; and (2) making preparations to bake its own. The appeal to the authorities was initiated by groups of worshipers. These local-level contacts sometimes came to resemble public bargaining. There were instances (usually in small localities) in which made a bakery and, at times, even flour mills were made available by the local administration for this purpose. The authorities usually ignored the Jews' requests and withheld official sanction; however, they did nothing to stop Jews from organizing on their own. According to one source, "The Soviet authorities instructed customs stations not to delay shipments of matzoh across the Soviet borders, including [those of] the annexed areas."[27]

In Lithuania, the authorities gave the Jews carte blanche to bake matzoh, and Passover, 1940, was celebrated in its most minute detail.[28] Those among the Jews who had observed the festival stringently before the war continued to do so in 1940 and 1941. However, more and more Jews wavered in their observance. Especially conspicuous were young Jews who ate in public restaurants, workplaces, and schools during the festival.

At Sukkot, 1940, the supply of *etrogim* (citrons, used in the holiday ritual) became an urgent question. It was no simple matter, because citrons had to be imported and connections with supplier markets had been severed. Again, however, a remedy was found. In the summer of 1940, one Chabrutsky, one of the most prominent activists in the synagogue of Moscow, visited Lvov; the local Jews asked him to help them procure citrons for the festival. Rabbi Petchenik described what happened:

Even though it seemed impossible, Mr. Chabrutsky pulled it off. Chabrutsky traveled to the Caucasus, found a place where citrons are grown, and, notwithstanding the tremendous difficulties, brought them to Lvov together with affirmations of rabbis there that the citrons were kosher. . . . I remember the lengthy queues that formed around the beit midrash in Lvov when the blessing over the citron was recited. . . . I witnessed in the "temple" of Lvov, where no one had evidently seen a citron before, how people pressed forward to lay their hands on one. . . . Even Red Army soldiers turned out to see the citrons, and everyone lauded and praised Mr. Chabrutsky for the way he had sanctified God's name.[29]

In Latvia, the authorities, after special intervention by one M. Dubin, allowed the Jews to clear palm fronds and citrons through customs for Sukkot in 1940.[30]

Because relations with Jewish communities abroad were weakening steadily, and because Jewish calendars had not been printed in the USSR for many years, such calendars became a highly prized commodity. The calenders were composed and distributed among the Jews by specially recruited experts.

Evidence of the sense of alienation that beset the Jews in the annexed areas, and the importance of the Jewish "calendar" in view of this, is an excerpt from the last known letter penned by historian Simon Dubnow, who lived in Riga at the time, dated March 5, 1941, to his friend Yosef Meisel in Jerusalem: "Your letter of January 6 reached me about two weeks ago, and, like any other letter that comes from a great distance, it was an important event in the life of a man who's incarcerated in the prison of Europe, encircled in fences of war. Even in the neutral countries. . .we are cut off from our spiritual wellsprings. Thus, for example, I succeeded in obtaining here, after a difficult search, just a small "penny" calendar for the year 5701 (1940/41)—representing our entire "literary outpouring" this year. Overseas newspapers do not arrive. We know only one one-thousandth of what's going on, and even this in a special form for the news media in our localities."[31]

The Soviet authorities, as previously stated, did not recognize the formal, juridical status of the rabbis; they deprived the clerics of all official civil functions, which they reassigned to general governmental services. This was especially salient in the recording of births and officiating at marriages. Most Jews, however, were so used to this combination—official governmental functions and the element of religious law—that they regarded it as natural.

Most Jews continued to have their infant sons circumcised under religious law, using private circumcisers; they were not content to register their children and their national affiliation with some government office. Ritual circumcision was done in family circles and, at times, in synagogues. Only a handful of Jews, casting their allegiance with the new regime and the Communist Party, are known to have vacillated in the matter of circumcision. A substantial proportion of Jewish Communists circumcised their sons, either reluctant to sever the thread of generations or unable to withstand the pressure from relatives and the Jewish milieu.

Bar mitsva ceremonies also continued as usual. Here, however, the ramparts were more prone to fissure. Growing numbers of non-Orthodox parents eschewed this ritual in the synagogue, limiting themselves to a celebration at home. In response to pressure at school—from the Pioneer movement and the fierce anti-religious propaganda of the Komsomol—many youngsters stopped laying *tefillin* (prayer phylacteries) after becoming bar mitzva.

Weddings as prescribed by religious law continued; some Jews insisted on meeting this requirement even when they had to do so furtively and modestly. Hardly any Jews contented themselves with civil registration only.

When the kehilla system was dismantled, the Jewish cemeteries were handed over to the municipal Soviet authorities, and the kehilla workers became municipal employees. Apart from this formality, no changes seem to have been made in the process and nature of Jewish interment.[32] Although the authorities rarely interfered with funeral arrangements, they undoubtedly meant to vitiate the religious aspect of this rite, especially when the deceased had been Orthodox.

Upon the death of the head of the Va'ad Hayeshivos (main office that served and represented the yeshivot), Rabbi Hayyim Ozer Grodzinski of Vilna, the censor banned the printing of outdoor death notices; the Jewish press disregarded his death. One of Rabbi Grodzinski's admirers, Samuel Rothstein, describes the funeral:

> Dozens of yeshiva men and rabbis formed a vigil, reciting psalms around the burial litter. . . . Several functionaries gathered at the Va'ad Hayeshivos building, discussing the funeral arrangements and spreading the word throughout the Diaspora. When they decided to send telegrams to Warsaw, Lodz, and Cracow, they also decided not to cable Bialystok, Lvov, and Grodno, which were in the Soviet-occupied zone, for the recipients of such cables would be in danger. . . . They decided to hold the funeral on Sunday, without asking the authorities for a permit.
>
> The authorities did not interfere, and even sent several dozen members of the Red Guard to oversee the arrangements. . . . All the shops (including those of the Christians) were shut. . . . The yeshiva men encircled the burial litter, forming a living chain. . . . Laboriously they made a path for the litter, and as they advanced toward the cemetery, a distance of several kilometers, the number of escorts multiplied further. Hardly a Jew stayed home. . . . As the corpse was readied for burial, more than 40 rabbis delivered eulogies in the funeral center. . . . Everyone chose his words carefully. Only the *maggid* (preacher) of Vilna, Rabbi Moses Zhukhowitz, made brief mention of matters that had been causing distress; immediately a member of the Red Guard approached him and ordered him to end his talk.[33]

Although burial was conducted without fee as a municipal service, the families habitually paid Jewish employees for providing various cemetery services, thus augmenting the modest salaries they received from the city. The municipal administration provided a standard gravestone for a small payment but permitted the erection of alternative stones financed privately. Burial services and gravestone unveiling ceremonies were held in the cemeteries, and families returned there to commune with their loved ones on the *yortsayt* (the anniversary of the death). They also recited *kaddish,* and even those who visited synagogues irregularly made sure to attend *yizkor,* the memorial service recited on festivals.[34]

The hasidic movement played an important role among Jews in all the annexed areas. This was especially so in Eastern Galicia, where Reb Yisroel had held court in Ruzhyn and sired the Sadigora dynasty and its offshoots in Galicia and Bukovina. The Eastern Galician towns of Czortkov and Husiatyn were home to courts of *tsadikim* (charismatic hasidic leaders). Additional dynasties and courts flourished there, chiefly of "grass-roots" tsadikim. The hasidim flocked to their rebbe to participate in communal feasts at festive occasions, to hear his erudite sermons, and to inform him of their joy and, especially, their woes. The rebbe, in turn, visited his adherents in various communities; his hasidim treated his arrival as a festival, sparing no grandeur and seeking shelter, as it were, in his presence.

Officially, the Soviets did nothing that would tarnish the luster of the rebbes. However, the latter were unable to maintain their practices as before. They could not visit their followers as freely as they had before September, 1939. The numbers of hasidim who crowded into the courts regularly diminished, and the rebbes and their families met with economic difficulties. Nor could rank-and-file hasidim, now wage earners in public government frameworks, visit the rebbe as freely as before the occupation. When trouble struck, however, the rebbe remained the religious legal authority to whom the hasidim turned in their distress. Thus, although relations within the hasidic movement contracted, they remained quite vibrant.

Community rabbis, too, lost much of their status. The diary of the rabbi of Bendery, describing the hardships suffered by the chief rabbi of Kishinev, Rabbi J. L. Zirelson, provides a graphic example:

... I was in Kishinev today and I visited Rabbi Zirelson, a long-time friend. What a terrible sight he was. They had felt no pity even for this old man. They deprived him of his spacious flat and expropriated his rabbinical court, leaving him only one room in which he arranged his vast library and sat there, lonely as a willow in the forest. The rebbetzin had died two weeks previously, and he, childless, was utterly alone, with no one to tend to him. Only after some individuals made special efforts was an old woman found to visit him and cook him his meals. . . .

I asked the few remaining pious Jews in Kishinev why they failed to visit the rabbi and take care of him. They were afraid of the government, they replied, since Rabbi Zirelson was considered a blatant enemy of the people. Then I realized, too, that their plight was even worse than ours in Bendery. Since Kishinev was the capital of the state, everyone was watched with eagle eyes. I went home depressed and angry.[35]

The head of the *kollel* (yeshiva academy for married men) in the Bessarabian town of Akkerman (Cetatea-Alba, or Volgorod) met a similar fate, as described by a member of this community:

True, the new Soviet rulers did not recognize the elderly rabbi. They left him alone. But his community of Jews, too, whose spiritual and religious leader he had been for decades—they too left him to his own devices and totally neglected him. . . . Only a handful, those closest and most loyal to him, still gave thought to their aged mentor.[36]

This is not to imply that all congregations neglected their rabbis. A large number of communities, especially the smaller ones, stood by their rabbis and organized to help them.[37] Neither does it imply that the authorities had declared total war on the rabbis. Their major intent was to strike at the clerics' status and image. One example is the affair of Rabbi Benzion Bogen of the town of Braynsk, Bialystok district. When this clergyman sought to obtain work as a bookkeeper, a local woman activist told him: "When the rabbi proclaims in public that he's a non-believer, he'll be allowed to work." The clergyman turned this down vehemently and, after appealing to the supreme institutions of the Party, he got the job he wanted and was even excused from work on the Sabbath.[38]

When the Jewish educational system was dissolved, the religious schools were not spared. Whereas the Polish authorities had occasionally accredited the yeshivot and heders, the Soviet regime did nothing of the kind. At first the Soviets were somewhat tolerant of these institutions, but in 1940 they evidently began to enforce regular and universal enrollment in the official schools. Orthodox parents responded by sending their children to unofficial afternoon heders in synagogues or private homes. In Lvov, officials pressured the Orthodox community to disband the yeshivot and heders, on one occasion arresting a Jew for maintaining a heder.[39]

Officially, the yeshivot were left unscathed because the Soviet authorities regarded them not as educational institutions but as settings of religious activity. Some continued to exist, although under difficult conditions. Some yeshiva students worked by day and pursued their studies at night. Several yeshivot staged an organized departure from Poland—rabbis, students, and all—crossing into neighboring Lithuania, where immigration was still feasible. When Lithuania became a Soviet republic, these yeshivot, as well as the indigenous ones, found themselves in a grave predicament. One by one, the exiled Polish yeshivot and their 2,500 students (including the Mir Yeshiva with its enrollment of 300) were ordered to vacate the large peripheral cities and scatter in the towns. There, too, under harsh conditions that included malnutrition, the students and their rabbis persisted in their studies and intensified their efforts to obtain Soviet exit visas and entrance permits to Palestine, the United States, and other foreign locations.[40] The Soviet authorities did not obstruct these efforts; indeed, they acceded to the entreaties of various institutions and individuals around the world, including the chief rabbi of Palestine, Isaac Herzog, "to allow refugee yeshiva students to emigrate via Odessa"[41] and subsequently via Vladivostok. The latter route was used in January, 1941, for the departure of various groups including 227 students of Mir Yeshiva. Several hundred students and rabbis from the yeshivot of Lublin, Kletsk, Baranowicze, Kamenets, Novogrudek, Bialystok, and other localities followed their lead.[42]

These and other Polish refugees continued to flee Lithuania until April, 1941, about two months before the Nazi invasion. The remaining yeshiva students, including the local ones, were unable to emigrate.

The grand, new home of the Knesses Yisroel yeshiva in Slobodka was used to accommodate a large clothing factory; its students were forced to crowd into the small Ohel Moshe yeshiva nearby, as they had before.[43] By the spring of 1941, all that remained of Knesses Yisroel were 30 students, most from small towns, and their mentor Rabbi Yehezkel. It was then that officials marched into the yeshiva and ordered it to shut down. The Telz yeshiva met a similar fate at roughly the same time (April, 1941), although it continued to operate clandestinely in neighboring small towns.[44]

Summing up, the Soviets' religious restrictions and prohibitions were gravely detrimental to an overwhelming majority of the Jews in the annexed areas. For many, the restrictions were merely one link in a chain of constraints foisted on them by sovietization. For the Orthodox, however, these were decrees that were unacceptable in any way or fashion, to be resisted at pain of death.

It is worth noting that the authorities were not as committed to total conformity on religion as they were in other areas, such as culture and the economy. They left a small amount of breathing room for those whose lives and essence revolved around their religion. The major beneficiaries of this lenience were the elderly and the ultra-Orthodox, who congregated around synagogues, yeshivot, hasidic courts, and so on. Forced into the tight confines of these frameworks, they continued to live almost as before, although the pressures of the new realities caused considerable erosion in their ranks. Compared with the vigorous, uncompromising war on religion carried out previously in the Soviet Union, including persecution of clerics, the attitude of the regime in the annexed areas was perceptibly moderate and, in any case, selective.

Conspicuous differences between the annexed areas in the application of policy and the degree of brutality that accompanied it also suggests that much was left in the hands of local officials and authorities.

Ceremony of adoption of Jewish High School No. 11 (one of two Jewish high schools in Kovno) by the silver factory in the winter of 1940. The speaker was Mayer Lappin, secretary of the Komsomol Youth Movement at the school; *(top, below the picture of Stalin)* the members of the Praesidium; *(bottom)* the workers and pupils of the school. *(From the author's personal collection.)*

General Yaakov Smushkevitch *(bottom row, center),* twice-decorated hero of the Soviet Union, during a visit with his family in Rokishkis, Lithuania, 1940. *(Courtesy of Isaak Kowalski,* Anthology of Armed Jewish Resistance, Vol. 2, *New York: 1987, p. 358.)*

N. Frankel, aged 83, and T. I. Maklovsky, aged 73, in December of 1939. They were weavers in a textile factory in Bialystok; both received retirement pensions from the Soviet Union. *(From* Der Shtern, *Kiev, Dec. 30, 1939.)*

Two comrades in the Workers' Guard patrol in Kishinev, 1940, a few hours before the Soviet annexation (i.e., the entrance of the Red Army forces). *(From* Der Shtern, *Kiev, July 11, 1940.)*

V. Tseitlin, stage director *(photo on left),* and Rachel Berger and V. Leiboshutz, actors, in a performance of Sholom Aleichem's play *Stempeniu* at the State Yiddish Theatre in Kovno, 1941. *(From the author's personal collection.)*

Young Jews in Lvov (Lemberg), Eastern Galicia, enlisting in the Red Army in July, 1940. *(From* Der Shtern, Kiev, *July 4, 1940.)*

פראלעטארישער טעאטער
די
א מיטקעמפער פאר סאָציאליזם

Jewish members of a traveling Yiddish theater in Vilna, taking part in the elections of the People's Sejm (parliament) of Lithuania in July, 1940. The banner reads, "Proletarian Theater: Comrades in the Struggle for Socialism." *(Courtesy of Leyzer Ran; reprinted from* Jerusalem of Lithuania, Vol. 2, *illustrated, documented, and arranged by Leyzer Ran, New York: 1974, p. 425.)*

Peretz Markish, *(seated, third from right),* with the Jewish Writers' and Poets' Group in Lvov (Lemberg), Eastern Galicia, 1940. The others are *(first row, seated, from right)* Tanya Fuks, Nusha Imber, Markish, Alter Katzisne, Yehoshua Perle, Nahum Bomze; and *(standing, from right)* Hirsh Weber, Shmuel Jacob Imber, M. Herzog, Sonya Friedman, Ber Shnapper, Israel Ashendorf. *(From the author's personal collection.)*

Placard in Lithuanian, Yiddish, and Polish, concerning the People's Sejm (parliament) elections in Lithuania, July, 1940. The placard reads, "Worker! Vote and recruit others to vote for the candidates of the Workers' Union." *(From the author's personal collection.)*

„א גאַנצן לעבן האָבן זיי געטראָגן פאַר יענעם, איצט טראָגן זיי פאַר זיך"

An illustration from the Kovno Jewish daily newspaper *Folksblat* (August 9, 1940), on the opening of a reading room in the name of R. Charny by the Porters' Union. The caption reads, "Throughout their life they carried for others, but now they carry for themselves." *(From* Folksblat, *Aug. 9, 1940.)*

פירט דער ארבעטער די מיזן...
מיט א שמייכל אױף די ליפן

ויצט ר' מאטע אין דער סקוה.
הי א הײליקע רעליקװיע

"קאמף" (ריגע). 1 ביולי 1940

A political cartoon from the Riga Jewish daily newspaper *Kamf* (July 1, 1940), showing a Latvian worker pushing a wheelbarrow containing a *mikve* in which three Jewish clerics, a Jewish businessman, and a drunken Latvian army officer are bathing. The worker is dumping them into the garbage. The caption reads, "Rabbi Motte is sitting in the *mikve* as a holy relic, and the worker is pushing them with a smile on his lips." *(From* Kamf, *July 1, 1940.)*

Cover *(top)* and certificate of identification *(bottom)* of Aron Garon (Aronas Garonas), editor of *Shtraln* ("rays"), the only Jewish weekly in Eastern Europe from 1940–41; it was published by the Lithuanian Komsomol. *(From the author's personal collection.)*

Photograph of Stalin on the cover of the Yiddish daily *Der Emes* (May 7, 1941), an official organ of the Central Committee of the Lithuanian Communist Party. *(From* Der Emes, *May 7, 1941.)*

П О С Т А Н О В Л Е Н И Е

/на арест/

Гор.Кишинев "22" июня 1941 года. Я ст.оперупол-
номоченный 1 отделения Отдела 3 Управления НКГБ МССР – мл. лейтенант
Госбезопасности – СОКОЛОВ, рассмотрев поступившие в НКГБ МССР мате-
риалы о преступной деятельности ЗИСМАНА Маркуса Самсоновича, 1921г.
рождения, уроженец с.Ламбровены, Сорокского уезда, прожив. в г.Ки-
шиневе, по ул. Киевской №119.

Н А Ш Е Л

что он являлся членом ЦК к.р. сионистской орга-
низации "Гордения" в Бухаресте. Прибыл он на территорию МССР после
установления Советской власти в Бессарабии с заданием сионистского
центра проводить нелегальную сионистскую работу. В настоящее время
занимается организацией к.р. нелегальных сионистских группировок
в г. Кишиневе.

П О С Т А Н О В И Л

ЗИСМАНА Маркуса Самсоновича, 1921 года рождения
проживающего по Киевской ул. дом 119 – подвергнуть аресту и обыску

Photographs and document of a Bessarabian Jew arrested by the Soviets and imprisoned at Kishinev on June 22, 1941, the day of the Barbarossa Operation—the invasion of the Soviet Union by the German Nazi forces. *(Courtesy of M. S. Zisman; reprinted from his book* Gesher Arokh *("a long bridge"), Tel Aviv: 1994, p. 73.)*

8

Refugees in a Temporary Haven

The outbreak of the brief German-Polish war caused tens of thousands of Jews and non-Jews to flood the eastern provinces of Poland in attempt to avoid exchanges of fire and the heavy German bombardment of civilian population centers as the Wehrmacht advanced eastward. The outflux gained strength with the first reports of German mistreatment of Jews in Czestochowa, Wyszkow, Krasnocielc, and other localities and reached a climax when the Polish military and political systems collapsed and the Wehrmacht mounted a siege on the capital, Warsaw. On September 7, 1939, the government of Poland urged civilians to relocate behind a new defense line on the eastern side of the Vistula. Masses of Jews responded. The highways and back roads from Lodz to Warsaw, and especially those from Warsaw to Bialystok and Lublin, were clogged with refugees who progressed on foot under heavy German bombardment and gunfire that took many lives.

When the Red Army entered the eastern provinces after September 17, the flight to the east gained further momentum. This time nearly all the refugees were Jews—public figures who had participated in political actions against the Nazis, members of the anti-German boycott committees, and Communists and leftist activists, some just released from Polish prisons. Refugees continued to reach the Soviet-controlled zone even after the frontier between it and the German-occupied area had stabilized. Once entering the Soviet zone, they continued to wander about for some time. Finally, however, most of them congregated in major cities such as Lvov, Bialystok, Rowne, and Luck, where, they hoped, jobs and housing would be easier to find. Not surprisingly, it was estimated (at least in the autumn of 1939) that nearly 50 percent of the Jewish population of several cities were refugees.[1]

As for the total number of Jewish refugees in the eastern reaches of Poland, estimates published at the time mentioned figures between 150,000 and 1,000,000.[2] The most reasonable number would seem to be 300,000,[3] roughly 25 percent of the Jewish population of eastern Poland.

THE FOUR STAGES OF REFUGEE MIGRATION

The flow of refugees into and out of the areas incorporated into the Soviet Union in 1939–1940 can be divided into four periods.

Period 1—September 1, 1939, until September 17, When the Red Army Crossed the Eastern Border of Poland

This period marked the climax of the German ground and aerial offensive, in which the civilian population suffered heavy losses. Among the refugees who fled to eastern Poland to ride out the storm, many had been born in these provinces and had immediate or more distant relatives there. Another category of refugees in these areas (especially Eastern Galicia and the vicinity of Vilna) were Jews who sought to emigrate via Romania or Lithuania. When the government ministries announced their official evacuation, growing numbers of members of political parties and various organizations joined them.

Period 2—September 17, 1939, Through October 31, 1939

The new frontier, set forth in the German-Soviet pact of September 28, 1939, was sealed on the latter date. Even though the two occupation zones were clearly demarcated by the end of this period (using natural borders such as the Bug and San Rivers), refugees were able to cross into the Soviet zone with relative ease. Moreover, the Soviets permitted and encouraged Jews to join Red Army units as they retreated from various locations under the Soviet-German accord.[4] Sometimes the Soviets even provided transportation.

Some 6,000 Jewish refugees had reached Vilna by this time, especially after the Soviet decision to assign these areas to neutral Lithuania became known. They included 400 Zionist *halutsim* (pioneers) in training, hundreds of yeshiva students, and dozens of Communist Party activists, writers, and journalists.[5] The waves of departure from this city became particularly strong in the second half of October, just before the Lithuanian army entered the city.[6] This time most of the uprooted were young Jews with little money and with leftist leanings; among them were writers and poets such as Leizer Wolf and Shmerl Kaczerginsky. Some had been active in the Workers' Guard and similar groupings; their departure was driven by ideology and a wish to live under the Soviet regime, with which they were enamored. Others, jobless and destitute, hoped that the Soviet areas would offer better opportunities than tiny Lithuania. The mass migration from Vilna lasted several days and continued after the official Soviet withdrawal. It gained momentum after pogroms erupted in Vilna as the Lithuanian army entered on October 28. Only on November 11, eleven days after the Soviets officially sealed this section of the border, was the hemorrhage stanched; by this time, 2,000–3,000 people had left Vilna for the Soviet areas. Many migrated south toward Bialystok and Baranowicze and even as far as Lvov; most, however, turned east, taking the shortest route to the Soviet border. Some of these refugees were unable to go any farther than the small towns of western Belorussia.[7]

Jewish refugees from Poland also attempted to enter the Soviet-occupied area by crossing into northern Romania, especially in the vicinity of Czernowitz. Here, however, the Soviet authorities were not eager to admit them, at least not at this stage.[8] By this time the Germans had begun to transport Jewish refugees from Czechoslovakia and Austria into Wolhynia and Eastern Galicia (western Ukraine), mostly via a concentration camp near the town of Nisko (west of the San River, which marked the German-Soviet frontier). Some refugees escaped from Czechoslovakia when the war began, crossing the border on their own initiative. When caught by Soviet border patrols, members of both groups—those from Central and Eastern Europe—were interned, accused of espionage, and banished to the interior of Russia.[9]

Among the masses of refugees who continued to flow into eastern Poland at this time, one group was notably organized and enthusiastic: political prisoners who were liberated from Polish prisons and concentration camps when the war broke out. They were often rudely received by Soviet officials, who rebuked them for having "deserted the arena of struggle."[10]

Another reason for the ever-growing numbers of Jewish refugees in the Soviet-controlled areas was the Nazi practice of expelling Jews and forcing them to cross the border.

Period 3—November 1, 1939, until the Spring of 1940

By now, elections had been held for national assemblies in Bialystok and Lvov, and the Soviets' sealing of the frontier was common knowledge. The stream of Jewish refugees from the German zone diminished. No longer was it a frantic flight into the unknown, as in September and October; instead, it was an exercise in border-running, clearly meant to escape the rising tide of persecution and mistreatment in the German-occupied areas. Although the frontier was more carefully guarded now, it was permeable here and there. Furthermore, the Red Army border forces did not behave consistently along the frontier; it is reasonable to assume that Soviet policy in this matter had not yet coalesced. In some cases, Soviet border sentries who encountered Jewish refugees fired into the air—mainly to impress the Germans across the border.[11]

In other cases, atrocities were committed along the frontier. In one instance, 1,400 Jewish refugees, chiefly women and children, stumbled into a no-man's-land near the town of Brok, where German guards beat them, robbed them of their belongings, and forced them to move toward the Soviet side. The Soviet sentries refused to admit them, yielding only after heart-rending entreaties. In the area between the Malkinia railroad station and Zaremby-Koscielne, Soviet sentries forced thousands of refugees to return to no-man's-land. Two days later, the refugees infiltrated the Soviet zone, undisturbed by the sentries.[12] In late November, 1939, Soviet border forces were explicitly ordered to turn back any Jews who approached from the Nazi-occupied area. Even after this, however, Jewish refugees continued to reach the frontier, singly and in groups. Some were helped by border-runners, but most fled in response to the German mass expulsions, accompanied by murder and physical abuse by soldiers and police. These expulsions became more frequent in the second half of November, 1939, and reached a climax on December 2, 1939. It was then that several hundred survivors out of approximately 2,000 Jews from the towns of Hrubieszow and Chelm reached the town of Sokal on the Bug River after a murderous six-day march. The Germans forced them onto a bridge in order to move them to the Soviet side, the Soviet guards pushed them back, and so on. In the end, a few succeeded in slipping into Soviet territory; the rest, although interned, were not handed back to the Germans.[13]

The flow of refugees slackened markedly in early 1940. In addition to stringent Soviet patrols and technical measures taken to seal the frontier as tightly as possible, the refugees responded to decrees and restrictions that the Soviets had introduced in their occupation zone as part of the sovietization process. Some refugees began to return to the German zone, and their numbers became considerable in the spring and summer of 1940.

Period 4—June, 1940, When Red Army Forces took over the Baltic Countries and Northeastern Romania, until the Wehrmacht Invasion of the USSR

A new group joined those who attempted to distance themselves from war and persecution in German-occupied western Poland: Jewish refugees seeking to enter Bessarabia and Northern Bukovina after the Soviet occupation of these areas. Families had been torn apart abruptly, some members remaining on the Romanian side (the west bank of the Prut River) and some in the Soviet zone. Other families had been ripped in half when Northern Bukovina and the vicinity of the town of Akkerman (Cetatea-Alba or Belgorod) was incorporated into the Ukrainian SSR.

The problems in Bessarabia and Northern Bukovina multiplied, as did their gravity, when thousands of Jews who were native to these areas began to return after permanent or temporary residence in Bucharest or other locations in central and western Romania. Their motives were diverse, including family, ideology, and livelihood.[14] Some reached these areas under Soviet-Romanian repatriation arrangements; others did so by other means such as border-running. Hundreds of Jews were streaming out of Bessarabia and Northern Bukovina at this time, in the footsteps of retreating Romanian officials and troops (the latter harassing them as they went). Most of these Jews were property owners, industrialists, members of the liberal professions, or bureaucrats in the Romanian monarchy. Activists in Zionist movements also set out for Bucharest and other localities in Romania.[15]

The Soviet authorities soon began to crack down on the influx of Jews to the Romanian areas that they now controlled. Many Jews who were native to these regions applied retroactively to the Soviet Embassy in Bucharest for permission to enter, and were turned down.[16] Only a few managed to slip into Bessarabia. Among those who failed, some were caught and exiled; others were shot by Romanian gendarmes.[17]

When the USSR annexed the Baltic countries, many emigrés from these areas, including Jews, returned with official Soviet encouragement from various European states—especially France, which had meanwhile been occupied by the Germans.[18] Organized groups of Baltic nationals who had gone to Spain to fight on the Republican side in the civil war also returned now from France.[19]

The refugees, mostly young men and teenagers, reached the eastern provinces with nothing but the shirts on their backs. Psychologically, too, their condition was desperate: they were agonizingly concerned about the fate of families left behind under German rule.[20] In general, the local Jewish population received them warmly, providing them with warm meals, overnight accommodations, and such medical assistance as local conditions permitted. For example, when hundreds of Jewish refugees reached Ostrow-Mazowieckie (Bialystok area) in the very first days of the war, the local rabbi immediately called emergency consultations, after which the community set aside some money for food and instructed several people to arrange for shelter. When the Germans overran Ostrow-Mazowieckie about a month later, the local Jews joined the ranks of the refugees. This pattern recurred in many other localities in the German-occupied zone. Under the circumstances, however, most of the burden of absorbing the refugees was shouldered by the veteran Jewish communities in Wolhynia, Polesie, and Eastern Galicia. Tens of thousands of refugees were attracted to these areas, especially major cities such as Bialystok, Lvov, Luck, Kowel, Pinsk, Kremenets, and Brest. The influx gained strength after the Red Army arrived, with the result that the cities teemed with hundreds of thousands of refugees, all homeless and destitute.

Yeshivas, synagogues, schools, and other public institutions, and private homes were pressed into service as refugee housing. By September 17, as the Soviet administration became consolidated and the kehillot were abolished, the synagogue was the only surviving framework for Jewish public activity and, as such, the most important center for the organization of refugee relief. Generally, these efforts focused on sleeping arrangements and medical and material aid. Several communities set up public kitchens. The authorities initially accepted this; several weeks later, however, they shut down these facilities on the grounds that "there's no place under the Soviet regime for charitable institutions."[21] Testimonies and memorial books describe various ways in which local communities mobilized to help the refugees:

> In Eastern Galicia . . . some of the local Jews fixed up shops and warehouses as housing. . . . A refugee care committee was founded. All of this was done surreptitiously, because the Soviets banned the existence of societies, even charitable ones. . . . Three members of the committee set out on a secret mission to other towns to collect funds for the refugees.[22]

The western Belorussian town of Volkovisk has been described as a transit station for refugees migrating eastward:

Synagogues, schools, and other public institutions such as Linath Tsedek and the municipal hospital were made available to them. All local Jewish organizations and institutions, as well as individuals, labored relentlessly to provide the refugees with relief, to the point of sharing their last loaf of bread.[23]

As housing shortages worsened, it became necessary to house the refugees in synagogues. In the Wolhynian town of Luck, the military commander of the town objected to this practice, citing regulations meant to safeguard "places that serve religious ritual" from damage. He ruled that the worshipers had to give their written consent.

Indeed, housing was one of the refugees' gravest problems, especially in the major cities where their numbers reached into the tens of thousands. Conditions in Lvov were so grim that liberated prisoners preferred to stay in jail for lack of alternative accommodations.[24]

A Jewish actor who had fled Warsaw described the situation in his memoirs:

Bialystok was crowded to the point of explosion. Thousands of refugees had nowhere to sleep. Many of them spent their nights loitering outdoors, slumbering on park benches, standing in some gateway, or leaning against a wall. At dawn, they queued up for the beds of people who had found a place to sleep that night. Thus many householders rented out their beds to "day sleepers" and "night sleepers." . . . The situation worsened as time passed, and [the refugees] were forced to get by on less sleep. No longer were beds rented out for day-sleeping and night-sleeping, but for a few hours only, and even this at top dollar.[25]

The refugees' meager resources were running out. Their plight became even more grievous when the Polish currency was replaced by the Soviet ruble ("the currency reform"); this turned them overnight into beggars. To keep themselves alive, they would congregate in local flea markets and sell anything they had managed to bring along: bits of clothing, underwear, shoes, and personal articles. Some of the refugees, taking their lives in their hands, began to slip into the German occupation zone, returning with various commodities that Soviet clerks and soldiers would snap up at any price. Some local residents began to resent and envy the refugees for their speculative commerce and excessive purchases of staples, which caused prices to skyrocket. Similarly, refugees were increasingly resentful of the local Jewish population for treating them "like bums."[26]

Naturally, the refugees tended to stay together in their new places of residence, and residents of particular towns were conspicuously inclined to do so. An organized group of artisans reached Luck from Chelm, which had fallen to the Germans, leaving their wives and children behind. The members of this group, carrying a faded red flag that they had saved from the 1905 revolution as a talisman, refused to avail themselves of public support. Instead, they formed a commune, found jobs, and pooled their income.[27]

Many of the refugees congregated in towns near the German frontier, where they lived under harsh conditions. From these locations, they hoped, they could eventually return home more quickly; also, until that became possible, it was possible to stay in touch with home by sending letters with border-running couriers. Bialystok was a case in point. Because it was so close to the German-controlled zone, it became an important communication center between the refugees and their families on the German side:

> The street was the refugees' meeting place. . . . There was a wall covered with a facade of boards, plastered from top to bottom with miscellaneous pieces of paper large and small, in Polish and Yiddish. These were notices about people who had perished during the escape, or requests from refugees for information about relatives. . . . The messages were almost always the same: I'm looking for my brother, M. R. . . . , who left Lodz together with me on September 6 and disappeared during the bombardment. If you know anything about him, please tell me. . . . Here one finds Jewish students who pose as peasants, deliver letters to Warsaw, and bring replies from there for five zlotys. Here is where one hires wagoners to bring relatives over from the other side.[28]

In their contacts with Soviets (Red Army soldiers and officers, militiamen, and so on), refugees were offered much sympathy, commiseration and, on quite a few occasions, genuine assistance. There were also cases, although relatively few, in which the initial encounter with Red Army troops left a bitter aftertaste, especially when the refugees assumed that, as victims of Hitler's persecution, the Soviet regime was their ally.[29] Be this as it may, the testimonies and memoirs leave no doubt that both the Soviet military administration and the subsequent civil administration gave thought to the refugee problem from the very start. In the town of Ludmir, for example, the military authorities made motor vehicles available for refugee transport. For a certain time, too, the refugees were allowed to ride the railroads at no charge.[30] Military administration officials were also known to cooperate with local refugee relief groups founded by Jewish public figures in Lvov, Przemysl, Luck, and elsewhere.

Aware of the plight of the masses of refugees in Bialystok, key members of the former Polish Communist Party convened in this city in October,

1939, for an informal discussion, following which the appropriate Soviet agencies were asked to help set up a public committee for the refugees. In early November, the authorities in Minsk endorsed the establishment of this committee, along with a recommendation that Joseph Lewartowski serve as its chairman. Hersh Smolar describes Lewartowski's activity:

> Lewartowski did not have permanent headquarters; he would walk, together with elected members of the committee who joined him, from one yeshiva to the next. Wherever refugees gathered, he would hear them out, give them an address where they might find a place to sleep, and offer some material assistance (from Soviet funds), especially for the children. The refugee committee made sure that its work was rehabilitational in nature, not philanthropic . . . but it was not destined to continue for long.[31]

More durable were two officially sanctioned institutions, *kompombezh* (refugee assistance committee) and *gorkombezh* (municipal refugee committee). These were set up for the general refugee population, an overwhelming majority of which was Jewish.[32] Agencies of these types were formed in late 1939 and early 1940 in numerous towns; Bialystok, Brest, and Grodno are only three examples. Ostensibly they were meant to tend to the refugees' needs—social affairs, food, clothing, medical help, housing, and so on. In fact, they were also intended to help the authorities regulate manpower according to the needs of the economy and to keep the government security services abreast of the state of this community.

One of the first actions of the gorkombezh in Bialystok was to register the refugees, even though many of the newcomers had already registered upon reaching the city. The action, taken on February 1–2, 1940, left the refugees quite unsettled and agitated, as some of their number—mostly Party activists, former army officers and bureaucrats, and the like—had recently been singled out for arrest. The refugees were also afraid that their registration would be followed by transport to the interior for labor, and they suspected that such labor, voluntary thus far and chosen by many thousands of refugees, would become compulsory (see below). To mitigate their irritation, *Bialystoker Shtern* printed the following article:

> Thirty thousand refugees have recently been sent to labor in Soviet factories,[33] but many refugees still remain in town, some dwelling in private homes, others in [public] dormitories. In order to determine the precise number of refugees remaining in Bialystok, a compulsory registration of refugees, those who are working and those who are not yet working, has been declared. The purpose is to prepare the refugees for work nearby. . . .

The municipality has acted vigorously to solve the refugee problem in Bialystok once and for all.[34]

The local authorities in Bialystok were especially interested in using the masses of refugees to help revitalize the town's economy. According to Hersh Smolar, who was deeply involved in local public activity throughout this period, nearly 11,000 refugees were put to work in Bialystok by January, 1940.[35]

These examples, however few and isolated, suggest that the nature of governmental actions to absorb the refugees depended somewhat on the personalities and motives of the responsible local officials. There is no doubt, however, that the factor of greatest importance in the successful integration of the refugees was the extent of local economic possibilities. Wolhynia is an excellent example of an undeveloped area that nevertheless absorbed numerous refugees with considerable success. An agrarian region, Wolhynia seemed poorly suited to Jewish refugees. Nevertheless, jobs for this community were gradually found. This accomplishment was helped along by several factors:

1. The Polish regime had treated health services with terrible neglect. As soon as the Soviets introduced or expanded their own government health services, there were vacant positions for physicians, pharmacists, other professionals, and the administrative workers that such services required. Integration of refugees was relatively easy: there was no language problem, and thus, too, the patients and the authorities were able to communicate. Wolhynia therefore profited in two ways: it acquired not only an extensive network of clinics and medical institutions but also top-notch physicians who had fled the cities of western Poland.

2. The school system expanded on all levels, including primary and, especially, secondary, post-secondary, and vocational. So many teaching positions opened up that refugee teachers could not fill them all. Thus all refugees with higher education, such as lawyers, were invited to retrain as teachers. Most of the new pedagogues specialized in foreign languages, natural sciences, and mathematics. Refugees who were assigned to Yiddish-language schools, and who had a good command of this language, found the changeover relatively easy.[36] Others attended evening language courses and lectures on the fundamentals of pedagogy. Members of the latter group were ordered to participate in supplementary courses in the 1940 summer vacation.

3. In view of the nature of the Soviet economy, bureaucracies ballooned everywhere. Thus many refugees found jobs as clerks, warehouse attendants, and so on.

4. The industrialization policy and the promotion of artisanship created jobs for refugees with technical training, including some in small enterprises. Some refugee craftsmen joined existing artels; others attempted to set up new ones.[37]

The Wolhynian pattern recurred with greater vigor in more developed and industrialized areas. Throughout the areas, without exception, the burgeoning government apparatus required experts in various fields, especially professionals such as doctors, engineers, teachers, accountants, and economists. Most refugees who possessed these credentials and were interested in working in their places of residence found jobs that suited their skills, more or less. The same was true for mechanics, electricians, printers,[38] and other craftsmen. Because qualified chemists were in notably short supply in eastern Poland, demand for refugees with training in this field was intense; some even advanced rapidly to senior echelons. Trained workers from the textile plants of Lodz and Warsaw also had little trouble finding work in the revitalized textile industry.

Refugee college students who could prove that the war had interrupted their studies were allowed to enroll in the University of Lvov and other institutes of higher learning. All of them were exempt from tuition fees; many were given dormitory housing and stipends that sufficed for a modest standard of living.

RECRUITMENT FOR LABOR IN THE SOVIET INTERIOR

Despite the incomplete (and largely improvised) efforts made to integrate the refugees into the economic and social life of Belorussia and the Ukraine, hundreds of thousands of these individuals remained homeless and jobless, causing a distressing problem. Nor did this general situation change after November, 1939, when the first vigorous official measures meant to stem the flow of refugees were taken.

Also, beginning in late 1939, the refugees were officially offered work in the Soviet interior. Labor recruitment bureaus were opened in several cities in western Belorussia and the Ukraine.[39] Municipal bulletin boards and the local press carried advertisements urging the refugees to sign up. Illustrations and photographs posted in public places and storefront windows depicted factories in the city of Magnitogursk in the Ural Mountains, oranges in the Crimea, peaches in Uzbekistan. Those willing were promised good pay and assured that all their needs would be met.

The refugees regarded the campaign as an invitation to a voyage into the unknown. Nevertheless, despite their jitters, about 40,000 persons registered by March, 1940, according to the local press.[40] Some were sent to the coal mines in Donbas, to foundries in the Ural Mountains, and to miscellaneous factories in the Ivanovo area. Others went to *sovkhozes* (state-owned farms) and kolkhozes in the Ukraine, Kazakhstan, and other localities. A few, mostly highly skilled craftsmen, were "left behind," placed near the major cities of Belorussia and the Ukraine (Kiev, Poltava, Minsk, Vitebsk, Mogilev, and others). The recruitment, orchestrated by high-ranking representatives of the economic ministries in the Ukraine, Belorussia, and the RSFSR, was accompanied by exuberant propaganda in all the media. The newspapers printed dozens of enthusiastic letters sent by refugees who had reached their destinations in the Soviet heartland. *Der Shtern* established a special column called "Unemployed from the Western Districts of the Western Ukraine Tell About Themselves." Here one could read letters from refugees from Poland who had reached workplaces in the USSR. *Bialystoker Shtern* published letters under headlines such as "We Were Warmly Received"; "We Work and Study"; "They Take Care of Everything"; "I Earn 500 Rubles a Month"; "We've Been Reborn"; and "We're Happy."

Testimonies of refugees who accepted the Soviets' job offers, and the memoirs of relatives and acquaintances who stayed in contact with them, suggest that the contents of these letters were quite inconsistent with reality. Shlomo Shtokfish, a furniture maker and veteran Communist from Lublin who had reached Kowel as a refugee, eagerly volunteered for work in the western Ukraine. Once he reached his post—a base where trucks were overhauled—he met with totally different circumstances, as he describes in his memoirs:

When we became sufficiently expert in this craft as to build three truck chassis per month, each of us earned 600 rubles per month, compared with others who worked at covering roofs or building fences, who earned only 250–300 rubles per month. People who had plied typical Jewish trades such as shoemaking, tailoring, hatmaking, and so on, suffered more than anyone else. They had become unskilled workers, were put to grueling toil, and didn't earn enough even to buy food because of the high work quotas they were forced to meet. . . . Because of the war with Finland, food supplies diminished severely and the attitude toward us also became tougher. They stopped treating us as newcomers, instead complaining about why we did not behave as if born into Bolshevism. I received a letter from my younger brother and his wife, who, like me, had volunteered in Kowel. They were sent to the forests near Moscow, where, in the winter, in bitter cold and without warm clothes, they were sent out to cut timber. Many of the workers there got sick, came down with frostbite, or were injured in accidents, and everyone ran away. Things were even worse in Donbas, where special elements of Communists or loyal sympathizers had been sent to the coal mines. At first they worked in the mines with great enthusiasm, performing so excellently that the local miners were displeased. They were increasingly mistreated and harassed by the locals, and their wages, based on work quotas, were withheld. So, after a few weeks of dangerous, grueling labor, most of them quit and fled, denouncing the Soviet Union and its methods with juicy profanity. After all, not only couldn't they afford food with their wages, they were treated like prisoners. Even letters sent to them *poste restante* were delayed.[41]

Many of the volunteers found conditions to which they were not accustomed and that they were not willing to accept: shortages of basic conveniences, especially sanitary needs; difficulty in obtaining basic commodities; and shared dormitories instead of the apartments promised them. This caused endless quarrels with neighbors. It is no wonder that many decided to flee their workplaces and return to their temporary places of residence in western Belorussia. Some returned from the USSR almost naked and barefoot, having had to sell their clothing and footwear to finance their escape and their needs along the way.

Even though the Soviet Union had rather strict laws against leaving one's workplace and domicile, the number of refugees who did this grew from week to week, until it became a mass phenomenon. The Kiev railroad terminal became a gathering point for escapees from various parts of the USSR; the Minsk railroad terminal served a similar function for persons fleeing workplaces in the Ural Mountains. Calling on their experience in pre-war Poland, these people, reinforced by "deserters" from other areas, decided to hold a demonstration: in Minsk, they turned out on Sovetskaya Street in Minsk with their wives and children, seating themselves on the ground across from the government building, near the statue of Lenin.[42] In this case, the authorities refrained from instituting police action against them, instead sending them on to other cities and towns, group by group.

"PASSPORTIZATION" AND ITS CONSEQUENCES

The failure of the volunteer-labor campaign was much more than one of administration and logistics. For many of the refugees, it expressed ideological and economic disillusionment. For the authorities, it branded the refugees as a group of ingrates; after all, they had been given privileges that were ordinarily denied to local residents. The failure did much to sour relations between the authorities and the refugees. The waters became even muddier when the economic policy was toughened. One of the targets here was the black market, in which the refugees were over-represented.

The most significant disruption of relations between the authorities and the refugees (often sealing the fate of the latter) was inspired by the refugees' strong loyalties to their former homes in the Nazi-occupied areas. Although this was a natural, human phenomenon, the Soviets frowned on it, taking the view that "whoever isn't with us is against us."

This is why "passportization"—distribution of Soviet "internal passports" (identification cards)—was so important. It was first done in the western Ukraine and western Belorussia in early 1940, mainly as a routine administrative action stemming from an edict issued by the Supreme Soviet in Moscow on November 29, 1939, that entitled refugees to apply for Soviet citizenship on an individual basis. A large majority of applications were accepted, and the former refugees received new ID cards. Most of these documents contained restrictive clauses denying their holders the right of residence in large cities and frontier areas (defined as anywhere within about 100 kilometers (60 miles) of the international border). Nevertheless, the offer of naturalization was unquestionably an exceptional gesture under the circumstances of the time, when many other countries refused to provide thousands of Jewish refugees with temporary residence permits!

At this time (in early 1940), only some refugees (by no means a majority) chose to effect their naturalization rights. Most of the refugees, especially those with families on the German side, preferred not to decide, thereby leaving themselves the option of obtaining temporary haven. In part, this was owing to their reservations about accepting the new internal passport with its restrictive clauses. However, there was another crucial factor: by accepting the Soviet passport, they would forfeit not only their previous Polish citizenship but the possibility of ever returning and being reunited with the loved ones whom they had left behind. Some refugees, eschewed Soviet citizenship lest they not be allowed to leave the USSR when it became practical. For the moment, those who turned down Soviet citizenship were not penalized; for example, they could live wherever they wished.

The refugees' ferment on the subject of family reunification increased perceptibly at that time. Many were tormented by yearnings for their loved ones and feelings of guilt for having abandoned them. Much of this was caused by the frequent letters and poignant greetings sent from the German side, containing explicit allusions to the fact that the refugees were very eagerly awaited. Some letters were phrased more subtly: "Quiet has returned, the decrees have passed, we are living, working, doing business, making a living. So please try to come home."[43]

Indeed, quite a few Jews crossed back into the German zone, returning to their homes in Warsaw, Lodz, Cracow, and other localities, preferring to die there than to live where they were.[44] Many would-be escapees were apprehended by Soviet border guards; most of them were charged with espionage for the Germans or similar accusations, and were sentenced to prison terms ranging from three to eight years.[45]

Because running the border was so difficult, many refugees sought a legal way to leave. Opportunities to do this were available, because mixed Soviet-German repatriation committees had been set up in a string of cities in the western Ukraine and western Belorussia. Most applicants to these committees were ethnic Germans who had resided in these localities for centuries and wished to cross into the German-controlled zone under the Soviet-German agreement. Although the agreement made no explicit reference to the inclusion of Jews, many applied anyway, aware that the committees were willing (at this time) to register refugees of any stripe.

Thus, lengthy queues of Jews trailed outside the offices of the mixed committees in Bialystok, Lvov, and other cities. Many of these refugees must have been aware of the persecutions of Jews in the Nazi-controlled area, the establishment of ghettos, the yellow-patch requirement, and so on, but each had his or her own reasons for wishing to return. A large majority of them were men who had fled from Warsaw and other towns in central and western Poland in the first days of the war, leaving wives and children behind.

It soon became clear that the mixed committees were discriminating against the Jewish applicants, either by refusing to sign them up or by withholding exit permits. Only a few hundred Jews managed to leave the USSR in this fashion. Even fewer were allowed to cross into the German side,[46] and the large majority sank into disillusionment and despair.

There is no doubt that the Soviet authorities were surprised to find the Jews so eager to cross into the Nazi occupation zone. Nikita Khrushchev, Secretary-General of the Communist Party in the Ukraine and the supreme leader in the western areas of this region, pointedly articulated a typical Soviet response to this phenomenon in his memoirs:

Serov [the head of the NKVD in the Soviet Union] described to me the following spectacle: in front of the office where residents signed up for permission to return to Polish territory tailed lengthy queues. When I inspected them from up close, I was astounded to see that most of the people in the queue were Jews. They tried to bribe the Gestapo men for permission to return to their homes at once.

Khrushchev reacted to this in the following way:

The Gestapo agents delightedly pocketed the bribe and enriched themselves, sending these miserable people straight to the gas chambers. Our hands were tied. They wanted to go home. Perhaps they had left relatives behind in Poland; maybe they simply wanted to return to the place of their birth. They must have known how the Germans treated Jews who fell into their hands.[47]

The Jewish refugees were aware of the bemusement of the authorities, and of the local Jewish population, at the sight of their great fervor to return to the German-occupied zone. When asked, they were wont to reply apologetically: "I'm not going to Germany; I'm going to my family—my wife and children."[48]

The names of refugees who registered with the repatriation committees were presumably forwarded to the internal security agencies, thus marking these individuals as "unreliable elements" in Soviet eyes. After the fact, at least, the Soviets used the passportization campaigns and the registration and repatriation committees as tests of allegiance.

After this stage, they evidently decided to subject all the refugees to a similar but more difficult test, announcing a comprehensive and compulsory refugee census. All refugees who had not yet exchanged their Polish ID cards for Soviet internal passports were ordered to report to one of the militia stations and declare, voluntarily and under their personal signature, either their acceptance of Soviet citizenship or their desire to return home (to the German-occupied zone). No third option was offered. Not surprisingly, the refugees complied "with fallen faces and stooped backs . . . as if signing their own death warrants."[49] Most of the testimonies, community memorial volumes, and personal memoirs that mention this episode suggest that a large majority of Jewish refugees opted to return home, where the Nazi tentacles awaited them. Their major motives were yearnings for family and disillusionment with life under Soviet rule.[50]

INTERNMENT AND DEPORTATION

Ever since the early passportization campaigns in western Belorussia and the western Ukraine, the refugees were deeply apprehensive about the possibility of official Soviet retribution. These fears mounted when the authorities forced them to accept or reject Soviet citizenship. Talk of "white nights"—a euphemism for the mass deportation of refugees to Siberia—became increasingly frequent.[51] To assuage the refugees and deter them from applying for mass repatriation to their (German-occupied) areas of origin, Gershman, secretary of the Communist Party in the Bialystok area, requisitioned a spacious auditorium in this city, convened a large number of refugees, and solemnly promised that the government would never force them to accept Soviet citizenship. "After all," he explained, "the Soviet regime does not need to naturalize you at all." Although there is no way to estimate the number of refugees who rejected Soviet citizenship, it is reasonable to assume that they were a substantial majority.[52] Similarly, one cannot ascertain whether certain groups among the refugees (the young, the old, and so on) were more likely than others to reject citizenship. Nor can one determine whether their decision was affected by such criteria as degree of economic integration into the Soviet system. The only permissible assumption is that family reunification was a very important consideration for refugees of all types.

Perhaps, too, refugees who had found work and secured their livelihood were more inclined to accept Soviet citizenship. This hypothesis appears to be especially valid for refugee students who had been admitted to institutes of higher education, since, as previously stated, young Jews were usually admitted without restrictions and despite their being refugees. When passportization began, they, too, were prodded to make a decision; they were informed in no uncertain terms that the acceptance of Soviet citizenship was a prerequisite for their continued studies. It was equally clear that they had no chance at all of continuing their studies under the Nazis. Moreover, the Soviet schools provided them with a small stipend and housing, thus sheltering them from the difficulties that the other refugees faced.

In and around May, 1940, the local press began to run articles denouncing the refugees for excessive peregrination, shirking regular work, and playing a major role in the black market. The daily *Bialystoker Shtern* bluntly warned the refugees of what might await them in an editorial headlined "Sweep Out the Garbage."[53] Many refugees, terrified, drew the necessary conclusions and quickly moved on to some other town or area.

Immediately after the census, in the six weeks beginning in mid-May, 1940, the internal security services raided urban refugee concentrations and carried out mass arrests. Within a few days, during which some of the detainees were briefly interrogated, nearly all of them were loaded on to freight cars and exiled deep into the Soviet Union. Most were unattached males who lacked Soviet internal passports; within a short time, a similar dragnet was set for their relatives. The climax of this operation, evidently planned and prepared down to the most minute detail far in advance, took place in the last week of June, 1940. These deportations lasted four days and four nights in Lvov, roughly three days in Bialystok, and for shorter periods of time in smaller refugee concentrations. All NKVD units in western Belorussia and the western Ukraine took part, backed by additional detachments from the USSR and numerous Party activists and Soviet functionaries employed by national governmental services.

Trucks and wagons had been requisitioned to transport the deportees to concentration compounds and thence to railway stations. Three-man squads visited the refugees' places of residence and carried out arrests on the basis of the lists with which they had been equipped.[54] Those arrested were given 15 to 20 minutes to pack their belongings, which were rarely allowed to exceed 40 kilograms (88 pounds). Mistreatment and brutality were rampant. Up to 150 persons were packed into railroad cars meant for 30 to 40 only. The cars had neither heating nor toilets. As the trains spent several weeks inching into the Soviet interior, the deportees often were without water and food and suffered the effects of hunger, dehydration, cold, and disease.

Reports of the deportation drove many refugees into hiding. Indeed, some of those listed for exile were not found at home when the agents visited; they were able to return and go on until the next sweep. In quite a few cases, family members who were away when their relatives were herded into the freight cars reported *voluntarily* to the police station or the railroad depot. There were also instances of escape from collection points and train stations, and even from railway cars in mid-journey.[55]

In some cases refugees who possessed Soviet internal passports also were swept up for deportation. This was presumably caused by errors on the lists of exile candidates. The authorities did not always take the trouble to investigate these fateful mistakes. In early July, 1940, for example, "dubious cases" rounded up in Lvov were interned in a former army barracks for sorting and investigation. After spending two weeks sleeping on the floor and surviving on a daily ration of 600 grams (roughly 2.5 ounces) of bread and a bowl of thin soup, nearly all of them were exiled into the Soviet interior like everyone else.[56] Only those who had special occupational skills, such as physicians, were released.

It is worth noting that the indigenous Jewish population manifested its solidarity with the refugees in various conspicuous ways, including offers of substantive assistance. When postcards bearing the exiles' addresses began to arrive, local Jews sent parcels to those whom they knew. Most such assistance was private, originating in acquaintances between local Jews and refugee families before their exile. These contacts usually lasted until the Soviet-German war broke out in June, 1941.

The Soviet authorities disclosed no information about the mass exiling of refugees; official data on the scale of this operation and the national/ethnic composition of the deportees have never been published. The data cited by western Polish sources in this matter are tendentious and excessively general.[57] It is therefore difficult to determine the proportion of Jews among the exiles. However, the testimonies of people who took part in the refugee census and deportations leave no doubt that the proportion of Jews among the deportees was immeasurably higher than their share of the population of western Belorussia and the western Ukraine. So salient was this phenomenon that the deportation of December, 1940, seemed to have been intended specifically for Jews (approximately 200,000 Jews were exiled at that time).[58] Although subsequent events showed that the deportees often were more fortunate than those left behind, the deportation was perceived at the time it occurred as a major disaster and left bitter memories. Many refugees who experienced this ordeal regarded the census and deportations as a carefully crafted trap, with which the Soviets intended to solve the refugee problem as they had solved those of other population groups whom they defined as "enemies of the people."

Whether the deportations had been planned before the internal passport campaign or was a consequence of it, no one disputes that it was the dénouement of a lengthy series of Soviet attempts to solve the refugee problem in a constructive and humane fashion, at least in Soviet terms of the time. As for the mass deportations, there is no doubt that the Soviets were insufficiently concerned with the spiritual well-being and special needs of the Jewish refugees—if they took these factors into account at all.[59]

Lithuania as a Gateway to the Free World

As soon as the Soviets occupied the eastern areas of Poland, Jewish refugees began petitioning the military authorities for exit visas in order to emigrate. At that time, the borders of the USSR were almost hermetically sealed to citizens who wished to go abroad, with the exceptions of government and Party emissaries; for this reason, applications by residents of the annexed areas, were turned down. Aliens who found themselves in Poland when the war broke out, and who had valid passports, did have some possibility of receiving permits to leave the Soviet-ruled areas. Some of these individuals carried documents from Palestine (*Eretz Yisrael*), including nine emissaries of He-haluts and other Zionist movements who had traveled to Warsaw after participating in the August, 1939, Zionist Congress in Geneva. Trapped in the Polish capital on the day that World War II erupted, they attempted to return to Palestine via Romania but were not allowed to enter the latter even though they had British passports and Romanian visas. It took them two months to find their way to Odessa, where they boarded a ship to Palestine.

By this time, the rumor had spread that the Soviets would soon reassign Vilna to the neutral Republic of Lithuania. If the rumors were true, a gate of hope might open, a window through which one might communicate with the rest of the world and even depart for foreign shores.

Author Benzion Benshalom described the nature of this story and its immediate reverberations:

Who spread the word from place to place, from person to person? Who gave it wings? I'll never know. The report spread with the speed of lightning, reaching all cities and towns in the western Ukraine and western Belorussia. From mouth to ear it was transmitted and nevertheless was borne on birds' wings. Flickerings of joy had been ignited. . . . People spent the summer dreaming and making plans. Faces were aglow, eyes ablaze, hearts feverish. Vilna![1]

Within a few days, "Vilna fever" had infected many of the refugees in the Soviet area of Poland, especially those who had previously decided to emigrate by any possible route, including the Romanian border. Now they reversed direction, moving northward on trains, cars, wagons, and even on foot. Local Jews joined the stampede, motivated largely by a quest for ideological fulfillment and fear of persecution (for example, members of Zionist movements, yeshiva students, and pious Jews who sought to sustain their lives of devotion undisturbed). Now they joined the refugee population, albeit voluntarily, and rushed to Vilna by any means available before it would be too late. In fact, the flow did not cease even after the Soviet-Lithuanian "honeymoon" had ended and the borders in this sector, too, were sealed.

THE INGATHERING OF POLISH REFUGEES TO VILNA (OCTOBER, 1939–JUNE 15, 1940)

Although the Soviet transfer of Vilna to Lithuania seemed unusual, this city had known many changes of government and rule in its history. Between September 1, 1939, the day that World War II broke out, and June 22, 1941, when the Germans invaded the USSR, it was a place of refuge, the only one of its kind in Eastern Europe, luring thousands of Jews from the Polish provinces that the Germans and Soviets had appropriated.[2]

A large majority of the Jewish refugees who reached Vilna in the first stage of this period—from the time the war broke out until October 28, 1939, when Vilna was handed over to the Lithuanians—either had been born in Vilna or had relatives and friends there. Vilna was relatively quiet, far from the front, and a springboard to neutral Lithuania in time of need. However, few fled to Vilna for these reasons. The influx of refugees from all parts of Poland (including the eastern provinces) became massive after the imminent transfer of the city to Lithuanian control became known. Since the Romanian border was virtually impermeable, Vilna was the only remaining escape route from occupied Poland.

Some refugees reached Vilna in an organized fashion. Conspicuous among them at the initial stage were groups associated with Zionist youth movements and training communes throughout Poland; by late October, nearly 400 such refugees had settled in Vilna. Approximately 1,000 yeshiva students and their rabbis arrived in a similar way,[3] as did Zionist leaders, activists, and halutsim, and members of the Bund (a socialist, non-Zionist Jewish party that was active mainly in Eastern Europe between the two world wars). Joining them were public figures, industrialists, owners of large businesses, and individuals who had close relations with Polish governing institutions. In all, these refugees embodied much of the political and intellectual elite of Jewish Poland.

The ingathering of Jewish refugees in Vilna during the period of Lithuanian rule reached its peak in late 1939, as shown in the table.[4] Even assuming that some Jewish refugees who reached Vilna and Lithuania did not register with the Refugee Committee,[5] these data are indicative of the movement of refugees at the time. In February, 1940, the Lithuanians and the Soviets tightened border security and stanched the flow. In June, 1940, just before the Red Army overran Lithuania, the influx dwindled to nearly zero. By this time, however, an estimated 14,000 Jewish refugees from Poland had reached the Vilna area,[6] about 70 percent from the German-occupied areas and the rest from the Soviet-controlled zone. Many of the latter were members of the aforementioned organized groups: 2,065 members of the Zionist pioneering movement, which operated in Vilna under an umbrella organization called *Kordinatziya* (a coordinating committee representing He-haluts, Ha-shomer ha-Tsa'ir, and Ha-no'ar ha-Tsiyoni);[7]

TABLE 9.1   Refugees Listed with the Refugee Committee by the Vilna Kehilla

Month		Men	Women	Children	Total
October,	1939	1,446	178	22	1,646
November,	1939	1,310	284	81	1,675
December,	1939	2,274	746	249	3,269
January,	1940	2,385	718	151	3,254
February,	1940	143	59	22	224
March,	1940	78	42	23	143
April,	1940	52	27	15	94
May,	1940	31	19	15	65
Total (%)*		7,719 (74.5)	2,073 (20)	578 (5.5)	10,370 (100)

*Percentage of all refugees.

approximately 1,000 members of Betar, the Irgun Tsva'i Le'umi (IZL), and the Revisionists;[8] 2,440 yeshiva students led by 171 rabbis;[9] 300 members of Left Po'aley Tsiyon;[10] and 561 members of the Bund.[11] Others included 100 writers and journalists with their families, plus many teachers, actors, and artists.

What all these groups had in common was that most settled into organized frameworks in Vilna (at least at first): yeshivas or synagogues, communes or Zionist training collectives, *heymen* (homes) or *internatn* (dormitories). Even those who succeeded in obtaining their own housing (mainly by subleasing) continued to stay in touch with members of their groups, especially when the group patronized certain public kitchens, clubs, or cafes.[12]

In terms of age distribution, gender, and occupational composition, these refugees were unusual. About half of them were between 20 and 30 years of age. By occupation, they had worked in crafts (20 percent), industry and trade (8 percent), liberal professions (7.3 percent), literature and the arts (12.6 percent), agriculture (1.3 percent), and religious functions (1.6 percent); 9.3 percent were unskilled, 22.6 percent were students, and 17.5 percent reported no occupation.[13]

As noted above, a large majority of the Jewish refugees in the Vilna area had left their homes voluntarily. Their motives were threefold: the chance to emigrate to or resettle in Eretz Yisrael, inability to adjust to life in the Soviet areas, and fear of personal persecution. Hardly any intended to settle in Lithuania; they regarded the country as a transit station only.

The response of the Jews of Vilna to the distress of their brethren from Poland was immediate, general, and warm. Their assistance was spontaneous and formal. The kehilla committee and subagencies were the most active in this field; the Va'ad Hayeshivos, led by Rabbi Hayyim Ozer Grodzinski, also offered some of its resources.[14] No less important was the assistance of Lithuanian Jews in brokering and intervening with the authorities on the refugees' behalf. A "special coordination committee," representing all the institutions that provided relief for Jewish refugees, discharged this duty.[15] The committee was headed by Dr. Jacob Robinson, an outstanding lawyer with excellent connections in Lithuanian government circles.

Several worldwide Jewish welfare organizations helped improve the refugees' lot. The most important of them were the American Jewish Joint Distribution Committee (AJJDC) and the Hebrew Immigrant Aid Society (HIAS), which financed most of refugees' basic needs and, in so doing, enriched the Lithuanian state treasury by nearly one million dollars.[16] An agreement was reached for the use of relief moneys from abroad, thus distancing Lithuanian agencies from the internal affairs of the Jewish refugee community. The representatives of these organizations included Moses Beckelman (AJJDC), A.I. Kaizer (Association of Polish Emigrés), and Dr. Samuel Schmidt for the Rescue Committee of the American Union of Orthodox Rabbis (United States and Canada).[17]

The worldwide Jewish relief organizations usually cooperated constructively with local groups such as the Va'ad Hayeshivos, the Kordinatziya, and others. An exception in this sense was the Bund, whose representatives among the refugees wished to avoid the general framework of the Jewish refugee committee. Only after exhausting, protracted negotiations with the AJJDC did they reach an agreement: while they would not join the committee, they would collaborate with it in the distribution of relief funds among their members.[18]

The local Jewish organizations, including the political parties and youth movements, admitted many activists and members of affiliated organizations who arrived from Poland as refugees. In general, Vilna Jewry benefitted from the presence of newly arrived well-known Polish Jews. The finest actors and directors from the Jewish theaters in Poland now performed on local stages; the best authors of Jewish Poland contributed articles, essays, memoirs, and short stories to the Jewish press in Kovno and Vilna. Thus Lithuanian Jewry profited from this encounter with the Polish refugees, if one overlooks the tragic situation that had made it possible.

SOVIET RULE (JUNE 15, 1940–JUNE 22, 1941)

The circumstances and status of the Jewish refugees, especially with respect to their chances of emigrating, changed substantially when the USSR took over Lithuania. The change became more pronounced on August 3, 1940, when Lithuania became a full-fledged Soviet Socialist Republic. By this time, about 3,200 Jewish refugees who had originally settled in Vilna relocated willingly, if not voluntarily, to the outlying cities. Many of them belonged to organized groups, including yeshiva students and their rabbis, most of whom moved to district capitals,[19] and members of the Zionist training collectives, some of whom resettled in agrarian regions.[20]

Jewish refugees from Poland, like the Jews of Lithuania, reacted to the arrival of the Red Army with mixed emotions. Some participated in assemblies organized by Communist activists, in which the people's government was urged to solve their problems, inasmuch as they were victims of the "imperialist war."

In very first week of the Soviet presence, the Ministry of the Interior informed the Jewish and Polish refugee committees that refugees would no longer be resettled in the peripheral towns. The authorities also disclosed that talks were being held concerning the possibility of providing work "for all refugees, thereby making them useful elements rather than burdens on the state or supplicants for philanthropic aid." Indeed, the refugees were informed a few days later that anyone aged 17–60 was entitled to register at the labor exchange, like any jobless citizen.

Although the political upheaval terrified many of the refugees, especially those who had reached Lithuania with intent to emigrate, its impact on day-to-day life was small. Nothing really changed, at least on the surface. The civilian and military authorities seemed to take a more favorable attitude toward the training collectives, and even paid courtesy visits. The general premonition, however, was that the arrangements made under the previous regime, including the autonomy of various refugee groups differentiated by their values or ideologies, would soon be revoked. Indeed, in the summer of 1940, the Jews' political parties, movements, and cultural and social organizations were abolished, followed by the yeshivas and the training communes.[21] The casualties included the World Zionist Organization Palestine Office and the HIAS agency, which had devoted most of their activity to emigration. Surprisingly, the AJJDC representative Moses Beckelman, succeeded in reaching an agreement with the new executive board of the Lithuanian Red Cross. The Red Cross agreed to continue distributing money to the Jewish refugees, more or less along the previous lines, on the assumption that the AJJDC would reimburse it when the flow of American money resumed. This arrangement, which ensured the AJJDC agency in Soviet Lithuania a substantial line of credit, lasted for five months (until early November, 1940); it provided the agency with some 450,000 litas (roughly $45,000), which really came from the state treasury of Soviet Lithuania.[22] The actual distribution of money to the Jewish refugees was left largely in the hands of the AJJDC agency. In early 1941, when everyone understood that the financial transfers from the United States would probably not resume, the Soviet authorities "washed their hands" of the episode and allowed Beckelman to leave Lithuania and the USSR.

It was during this time that the Soviet Lithuanian policy toward the refugees, including exit and naturalization procedures, took shape. On December 30, 1940, the Council of Commissars of Soviet Lithuania announced its decision to naturalize any war refugee from what had been Poland who desired Soviet citizenship. By January 30, 1941, all war refugees in Soviet Lithuania were ordered to register.

There is no doubt that the refugees were somewhat disquieted when they learned of these decisions, which the general and Jewish press rushed to disseminate.[23] Most of them were well acquainted (some by personal experience) with the passportization campaign in the western Ukraine and western Belorussia and with the mass deportations that followed. At roughly that time, also, the authorities decided to shut down the separate national institutions that had cared for the refugees (including all departments and branch offices of the Jewish Refugee Committee),[24] transferring all their assets and equipment to the People's Commissariat for Social Care. With this, the existing frameworks of refugee care were destroyed. A fateful watershed in the attitude of the Soviet Lithuanian authorities toward this public had been crossed. The new rules were two: those wishing to remain were assured treatment no different from that given to non-refugees; the others, especially those who explicitly indicated that they wished to emigrate, would be given separate treatment—with all the risk that this implied in view of past experiences.

ESCAPE FROM LITHUANIA

The refugees now clamored to leave Lithuania at any price. In response, the emigration agencies—chiefly HIAS, HICEM, and the Palestine office (of the World Zionist Organization, which coordinated and supervised the practical aspects of Jewish immigration to Palestine)—stepped up their efforts to find unusual routes to Palestine, America, and other destinations. Complicating their efforts were the labyrinthine, volatile circumstances of wartime Europe. Many institutions and individuals (e.g., the Jewish Agency, Agudath Harabbonim (Union of Orthodox Rabbis) of the United States and Canada, and Rabbi Isaac Herzog in Jerusalem) participated in these efforts at various stages. Of course, the refugees themselves did what they could, singly or in organized groups. The government of Lithuania collaborated to some extent, since it was interested (chiefly for domestic political reasons) in disposing of the refugees, whom it regarded as a foreign, unstable element. In this sense, the governments of independent Lithuania and Soviet Lithuania were virtually indistinguishable; the changeover in the summer of 1940 made almost no difference to the refugees.

During their brief occupation in the autumn of 1939, the Soviets had prohibited all departures of non-residents, including Polish refugees, from Vilna. The situation improved when Vilna was reassigned to sovereign

Lithuania, but the flow of emigrants was slight, mainly because the destination countries refused to admit Jewish refugees. The HIAS office in Vilna reported that 735 entry visas were issued during that time, of which only 543 were used: 406 to Palestine, 46 to British Commonwealth countries, 41 to the United States, 37 to Latin America, and 13 to other destinations. The immigration certificates for Palestine were obtained under an agreement signed by the Palestine Office in Kovno with the Scandinavian airlines and other local agencies, following strenuous negotiations assisted inter alia by the Chief Rabbi of Sweden, Dr. Marcus Ehrenpreis. The emigrants to Palestine were flown from Riga to Stockholm and thence to the Netherlands or Marseilles, where they boarded ships for the run to Haifa. The German invasion of the Netherlands and Belgium on May 10, 1940, shut off one of these escape routes; their occupation of France eliminated the other. This left only one practical way out of Lithuania: via the USSR. This required a Soviet transit visa, a document obtainable only at the end of a lengthy, complicated process.

On June 15, 1940, when the Red Army marched into Lithuania and the first steps toward full sovietization were taken, it seemed as if the Polish refugees' dreams of escape had been dashed. Lithuania, previously a neutral island in the tumult of the war, now fell like a piece of ripe fruit into the hands of the Soviets. The masses of refugees were trapped. Many felt that the Soviet "gilded cage" had been shut totally and irrevocably.[25] The gloomy assessments must have become grimmer still when the new Lithuanian government took the following administrative decisions, which had an immediate impact on refugees who had intended to leave:

1. Institutions and organizations that had handled emigration matters were dissolved.

2. Foreign legations and consulates in Kovno were shut down, and those in Vilna were transferred to Moscow.

3. Distribution of safe-conduct certificates, attesting to the refugees' status as stateless persons, was halted.

Especially noteworthy among the many actions taken at the time was an initiative taken by a group of refugees who headed the Palestine Office in Warsaw, who continued to run this institution in Lithuania under semi-underground conditions.[26] They had managed to contact (by means of a well-known Jewish figure from Kovno, Dr. Elhanan Elkes) the Soviet legate in Lithuania, N. G. Pozdnyakov, and the deputy prime minister of Soviet Lithuania, P. Glovackas. In late June or early July of 1940 (i.e., when refugees who wished to leave the Soviet occupation zone in eastern Poland were being deported to the USSR), Elkes introduced Glovackas to a staffer in the Palestine Office in Warsaw, Dr. Zorach Warhaftig, identifying him as "the representative of the refugees." Following this conversation, Glovackas asked for and received a detailed memorandum on this subject, along with something more important and dangerous: a list of approximately 700 refugees (nearly all of them Zionist halutsim) who wished to emigrate.[27] The memorandum described the Jewish refugees as culturally and politically alien, adding that, in view of their occupational and economic characteristics, it would be difficult for them to integrate into the economy and society of Soviet Lithuania. So why not let them go, especially since some of them already held entry visas to other countries and the cost of their transport was being covered by Jewish organizations abroad?

The participants in this scheme feared that their ruse might backfire ("writing ourselves a ticket to Siberia," as they described it). In August, 1940, however, Moscow answered in the affirmative: any refugee who possessed an entrance visa to any country would be given an "exit permit" (a transit visa through the USSR) as well.[28] At about this time, Ivan Maisky, the Soviet ambassador to London, responded in a similar fashion after Rabbi Isaac Herzog of Jerusalem had asked him to permit the emigration of yeshiva students who had reached Lithuania from Poland as refugees.[29]

Refugees who wished to leave the Soviet Union had to do the following:
1. Prove their refugee status, since only refugees were allowed to go abroad.[30]
2. Present an entrance visa to the destination country and transit visas en route thereto.
3. Obtain a permit to cross the Soviet Union from the People's Commissariat for Internal Affairs (the NKVD).
4. Present the transit visa to Intourist, the Soviet travel agency, which would determine the travel schedule, terms of payment, food and board arrangements on the way, and so on.

As time passed, Intourist played two important roles: brokering between the refugees and other Soviet institutions, and maintaining a liaison between the refugees and the foreign legations in Moscow.

The dream of departure began to come true in early September, 1940, only a few weeks after the Soviet Union had officially annexed Lithuania. It was truly hard to believe: Polish refugees, some of them recently sentenced to prison or banishment to inhospitable lands, were now allowed to cross the country in spacious railway cars, enjoying Intourist services, staying at grand hotels in Moscow, sometimes even venturing on visits to interesting sites in the Soviet capital—all with official sanction. The honeymoon lasted a few months, including ups and downs and protracted stoppages. The frequency of departure was determined mainly by the pace at which transit visas were issued; the route was dictated by the location of the country of destination and the willingness of transit countries to allow the refugees to cross through.

Travel Routes for Polish Refugees

By early 1941, three main travel routes for the emigration of Polish refugees had taken shape:

VILNA-MINSK-MOSCOW-VLADIVOSTOK, AND THENCE BY SHIP TO SOROGA AND KOBE IN JAPAN

This route, used between September, 1940 and April or May, 1941, involved two weeks' travel; it was usually chosen by those whose real (e.g., the United States) or fictitious (e.g., Curacao) destination was in the West. Refugees headed for Palestine also used this route.[31]

In all, 2,500–3,000 persons left Soviet Lithuania by the Moscow-Vladivostok-Japan route.[32] Only a few of them succeeded in reaching the United States; most spent the war in Kobe or Shanghai.

VILNA-MINSK-MOSCOW-KIEV-ODESSA, AND THENCE TO ISTANBUL

This route was taken mainly by those whose destination was Palestine and who had succeeded in obtaining Turkish transit visas. The Turkish authorities agreed to provide Jewish refugees with such visas in early 1941, and there is reason to hypothesize that this act so impressed the Soviet authorities that they, too, resumed the issue of exit permits after a protracted moratorium.

Busy traffic on this route began in December, 1940. From then until March, 1941, the immigration to Palestine of Polish refugees from Soviet Lithuania was at its peak. The refugees set out in groups of 50 (one group per week) until the total reached approximately 700 individuals.[33] Nearly all of these were Zionist halutsim whose names appeared on the list presented to the Soviet authorities. In all, about 2,400 persons, including more than 500 halutsim immigrants to Palestine, left Lithuania on the Moscow-Odessa-Istanbul route.

VILNA-MOSCOW-IRAN-INDIA-TRANSJORDAN

This route to Palestine took shape gradually. Most of the travelers had obtained Iranian transit visas in Moscow, and when they reached Iran they were issued transit visas for Transjordan and India.[34] This option seems to have been used by no more than several hundred refugees.

In all, 4,500–5,000 refugees left Soviet Lithuania by these three routes between September, 1940, and April, 1941, compared with roughly 400 who left autonomous Lithuania between November, 1939, and June, 1940.[35] The departure of refugees from Soviet Lithuania, which began almost surreptitiously, took place with great public fanfare in its final stages. This magnified the impact of its termination in early February, 1941, just before the official deadline for the acceptance of Soviet citizenship by those refugees who desired it.

EMIGRATION OF REFUGEES FROM SOVIET LITHUANIA: CONTRIBUTING FACTORS

The issuance of departure permits for refugees in Lithuania was markedly exceptional behavior for the Soviet regime of the time.[36] Because authentic Soviet sources are inaccessible, one cannot explain this action in unequivocal terms. However, the major factors that contributed to this strange decision and its implementation are known and evident. These factors (which, for all intents and purposes, are one) included the refugees themselves, the institutions and individuals in Lithuania and abroad who helped them, and, most important, the Soviet authorities' own interest in succumbing to the pressure.

In their eagerness to emigrate, the refugees took various and sundry initiatives. A Warsaw writer who resided in Lithuania at the time describes something of the emigration fever that gripped the refugee community:

They ran to the telegraph station and sent a few words to relatives near and far, to friends, or to any address at hand. They literally went to such lengths as to find relatives six feet under. They'd cable someone in Argentina and ask him to cable John Doe in Chicago, asking this John Doe to ask another John Doe in South America about the whereabouts of the former brushmaker from Mezhirichi (Miedzyrzecz) who had previously emigrated from Poland. They assumed that this former brushmaker from Mezhirichi had become a millionaire by now. Now, even if he's a millionaire he's still a relative, and such a relative is surely capable of sending money and even an entry visa, too. Many tried their luck this way, and wonder of wonders: luck often went their way and brought them salvation.[37]

The refugees were extremely resourceful and inventive in their hunt for the documents they needed. Making the rounds of the consulates in Lithuania, they succeeded in obtaining from the Dutch legation a restricted entry visa to the Dutch colony of Curacao, on the basis of which the Japanese consulate agreed to issue transit visas entitling the refugees to cross Japan. In turn, the Soviet authorities provided visa via Siberia and (most important of all) exit visas from the USSR.

Rabbi Isaac Levin of Lvov described the Curacao affair as he and his wife Peppy, *née* Sternheim, from Holland, experienced it during their stay in Lithuania:

We thought to apply to the Dutch consul for an entry permit. . . . The Dutch consul in Kovno, Jan Zwartendijk . . . said he wasn't authorized to issue such a visa. Following his advice, my wife wrote to the Dutch ambassador in Riga. . . . The ambassador answered that, regrettably, it was impossible to give us a visa, to Java or to any other location. . . . She wrote back, telling him the following: If you can't give us an entry permit, perhaps in some other way you could provide us with a letter that we could use to get some kind of permit there. He replied that it was impossible for Java, and even for Sumatra and Curacao, since visas weren't even issued for those places; any entry was at the discretion of the governor. . . . My wife wrote him a letter asking him to state in writing that for Surinam and Curacao one did not need a visa at all. He replied that all he could do was to write that Surinam and Curacao do not require a visa. . . . We realized that this alone would solve our problem. . . . My wife went to the Dutch consul in Kovno, showed him the letter, and asked him to copy what the ambassador had written. Here is what he wrote: "The Dutch consulate in Kovno hereby confirms that entry to Surinam, Curacao, and other Dutch colonies in America does not require an entry visa." . . . This was in Kovno on June 22, 1940. Mr. Zwartendijk [the consul] signed it. My wife went straight to the consul of Japan, and on July 26, 1940, he gave her a transit visa for Surinam via Japan. He signed it. It took a few litas to accomplish this. . . . That was something one had to do in order to obtain an exit visa from Russia.[38]

The continuation of this testimonial, corroborated by other sources, proves that other refugees, especially yeshiva students and their rabbis, made use of the Dutch consul's precedent. In principle, the yeshiva deans were not eager to let their students "put aside their holy labor and go out to hunt for documents and visas." However, after realizing how important it was, some of them (e.g., the head of the Mir Yeshiva) agreed to invest some of their meager funds in the venture, allowing students to travel to Kovno where they might obtain the documents.[39] The heads of other yeshivas (e.g., Kletsk, Kamenets, and Baranovicze) disparaged the "Curacao adventure" and regarded the dummy visas as useless.[40]

The Zionist training collectives and other refugee groups went about this with great vigor. Although the Soviets had dissolved their organizational frameworks, their activity in obtaining emigration documents did not cease. Now, however, the members themselves had to scurry from office to office in Kovno.[41] Awareness of the crucial need to petition the bureaucracies mounted further with the approach of the deadline for the consulates' closure in the fall of 1940. Even after this, with many applicants still in need, desperate refugees "used all kinds of techniques, as one may do when in mortal peril, to forge the genuine visas that were affixed to the documents."[42] Disregarding the obvious danger, local Jews helped to forge documents and deliver them to those in need.[43] Not surprisingly, some of these local Jews attempted to ride the wave of departing refugees,[44] since, as citizens of Lithuania, they were not allowed to depart legally.

Several institutions and individuals took highly appreciated initiatives, working systematically and rather successfully to help refugees leave Lithuania. Especially noteworthy among them was the AJJDC and its agent in Lithuania, Moses Beckelman.[45] One reason for the accomplishments of the AJJDC was the large sums of foreign exchange that it had deposited with the state treasury, as the reader will recall. The local branch of HIAS-ICA (Jewish Colonization Association), headed by the veteran functionary Isaiah Rozovsky, played a similar role in financing travel expenses and the supply of the requisite documents. The chief rabbi of Palestine, Isaac Herzog, acted energetically to alert public opinion and government officials in Palestine and England to the problem of the Polish yeshiva students trapped in Lithuania. His lengthy meeting with the Soviet ambassador to London, Ivan Maisky, in February, 1940, was especially effective, even though the Jewish establishment in England (and even some Palestinian Jewish leaders) expressed misgivings about contact with the Soviets in this sensitive regard.[46]

Until Lithuania was sovietized, the Palestine Office in Kovno handled most of the transport needs of refugees who held Palestine immigration certificates. When this office was closed, the Jewish Agency and its agent in Istanbul, Chaim Barlas, took over. After a series of measures, the Jewish Agency mission persuaded the government of Turkey to allow Jewish refugees to cross through, as long as these were foreign nationals "who were subject to persecution in their countries of origin." The mission also conducted protracted and complex negotiations with the Soviets, which resulted in an agreement with Intourist for the transport of emigrants via Moscow and Odessa to Istanbul, and thence, using another ship, to Haifa. This allowed the flow of refugees from Soviet Lithuania to resume in early December, 1940.[47]

Other activists on behalf of Jewish refugees from Lithuania on their way to Palestine included the chief rabbi of Sweden, Dr. Marcus Ehrenpreis; the chief rabbi of Egypt, Nahum Effendi; businessman Joshua Pollak; and Simeon Brodie in Istanbul.[48]

Two American Jewish organizations deserve special mention for their accomplishments in obtaining entry visas to the United States. One was the Jewish Labor Committee under Jacob Pat. This committee, with the help of American trade unions, attempted to persuade President Roosevelt to instruct the American legate in Lithuania to issue "rescue visas" for refugees whom it recommended, chiefly Bund activists. The other was Va'ad ha-Hatsala (Rescue Committee), an agency of the Agudath Harabbonim (Union of Orthodox Rabbis of the United States and Canada), headed by Rabbi Eliezer Silver. This committee, established in November, 1939, in an emergency conference of Orthodox rabbis, managed to raise $140,000 in about half a year. The funds were pledged to relief for refugee yeshiva students and rabbis in Lithuania. The committee also recruited well-known personalities and senior officials, who helped to obtain hundreds of entry visas to the United States.[49] In the fall of 1940, Agudath Israel, in concert with Keren Hatorah, established a relief organization called Ahi-Ezer, also devoted to the rescue of yeshiva students and rabbis in Lithuania.[50]

Although these initiatives were quite important in terms of Jewish solidarity, there is no denying that their results were meager. One reason for this was lack of coordination among the sponsoring groups, in view of the worldwide state of war.[51]

The relatively large outflux of emigrants via the USSR and Japan (and, to a lesser degree, via Turkey) became possible, as stated, because several consulates in Kovno provided thousands of entry permits and transit visas relatively smoothly—just as the Soviet authorities were pressuring them to quit the city. The British consul, named Gent, not only agreed to regard a report concerning the paving of a road from the USSR to the Turkish border as sufficient reason to issue exit visas to Palestine, but also agreed to hire members of the Palestine Office in Warsaw to draw up the necessary documents. In addition to the 250 Palestine visas stamped on the refugees' passports, the consulate provided about 550 "notification letters"[52] for refugees who lacked passports. Gent also was willing to give the Palestine Office people blank sheets of letterhead, imprinted prominently with the British crown, so that they might produce additional "notification letters" when necessary. This sympathetic attitude, above and beyond the convention among British diplomats at the time, is especially striking in view of the consistent refusal of the British legation in Moscow to provide Jewish refugees in Lithuania with entrance visas for Palestine.

The honorary consul of the Netherlands in Kovno provided special permits facilitating entry to Curacao, Surinam, and the other Dutch islands in the Caribbean. The price charged was symbolic. The consul took this action with the knowledge of the Dutch *charge d'affaires* accredited to the Baltic countries, F. N. de Decker, who was seated in Riga. When the Dutch consulate in Kovno was forced to close, refugees were provided with another 1,000 permits of this kind by the Dutch consul-general in Stockholm, A. M. De Jong.[53] When the Soviets insisted that these permits be forwarded directly to Intourist, De Jong acceded but suggested ways of making the transfer more efficient, even though it entailed additional work. He discharged this voluntary duty assiduously, with a sincere desire to help the refugees, of whose plight he was aware first-hand. In all, the Dutch consuls in Kovno and Stockholm issued 2,500 permits.[54]

Another diplomat in Kovno who displayed a special attitude toward the refugees was the Japanese consul, S. Sugihara. Even though he almost certainly knew that the Dutch visas to Curacao and Surinam were contrived, he agreed, for the negligible sum of two litas (20 cents), to issue Japanese transit permits based on them. Once the refugees obtained this document, the Soviet authorities were willing to grant them exit permits. It is no wonder that the refugee community held this man in very high esteem. In his memoirs, Sugihara described what he did and why:

Early one morning in August, 1940, there was an unusual commotion in the street next to the consulate. I peered out of my apartment window and saw that a crowd of refugees had gathered along the fence. These were people who had fled from various localities in Poland that already faced the menace of Nazi invasion. The number of refugees in the street grew and grew. Tears in their eyes, they begged for Japanese transit permits so they could reach other continents via Japan. When asked about their final destination, most indicated Latin America, the United States, or Palestine. The refugees—men, women, and children—were deathly tired and spent. It was not clear to me where they succeeded in sleeping those days: at the train station or simply outdoors in the unfamiliar city. I made inquiries with the

Soviet consulate about obtaining Soviet visas so the refugees might cross the USSR to Japan. The consulate workers explained to me that they were willing to provide these transit permits on condition that the refugees obtain the Japanese visas first. As all of this was taking place, I already knew that my term of service in Kovno would end in another month or so. In the meantime, the number of refugees requesting Japanese visas continued to grow. On August 10 or thereabouts, I decided there was no point in further contacts with Tokyo. On August 11 I decided, on my own counsel and full responsibility, to distribute Japanese transit visas to the refugees, irrespective of whether or not this or that individual possessed or lacked the requisite documents.[55]

After the war, Yad Vashem, the Holocaust Martyrs' and Heroes' Remembrance Authority, awarded the three aforementioned consuls the title *Righteous Gentile*—for good reason.

As important as the actions of the foreign consuls and agencies were, the ultimate decisions were taken by the Soviet authorities for considerations of their own. One presumes that whenever these actions coincided with Soviet local and global interests, the Soviets were more inclined to respond, albeit with controlled, small steps. Often measures taken by the Soviet authorities were devoid of logical consistency and hardly seemed to serve even Soviet interests efficiently. For example, the authorities did not forbid contact by refugees with foreign countries for the purpose of expediting their departure;[56] however, numerous Soviet functionaries tried to persuade the refugees, dangling various promises and temptations, to stay put.[57] At times, the security services summoned refugees who already held exit permits issued by these institutions, subjected them to painstaking interrogation, and in some cases, incarcerated them for days on end.[58]

Procedures for the issuance of exit permits were also inconsistent. In some cases, would-be emigrants were summoned personally to the NKVD offices, where they were given their permits with relative alacrity, enduring only a brief, gentle, perfunctory interrogation. In other cases, however, refugees were summoned repeatedly for many weeks, "including orders to report for talks at two or three o'clock in the morning." Sometimes refugees waited outside for eight, nine, or ten hours until an NKVD officer invited them in. If they were not present at that very moment, they would have to wait several weeks for a new appointment. Applicants for exit permits were "told 'yes' and then 'no'; then they would be arrested."[59] At first, they had to pay in dollars for part of their train fare; when the fares went up considerably, most of the increase was the foreign-currency increment. Since the possession of foreign currency was a major offense, the refugees had to resort to the black market, where the exchange rate spiraled with dizzying speed in response to the brisk demand. When refugees asked the Soviet clerks in astonishment: "How? Aren't dollars prohibited in this country?" they were told, "In this office, everything's done in dollars."[60]

Would-be emigrants had to fill out lengthy and detailed questionnaires and produce a curriculum vitae. The Soviet bureaucrats who dealt with the refugees' "autobiographies" knew full well that they were a well-crafted hodgepodge of facts and half-facts. The authors' goal was to strike a delicate balance, providing neither a reason nor a pretext for rejection while avoiding falsehood and the complications that this would cause. Nevertheless, the officials insisted on receiving these documents.

"Why did the Soviet government need the autobiographies of the merchants of Warsaw, Bialystok, and Lodz?" one of the refugees asked in his memoirs. "One reason for sure: to laugh. They must have laughed when they read the new poems by the new poets. There was plenty there to laugh about."[61]

These contradictions and oddities in official practices continued almost until the end of the nearly year-long honeymoon. The cognoscenti among the refugees attributed this jumble of contradictions to "irregularities for which the Soviet ministries at the time were noted," and for which various explanations were offered.[62] One may, of course, ascribe these contradictions to Soviet ineptitude and inflexibility in handling the refugees' departure. After all, the operation, in its substance and magnitude, was highly exceptional in the USSR at the time. In other words, even after the central government decided to allow Polish refugees in Soviet Lithuania to leave, the bureaucracies found the decision hard to digest.

Because Soviet historiography says almost nothing about this unprecedented decision to allow thousands of persons to leave the country, it is difficult to know how and why the decision was made. One may surmise that one consideration was the possibility of exploiting the exodus from Soviet Lithuania to plant Soviet spies in the "capitalist" world.[63] The Soblen affair (described later) supports this inference, and the memoirs of erstwhile refugees suggest even more strongly that it was true. Many refugees in Lithuania who requested exit permits were asked in their interrogations "what they could do for the USSR after reaching their destinations."[64] The Soviet intelligence services even tried to recruit local Jews who attempted to slip into the emigration wave. For example, the commissioner of Betar in Lithuania, Joseph Glazman, was offered a unique political/intelligence deal in which he was asked, in essence, to orchestrate military collaboration between the IZL (Irgun Zva'i/Tsva'i Leumi—Etzel, or "the Irgun") and the major Soviet security agencies, in view of the anticipated Soviet-German war.[65]

The Soblen affair strongly suggests that the intelligence consideration made the senior Soviet echelon more willing than it would otherwise have been to allow the Polish refugees to leave Soviet Lithuania. However, additional considerations cannot be ruled out. There are indications that well-known and responsible people among the refugees in Lithuania were exploited, directly or indirectly, for Soviet propaganda purposes. It is surely no coincidence that several famous rabbis, after they had emigrated, praised the Soviet attitude toward the Jews. Their remarks were published in the Jewish press. An example is the Modzhitzer rebbe (head of the hasidic court in Modzhitz) after he reached the United States.[66] The Soviet authorities are known to have told departing refugees that "a Jew who leaves Russia can also be a goodwill ambassador," adding that "something bad might happen to other Jews about to leave" if the truth about Soviet life became widely known.[67]

Another factor was the concern of institutions and individuals abroad. Their strong interest in the refugees and their fate magnified the importance of the refugee community among officials who pondered the implications of this issue for international relations and world public opinion. The diplomatic legations in Lithuania, which apprised foreign agencies on developments in Lithuania and the fate of the refugees in particular, were especially important in this sense.

Moreover, the special status of the Lithuanian SSR vis-à-vis the Soviet-occupied areas of Poland and Romania, coupled with the conciliatory stance of the Communist Party of Lithuania toward the Polish element in the country, certainly affected the considerations.

Still another factor, beyond all doubt, was the lesson learned from the abortive effort to "productivize" Polish refugees in western Belorussia and the western Ukraine. The consensus in the Soviet establishment was that most of the refugees were non-productive and would be difficult to integrate; moreover, they were liable to cause political, economic, and value ferment. The refugees shared this view and expressed it in official memoranda, depositions, and personal talks with Soviet officials. Practically speaking, this attitude may have inspired officials to attempt to dispose of the refugees, either by mass exile to Siberia (as was done in Belorussia and the Ukraine, causing no small detriment to the image of the Soviet regime) or by allowing them to emigrate, an act from which the Soviets might benefit in the economic, propaganda, and security senses.

By providing some refugees with exit permits, the authorities were able, with no unnecessary dislocations, to filter out those who wished to leave the USSR. The refugees were informed of the possibility of Soviet naturalization only at the end of the period reserved for exit permit requests (February, 1941). This prevented the recurrence in Soviet Lithuania of a phenomenon that had caused much embarrassment in the western Ukraine and Belorussia: the nearly total refusal of Polish refugees to accept Soviet citizenship, lest this deprive them of their chance to leave. From the refugees' standpoint, it eventually became clear that the choice of Lithuania as a refuge and a gateway for emigration was largely correct.

AFTERWORD: THE SOBLEN BROTHERS AFFAIR

Robert (Reuben Leib, born 1900) Sobolevich and his younger brother Jacques (Jacob Abraham, born 1903) were the sons of an affluent industrialist, Samuel Abba Sobolevich, from the southern Lithuanian town of Vilkaviskis. They had another brother (Berl or Boris) and two married sisters. Robert and Jacques became active in the Communist Party in Lithuania in 1919[68] and were arrested on several occasions for participating in demonstrations and similar activities. In the 1930s, they left the country to study. Robert earned a Ph.D. in psychology at the University of Bern and returned to Lithuania with his wife Dina (née Volberg), who held a degree in medicine. In the late 1930s, he opened a private practice in Kovno, where he worked until 1941. It was widely rumored that he had been a member of a Trotskyist cell.[69] Jacques, who studied economics and law at the University of Leipzig and the Sorbonne, went to Moscow in the mid-1930s and, according to rumor, was appointed editor of a Comintern journal.

When the Soviets tightened their grip on Lithuania at the beginning of World War II, Jacques arrived from Moscow and Robert paid a brief visit to Moscow. In early 1941, the Jews of Kovno were astonished to learn that the entire Sobolevich family, including Robert and Jacques, along with several family friends (nearly 20 persons in all) had been allowed to leave the USSR and emigrate to the United States via Japan.[70]

It was baffling. Not only were they local Jews and not refugees; they were public figures, well-known, and affluent, the kind of people whom the authorities loved to harass. The next rumor resolved the puzzle: their departure had been brokered by the Soviet security services.[71]

The group traveled to Vladivostok via Vilna and Moscow, continuing from there to Kobe and Shanghai. From Shanghai they boarded an American ship and reached San Francisco on October 20, 1941. At this point the group broke up, some settling in New York, others in Boston and Montreal. The two brothers changed their names to Soblen, and Jacques went into the brush business. In 1947, both brothers received American citizenship. Dr. Robert Soblen started a private practice that consumed most of his time; he and his wife also worked for a government hospital in Rockland County, New York.

In 1957, after protracted FBI surveillance, Jacques and his wife Mira were arrested on charges of military espionage for the USSR. According to the prosecution, Jacques had taken over from Vasily Zvilin, the Soviets' head spy in America and the third secretary in the Soviet Embassy. Jacques was sentenced to seven and one-half years in prison, and Mira to five and one-half years. Robert was arrested on similar charges about four years later. Convicted of having forwarded important information to the Soviet Union, he was sentenced to life imprisonment. While out on bail, however, he fled to Israel, was extradited, and committed suicide on the aircraft returning him to the United States. In the course of their trials, it was found that Laurenti Beria, chief of the Soviet security services, had singled them out for intelligence work in the United States. It seems that Beria had also devised a cover for the "moles" by building around the brothers a group including parents, siblings, other relatives, and friends, some of them well-known public figures. The ruse worked beautifully, one reason being that the Sobolevich family had acquired American entry visas through the intervention of a relative with clout in U.S. government circles.[72]

There is no way of knowing how many agents the Soviets planted in the controlled outflux of Polish refugees from Soviet Lithuania. One may presume, however, that the Soblen cell was not *sui generis* and that some of its counterparts have never been uncovered.

10

The Encounter with Soviet Jewry

Soviet Jewry was shocked and silenced by the Ribbentrop-Molotov pact. Especially jolted were those who, for an entire generation, had taken the Soviets' anti-Fascist indoctrination at face value. The bizarre Soviet-German alliance plunged these people into a grave crisis of values. For some of them, the rapprochement weakened their identification with the Soviet regime and put their ideological and moral allegiance to the test.

Needless to say, Jews in the annexed areas, found it difficult to acquiesce to the new reality—namely, that the Soviet state, which had saved them from the menace of Nazi occupation, had taken a neutral if not friendly posture toward Hitler's Germany. However, even they were too stunned by the transformation that had overtaken their lives, and too preoccupied with adjusting to their new circumstances, to respond.

It was against this background that the two Jewries, that in the annexed areas and that in the Soviet Union proper, in Eastern Europe, resumed direct contact after many years of separation. True to the nature of the Soviet regime and its sensitivity to the issue of Jewish nationality, the Soviet press and literature of the time had little to say about the reunion. To obtain a more comprehensive picture, one must rely largely on memoirs, even though nearly all literature of this type was written by people from the annexed areas who were hardly objective, especially in political and personal matters. These memoirs, coupled with the Soviet Jewish press and literature of the time, provide copious information on Jewish cultural life in the annexed areas. The vital importance of these sources for an understanding of relations between the two Jewish communities is discussed at greater length at the end of this chapter.

SOCIAL RELATIONS

Exploratory contacts began at the very start of the annexation process, when the experience was an intriguing and exciting novelty for both sides. These feelers were absolutely spontaneous, initiated mainly by Jewish soldiers in Red Army units that entered the Jewish-populated parts of eastern Poland. For local Jews, the spectacle of Jews in officers' uniform was unforgettable. Similarly, the sight of the Jews of Janow, greeting the Red Army in their prayer shawls, was something that had many of the Jewish-born Soviet troops had certainly never before beheld.[1] For the latter, the encounter with the authentic Jewish community of Poland reinforced pride and fraternity. Traditional Jewish life had been so diluted in the USSR as to have become a distant memory, as Soviet Jews were wont to admit nostalgically:

On Passover of 1940, I had an opportunity in Bialystok to converse with a Soviet officer, D. On the eve of the festival, this Jew went into the synagogue to see, as he said, "what's going on there, in a house that's so brightly illuminated." He was surprised to hear that this was the eve of Passover, that Jews gathered here to pray and celebrate the festival of freedom. For 20 years he had not even known when this holiday fell.

A Jewish Red Army officer, Hirsh Shvartzman, reached the Bessarabian town of Orhei (Orgeyev) with the 266th Artillery Brigade in August, 1940. There he conversed with local Jewish intellectuals, visited them in their homes, and even lived with them for some time. The relationship that developed, however, was not altogether smooth:

My first landlord, Joseph Pagis, was a nice man. I continued to visit him often even after I had moved out. On one of my visits, I found him very nervous and upset. He spoke to me sharply: "You'd better not talk too much." I didn't understand what he meant, but since I thought of him very highly, I did not respond. Then he hinted to me that the NKGB (the secret police) had summoned him for an interrogation, in which one of the subjects discussed was me. Another case: On May 1, 1941, after participating in a military parade in the morning, I visited several families. Two or three days later the NKGB agent in our brigade confronted me, describing in detail where I had been on the festival days, whom I had met, and even what I had spoken about. Since I was a loyal Communist at the time, I had neither disclosed military secrets nor said anything derogatory about the regime, so nothing happened to me. But I realized then that quite a few of my "friends" were undercover agents for the NKGB. . . .

Our brigade had three or four Jewish officers. We visited the synagogue together several times. We spent only a short time there; we did not pray or take part in any ritual. At the time, I felt no need for this. For a Red Army officer, it was a dangerous thing to do.

Once or twice I heard radio broadcasts from Jerusalem while visiting my landlord, Dr. Markovitz. . . . Although I was a loyal Communist at the time, as I've said, I was very sympathetic toward Zionism, Palestine, and the Hebrew language. Once I bought something in a shop—a razor, I think—that was made in Palestine. The label had a few Hebrew words on it. I kept that label for almost two years. I lost it during the war.[2]

The two Jewries shared the Yiddish language, with which Soviet Jewry articulated its yearning for Jewish life. Here and there, Soviet Jews formed relations with Jews from other countries who had found themselves in the USSR inadvertently. A Palestine emissary who was allowed to return to Palestine via the USSR described the eagerness of many Soviet Jews to stress the value of their labors in the USSR. Repeatedly and with emphasis, they insisted that Soviet Jews lived well, lacked nothing, enjoyed full opportunities, and suffered no discrimination. The impression they conveyed was that they were truly satisfied.

Many Soviet Jews were sent west to the annexed areas as administrative and economic clerks in the civil and military bureaucracies. Trained by and immersed in the Soviet system, they were almost totally ignorant of Jewish values. Author Moshe Grosman described an encounter with three such Jews from Homel (Gomel), Mogilev, and Vitebsk:

They run the administrative institutions in Bialystok. They go to their headquarters to submit reports. The three of them knew each other previously. Now they talk about their businesses, about women, about food. They set up their meal in mid-conversation. They place a suitcase on their knees, spread a tablecloth over it, and lay their food on it. The meal begins with a jigger of schnapps. . . . The three of them look almost alike: military khaki shirts, wide leather belts, gleaming boots, everything tailored to fit. Their faces are satisfied, radiating pleasure. Their features are crude, the backs of their necks fat and red, shaven silky-smooth, with the customary straight line. As they talk, drink, and gorge themselves, they turn to a Jew from Slonim who sits across from them, his face wreathed in a beard and sidelocks, and invite him to join the feast: "Old man, would you like to help yourself to a piece of ham? It really fills you up!" As they say this, they burst into the rude and callous laughter of drunkards. The Jew from Slonim, unwilling to go down to defeat, answers sharply: "Once the Jews of Russia were dear Jews; they produced renowned, respectable people. Today's Russian Jews are totally different." One of the three replies: "Don't worry, rabbi. Today too, some of us Jews are great and important people; there are more of us now than in the past! . . . What used to be is forever dead and gone." . . . He points to the muscles of his arms. Then, as if to justify himself, his comrade adds: "Some of us are religious, too. For example, my mother lights candles every Friday night. On Passover she eats only matsa [unleavened bread], and on Yom Kippur she fasts and attends synagogue."

Like all Soviet citizens from the east who flooded the annexed areas, the Jews, too, snapped up all the goods and commodities that they could find. Their clothing was shabby and threadbare, and their demand for food products knew no bounds. Many were assigned key positions and ruled with a high hand. The locals came to resent the arrogant, contemptuous "easterners," who habitually dissembled about the high standard of living in the USSR (*U vsyo nas yest!*—We've got everything!). In day-to-day contact, however, the local Jews frequently saw direct and implied indications of what the "easterners" truly felt.

Many relatives of Jews in the annexed areas had remained in Soviet territory after World War I, and contact with them had been lost. The new situation presented an opportunity to restore family ties. The first to experience this were the Soviet soldiers of Jewish origin. A Palestinian Jew who found himself in Vilna at the time described the poignancy of these family reunifications in his diary:

A Vilna-born Jewish soldier in the Soviet army made inquiries about his sister, whom he had not seen in 25 years. In the usual way, a group of curious onlookers formed around each soldier, and *a fortiori* around each Jewish soldier. One member of the group that gathered around him was a Jew who remembered the person in question at once, for his sister had lived in the same court. He ran straight home and brought her to her brother. . . . Hundreds of people stood around them, sharing their delight. I saw them embracing: she, a Jewish woman well along in years, and he, a Red soldier wearing a gray jacket and a steel helmet. . . . How many brothers and sisters, acquaintances and friends met during those days in Vilna?[3]

Such encounters fueled hopes and triggered a wave of advertisements in the "Searching For" departments of the Jewish newspapers. The actual results of the ads were scanty, either because the newspapers failed to reach the relatives in the Soviet Union, or because the relatives were no longer alive or refused to identify themselves. Fear of contact with "foreigners" was so rampant in the USSR that Jews often were reluctant to restore bygone family relationships.

Personal letters sent to relatives at old addresses in Russia were sometimes answered in the grammatical third person, the respondents begging to be left alone. When replies from relatives in the USSR had patriotic significance of some kind, the newspapers printed them.[4]

Owing to the restrictions on private travel in the Soviet Union, as well as between the USSR and the areas across the old border, there were few visitors from the east. One of them was General Jacob Shmuskevich, a hero of the Spanish Civil War and the Russo-Japanese War. After 21 years away from his native Lithuania, he landed in his home town of Rakishok (Rokoskis) in a military aircraft in October, 1940. A waiting limousine then chauffeured him to the home of his father, the tailor Velvel Shmuskevitz. Even though his four-day visit was defined as purely private and familial, he was given a festive and emotive reception in the town hall. As word of the arrival of "our Yankl" reverberated, not only the Jews of Rakishok but also many Jews throughout Lithuania treated the visit as a source of pride, pleasure, and satisfaction.[5]

Travel restrictions also kept all but a few Jews in the annexed areas from meeting Soviet relatives in their places of residence. The few exceptions in the early annexation period usually were refugees who had volunteered for labor in the Donbas region and other locations in the USSR. One of these individuals, finding himself in the capital of the Ukraine, related:

We began to acquire Jewish friends. Kiev was a Jewish city with a large, well-stocked Jewish library, a daily newspaper, and a Jewish theater where the Jewish play *Bar Kokhba* was being staged at the time. Even though the theater was packed with Jewish subscribers, the manager was kind enough to let us in and offer us seats brought in especially for us. We watched the grand production, which followed the original text with the exception of a few revolutionary clichés thrown in. . . . A young Jewish couple invited us to their home to celebrate the October Revolution, even though their parents, who lived with them, were upset with them for having brought a foreigner into their home. I had a rather good meal there and washed it down with Soviet champagne. . . . The hosts proved to be good people and warm Jews . . . and I have visited them regularly ever since.[6]

Jews in the annexed areas who visited the Soviet interior in official capacity described similar encounters in their memoirs.

CULTURAL RELATIONS

Education and culture were the fields in which relations between Soviet Jews and their counterparts in the annexed areas were most extensive and fruitful, since these domains were so widely diffused. Jewish cultural and educational activity, as previously stated, had been declining in the USSR in the late 1930s, whereas in the annexed areas it was officially promoted and assisted. Thus, Soviet Jewish activists and creative artists regarded the new territories as a new, promising arena in which to operate. About a week after the Red Army entered the western Ukraine and western Belorussia, Jewish writers assembled in Kiev to discuss the need to "create mass political literature and *belles lettres* in Yiddish for the masses in the western Ukraine, all in the near future."[7] Participants in this consultation expressed a wish to prepare a set of Yiddish-language pamphlets on Soviet life. (According to reports, sizable quantities of books, including the works of Lenin, had already been sent there.) The Moscow Writers' Club held a similar discussion at roughly the same time, after its members were shown a report by Itzik Fefer and Fayvl Sito on their visits to western Belorussia.

The Soviet Union had three Jewish Yiddish-language daily papers and four monthly journals at the time. In the annexed areas, four dailies and two literary biweeklies (*Shtraln* in Kovno and *Ufboi* in Riga) appeared throughout this period, albeit in various metamorphoses. The newspapers in the annexed areas published poems and short stories by Soviet authors such as Itzik Fefer, Peretz Markish, Shmuel Rassin, Dovid Hofstein, Leib Kvitko, Feivel Sito, and Ziama Tellesin. Authors from the annexed areas were allowed to publish in the Soviet journals; 16 of them even had works published by Soviet publishers, along with introductions by "veteran" Soviet Jewish writers (see pp. 132–139).

Important personalities in Soviet Jewish literary and artistic circles tried to explain their interest in and relations with their colleagues in the annexed areas as a matter of party and state interest. One of them was the author Dovid Bergelson. At a conference of authors and artists in Minsk in May, 1941, several months after the annexation, Bergelson stated:

Now that we've have acquired a large number of new Yiddish readers, we must act with alacrity to help the liberated masses rehabilitate themselves and integrate into the new socialist life. The Soviet regime and the Party have entrusted us with an important, weighty task, and we are dutybound to discharge it faithfully. Soviet Russia has enriched itself with a group of talented Yiddish-language authors and poets who have arrived with the liberated masses. The mission of papers and the journals is to help these new writers understand the new life and support it in their creative endeavors.[8]

Jews from the east, nearly all of them former teachers discharged from the Soviet Yiddish educational system in the Ukraine and Belorussia in the late 1930s, were sent to help sovietize the education system in the annexed areas. This gave them new opportunities for action. Within the new framework, these teachers, some newly appointed as school principals, imposed Soviet ideology on the faculty and the student body. A few of them, influenced by the approach taken by the *Yevsektsia* (the Jewish section of the Communist Party, active in the USSR between 1918 and 1930), spearheaded the campaign against Hebrew—a "reactionary language, unfit for use." Principals and teachers brought in from the Ukraine wielded two kinds of authority: professional and political.

Part of the sovietization of the educational system was the "adjustment" of textbooks in view of the new subject matter. This triggered an abrupt upturn in the fortunes of Yiddish-language publishers and printers in the Soviet Union. Among Jewish culture activists in Moscow, however, the sudden demand for Yiddish-language books (textbooks and others) evidently touched a nerve. Local Jewish authors, frustrated by the steady decline of Jewish education in the USSR, were both energized and traumatized by the new developments. Golde Frades, a veteran Moscow writer for the Soviet Jewish dailies, commented:

It's been a long time since the *Der Emes* publishing house has held such interesting meetings. . . . The detailed, serious, and painstaking debate showed the high degree of responsibility that the purveyors of culture in Moscow felt for the quality of Jewish schools.[9]

A visit to Moscow in the summer of 1940 (after nationalization) by the director of a large Jewish press in Kovno resulted in genuine achievements. First, the director made a courtesy call at the *Der Emes* publishing house and was warmly received by its manager, Leib Strongin, and several important Jewish authors. When the hosts expressed avid interest in events in Lithuania, especially Jewish life, the visitor realized that they wished to publish their works and those of their comrades at the printing presses in Lithuania, because of their technical capabilities and high-quality paper. During the visit, both parties agreed to publish Soviet *belles lettres* and children's literature in Lithuania; indeed, Strongin reached Lithuania a short time later with an order so large as to eliminate unemployment among Jewish printing workers.[10]

Another area of mutually advantageous relations between Jews in the USSR and the annexed areas was the theater. The Soviet Jewish theater still retained much of its vitality at the time, including some of the momentum of its growth years. As already noted, there were ten active governmental Jewish theaters in the USSR at the time that the Red Army entered eastern Poland. The authorities viewed the Jewish theater favorably, since theater was considered an especially important medium of indoctrination. Thus the authorities apprised the Jewish actors in the areas of the new line, with a measure of arm-twisting thrown in.

Of the 36 plays by Jewish playwrights performed in these areas, 13 were written by Soviet Jews. An example is P. Markish's *The Ovadis Family.* "By means of this work," the press asserted, "the Jews of the western Ukraine have seen for the first time healthy Jews such as these, young Jews clutching weapons, something that can happen only under Soviet rule."

Soviet Jewish directors were invited to visit the western areas and take part in Jewish theatrical production there. Soviet Jewish actors joined the casts after receiving invitations to perform in the Jewish theaters in the annexed areas. In the middle of 1940, a group of actors from Dniepropetrovsk joined the Jewish governmental theater in Lvov after the cast had quit and the Yiddish theater in Dniepropetrovsk was shut down. Initially, there was perceptible tension between the newcomers from Russia and the local actors. One reason was that the two groups held different beliefs about the substance of Jewish theater; the authorities seemed to think that the importation of Soviet Jewish thespians would accelerate the sovietization of the Jewish theater in Lvov.[11] To make sure of this, theater directors from the Soviet Union were installed alongside Soviet Jewish playwrights, directors, and actors. Management of the Jewish governmental theater in Lvov was transferred from Ida Kaminska to people from the "other side," i.e., the Soviet side. The last manager of this theater was Jacob Zaykin, a Soviet Jew who held this position until the war with Germany broke out. A member of the Communist Party, Zaykin was elected to the town council of Lvov in late 1940. Soviet Jewish stage director B. Z. Serebrenyak was installed as the artistic director of the municipal Jewish governmental theater of Tarnopol. Soviet Jewish actor Y. Rokitin took over the management of the Jewish governmental theater in Bialystok; a Jew from Minsk named Shuster was named the administrative director.

In addition to this importation of theatrical talent from the east, Soviet troupes from the eastern Ukraine were sent on performing tours of the western areas. For example, the Jewish theater in Kiev presented Goldfaden's *Zvey kunyleml* ("two eccentrics") and *Bar Kokhba* in Czernowitz in the spring of 1940. The Jewish governmental theater of Minsk performed *Shulamis* (Yiddish for the Hebrew name Shulamit) in Bialystok in the summer of that year. The Jewish troupe in Vinitsa performed in the Eastern Galician town of Zloczow and elsewhere.

Concurrently, Jewish troupes from the annexed areas performed in the Soviet Union. The Jewish governmental miniature theater, with the participation of Shimon Dzhigan and Shumacher, performed successfully in several Soviet cities, including, Moscow.[12] The manager of this theater, Moshe Broderson, described in a letter to *Vilner Emes* the warm reception that his actors received throughout the USSR; he also mentioned their encounter with the famed actor S. Mikhoels and numerous authors in Moscow. The theater personnel were in Odessa when the war with Germany broke out; they moved on to Kharkov and then broke up into small groups in Central Asia.

While visiting western Belorussia and the western Ukraine, S. Mikhoels selected a group of young men and women for enrollment in the Jewish School of the Theater in Moscow, which he headed. They pursued their studies in Moscow until the war broke out.

Many important Yiddish-language authors in the Soviet Union invoked motifs connected with the lives and circumstances of Jews in the annexed areas. The heroes of Peretz Markish's drama *Kol Nidre* (first presented just before the war at the Jewish theater in Kiev) are Arye Baal-Pinkes and his daughter Hadassah, who dwell in a small town in Poland. The day before Yom Kippur 5700 (1939), Arye shelters a Polish governor in his home, even though the official had interned and tortured his daughter Hadassah for Communist revolutionary activity.

VISITS BY AUTHORS

In contrast to the spontaneous enthusiasm of ordinary Soviet Jews at the sight of their brethren in the annexed areas, the response in institutional and official circles was restrained and controlled. This was especially evident when Soviet Jewish authors and poets visited western Belorussia and the western Ukraine after these areas were annexed. To avoid suspicion of nationalist leanings and deviation from the general line (which stressed the "liberation of the Belorussian and Ukrainian brethren"), these litterateurs and other prominent Soviet Jews restrained their emotions and subordinated their connections with their compatriots in the liberated areas, as prescribed by the official framework. Several days after the Red Army entered western Belorussia, the daily *Der Shtern* printed a warmly phrased advertisement greeting the Red Army and signed by Jews born in the western Ukraine who held important positions in Kiev. The same edition of *Der Shtern* cited the Jewish masses in western Belorussia and the western Ukraine as partners in the fate of their non-Jewish neighbors in these provinces: "For all practical purposes, the Polish government continued to pursue the Czarist policy— harassment of minorities—with respect to the Jews, too."[13]

Even before the end of 1939, a pamphlet named *Di bafrayte brider* (The Liberated Brethren), containing 22 Yiddish-language works by Soviet Jewish authors and poets, appeared in Minsk.[14] Only six of the entries were unequivocal about their Jewish origins (i.e., using the word "Jew" or presenting characters with Jewish names or descriptions). The subject was treated gingerly even in these cases. In contrast, conspicuous national motives appeared in an article by A. Reznik, "We Extend You a Fraternal Hand." This piece made explicit mention of the Jews' sufferings in Poland (along with those of the Belorussians and the Ukrainians, of course) at the hands of the malevolent landowners' regime. "The Soviet regime has given you, dear brothers, the human rights that you had lacked thus far," the author concluded.

In the same collection, the poet Z. Tellesin articulated in verse his ardent desire to reestablish contact with his brethren, noting that these brethren are the Jews. To ward off the evil eye, however, he mentioned the Belorussians first: "There dwell my brothers, the Belorussians and the Jews." Poet H. Shvedik outdid himself in his poem "One of These Days," in which, when visiting towns such as Rowne or Slonim, he encountered "the age-old Jewish sadness," meaning "the sadness of these perpetual wanderings . . . the sadness of a homeless people, dispersed among all the nations."

It is worth restating that only a few entries in the collection contain even these modest, cautious manifestations of solidarity. This, to a large degree, reflected the tragic dilemma that subsequently typified the attitude of veteran Soviet Jews toward their fellow Jews in the annexed areas.

Authors in the annexed areas held their visiting colleagues in awe, in view of their artistic and professional quality, their official status, and the opportunity they had been given to obtain their assistance. However, the locals also sized up the Soviets' limitations very quickly. The visitors were not only careful and circumspect in conversation, they were also distressingly poor. Among the numerous testimonials of Jews from the annexed areas that articulated this impression, one of the most effective was that of Joseph Rubinstein in his Yiddish-language poem "Megiles Rusland":

In those days we were visited by a large number of authors, Jews and Russians alike. Most of them came to buy clothing and footwear, and were puzzled about how wealthy we were. . . . Feverishly these authors from Moscow snapped up shoes, shirts, women's hosiery, and even underwear. Since time was passing and they'd soon have to return, they rushed to buy everything they saw.[15]

After the new regime stabilized, Soviet Jewish authors and artists began to interact directly with the Yiddish-speaking and Yiddish-reading public in the annexed areas. Both sides benefited from the encounter: the local writers used these contacts as "seals of approval" in their efforts to publish their works, and the Soviet Jewish authors found new subject matter and, more important, a new public for whom to write.[16] It has therefore been argued that the eruption of World War II in September, 1939, and the resulting Soviet annexation, "saved Yiddish-language Soviet literature and delayed its extermination."[17] As far-reaching as this assertion sounds, it is defensible. By inference, one may add that the annexation helped reinforce Soviet Jewish culture in general.

Contacts between the Soviet Jewish authors and their colleagues in the western areas were manifested, as previously stated, in frequent visits. The travelers were usually easterners, especially veteran authors of stature. The main reason why they thronged the annexed areas was "to bask in the warmth of a large Jewish community" that still radiated something of indigenous Jewish culture. Others visited in search of relatives, a rare book, and so on. A widely invoked reason for visits was "to prepare the bearers of local culture, especially the authors and poets, for the new Soviet realities and for writing in the Soviet spirit."[18] Some participated in missions representing others. An example was an elite group of Jewish authors who reached Bialystok in February, 1940. The purpose of the mission was to encourage the Jewish public to take part in elections for Soviet institutions, and the travelers had received a detailed briefing to this effect by the secretary of the Belorussian Communist Party, P. Ponomarenko. Jewish authors and poets from Kiev visited Lvov under similar circumstances, participating with local colleagues in a large literary affair at the government Jewish theater in that city.

In their official appearances, the visiting authors were unwilling or unable to speak their minds. Often they contented themselves with statements of courtesy only, or with shopworn platitudes culled from the contemporary Soviet political lexicon—mainly lavish praise for "Comrade Stalin."[19] Soon, however, the veteran Soviet Jewish litterateurs realized that their western colleagues were not as pitiable and in need of preaching as they had thought:

They suddenly understood that the tears they shed for our fate were in vain. The opposite was the case—shouldn't *you* be consoling *us*?—the poet Rassin whispered. We had no idea what you had and still have. You are better off than we are: you have schools where they still study in Yiddish; everything of ours is padlocked. Not a trace remains. Truth to tell, we could fill more than one school, but they won't let us; the government prohibits it.[20]

In public, the same Rassin sang a different tune:

Afterwards, he recited some of his poetry at a gathering of poets: "How exalted and lovely are Stalin's utterances, how valorous his army. . . ." Thus we saw him, the sensitive lyricist, reiterating that worn-out refrain, and I indeed felt his agony.

Peretz Markish, a favorite of Jewish audiences in Poland, fondly remembered for his performances there in the 1920s, addressed a group of Jewish authors in western Belorussia with the following:

Our country, which sustains 183 million Soviet citizens, will never forget the authors who fled that well-known place of mayhem, reached this locality, and entrusted their fate to our healthy, strong Soviet hands. We welcome you with open arms, and you—welcome us with open hearts![21]

Markish went on, however, to warn his audience "not to become opportunists, cheap yes-men," for this was altogether unnecessary. "In any case, we'll know who toes the line, since in these matters we understand more than enough and are vastly experienced in this field."

Such visits almost always included "literary evenings," on which local authors would recite their works and guests would venture their opinions. Even at this early stage one could discern the great difference between the visiting authors' ideational and aesthetic norms and the official criteria under which they were supposed to criticize the works recited. One of the critics, Dovid Sfard, described this in his memoirs:

The extent of the gap between truth and utterances was different for each of them; each expressed it to a different degree and in a different way. With Markish, it was the abyss between the raucous enthusiasm and officiousness that typified the beginnings of his appearances, as if he wished to drown himself out, and the slack and slightly ironic conclusion. With Fefer, it was the contrast between the serious, quiet tone of voice that he used when he spoke officially, and the facetious smirk on his face. With Bergelson, it was the excessively serious tone of voice in which he uttered his loyal-author platitudes. Others, such as Kvitko, Kushnirov, and Halkin, were sometimes struck dumb with embarrassment, falling into miserable silence, occasionally swallowing everything said whole.[22]

According to Sfard, only Der Nister ("the Concealed One") maintained total silence. Only on rare occasions, after everyone had said his piece, would he murmur to someone, "as an aside and *sotto voce,* some heavy and grayish word like a hunk of solidified lava." None of the visitors was at peace with his official message. The guests' authentic, normative Jewishness was like an underwater stream gurgling under strata of foreign matter hauled in from a far-away, alien place.

Not surprisingly, in view of the tension that pervaded these encounters, local authors and visitors frequently clashed when the former pressed the latter to the wall with embarrassing objections and queries. One such incident took place during a lecture by Professor I. Nussinov in Bialystok on "positive national motifs in literature." When he cited the Ukrainian hero Bogdan Chmielnicki as an example of such a motif, the audience began to cough and sneeze. When it came time for questions and answers, someone handed the moderator the following question: why does the Soviet Union praise this hooligan, who murdered thousands upon thousands of Jews, even screening a film on his heroic exploits in disregard of his anti-Jewish atrocities? The moderator fell into an embarrassed silence, whereupon Nussinov answered that the film did not have to state everything explicitly. Now, if this was true with regard to Chmielnicki's greatest achievement—orchestrating the Russian annexation of the Ukraine—there was surely good reason to disregard other, less laudable actions of his. This was evidently an allusion to the Soviet-German alliance, signed a short time previously. Then Nussinov added: "All politics, and *a fortiori* socialist politics, has its own ways, norms, and rules. Insofar as they are politically important and worthy of the construction of a new socialist society, so should one conduct oneself, and that's how it will be in the future, too!"[23]

Author and journalist Tania Fuks described a similar incident that took place at a social affair at the Writers' Union in Lvov, where Jewish authors from the USSR were feted, with the expectation that they would help support Jewish education in Eastern Galicia:

I demanded the floor and asked: For whom, really, do the Jewish writers write? Today's readers are already mere vestiges of the old generation, and they are not particularly young either. Who will be reading Yiddish five years from now? After all, they don't teach Yiddish in the Jewish schools anymore. I told them what's happening in my school, the last high school in Lvov. The other school had gone over to Ukrainian before this. . . . I hoped that the guests, the Jewish authors, would perk up at once and begin to do something. Instead, they took the matter quietly and placidly, arguing: "We believe in the Soviet policy on national minorities, and whatever the government does, it knows what it's doing." . . . We could not figure this out.

In this context, Tania Fuks described yet another incident in Lvov, this time at an evening affair in the memory of I. L. Peretz at the Jewish Archives, attended by a large audience of local Jews and visiting authors from the USSR.

In their lectures on Peretz, the guests spoke with a strange coldness, using a tone that we were not accustomed to use when speaking of our classical authors. The people in the audience looked at each other and continued to sit there, as if embarrassed. Then Alter Kacyzne took the floor. He was an excellent orator, but he gave the kind of speech that I had never heard before. It was more a prayer service than a speech, so imbued was it with adoration, emotion, and love. The auditorium fell into a bizarre silence; people were agitated to the point of tears. Only our guests, it seemed, were ill at ease. In any case, they no longer felt at home here after Kacyzne's verbal cadenza. A kind of dualism began to coalesce in all fields: "we" and "them," "we" the locals, and "them"—those who arrived from the Soviet Union: from Kiev, Kharkov, Dniepropetrovsk, and places farther away. Eventually their numbers grew greatly. "They" treated us like inferiors, while "we" were not yet so lowly as to appreciate "their" behavior. There were even moments of sorrow: after "we" had done all the work and set everything up, "they" came in and begin to set the tone.[24]

At times, however, the two groups managed to "break the ice," forming islands of rapprochement in the sea of estrangement. On one such occasion, Dovid Sfard took part in a grand affair marking the 60th birthday of the noted Belorussian Jan Kupala, by virtue of his position as deputy chairman of the Writers' Union in Bialystok. The participants included distinguished guests from all parts of the USSR, including S. Halkin, the Soviet Jewish author and playwright, and S. Berlinsky, the Yiddish author from Poland.

Following the custom in affairs of this kind, alcoholic drinks were served and consumed until many participants, including the master of ceremonies, were tipsy. Dovid Sfard describes what happened then:

When the orgy reached its climax, S. Halkin said to me: "Let's get away from these drunken goyim and find ourselves a corner of our own." We found an empty room and sat down, the three of us—Halkin, Berlinsky, and myself—and began to sing melodies of the sort chanted at the afternoon Sabbath feast. At first we sang very quietly, but then it reached a crescendo. Within a few minutes the rest of the authors gathered around us, and joining in at the top of their lungs.[25]

Some Soviet Jewish authors were so moved by their warm contact with local Jews that they disclosed their true thoughts. Hersh Smolar, a senior official in the Belorussian Writers' Union and a member of the *Bialystoker Shtern* editorial board, helped organize a reception for the first group of Soviet Jewish authors to visit the Belorussian capital. During the reception, Peretz Markish asked for a private meeting with him and made the following shocking disclosure:

We can be frank with you. . . . We've known you for some time now. . . . So please remember: not a word of this to anyone! . . . What happened to us is going to happen to you. They'll leave you alone for a little while, a year or two, maybe more, and then they'll wipe everything out.

Markish told him that before reaching Bialystok he had been in Minsk and was received by Ponomarenko, who told him with biting cynicism: "The fate of the western provinces will be no different from that of the eastern ones. All the fuss and bother will be over and done with, and the people will understand—we'll help them—that their future is tied to the culture that the entire Soviet people accept."[26]

The complex relationship between the Jews in the annexed areas and the Soviet Jewish writers—and within the latter group—had an especially potent impact on Zelig Akselrod, a lyric poet and editor of the literary journal *Shtern* in Minsk, whose official functions frequently took him to Bialystok, Vilna, and Kovno. From the very beginning, Akselrod attracted much favorable attention in Jewish public circles, particularly among authors. However, his inability to adjust to the new realities, and his identification with authentic Judaism, led to unusual behavior that hastened his demise as soon as the authorities focused on him. For example, in a concert of operatic selections by the renowned cantor Moshe Koussevitzky of Warsaw, Axelrod was one of the first in the audience to demand that the cantor sing "Kol Nidre." When he visited Vilna and Kovno in early 1941, he tried to prevent the closure of *Vilner Emes,* thus incurring the wrath of the Communist Party secretary of the Writers' Union in Minsk, who had accompanied him on the visit. In Lithuania, he apprised local Jewish functionaries of the eradication of the Jewish schools in the USSR and warned them to expect similar moves in the annexed areas, including Lithuania. The only way to prevent this, he said, was to instruct parents to insist in writing, in detail, that Jewish education continue.[27] Akselrod evidently paid for these and other similar actions with his life. According to rumor, he was shot in June, 1941, for disseminating "Jewish nationalist propaganda." Indeed, the personality and fate of this poet embodied the tragic nature of the contacts that Soviet Jews nurtured and maintained with their compatriots in the annexed territories.

Some Jewish writers from the annexed areas also visited the Soviet Union. In early 1941, I. Ashendorf, Nachum Bomze, and Yehoshua Perla set out from Lvov for a visit to Kiev. The threesome recited some of their works at a literary evening held in their honor at the local Writers' House. At roughly the same time, another group of performing artists from Lvov visited Moscow; this group included Alter Kacyzne, Rachel Korn, B. Snapper, H. Weber, and J. Rubinstein. A literary feast was held in their honor at the Writers' House, and the guests recited their works. They also visited the *Der Emes* publishing house and the central committee of the Journalists' Association.[28] Another encounter was held on April 11, 1941, in Moscow, with the board members of the journals *Oktyabr* and *Shtern.*

In addition to the reciprocal visits, Jewish authors and artists from the annexed areas were invited to participate in national cultural events such as festivities marking the 90th birthday of I. L. Peretz.

These exciting and disappointing encounters were surely important and unique, but it should not be forgotten that only a very small proportion of Soviet Jewry was involved in them. One may estimate the number of Soviet Jews who came into direct contact with Jews in the annexed areas at only a few thousand; these included soldiers and various defense and other functionaries, whose relations with local Jews were not recurrent. However, there is no way of gauging the scale of indirect contacts (letters, newspaper accounts, rumors, and so on). The immediate impact of these contacts on the three million Jews living in the USSR at the time cannot be assessed. Neither can one estimate the cumulative impact of this encounter in subsequent times.

By way of general summary, one may state that the annexation of the western areas, with their vigorous Jewish population, did affect the veteran Soviet Jewish community, which was in a state of cultural decline. Jewish education and culture underwent something of a rebirth in the annexed areas. The main beneficiaries of this cultural flowering in the annexed areas were public institutions and enterprises such as publishing houses, cultural institutes, newspaper editorial boards, and theaters. Jewish authors, educators, and various purveyors of culture (some famous and others less so) profited as well.

Many institutions and individuals pledged themselves to help the Jewish population in the annexed areas, chiefly with respect to culture and education. Admittedly, they were encouraged in this endeavor by major authors, but their inner motivation was strong. The vision that drove the Soviet establishment was unilateral and evidently technical and political; however, the encounter of Soviet Jews with their compatriots in the western areas was a profound, impressive, two-way experience on the national level. Soviet Jews often derived profound encouragement and psychological strength from these encounters, which they invoked in their struggle with the specific difficulties of Jews in Soviet society. At times the Soviet emissaries, ostensibly representing the establishment, identified more with their brethren in the west than with the institutions that had sent them. In other cases, the Soviet Jewish visitors to the west took an authoritarian attitude, either out of excessive allegiance to their official capacities or because they regarded themselves as custodians of the local Jews. Both attitudes, however, were ambivalent.

In general, the annexation of the western areas reinvigorated Soviet Jewry and straightened its cultural "spine." This evidently clashed with Soviet policy, which aimed to vitiate the Jews' national distinctiveness and encouraged the community to assimilate. Accordingly, there is reason to surmise that the relative honeymoon enjoyed by some members of Soviet Jewry as a result of their contacts with Jews in the annexed areas was fated to be short-lived from the outset.

11

Zionist Underground Activity

Many Jews, confident that the changes following the Soviet annexation would be long-lasting, preferred to adjust to the new circumstances. Quite a few collaborated with the authorities, some out of ideological identification and others for reasons of sympathy and gratitude. Over time, however, the sense of relief dissipated and the Soviet regime wore out its welcome. Passive resistance increased, and some Jews actively opposed the arrangements imposed by the new regime. They refused to work on the Sabbath, adhered strictly to religious customs, crossed the borders between annexed areas, maintained contacts with foreign countries (even transferring information), and criticized the regime (behind a smoke screen of jokes and other devices). This unwillingness to acquiesce was especially prevalent in groups and organizations that previously had been known for nonconformism. Some of these now merged into new underground frameworks in order to continue inculcating their ideologies and values. Their operational goals were to meet needs that had not changed, using methods and means dictated by the conditions of the time.

Unlike non-Jewish resistance groups affiliated with the majority peoples (e.g., Ukrainians and Lithuanians), Zionist groups did not reject the fact of the annexation of their areas of residence. Even so, their positions and behavior in response to Soviet anti-Zionism constituted acts of organized resistance, however passive most of them were. Obviously, the Soviet regime would not tolerate the existence of any organization that it did not recognize, especially political associations. Even the Bund organizations were disbanded at this time, many of their activists moving to social or trade-union activities sponsored by the new regime. This is why the Zionist groups that insisted in remaining active had no choice but to go underground. In due course, the very term *underground* became a specific synonym for clandestine Zionist activity of various kinds by Jews in the annexed territories.

Just before the war, talk of emergency plans had been rife among the Jews of Poland, especially those who belonged to political parties and youth movements. Most such discussions pertained to the prospect of war between Poland and Germany. Because few considered the possibility of a Soviet occupation, the Jews gave little thought to such an eventuality and how they might respond to it.

Within weeks after Nazi Germany pounced, overwhelmed the Polish army, and flooded the western part of the country, masses of refugees rushed from western and central Poland into the eastern reaches of the country. Conspicuous among them were numerous groups composed of members of Zionist *hakhsharot* (training collectives), youth movement members, and political activists. Most of these maintained their organizational integrity as they advanced on foot. Thus, when Red Army forces poured into eastern Poland, they found a population larger than the local one, including Zionist youth movement members from all over the country and activists and leaders of most political parties and associations that existed on the Jewish scene. The latter group included most members of the central committee of the Bund, who had congregated in Bialystok and Brest; the central leadership of He-haluts ha-Tsa'ir–Frayhayt and He-haluts, which had fled to Kowel and Luck; the Ha-shomer ha-Tsa'ir leadership, which had relocated to Rovno; that of Ha-no'ar ha-Tsiyoni in Pinsk; that of Gordoniya in Luck and Rovno; and several commissioners of Betar and cell commanders of the IZL in Lvov and Luck. Concurrently, a considerable number of leaders and luminaries of the religious Zionist parties, the Bund, the Folkists, and other groups had reached Vilna or were en route to the Lithuanian capital.

The sudden advent of Soviet rule, known for its fierce opposition to much of the Jewish political constellation, engulfed the leaders of the Jewish organizations in confusion and dread. Bund leaders, it transpired, were in danger of arrest from the moment the Red Army entered the areas. Soon the organizations and movements that intended to continue operating under the new circumstances realized that they were isolated from the Jewish rank-and-file and were no longer able to rely on anyone but themselves. Large political and public groupings that had once wielded power in the Jewish "street" now collapsed, making no serious attempt to survive. It is worth bearing in mind that several branches of Jewish parties, organizations, and youth movements had been closed since the war broke out because of the state of emergency. As for the dozens of Zionist training collectives in these areas, the situation was unclear at first, but they, too, ceased to exist within a few months. Several Zionist youth movements resolved (in a phrase that later became famous) "to disperse, not to liquidate." This was a tactical retreat, so to speak; it left the movements with the option of going underground and resorting to unusual methods of activity that the Soviet regime banned altogether. Those who chose this path would not be given a reasonable period of time for reasoned, quiet preparations; they would have to adjust to the new realities at once and build an infrastructure allowing them to remain active under various constraints and pressures. Several organizations had set up alternative or reserve leadership structures before September 17, identifiable as such by their suffix, the Hebrew letter *bet* (B) (e.g., Leadership B; Institution B). Other than these, most prewar preparations now seemed anachronistic and ineffective.

Such was the state of affairs in Poland, where the arrival of the Red Army had taken the country by total surprise. Jews in the Baltic countries and eastern Romania, in contrast, had been more aware of the possibility of a Soviet takeover. The thousands of refugees from Poland who had experienced Soviet rule had apprised the Jewish communities in these areas of the nature of the Soviet regime and its actions against pre-sovietization Jewish institutions and political movements. Thus, activists in some Jewish organizations and movements in the Baltic countries and the Romanian provinces, well aware of the danger they faced if certain items were confiscated by the security services, hastened to destroy or hide membership lists and organizational trappings such as emblems and banners, even before the regime had time to disperse the organizations. Again, the rule was dispersion, not liquidation.

While the preparations for such a contingency in Lithuania and the other Baltic countries had taken shape in these areas, the geographic circumstances of Northern Bukovina and Bessarabia left room for alternatives—namely, relocation to areas outside Soviet control, chiefly the "Regat" (Romania within its pre-World War I borders) and adjacent regions.

Zionist and other Jewish groups began to implement their "activity under any circumstances" resolution as soon as the Red Army entered, and the process continued at varying levels of intensity throughout the period of Soviet rule (i.e., until the summer of 1941—21 months in Poland and 12 elsewhere). During this time, about 2,000 persons were active in the underground metamorphoses of the Zionist youth movements. Socially and organizationally, this activity had its ups and downs. Often it resembled the kinds of activities that youth movements pursue in ordinary times, such as local rallies; however, there were also special operations, such as interregional activities that required the crossing of an internal border, with all that this implied.

THE UNDERGROUND PRESS

Hebrew culture and Zionism was a matter of great importance to the two million Jews who lived in these regions. For many of them, sovietization was traumatic: Hebrew schools were closed, Hebrew books removed, and all publications in Hebrew shut down. It is no surprise that some continued to cultivate Hebrew culture and Zionist values surreptitiously, despite the danger of arrest or deportation to Siberia. Most of those who carried on this work were young, former students of Hebrew schools and members of Zionist youth movements. Within a short time, they coalesced into well-organized undercover groups, most of which were direct outgrowths of older movements such as Ha-shomer ha-Tsa'ir, He-haluts ha-Tsa'ir, and Ha-no'ar ha-Tsiyoni. Some, were new, such as Herut (Freedom) and Irgun Berit Tsiyon (Alliance of Zion Organization [IBZ]), which arose in Soviet Lithuania in late 1940 (discussed later).

Like all underground groups that pursue political or ideological aims, these organizations needed expository material suitable for hand-to-hand transmission. This brought an underground press into being, chiefly for Hebrew publications that appeared more or less regularly, either printed or handwritten. Obviously, publishing under these clandestine conditions required elaborate organization, skill, and resources, if only because the materials required (chiefly paper) were both scarce and costly. Furthermore, these publications gave the NKVD (today known as the KGB—Kommissariat Gossudarstvennoy Bez'opastnosty) a convenient "handle" with which to trace the activities of the underground organizations that helped publish and distribute them. Hence few such movements were able to sustain their publishing efforts.

The most important Hebrew-language newspapers of this genre were *Deror* (Freedom) and *Mi-ma'amaqim* (Out of the Depths).

Deror was the organ of two movements that had merged: He-haluts ha-Tsa'ir and Frayhayt. The first issues were published in the western Ukraine under the editorship of Yitzhak Zuckerman. His colleague,

Scheindl Schwartz, managed to obtain the newsprint and distribute the publication in Wolhynia. In May, 1940, when Zuckerman left for Warsaw, Addek Golovner succeeded him as editor. Several copies were smuggled into Lithuania (especially Vilna and Shavli) for members of Herut, an affiliated movement there. When relations between the two became stronger, the paper was printed in Wolhynia for He-haluts ha-Tsa'ir and Frayhayt and in Lithuania for Herut. At this time the paper was readied for print by Mordechai Tenenbaum and Zvi Mersik, Zionist activists in Poland, and by Teddy Pik in Lithuania. The issues meant for the former Polish areas were smuggled into Lvov and Kowel by resourceful women couriers. *Deror* continued to appear until just before the German invasion in the summer of 1941, and it came out in at least seven issues (perhaps eight). No copy of the paper seems to have survived.

Mi-ma'amaqim was the organ of Ha-shomer ha-Tsa'ir in the western Ukraine and western Belorussia. Three issues appeared in the first half of 1940, when the underground activity of this movement reached its peak. It was printed in secret by mimeograph in Rowne, Wolhynia. The first issue, six pages long, contained the resolutions of the movement's inaugural meeting (on New Year's Eve, 1939) and an exhortation by the leadership to establish movement cells in the cities and small towns of the western Ukraine and western Belorussia. This issue was distributed in 20 localities ("only those where the members' loyalty was not in doubt").

The second issue was eight pages long and contained more diverse material: information on a secret meeting of the movement council in March, 1940, news about the Jewish world and Palestine, a review of the state of the war and international problems, and a comprehensive article on clandestine Zionist pioneering movements under the Soviet regime. The third issue appeared about a month later and contained 25 pages. Several pages of one copy of this issue survived and are kept in the Ha-shomer ha-Tsa'ir archives in Israel.

Local underground organizations sponsored several sporadic clandestine publications in Hebrew and other languages; these had a comparatively wider circulation. Examples include *Hayenu* (Our Life)—a biweekly published by young members of Ha-shomer ha-Tsa'ir in Nesvizh (western Belorussia)—and *Mi-gov riqavon* (Out of the Pit)—a mimeographed periodical published four times in Vilna by an underground Zionist group called the Hebrew National Movement. One of its editors was Ze'ev Evionski, a high-school student.

Several publications appeared one time only, including *Yoman ha-mesheq* (Farm Daily), published by the Ha-shomer ha-Tsa'ir collective in Vilna in early 1940, and *Mi-ma'amaqim* (Out of the Depths), published by the Bnei Aqiva movement in Kovno in early 1941 (a different publication than the *Mi-ma'amaqim* described previously).

The most salient publication at this time was undoubtedly *Nitsots* (Spark). Unique among the many underground publications, it appeared continuously for seven and a half years, well beyond the end of World War II, coming out in different places and surviving changes in regime.

Few Jewish communities suffered more from the Soviet antipathy toward Hebrew culture and Zionism than Kovno, Lithuania. In the autumn of 1940, when the USSR annexed this country, the Jews of Kovno were left with a handful of Yiddish cultural schools that ignored Jewish history, severed all ties with Palestine, and burned Hebrew books. The community's frustration gave rise to an apolitical underground group called Irgun Berit Tsiyon (IBZ). Its founders and members were high-school students. For most, this was their first experience with membership in a political group; in this sense the IBZ differed from the other Zionist youth movements that had gone underground. Only a few IBZ members had belonged to Ha-no'ar ha-Tsiyoni or Makkabi ha-Tsa'ir. In all, the new organization had about 100 members. Most regular activities, conducted in Hebrew, concerned Zionist and Palestine studies, listening to *Voice of Jerusalem* radio, salvaging Hebrew books, and so on. The first issue of the IBZ newspaper coincided with the organization's first party, held at Hanukka (December, 1940). The newspaper's name, *Nitsots,* was derived from the poem "I Did Not Win Light Out of Lawlessness," by Hayyim Nachman Bialik, an excerpt of which appeared under the masthead [free translation]:

One spark (*nitsots*) is hidden in my heart
A small spark—but all my own,
Not borrowed, not stolen,
It is inside me and part of me.

The first editor of *Nitsots* was Shimon Graz, 18 years of age, a founding member of the organization and the leader of its headquarters at the time. Initially *Nitsots* was handwritten on a single printed page. Sufficient copies of issues appeared almost every month to be distributed to most activists in the IBZ, along with "student clubs and school corridors" here and there. It reached hundreds of readers, mostly teenagers. *Nitsots* contained not only information about events in Palestine but also Hebrew poetry and literature and intellectual writings about Zionism and the Jewish people, such as excerpts from Yehezkel Kaufmann's book *Gola ve-nekhar* (Exile and Estrangement).

The first issues were duplicated by mimeograph; however, to avoid breaches of secrecy the publishers were forced to resort to using carbon paper for copying. In all, there were seven issues during the period of Soviet rule; the last appeared shortly before the German invasion of Russia. The eighth issue was published in the Kovno ghetto in October, 1941, about four months after the Nazis had overrun Lithuania.

INTERNAL STRUCTURE AND MODUS OPERANDI

The basic framework of organization in almost all the movements and regions was the "cell." Cells were subservient to rigid centralized hierarchies based on iron internal discipline for the purpose of compliance with unconditionally binding movement decisions.

Proposals tabled for discussion in the founding meeting of Deror, on December 31, 1939, contain characteristic features of this method. The subject was the establishment of a network of undercover cells, and the main points follow:

Members in the ranks are contacted through the chain of command. The district cannot be autonomous; in all respects it is subordinate to instructions of the province, and the degree of independence of the province, too, should be limited. No public appearance, demonstration, or propaganda activity should be allowed without the decision and approval of the "center." The center's decision is binding. The leader of the cell is directly responsible to the branch. He is the organization's image and emblem. Every cell leader inspects and tests his men.[1]

When Ha-shomer ha-Tsa'ir went underground, it chose—again in a New Year's Eve meeting—the term *gar'in* (Hebrew for "nucleus") to describe its basic unit. The gar'in was defined as "an operational unit with no more than five members aged 15–18." Candidates for the gar'in, male and female, had to meet several criteria: (1) acceptance of the principles on which the movement's activity were based; (2) the desire to follow this path and willingness to pledge unconditional allegiance to it; (3) confidence in one's fortitude to honor the undertaking in the previous clause.[2]

It was decided at this meeting to set up "one organizational framework named Ha-shomer ha-Tsa'ir in the Ukraine and western Belorussia" with "a small headquarters in Lvov," and "to confirm the provincial and district co-ordinators." Here, too, the organizational framework was rigid: the person responsible for an area customarily met only with the provincial coordinator, who met only with the district coordinator, who met only with members of the gar'in.[3]

Although this structure was meant to safeguard members from discovery and downfall, it also constricted their opportunities for social contact. Movement events, insofar as they continued, actually took place outside the underground cell or gar'in. Most settings, ironically, were prewar ones—in school, on the job, or in the evenings while strolling in the street. In this fashion the teenage members circumvented the rigidities of the organization.

At the peak of underground activity, Ha-shomer ha-Tsa'ir in the western Ukraine and western Belorussia had at least 30 cells with 400–600 members, including external hangers-on. Deror was approximately the same size; it had dozens of branches organized in groups of five.[4]

The two organizations drew up an interim account of their situation about six weeks after they went underground:

In the Soviet area, activity now takes place in a uniform framework for Galicia, Polesie, Wolhynia, and the Grodno-Bialystok vicinity, in place of the two separate frameworks for Poland and Galicia. . . . Only Ha-shomer ha-Tsa'ir and the Ha-kibbutz ha-Meuhad [probably another name for Deror, a kibbutz federation in Palestine with which Deror was affiliated; the alternate name was used for camouflage] are active. Ha-no'ar ha-Tsiyoni began some activities but evidently called them off for now. People who were in training collectives when the occupation began were steered in the direction of the border, about 90–95 percent of them to Vilna and a few toward Romania. The members today are youngsters, aged 16–17 or older, organized in small cells under centralized, top-down control. They've got to be very careful. Whenever one member of a cell leaves, the entire cell is disbanded. Only loyal, safe members have been organized thus far.[5]

The five-person cell method was emulated by Bnei Aqiva members who had taken up residence in Lvov[6] and by Ha-no'ar ha-Tsiyoni:

As for the Soviet occupation zone in Poland . . . there are nuclei dispersed throughout the occupation area and the work is centralized. Special emis-

saries from Vilna organized the nuclei, and some have stayed on. . . .
250–300 of our people are organized in these units in the Soviet occupation
zone of Poland.[7]

In Pinsk, a stronghold of Ha-no'ar ha-Tsiyoni, the young local leadership organized small groups that met in private homes. In Eastern Galicia, Ha-no'ar ha-Tsiyoni activity focused on contacts among the members, economic aid, job arrangements, and, in part, assistance in crossing the Romanian border. In the town of Ciechanowice (Bialystok district), members of several youth movements (Betar, Frayhayt, He-haluts ha-Tsa'ir, Ha-shomer ha-Tsa'ir) continued to operate for some time, camouflaged as a "song-and-dance troupe" organized for the ostensible purpose of entertaining soldiers and civilians.

In several localities, attempts were made to set up agricultural training centers under the guise of "productivization" projects for Jewish youth. The settings chosen were economically secure farms such as Czyzykow in Eastern Galicia; the nationalized estate of Baron Flondor in Northern Bukovina; and Margalaukas, Valakumpiai, Mikhalina, and Leopoltava in Lithuania. These ventures, however, were short-lived, mainly because of opposition by local peasants and Communist administrators.

The Herzliya movement (which Ha-no'ar ha-Tsiyoni was called in Latvia), moribund for some time after members had come under protracted surveillance, resumed activities in late 1940 on a limited scale. By this time, a few members had gone over to the Komsomol; others preferred to adjust to the new conditions and stay out of trouble. Most of this underground activity took place in Riga and Rezekne. One of the participants describes the secret assemblies: "We met at six o'clock in the morning, five members of scouts' age. We conversed, studied Hebrew. Of course, we took some precautions. The whole gathering took 40 minutes in all."[8]

Former members of No'ar Tsofi Halutsi (Pioneering Scouting Youth, known by its Hebrew acronym *Netsah*), Gordoniya, and other organizations in Latvia undertook similar operations, planning systematic underground activity in groups of three. Evidently, however, they had not managed to activate these frameworks in any orderly fashion by the time the war with Germany broke out.

Among the first to organize underground cells at this time were members of the farm collectives, who had been transferred from Poland to the Vilna center or dispersed in various locations in Lithuania.

Quite a few members of the Ha-shomer ha-Tsa'ir collectives had dispersed according to plan, maintaining their collective and movement relationship. By adhering to principles of discipline, financial collectivism, a strong work ethic, and efforts to emigrate to Palestine, these *kibbutzim* (training collectives) retained their vitality and allowed the elected central institutions of Ha-shomer ha-Tsa'ir to guide their steps. Thus the movement, even in dispersion, remained centralized under new tenets.[9]

A member of the He-haluts ha-Tsa'ir collective who reached Lithuania from Wolhynia described the dispersion of the members of his kibbutz in the town of Taurage:

The authorities drove us out, expelled us forcibly, seated us in trucks, and transported us to Kelm [Kelme]. However, we had already organized in groups—to stay in touch, emigrate to Palestine at some opportunity, and survive. In fact, we split into communes, each with ten or twelve members. . . . We had nowhere to work. . . . We began to travel to Shavli for construction work. . . . From Kelm we moved on to Yanova and gathered there, nine or ten members.[10]

When the IZL's quasimilitary formations were dissolved, some of their members set up small collectives in various parts of Lithuania, "doing hard menial labor in order to make a living and hang on until orders from their commanders came in."[11]

Several movements, implementing contingency plans, set up a "leadership B" composed of younger and less well-known members. Ha-shomer ha-Tsa'ir then disbanded its cell in Vilna, even though the authorities gave it their de facto approval on condition that it present them with a list of activists. Following this decision, the local Ha-shomer ha-Tsa'ir and refugee members of the organization set up a joint emergency leadership composed of Abba Kovner, Chaika Grossman, and Addek Buraks. Underground cells were organized, each comprising five hand-picked members.[12]

The Ha-shomer ha-Tsa'ir cell in Kovno underwent the same kind of experience. While some of the members broke ranks (several joined the Komsomol), it seems that all 25 counselors remained active in the underground, using the modus operandi handed down from headquarters.

The Betar cells in Vilna, Kovno, Shavli, Vilkomir (Ukmerge), and elsewhere converted to small undercover cells commanded by young people who were less well known in public circles. One of them, Yehuda Zupovich (whose nom de guerre in the IZL was "Kokhba"), subsequently led the anti-Nazi underground in the Kovno ghetto.

In the town of Shavli, a stronghold of No'ar Tsofi Halutsi, the last
conference of movement activists was held in the home of one of the
women members shortly after the Red Army entered. The 15 participants
decided to reconstitute the movement as an underground based on central leadership, strict discipline, and "inexhaustible willingness to meet
the movement's demands."[13] After they were initiated (reciting a written
oath), members were organized into three-person cells for underground
activity.

Conditions in the annexed Romanian areas were not significantly different. Shortly after the Ha-shomer ha-Tsa'ir branch in Czernowitz was dissolved, "the older groups of members in this branch split into small cells,
which were to stay in touch with each other and meet for ideological discussions." Most of these cells had five members or so. An activist from
Bucharest was recruited to manage the underground activity; when he failed
to arrive, three local members took over this responsibility,[14] forming a
"middle-management" echelon. This method was duplicated in Lipkany and
other localities, where liaison with the rank-and-file was restored in meetings between the leaders and small groups.

In the Betar cells in Czernowitz, several members established an underground framework: "Isolated cells were set up, each unaware of the others'
existence."[15] Four cells were set up at first, and one member of the "administration cell" was designated as responsible for each. Meetings with members of the separate cells were held in public parks, and, at times, in the
local cemetery.

Zvi Yavetz, in his memoirs, described the growth of the underground
operational units formed by high school students in Czernowitz:

We would meet surreptitiously, without our parents' knowledge, in public parks and in attics. We studied Hebrew, using Zionist books. We sang
"Paneynu el ha-shemesh ha-olah" [Our Face to the Rising Sun] and recited "El ha-tsipor" [To the Bird]. We did not know that such groups
existed in many corners around town. . . . I would estimate the number
of young members who were active during the Soviet occupation at several hundred.[16]

There is reason to surmise that nearly 2,000 persons were involved in
the underground organizations at the peak of their activity, including more
than 1,000 in the western Ukraine and western Belorussia, about 500 in
the Baltic countries (chiefly Lithuania), and the remainder in the former
Romanian areas.

By force of circumstance, the movements and organizations that coalesced for continued activity in the underground adopted conspiratorial methods. Sometimes these emulated the tactics of the "classic" historical revolutionary movements; in other cases they were devised haphazardly, reflecting the pressure of realities and relentless needs. As the organizations gained experience, so did their modus operandi grow in sophistication.

The first requirement was to equip major activists with new identities and documents. Because these leaders had to change residence from time to time, "safe houses" were needed. Some of the apartments chosen had back doors or abutted government institutions. Information about their location was shared on a need-to-know basis and confined to the most loyal movement members.

Meetings were held in locations such as public parks; some encounters took place in the street.[17] When national-level gatherings and conferences were held, the organizers and participants had to be doubly wary, since the presence of people from other areas required a permit.

As time passed, the habits and rules of clandestine activity became entrenched. The use of specific passwords and signals (e.g., a pen or a certain newspaper in one's pocket) was terminated. Members did not stop acquaintances on the street unless it was truly necessary. Any list or possibly incriminating piece of paper that was not vital was destroyed. Members were not brought to safe houses without good reason. In several localities impressive initiation ceremonies were introduced. Because one purpose of these rituals was to reinforce the conspiratorial mind-set, an oath of secrecy was devised.[18]

Members of the underground became quite sophisticated in correspondence with each other and with institutions and members abroad, especially in Palestine. As time passed, the movements developed a secret lexicon of terms and names for people and places. For example: "It seems as if Frumka wanted to go to Lipsky's with her friends and relatives, but she didn't make it because of the cold." This innocuous message referred to attempts by members of He-haluts in Warsaw to establish a route from Poland into Slovakia and Hungary in the winter of 1940. Shlomo Lipsky was the Ha-kibbutz ha-Meuhad emissary in Hungary; Frumka Plotnicka was the term for He-haluts and Deror. (Tosia Altman was the term for Ha-shomer ha-Tsa'ir.)[19]

Like all underground organizations, those discussed treated communication between the leadership and the outlying units with great importance. Vilna was the communications hub throughout this period, with few exceptions. By late 1939, liaison-couriers, mostly local activists, were streaming out of Vilna to expedite and assist the movement of members and activists to this city and to revitalize the movements in the former Polish areas, including the Soviet occupation zone. These emissaries also visited localities where underground cells or "nuclei" were already operating, boosting morale and gathering information that to be forwarded to headquarters.

As time passed, patterns of communication and contact developed on broader levels (e.g., provinces and districts). The tasks of the liaison agents included not only rehabilitation, encouragement, and guidance but also specific courier duties such as forwarding information, printed material, and relief funds. Some of these agents were young women who were especially important in the dissemination of underground newspapers and other printed matter.

Czernowitz initially was an important communications center, but its role gradually diminished until it was almost zero. In early 1940, members of underground youth movements in Northern Bukovina took the initiative to develop communications by mail. On January 12, 1940, when the situation on both sides of border had stabilized somewhat, the first letter was sent from the Romanian side. This missive, addressed to "loyalists of halutsic Zionism in the former Polish territories," contained news from the "outside" Jewish world and practical advice for members who wished to cross the Polish border into Czernowitz.[20]

At roughly this time, the emissaries of Ha-no'ar ha-Tsiyoni, Ha-shomer ha-Tsa'ir, Gordoniya, and Ha-kibbutz ha-Meuhad in Romania reached an agreement meant to help these movements "continue their halutsic [pioneering] Zionist activity under the circumstances of the new regimes in Poland" and "to facilitate the emigration to Palestine of adult members in these territories."[21] To meet these goals, the emissaries decided to establish two liaison committees, one on either side of the border.

These relatively intensive contacts between Zionist organizations on the Romanian side and their members on the Soviet side made Czernowitz a relay station, so to speak, for news from the "headquarters" in Vilna and the other former Polish areas. These reports reached as far as Palestine. The Soviet annexation of the Romanian provinces in the summer of 1940 brought this situation to an end. The Zionist movements—still attempting to sustain their activity in the underground—became vestigial and isolated, especially vis-à-vis their centers in Romania proper. From this time on, only one individual was smuggled from Romania proper into the Soviet-annexed area to encourage the local underground movements.[22]

In July, 1940, four members of Ha-shomer ha-Tsa'ir reached Czernowitz from the underground headquarters in Lvov, providing details about activity in the Polish areas. Two of these emissaries returned to Lvov with a few copies of the movement's weekly journal in Palestine. The other two took up positions in the local underground and did much to further communication between the leadership in Czernowitz and members in the surrounding smaller towns.[23]

At this time, Riga, the capital of Soviet Latvia, was an important center of communication between local activists (mainly affiliated with the General Zionists) and higher-level institutions in Palestine. This correspondence, in Hebrew and Yiddish, continued with hardly any interruption until the war with Germany broke out in June, 1941.[24] It even included weak, sporadic contacts with important members of Zionist movements in Switzerland. As long as postal service between Germany and the USSR was operating soundly, this correspondence involved members of affiliated movements in the German area of occupation.

OVERVIEW: THE FIVE STAGES OF UNDERGROUND ACTIVITIES

The activities of the Jewish underground movements in the Soviet-annexed areas may be divided into five stages.

Stage One, September–October, 1939: Attempts to Reach Palestine

This period was marked by futile attempts to smuggle members across the Romanian border in order to reach Palestine.

As movement activists and members congregated in eastern Poland, and as initial exploratory meetings were held with agents of the Soviet regime, a decision was made to send groups to the southern (Romanian) border. Members of He-haluts and Ha-shomer ha-Tsa'ir set up joint crossing points (more correctly, border-running points) in Horodenka, Kuty, and other locations. Security was maintained in various ways, including passwords, liaisons, and border-runners. In practical terms, very little was accomplished: only a few succeeded in crossing. Members of Aqiva, the IZL, and others who set out toward the Romanian border in organized fashion met a similar fate. This method was clearly shown to be unsuitable for the masses of members.

Stage Two, October, 1939, Through January, 1940: Mass Flight to Vilna

The restoration of Vilna to Lithuania became known even before attempts to cross the southern border were given up. Consequently, Jewish refugees from central and western Poland, along with political activists from eastern Poland, began streaming to this city, hoping that Lithuania, still independent and neutral, would prove to be an easier point of departure for foreign destinations, including Palestine. Therefore the organized movements decided to give this matter higher priority, sending couriers to the cells and branches to encourage them to join the throngs heading for Vilna and perhaps, thereby, bring the dream of emigration to Palestine closer to fulfillment. Several movements (He-haluts ha-Tsa'ir–Frayhayt, Ha-shomer ha-Tsa'ir, Gordoniya, Aqiva, and Ha-no'ar ha-Tsiyoni) collaborated in establishing a secret headquarters in Lida, a town not far from one of the main crossing points on the Soviet–Lithuanian border. Later on, these representatives and those of other organizations set up a central agency across the border, in Vilna, known as the Coordinating Committee of Halutsic Organizations, or Kordinatsiya (see Table 11–1). Members of other movements took part in the organized trek northward, including He-haluts ha-Mizrachi, He-haluts ha-Medinati, Betar, and the IZL, even though the last two were not represented in the Kordinatsiya. Members of the Bund and other organizations—including the yeshivas of Baranowicze, Mir, Kletsk, and other localities—started their own systems to move their activists and leaders to Vilna.

Within several months, much of the Jewish political elite in Poland, and, of course, the leaderships of the youth movements, had congregated in Vilna. However, while the former realized that they had become "generals without an army," the number of youth-movement members in Vilna grew each day, ultimately exceeding 2,000. Some of the newcomers became active in the corresponding movements in Lithuania, including IZL cells.

When the Soviets decided to seal their border with Lithuania, transit possibilities diminished; by January, 1940, the flow had almost totally ceased. Several movement activists who had manned the crossing stations were arrested, others were forced to flee. One of the few training collectives still op-

Movements Participating in the Vilna Kordinatsiya (Coordinating Committee of Halutsic Organization), April–May, 1940

Movement	Total Membership (April 4, 1940)		Training Collectives (May 10, 1940)		% of Palestine Immigration Certificates Awarded (April 17, 1940)
	No.	%	Collectives	Members	
He-haluts ha-Mizrachi	250	11.99	2		15
He-haluts ha-kelal-Tsiyoni A	240	11.51	4		13.5
He-haluts ha-kelal-Tsiyoni B	25	1.19	1		1.25
He-haluts ha-Medinati	35	1.67	1		2.5
Total, He-haluts	550	26.38	8		35.25
Ha-shomer ha-Tsa'ir	720	34.53	5	605	31
Deror (General Bloc)	600	2.77	3	510	26
Gordoniya	130	6.23	2	115	6
Aqiva	85	4.07	1	78	4
Total, other organizations	1,535	73.62	11	1,308	67.75
GRAND TOTAL	2,085	100	19		100

erating under Soviet rule in Poland, the Ba-minhara training kibbutz in Rowne, was liquidated at about that time.

Stage Three, January–May, 1940: A Time of Momentum and Growth

When most of the movement *aktiv* (activists) had been evacuated en masse to Vilna, Kordinatsiya, with more than 2,000 members, became a full-fledged organizational headquarters (indeed, it was termed the *rikkuz,* Hebrew for "congregation" or "concentration"). Aktiv was largely responsible for reviving the vestiges of the movements that remained in Nazi-occupied Poland. Despite the harsh terms of life in the German-occupied area, cells of 16–18 members had succeeded in coalescing there by their own initiative. They included young members of Ha-no'ar ha-Tsiyoni in Polesie, and Ha-shomer ha-Tsa'ir and Aqiva activists in Galicia, who followed through on their decision to continue operating in the underground.

Couriers from the Vilna rikkuz contacted these and other groups on several occasions—illegally, of course—to plan, guide, and stimulate activities. Two important meetings of this type were held around January, 1940, one in Rowne and the other in Lvov. (They were called the "Sylvester meetings," because New Year's Eve was known in these countries as St. Sylvester's Day). These sessions laid the foundations for underground activity in western Belorussia and the western Ukraine. Operations indeed gathered momentum, and two deserve special mention (alongside regular activities in scores of localities): underground publications, including six issues of *Deror* and six of *Mi-ma'amaqim;* and the convening of an interregional council to determine the ideological underpinnings of the Czyzykow farm (with the participation of a special representative from the Vilna rikkuz). Even though many plans drawn up were never implemented, for lack of funds among other reasons, it was a time of intensive activity and strong optimism. This period also provided a good opportunity to overcome fragmentation and heal old wounds. Thus, for example, some members of Gordoniya and Aqiva merged with the underground Deror movement at this time. (Deror itself was formed in a 1938 merger between He-haluts ha-Tsa'ir and Frayhayt; it emerged in its new metamorphosis in late 1939.)

Relations between the two constituent movements of He-haluts—Ha-shomer ha-Tsa'ir and Deror—were more complex and intricate. Although they discussed ways to effect greater cooperation to the extent of full merger, nothing came of it.

Stage Four, June–December, 1940: From Upheaval to a Glimmer of Hope

The Red Army entered the Baltic countries, Northern Bukovina, and Bessarabia in June, 1940. After annexing these areas, the Soviets ordered political parties and youth movements of all persuasions to disband. Some groups, especially in Northern Bukovina and Lithuania, anticipated the crisis and reorganized into underground cells administered by new institutions.

The Soviet annexation of Lithuania brought some 3,000 refugees from Poland residing in Lithuania (members of youth movements and the IZL) under Soviet rule. They responded by organizing small cells that met from time to time, communicated with each other, and stayed in touch with their parent organizations. These organizations, in turn, continued to exist for the moment; the Soviets even allowed them to promote the emigration of their members to Palestine.

A wave of arrests in the summer and autumn of 1940 decimated the World Zionist Organization leadership in Bessarabia and Latvia. In Lithuania, a similar operation at this time led to the internment of local leaders and activists, as well as refugees from Poland, including the commissioner of Betar in this country, Menachem Begin. Arrests of members of Zionist movements also became more prevalent in the Soviet-occupied areas of Poland and, especially, the western Ukraine. Unlike their counterparts in Lithuania, however, the movement activists in the western Ukraine had already embarked on underground activity. In Lvov, for example, seven members of the Ha-shomer ha-Tsa'ir leadership were arrested and prosecuted. Although the relentless sovietization measures caused great turmoil, the underground had opportunities to step up its collaboration. Thus, for example, a squad of activists from Lvov slipped into Czernowitz in a mission that proved to be quite important, to seek escape routes from the Soviet Union, if possible to Eretz Yisrael.

It was at this time (autumn of 1940) that an undercover unit of the Soviet security services contacted several leading Betar and IZL figures in Lithuania, including the commissioner of the local Betar organization, Joseph Glazman, even as other Soviet agencies were excoriating and persecuting the same individuals. Glazman was offered a unique deal: military collaboration in the expected war with Nazi Germany. During the resulting negotiations, the Soviet agents also mentioned the possibility of collaboration in anti-British intelligence activity in Palestine. This carrot-and-stick approach was used in other areas, such as contacts between Communist establishment figures and activists in Ha-shomer ha-Tsa'ir, Deror, and Po'aley Tsiyon.

In the autumn of 1940 a surprising glimmer of hope presented itself: Soviet Lithuania as an outlet to Palestine. Refugees there petitioned the Soviet authorities for permission to emigrate, pledging most of their resources and efforts to this mission. Such efforts were both overt and covert; they included the forging of documents and obtaining of foreign currency.

In everything they did to make emigration a reality, the Polish refugee members of movements and agents of political parties—who lived in Lithuania under semi-underground conditions—pressed their local colleagues into service. In this context, it is notable that even though Latvia and Lithuania had become full-fledged Soviet Socialist Republics, the authorities there were more liberal than those in the Polish and Romanian provinces that had been annexed to existing SSRs (those in the Ukraine were notably inflexible). This explains, in part, why Lithuania became and remained a center of communications between the annexed areas and overseas localities, and among the annexed areas themselves. The underground, of course, benefited from the situation and exploited it whenever possible.

Stage Five, December, 1940, Until June 22, 1941: Fragmentation Preceding the German–Russian War

In the beginning of this period, it became possible to emigrate to Palestine via Odessa and Turkey (there were also eastern routes, via Vladivostok and Iran). By April, 1941, nearly 1,000 persons had departed using this route. Most were members of Zionist movements who had reached Vilna in the mass flight from Poland, and they included many leading members and counselors of the youth movements. Their emigration, coupled with the departure of several movement leaders to Warsaw and the arrests of activists, weakened the underground activities in the annexed areas. Then, in another aspect of the same process, new activists and leaders—mostly people in their late twenties who had assumed their positions in the course of underground activity—began to vacillate. Several members of this group went on to lead the ghetto uprising movements; it suffices to mention two of them: Mordechai Anielewicz and Mordechai Tenenbaum.

In Lithuania, the unification tendencies in the Zionist underground were emulated by the young emigrants to Palestine. Two new movements came into being at the very start of this period, December, 1940. One was Irgun Berit Tsiyon (IBZ). Representing the merger of elements of Ha-no'ar ha-Tsiyoni A, Bnei Aqiva, Makkabi ha-Tsa'ir, and perhaps Gordoniya, IBZ was the publisher of *Nitsots* (discussed previously). This organization actually outlived the war. The second group, Herut, was the result of a merger between He-haluts ha-Tsa'ir and No'ar Tsofi Halutsi (Netsah) in Lithuania with members of Deror from Poland. Their newsletter, also called *Herut,* was initially shared by Herut and Deror, an affiliated movement in eastern Poland. This cooperation was short-lived, mainly because the cadre of Deror activists in Vilna and Luck was decimated by arrests. At this time, several members of Ha-shomer ha-Tsa'ir and Gordoniya were arrested in Czernowitz. In response, activists of all stripes went into hiding or concealed their past in various ways. Only on June 22, 1941, when the war broke out, did they resurface. The menace of Nazi occupation made all other dangers, including deportation to Siberia, seem trivial. Indeed, the German invasion prompted hundreds of movement activists and members to attempt to flee to the USSR in organized groups.

SUMMARY

Examination of the youth movements' conduct in the underground shows that, under the pressure of dynamic events and rapidly changing geopolitical realities, their activities occasionally transcended the vague goals articulated in decisions made at the beginning of the Soviet occupation. One of these goals—"dispersion, not liquidation"—was explicit. Various slogans were used: "keeping the ember alive," "surviving under any conditions and under any government," and so on. Reviewing the platforms and the ideational underpinnings of most movements that attempted to remain active under these conditions, and considering the operational consequences of these fundamentals, we find three major goals:

1. Facilitating the departure of as many activists as possible from the Soviet Union, in order to move them to Palestine or nearby destinations. This was also a preventive measure against persecution, pressure, political brainwashing, arrest, and disappearance.

2. Organizational, spiritual, and ideological activity. Essentially, this meant the cultivation of continuity, either within defined frameworks or

in the nearby periphery. The purpose was to fortify and augment members' fortitude in the senses of ideological and national consciousness, in order to withstand the Soviet doctrines and vigorous propaganda.

3. Moral and organizational assistance for the thousands of members left behind in western Poland—especially Warsaw—where, with hardly any leadership to speak of, they had to cope with Nazi terror. In pursuit of this goal, the movements sent several major activists back to the Polish capital, even though they had just fled this cauldron.

Comparison of the declared goals of several of the movements that operated in the underground shows that almost all of them pursued these goals, if perhaps with different phrasings and priorities. The same may be said with respect to activities. Much activity was ideological and cultural in nature, such as the continued use of Hebrew (including the writing of Hebrew books), discussions about Zionism and other themes in Jewish culture, listening to Hebrew programs on "Voice of Jerusalem" radio, and donating to the Jewish National Fund. More practical operations included the disposition of archives (hiding or burning them, depending on the circumstances), weapons training, publishing and dissemination of clandestine publications, assistance for members in trouble, including those languishing in prison or exiled to Siberia, and, especially, attempts to emigrate to Palestine. In several areas, emigration was given the highest priority. Sometimes the action was public and demonstrative—for example, public commemoration of the Maccabees' valor on Hanukka, and memorial ceremonies for Jabotinsky. It is impossible to describe here every action taken and assess every technique used; they would fill many volumes. Still, these matters are as fascinating now as ever. The material exists; perhaps the time has come to gather and publish it.

One final question deserves attention: did these activities and undertakings conform to the conventional model of a "classic" underground, or were they no more than a string of illegal activities? The available material on the subject suggests that the posture of at least some of the Zionist youth movements vis-à-vis the Soviet regime was far removed from the conventional underground model. These movements did not regard themselves as enemies of the regime, instead hoping that over time the regime would change its policies regarding Judaism and Zionism. They believed that the "tragic misunderstanding" between Zionism and Communism would eventually vanish. This posture was somewhat embarrassing to several Zionist movements of socialist coloration, especially Ha-shomer ha-Tsa'ir, although even they never doubted that their underground activities were in violation of Soviet law. A poster for May Day, 1940, issued jointly by Ha-shomer ha-Tsa'ir and Deror, serves as an example. The very authoring and dissemination of this poster was a serious counterrevolutionary act in Soviet terms, even though the contents of the poster were actually sympathetic to the USSR. Moreover, even though the Zionist youth movements were hounded by the security services throughout this period, none of them (not even Betar) professed hostile trends of thought, and all were careful to avoid any manifestation of anti-Sovietism. The problem of the attitude toward the USSR was so dominant and decisive that it led Deror and Ha-shomer ha-Tsa'ir to part ways.

Sovietologist and essayist Dr. Jehoshua A. Gilboa, who spent many years in the gulag (the network of labor and prison camps that stretched from Arkhangelsk to Yakutsk) for his activity in Ha-no'ar ha-Tsiyoni in 1939, asked whether it was an underground at all. He provided the answer himself: "It may have been a semi-underground in its internal activities and the protection of its ideological and spiritual purity, but [not] in the sense of explicit anti-government activity."[25]

The cumulative findings and information leave no doubt that the importance of the organizational activities and frameworks described above was much greater than its impact during the period under discussion. Their consequences were salient in at least the following areas:

1. Resistance during the Nazi occupation.

2. Strengthening the practical Zionist commitments of the large numbers of refugees and organizations that found themselves in the Soviet Union during the war.

3. Gathering the survivors of the Holocaust and bringing them to Palestine after the defeat of Nazi Germany.

4. The national awakening of Soviet Jewry in the last stages of World War II and thereafter.

12

Exacting Justice with "Hostile" Elements

As soon as the Red Army entered the western areas, the Jews began to harbor, along with a feeling of relief, apprehensions about life under Soviet rule. Especially anxious were those whose political and social views were contrary to Soviet norms. Indeed, despite the policy of relaxed tension and the smiles flashed by representatives of the new regime in the early going, the authorities regarded the Jews as "unreliable" and even "hostile." Before many days passed, Soviet authorities took various repressive police and administrative measures against the Jews, in addition to the decrees imposed on the population at large. These measures proved especially detrimental to much of the Jewish population. However, while the general decrees were explicit and overt, the police repression and harassment were usually subtle and hardly publicized. In fact, they were "preventive" measures taken against elements who, in the authorities' opinion, might do the new regime harm at some future time. In their actions against these elements, the authorities undoubtedly invoked the vast experience that they had amassed in their protracted struggle with population groups in the USSR proper in the 1930s.

The criteria by which individuals were defined as dangerous and as "enemies of the people" were usually based on their actions, views, and public and economic positions in the past (i.e., before the Red Army entered the area).

Even though the proportion of Jews among genuine anti-Soviet activists was small if not negligible, the security services' attitude toward them was sometimes informed by an antisemitic undertone that manifested itself in greater stringency toward the Jews than toward other peoples.

One of the conventional measures taken against former merchants, industrialists, and property owners was denial of the right to obtain responsible positions in the governmental and public system. The explanation given was that "our customs are different from yours in Poland. The merchant is the greatest enemy of the socialist regime. We can defend ourselves against our enemies but not against the merchant; we have to fight him constantly."[1] This principle, however, did not stop directors of Soviet governmental institutions, most of whom were brought in from the USSR, from hiring local shopkeepers and merchants in return for bribes.

Since most workplaces under the Soviet system were governmental or public, job-seekers in the proscribed categories were often forcibly idled or confined to petty occupations within the private settings that were still allowed to operate on the fringes of the economy. Fearful of being caught jobless, former business owners preferred to accept dirty, difficult work—anything, as long as it spared them the risk of being labeled "parasite."

The difference between Soviet theory and practice in these matters may be gauged by the case of Dr. Samuel Weiss, a lawyer from Slonim. "Anything that whoever thought or did under the Polish regime will not be held against him," the governor of the town proclaimed to anyone would listen. Therefore, "everyone will be given work in accordance with his skill and will be paid in accordance with his achievements." Even though Dr. Weiss, a well-known Zionist activist in Slonim, was seated at the presidium table while the governor made his festive proclamation, and even though he had defended local Communists in court when the Polish authorities had placed them on trial, he was barred not only from his profession but from all other forms of work. Subsequently, his apartment was confiscated and he was hauled off to prison.[2]

One purpose of the passportization campaign (discussed in Chapter 7), conducted in the annexed areas six to eight months after the Red Army came in, was to filter out residents whose social or political past was displeasing to the new regime. The authorities expressed such displeasure by marking the new ID cards with the numbers 11, 14, 38, or 39, depending on the region. These residents were henceforth subject to systematic administrative and economic restrictions that made them, in effect, second-class citizens. Practically speaking, this manifested itself in restrictions in the allocation of housing, study permits, and other matters. Those living in district capitals or areas near the German border were forced to relocate, usually to nearby small towns.[3] Also, these residents had to renew their ID cards each year, instead of every five years for everyone else.

Although the exact proportion of Jews among these "marked persons" cannot be verified, the number of Jews involved was undoubtedly very large. The incriminating ID numbers were given not only to the wealthy and to property owners, but also to merchants with medium-sized establishments, sometimes, even small retailers and shopkeepers—economic groups that embraced a sizable proportion of the Jewish population, especially in the cities.

Merchants in the Baltic countries were exempted from this social mark of Cain, evidently because passportization in those countries took place at the relatively late date of April, 1941 (about two months before the Germans invaded). In Bessarabia, in contrast, the method was invoked in the very first months of the Red Army presence.

In the former Polish provinces, the first wave of arrests, which concentrated on the public and political elite of the previous regime, swept up a large number of Jews. The victims were leaders of kehillot, members of town councils, and officials in now-outlawed political and party organizations. The leadership of the Bund and its satellites was especially affected at this stage. Two well-known Bund leaders, Henryk Erlich and Victor Alter, were reportedly arrested as early as October, 1939, along with Dr. Carol Eineigler, a leading figure in Lvov, and prominent activists in Slonim, Bialystok, Brest, Grodno, and Nezvizh. In Vilna, almost all local committee members and major activists were arrested, including Anna Rosental, a founding member of the Bund. Additional well-known public functionaries were arrested, including Aaron Tsintsinatus, editor of the Zionist newspaper *Tsayt* and an active member of Po'aley Tsiyon ZS (the "rightist" Po'aley Tsiyon, distinct from the Left).[4]

Jewish Vilna was shocked and horrified to learn of the arrest of the Attorney Joseph Tshernikov, a veteran journalist, Territorialist, and Folkist functionary who had made his reputation, among other things, for courageously defending Communists in Polish courts. Equally stunning was the arrest of the editor of the newspaper *Tog,* Zalman Rejzen, who frequently wrote pro-Soviet articles and reports. Tschernikhov and Rejzen were among the leaders of IKUF (Idisher Kultur Ferband), the Yiddish cultural league, which was set up at the World Conference in Paris in 1937 with the active participation of Jewish Communists. They were also board members of YIVO (Yidisher Visnshaftlikher Institut), the Institute for Jewish Research.

These arrests not only upset the local population, including those sympathetic to the Soviet regime; they also caused worldwide outrage and elicited a flood of appeals to release the detainees. They were not released, and several perished during the evacuation that followed the Nazi invasion of Russia. Others died under the harsh conditions of internment in the Soviet interior. Only a few survived their ordeal, after extensive peregrination.[5] This roundup of leading Bundists was undoubtedly another stage in the vicious and prolonged Soviet campaign against the Bund.

The authorities treated Zionist leaders similarly, if less harshly at this stage. Arrests of such individuals, like those of the Bundists, were selective for the moment. Jews in the vicinity and abroad were dismayed to learn of the detention of Dr. Emil Sommerstein in November, 1939. Sommerstein had represented the Jews of Eastern Galicia in the Polish Sejm and reached Lvov in the stream of refugees when the war broke out. At roughly this time, Professor M. Shor, a member of the Polish Senate and the Chief Rabbi of Warsaw, was arrested. He died about two years later in a prison in Uzbekistan. It was not clear whether Sommerstein and Shor had been arrested for their Zionist views or for having held high-ranking positions in the Polish administration. Either way, these initial arrests magnified the anxiety and perplexity of Jewish leaders in the annexed areas. Nearly all eschewed public activity and sought jobs of some kind, hoping that this would give them immunity. Some even tried to erase their traces by changing their place of residence.

In Nezvizh, the first wave of arrests claimed Joel Rozovski, chairman of the kehilla, head of the local World Zionist Organization office, and deputy mayor. In Pruzhany, the chairman of the World Zionist Organization office was arrested. In Bialystok, a sweep in late 1939 lasted several nights. At first the detainees were locked up in the local jail; after interrogation they were transported to Minsk. In Lomza (Lomzha), several Revisionists and a member of the Po'aley Tsiyon Central Committee were arrested. Some of these individuals also were hauled off to Minsk. In Brest, leaders of the General Zionists and Mizrachi and also the chairman of the Working Palestine (Eretz Yisrael) League were arrested.

The authorities, it transpired, had made preparations for these arrests and carried them out with the help of local Communists, who had drawn up detailed lists of Zionist activists, public functionaries, and individuals who had relatives in Palestine. The local Jews, discovering the scale of the arrests, were shaken, "until the town dignitaries saw fit to assuage the angry spirits by explaining, unofficially, of course, that most of the people arrested had

been charged with criminal offenses. [They added that] anyone found inno-
cent would, of course, be set free after the inquiry, since they wouldn't arrest people for nothing!"[6]

In Lithuania, the first dragnet swept up Reuben Rubinstein, a leader
of Lithuanian Jewry who had been the editor-in-chief of the Zionist daily
Di Idishe Shtime in Kovno for nearly 20 years. Rubinstein described the
experience in his memoirs:

On Friday night, July 12, 1940, after midnight, NKVD agents including a
Communist Jew came, ransacked my flat, poked around, turned over my
books and papers, threw all the written material into boxes, and handed me
a piece of paper: an arrest warrant.[7]

This warrant was one of hundreds issued for leading Lithuanian public
figures at the time. The intention was to neutralize elements that might in-
terfere with the People's Sejm elections, which were two days away. Only a
few Jews were arrested on this occasion, including newspaper employees,
heads of organizations, and activists in Zionist political parties. Most of
them were left to languish in various jails pending trial. A few were immediately exiled to the USSR. On August 1, 1940, the former chairman of the
Berit ha-Hayyal (Union of Jewish Army Veterans) in Poland, Dr. Miron
Sheskin, was arrested in Vilna; the commissioner of Betar in Poland,
Menachem Begin, and several of his colleagues met the same fate about a
month later.[8]

In Latvia, one of the first Jews arrested was the local Betar commissioner,
David Warhaftig. The Revisionist Party leadership was swept up later.[9]

One of the first to be arrested in Bessarabia was Isaac Milstein, the director of the Joint Distribution Committee office and the "Foundation," as this
organization was known in Bessarabia in the 1920s and 1930s. His arrest,
on July 7, sent the community into shock, since his staunch pro-Soviet leanings were well known.[10] About a week later, a group of Zionist leaders in
Kishinev and surrounding towns were arrested.[11] Apart from Jewish party
and organization activists, this wave of arrests included members of Romanian political parties, former governmental and municipal officials under
the Romanian regime,[12] and former members of the gendarmerie.

In Northern Bukovina, only a few Jews were arrested at this time. However, the eradication of Jewish community institutions in this area was
accompanied by a settling of scores. Thus, for example, a "liquidation committee" in Khutin ordered the six leaders of the kehilla (nearly all staunch

Zionists) to raise a "contribution" of 126,000 lei to offset the public funds spent to register the kehilla in the Jewish National Fund Golden Book. This project was intended to help young Jews meet the expenses of travel to Palestine and the like.[13]

After the initial post-annexation wave of arrests, the next sweep took place when the authorities moved swiftly to integrate the annexed areas into the USSR. In the western Ukraine and western Belorussia, there were at least two waves of arrests coupled with deportations at this time, in February and March of 1940. Most of the victims were Poles who owned farmsteads or estates, local peasants who had accumulated some wealth, and former high-ranking government officials—especially judges and prosecutors, and army and police officers. Members of the last group were deported to distant localities in the USSR.

Because the proportion of Jews in these population groups was miniscule, their representation among the persons arrested was also small. Here and there, however, Jewish community and party leaders were arrested and exiled, as were relatives of the first wave of detainees.[14] Also arrested were Jewish army officers (most of them physicians) who had fought with the Polish forces against the Soviet invasion in September, 1939. After the Red Army had taken them prisoner, they were kept with thousands of Polish officers in special camps in the Soviet Union, such as Kozelsk, Ustashkov, Starobelsk, and Vologda—the camps from which thousands of prisoners were subsequently taken to the forests of Katyn for execution.[15]

In the western Ukraine and western Belorussia, large-scale arrests began early in the morning of April 13, 1940, and lasted for several days. This sweep included persons who had once held positions of economic or political responsibility and families whose heads of household had been arrested and exiled in the previous sweeps. Indeed, the share of elderly, women, and children was conspicuously high.[16] Some of these persons were prosecuted under Article 58 of the penal code, which prescribed penalties for anti-Soviet propaganda. Most of them were exiled to Siberia or other locations deep in the USSR.

Jewish Communists were arrested at this time and accused of "Trotskyite deviations" and other similar offenses."[17] It is notable that Orthodox circles were not touched; at the present stage the Soviets did not regard them as an element that required mass arrests and deportation. However, certain individual Orthodox Jews were arrested, mostly rabbis suspected of "anti-Soviet" activity.[18]

The second wave of arrests and deportations, about eight months after the eastern Polish provinces had been annexed, did not spare the Jewish population. Advocate Leib Garfunkel, one of the major Po'aley Tsiyon ZS leaders and proponents of Jewish autonomy in Lithuania, was arrested on October 26.[19] On the night of April 1, 1941, Dr. Miron Sheskin, a leading Revisionist in Poland who had been interned in Lukishki Prison in Vilna— ostensibly for being a member of the British security service, a spy, and so on—was sentenced to eight years' hard labor. In all, 50 to 60 people were handed similar verdicts at Lukishki Prison including the commissioner of Betar in Poland, Menachem Begin, and various Zionist activists in Poland and Lithuania. Most were exiled to the Pechora area and other localities in the far north.

In Riga, Rabbi Mordechai Nurock, the Mizrachi leader in Latvia and a former member of the Latvian Sejm, was arrested on February 3, 1941. Also arrested was Rabbi Mordechai Dubin, a former delegate to the Sejm representing Agudath Israel and a confidante of the leaders of the old regime. Both were deported to the far reaches of Russia in the spring of 1941.

In Tallinn, Estonia, the head of the NZO (the Revisionists' "New Zionist Organization"), Pinchas Katz, was arrested after months of sporadic interrogations, of which he was allowed to disclose nothing, not even to his wife. This seems to have been the first political arrest of a Jew in Estonia. A short time later, five Revisionist and Betar leaders were arrested, taken to the northern part of the USSR, and tried for spying for Great Britain, among other "charges." Two individuals were sentenced to death by firing squad; the others were sentenced to ten years in the Gulag.[20]

In Bessarabia and Northern Bukovina, Jews were interned and exiled in similar mass operations in the autumn of 1940 and spring of 1941. Most of them were members of the liberal professions and former Romanian bureaucrats.

The dénouement of the mass deportations occurred on Friday night, June 13–14, 1941, throughout the Soviet-annexed areas, from Estonia in the north to Bessarabia in the south. Individuals and entire families were loaded onto trucks and wagons and transported first to railroad stations and thence eastward to distant locations in the USSR. This mass deportation evidently included hundreds of thousands, including many thousands of Jews. The Soviet authorities had succeeded in concealing their systematic, painstaking preparations for this operation until the last moment; the timing was apparently chosen to coincide as closely as possible with the estimated date of war with Germany.[21]

As for the criteria set by the Soviet security services for the deportation candidates, one may form an impression (at least in part) from orders issued by the Commissariat for Security Affairs in Soviet Lithuania to monitor "national and counterrevolutionary elements" among the Jews. The groups singled out for scrutiny included (1) leaders of all Zionist organizations and employees of the Zionist press, (2) leaders and journalists affiliated with the Bund, and (3) members of "militaristic Jewish organizations and fascist formations" (e.g., Alliance of Jewish Fighters at the Front, Berit ha-Hayyal, Betar, El Al, and the Revisionist Party). Also on the list were former industrialists and merchants, refugees, Trotskyites, and anyone who had been expelled from the Communist Party.[22]

Almost all Bund and Zionist leaders were listed, especially those aligned with the Revisionists and the General Zionists and (somewhat less so) those affiliated with the Socialist-Zionist camp. Only a few members of Zionist youth movements were exiled. Some of the deportees had been more or less integrated culturally or economically in the new system.

The second category, included prosperous merchants and major industrialists and bankers—people who were affluent and comfortable if not genuinely wealthy; occasionally, however (especially in the small towns), the list included the names of "people who had never earned enough to live on— families with lots of children." In contrast, the names of numerous Jews who were known to be extremely wealthy were omitted. This was almost surely the result of misrecording of names or similar errors. In other cases, people were placed on the list so as to settle personal accounts; for example, Jews and non-Jews were known to engage in denunciation for various reasons, including antisemitism.[23]

To gauge the way in which the mass deportation of "socially dangerous elements" was carried out, one can study the secret orders that the Deputy People's Commissar for State Security, Ivan Serov, sent to the Baltic republics. These orders suggest that the operation was to be implemented largely at night, "until dawn. . . . When entering the home of the deportee, the comrade responsible for the operational team should gather the family of the deportee into one room, taking appropriate measures to prevent any possible outburst." After verifying the identities of the family members, the team was to search the premises painstakingly for weapons, counterrevolutionary literature, foreign currency, and valuables in large quantities. "After the search, inform the deportees that, by decision of the government, they are about to be transferred to other parts of the Soviet Union." According to these orders, deportees were allowed to take with them up to 100 kilograms of commodities and objects of the following types: "(1) Clothing, (2) shoes, (3) underwear, (4) bedding, (5) dishes, (6) cups/mugs, (7) kitchen utensils, (8) enough food for their family for one month, (9) such money as in their possession, (10) a bag or boxes to hold objects."[24]

The operational team usually was composed of three people, at least one of whom was a local resident. Some of these local residents were Jews. Evidence in community memorial volumes and personal testimonials indicates that the operations were carried out in a similar fashion in all localities. These accounts confirm, among other things, that the deportations in certain localities continued even after the German–Russian war broke out. This was especially conspicuous in Estonia, where an exceptionally high proportion of Jews were deported because the Soviet armies withstood the Wehrmacht for several weeks. As many as 500 Jews were exiled from Estonia, including families, women, elderly, and children. Their homes were sealed with government padlocks; their relatives awaited their turn. It was under such circumstances of oppressive tension and fear that the German invasion began.

In Latvia, some 6,000 Jews were deported, including quite a few belonging to the sociopolitical elite. A day after the war broke out, about 250 Jewish refugees from Germany and Austria, including some Communists, were arrested and deported from Riga to Siberia, some accompanied by their Latvian-born wives. The deportations were assisted by specially recruited members of the Workers' Guard and employees of various institutions and factories.

Deportations of Jews from Lithuania at this time totalled about 7,000, including local residents and refugees from Poland and elsewhere.[25]

In Bessarabia, the deportations were rather indiscriminate. The authorities frequently swept up Communists, pro-Communists, and people with very low incomes.[26] The operation continued at full speed even after the war began; it ended only when the Wehrmacht was poised to enter the country.[27] In all, about 10,000 Jews were deported from Bessarabia, mostly property owners and political or public activists.[28]

The mass deportation in Northern Bukovina, carried out on June 13, 1941 and the days following, was not the first of its kind that year. Like this one, the previous deportations included a considerable number of Jews, especially those who had worked for the Romanian government. Now, in addition to non-Communist public leaders and activists, rank-and-file members of Zionist parties and the Bund were swept up. The transports also left room, of course, for industrialists, estate owners, merchants, miscellaneous business owners, lawyers, and doctors.

If many of the Jews in these areas had lived in constant fear thus far, the deportations of June, 1941, reduced them to blind panic. Thousands of people rushed to change their places of residence. Contributing to these reactions were NKVD cells that did not hesitate to drive the ill, as well as the healthy, out of their homes, promising them that they would find excellent doctors in their new places of residence, who would restore them to health.[29] The government news media described the expulsions in terms of the "resettlement" of thousands of enthusiastic volunteers, all eager to move into the Soviet interior. The war stopped the operation in mid-stream, although it continued for a few more days; in all, the authorities managed to deport about 5,000 Jews from Czernowitz and the surrounding towns.[30]

When the intention was mere interrogation, the authorities camouflaged their activities in various ways in order to prevent unwanted reverberations in the immediate vicinity. Only on rare occasions were people summoned directly to the NKVD. Ordinarily they were ordered to report to plausible locations such as a bank branch, an army recruiting station, the town council building, the Ministry of Education, or the income tax office. There they would be greeted by a security agent in civilian attire, who would say "Please follow me" or something equally polite. Only then were people led to the NKVD office.

Menachem Begin, living in a rural home near Vilna, was summoned to the municipal engineering department. When he failed to report, officials sought him out, ostensibly to find out why, and arrested him. A leader of the ZS in Lithuania, L. Garfunkel, was detained while visiting the Interior Ministry to apply for an exit visa from Lithuania, after having been told that an entry visa to the United States was waiting for him in Moscow.[31]

Public figures and activists in various political parties were summoned to the security services and interrogated at length, mainly at night, about their activities and those of others. A few people succeeded in evading continued interrogation by taking flight. Others committed suicide.[32]

Most of the prisoners were kept in separate cells. Interrogations, usually conducted at night, began long before the subject was incarcerated. The interrogations were sometimes accompanied by abusive language, beatings, and other humiliations, arousing fear and repugnance. Horror stories abounded about what went on between the walls of "the four-letter word" (as the NKVD or NKGB was called), and most of them proved to be true. The interrogations began in a rather friendly tone but sooner or later turned into a nightmare of the "we know everything" variety. The intent was to extract a maximum of information, even about matters that had taken place 20 or 30 years previously in political parties, schools, synagogues, community life, municipalities, and so on, including personal details about this or that citizen and his background. Needless to say, every person so interrogated had to describe his or her own past in great detail.

The major purpose of these exhausting investigations of party activists was to extract confessions about past activities that could be used against them in court. The accusations against Bund people usually had to do with collaboration with the previous reactionary regime. The charges against many of the political prisoners focused on something defined in the Soviet legal lexicon as "counterrevolution." The relevant item in the penal code was Article 58, which was divided into many subclauses. The investigators—Russians, Ukrainians, Lithuanians, and Jews—consulted a pocket manual containing data on all political parties and movements, including Jewish ones. Zionism was defined as "an agency of British imperialism whose main function is war on Communism."

A Russian investigator from Moscow who interrogated Reuben Rubinstein, a Lithuanian Zionist leader, pulled out a scrap of paper in one of the sessions and recited from it: "You Zionists are simple spies, British agents, and lackeys of international capitalism. You want to dispossess Arab laborers of their land and establish a bourgeoisie reactionary state in Palestine that will sell out to British imperialism and repress the peoples of the Middle East." The prisoner was asked when he had been taken on by the British secret service, what his monthly salary was, what information he had already forwarded to the British, and, most important, who his colleagues and partners in espionage were. When the subject responded with a puzzled expression and categorical denial of all charges, the investigator berated him: "Every Zionist functionary is a spy and an agent of a foreign government. You received money not only for forwarding military information but for waging war against the Communist revolutionary movement. With your speeches and articles, you've poisoned the souls of Jewish youth and thereby blocked their path to the revolutionary camp."[33]

Rabbi Mordechai Nurock, a Mizrachi leader and former delegate to the Latvian Sejm who was arrested in Riga in early 1941, described his interrogations as having focused on his having been:

1. A senior delegate to Zionist congresses.

2. A member of the Jewish National Fund board.

3. A leader in Mizrachi, the functions of which were to teach Bible and Hebrew.

4. The co-author of a memorandum on the condition of the Jews in the USSR in 1937.

When he attempted to mention his activity in the worldwide struggle against the Nazis, he was told: "Hitler is our friend and ally; we do not wish to hear anything against him."[34]

A series of accusations hurled in the face of Joseph Aronovitz, a member of the Bund party committee in Vilna, on November 15, 1939, is indicative of the nature of the anti-Bund efforts:

1. The Bund is a nationalist and counter-revolutionary party.

2. It had received money from many countries, including Poland, in order to wipe out the workers' movement.

3. It had, according to a Polish government proposal, collaborated with the PPS (Polish Socialist Party) in order to foment factionalism in the trade unions.

4. It had accepted money from industrialists for strike-breaking purposes.

5. It had set up nationalist trade unions in order to sabotage the unity of the proletariat.

6. It had provided the Polish secret police with lists of trade union members.

7. It had urged workers to fight against the Soviet Union.

8. It had helped General Zeligovski occupy Vilna in 1919.

9. Together with the PPS, it had urged Polish workers not to surrender and to continue fighting Nazi Germany.

10. It had collaborated with the Pilsudski and Sanacja factions (the latter was a political agency established by Pilsudski in 1927) to help Poland gird for war against the USSR.

11. Together with the PPS, it had planted spies in the USSR to provoke riots, destroy factories, and so on.

12. It had planted *agents provocateurs* in the Polish Communist Party.

13. Two of its leaders, Henryk Erlich and Victor Alter, who were also representatives of the Socialist Internationale, were spies and agents who had sold out to the bourgeoisie.[35]

The agonizing ordeal of protracted interrogation was inflicted on industrialists, merchants, bankers, and ordinary people who had acquired some wealth. Nor were these interrogations free of antisemitism.

Many of the lists of candidates for internment and exile evidently were compiled from documents that local authorities, central authorities, and various parties and organizations had not had time to destroy.[36] Whenever the security services thought the rosters of functionaries and public figures were incomplete, they consulted local Communists and sympathizers. There is no other way to explain how the security services were able to carry out arrests within a week or two of having reached the area. Moreover, the Zionists and socialists could not have been culled from the masses of refugees from western Poland on such a large scale without the assistance of Jewish Communists, who stalked them "like beasts of prey in the streets of Bialystok, Luck, Grodno, and Kowel."[37]

Subsequently, after nearly all political activists in or around the previous regime had been uncovered, the security services had no further need of the veteran Communists. Any information that they could not supply was provided by informers who reported everything going on in the here-and-now. Since the public was oblivious to the informers' relationship with the security services, the informers were both more efficient in their mission and more dangerous for their victims. They became even more menacing when the new regime settled in and spared no efforts to combine them into a permanent network.

In quite a few cases, ordinary Jews were forced to become informers after having been caught "misbehaving" (especially in economic matters). In the course of their interrogation, they were told that their punishment might be nullified or deferred if they would sign a commitment to help the security services by providing information or other assistance. This kind of entrapment not only fomented betrayal and treachery but also provided a convenient background environment for informing in the service of personal interests.

The incarcerations, interrogations, expulsions, and deportations plunged the public into an atmosphere of fear and dread. Circles that had originally greeted the new regime warmly now felt insecure. The delight with which they had greeted the Red Army was no more. Not surprisingly, many of the Jews "lived without a tomorrow; no one was sure what the morrow would bring."[38] This was especially true for those who were lumped together under the collective heading of "bourgeois," including not only the very wealthy but much of the middle class. The new regime persecuted them relentlessly, turning the arrests into a daily nightmare that came true with every knock on the door.

People stopped talking, even with acquaintances, except to chat about the weather. They refrained from meeting even with relatives. Trust in friends vanished. They didn't visit others' houses or admit guests to their own. They stopped telling jokes. They were afraid to listen to overseas radio programs, even if it wasn't explicitly forbidden. . . . People were reluctant to talk and hear about their past. . . . Jews in the town broke relations with kin in other countries and with people in Palestine, constantly fearing that they would be accused of Zionist activity or intelligence and espionage activities. Most people were so fearful in these matters that they lost their vigor and initiative. They began to stick to themselves, saying little, because everyone was suspicious of everyone.[39]

A palpable example of this is an excerpt quoted below from the letters of parents in the western Belorussian town of Brestowice to their son, Isaac Getz, in Chicago. On February 27, 1941, the father wrote:

It is no trivial matter for us to be on friendly terms with those overseas. As for your questions that I'm not answering—that's how it must be. The main thing that should concern you and us are family matters. In this context, I can tell you that we're all healthy, satisfied with Soviet rule, and lacking nothing. . . . Please, please understand me. . . . I advise you to write your letters delicately and with more of a family tone. Please forgive me for these remarks. . . .[40]

The last letter, written just before the war broke out, ends with the following plea: "Please don't regret that I write so little and of so little interest. . . . Understand me, and then everything will be clear to you. . . . It is much healthier to write sparingly. . . ."

Anyone who had ever quarreled or struggled with Communist groups, irrespective of his or her social class, now lived in a haze of concern and fear of retribution. Many who had good reason to fear mishap and misfortune now tried to obfuscate their identities, to the extent possible, by changing their mode of attire. People of means who had previously been careful to dress well now shuffled about in worn-out, shabby clothing. In Czernowitz, where more than half the population was Jewish, "one could no longer meet well-dressed people in the streets," in the words of a report from the fall of 1940. "People of the upper and middle classes are afraid to show their faces."[41] In the cities and towns, it became fashionable to wear boots instead of shoes. "It was a sad joke," a contemporary account from the western Belorussian town of Volozhin related, "to see important property-owners going about in boots, taking off their starched-collar shirts in favor of the Soviet *gymnastyorka* (semi-military khaki shirt) even without an order from on high."

One of the most accepted ruses to blur the past was to change residence or to move to a far-away city. Not everyone who feared arrest and persecution, however, was able to part with his home and community. Furthermore, many still secretly hoped that, everything notwithstanding, they would be spared. After all, the arrests were selective. Thus most of the Jews stayed where they were, despite the arrests, deportations, and expulsions. In a few cases they tried to avert the danger by attempting to bribe local officials or beseeching "higher authorities," including Stalin.[42]

Had the war with Germany not broken out, the waves of arrests and expulsions would probably have spread to additional sectors of the Jewish and non-Jewish population. As it was, the Red Army beat a hasty retreat; the security services were forced to stop the arrests and deal with the transfer of those already interned.

In addition to the mass internment and deportation of "enemies of the people" for so-called political and social reasons, many Jews became victims of the new regime's struggle against the perpetrators of "black market" dealings and other economic offenses. Indeed, a black market in commodities—with hoarding, price gouging, and "speculation"—followed the Soviet regime into the annexed areas. This was owing in part to the state of war and the movements of armies in the area, which disrupted supplies to urban centers. Such circumstances, of course, encourage hoarding. Compounding the problem was the influx of refugees; all those extra mouths to feed exacerbated the logistical problems that had always bedeviled the Soviet army.

Jews took up position among the black-market transactors for other reasons as well. Most Jewish breadwinners in the annexed areas, as the reader will recall, had been merchants and craftsmen. This community had now been overtaken by a regime that sought to apply socialist principles by means of mass expropriation and nationalization. Whereas more powerful merchants and industrialists had been summarily stripped of their property and inventories, shopkeepers and even smaller retailers were given a reasonable period of time to contend with the nationalization policy on their own. In many cases, their immediate response was a desperate attempt to keep their modest possessions away from the regime—which defined any such attempt as the criminal offense of hoarding. In this matter, the authorities had no pity even for peddlers and small shopkeepers who had hardly scraped by under the old regime. No did the attempt to channel these masses of self-employed breadwinners into other occupations solve the problem altogether. Often those who accepted salaried jobs did not earn enough to support their families; consequently, they were inclined to dip into government property and trade in it. This further widened the circle of black marketeers.

The Soviet regime responded with a swift crackdown, condemning these "speculators" as "enemies of the people who sabotage the economic revitalization and dispossess the masses of laborers of their money." In their enthusiastic pursuit of speculators, gougers, and hoarders, the authorities did not always distinguish between major players and "small fry." By all indications, the only important rationale in the application of punishment was deterrence.

Another factor in the persecution of economic offenders was personal revenge. For example, a Jewish shoemaker in Nezvizh informed on a Jewish competitor for having "speculated" with a package of yeast; the latter was sentenced to a year in prison.[43]

The press covered the anti-speculation campaign at great length. The names of offenders, the details of the charges (including the specific offense under the Soviet legal code), and, of course, the verdict, were reported in prominent locations and in outsize bold print.[44] At certain stages of the occupation, the authorities failed to distinguish between political opponents and economic delinquents; both were branded "opponents of the regime" and exiled with their families to Siberia.

According to Polish sources (closely connected with the Polish government-in-exile in London), 30 percent of the 1,150,000 individuals arrested and deported from Poland to the USSR in the Second World War were Jewish. In other words, 345,000 Jews were exiled from Poland alone during this period.[45] This figure seems to be an exaggeration; furthermore, there is no doubt that as many as two-thirds of these people were refugees from the western and central parts of the country. Data from various locations and sources suggest that the number of local Jewish residents of the eastern provinces of Poland who were arrested and exiled to the Soviet interior probably did not exceed 5 percent of the Jewish population of these areas, i.e., approximately 60,000. By region, 30,000–35,000 had resided in Eastern Galicia and Wolhynia, and 25,000–30,000 in western Belorussia.

The proportion of similarly affected Jews in the other Soviet-annexed areas was roughly the same, although these deportations took place at later dates. In absolute terms, the approximate numbers were 7,000 in Lithuania, 6,000 in Latvia, 500 in Estonia, 10,000 in Bessarabia, and 6,000 in Northern Bukovina.

In all, nearly 100,000 Jews were arrested and exiled in 1939–1941, i.e., about 5 percent of the local Jewish population in the Soviet-annexed areas. Many of the deportations (especially in the Baltic countries and the former Romanian areas) took place just before the war with Germany broke out and afterward. Even more people would have been deported were it not for the hasty Red Army retreat from the advancing Wehrmacht in the summer of 1941.

13

The German Invasion

On June 22, 1941, at dawn, Nazi Germany launched a blitzkrieg against the Soviet Union across the entire length of the frontier. The assault included the flanking of large centers in a pincer movement meant to cut them off, coupled with heavy bombardment of military and civilian targets. These operations were preceded by crushing strikes by the Luftwaffe and Wehrmacht against the civilian population of the Soviet-annexed areas. Cities with large concentrations of Jews, such as Riga, Kovno, Bialystok, Rovno, and Lvov, suffered heavy air raids. The rapid German attacks caused widespread pandemonium, as whole sections of the front were rendered defenseless.

Most attempts to repulse the invaders failed, and the Soviet defense lines, particularly in the north (from Latvia to Wolhynia), crumbled and collapsed. Although the Red Army was slightly more successful on the southern front (from Wolhynia to Bessarabia) and in the northernmost section of the Baltic coast (Estonia and several islands in the Gulf of Finland), overall Soviet resistance was no match for the Germans. Lithuania was overrun in a few days; Latvia and Belorussia within a week or so; the western Ukraine, Eastern Galicia, and Northern Bukovina within two weeks; Wolhynia within three weeks; Bessarabia within a month; and Estonia within two months.

The possibilities for escape and evacuation from the areas engulfed in the fighting were determined chiefly by the time that lapsed between the onset of the invasion and the completion of the conquest. Other factors, discussed later, included enclaves that the rapidly advancing German forces left in their rear, with whole cities and towns still under Soviet control. Thus, for example, the Germans took Dvinsk (Daugavpils) in eastern Latvia on June 26, three days before they entered Liepaja in western Latvia. The easternmost township in the Polesie region was captured on June 26, three days before the fall of Pinsk to its west. The town of Nesvizh, situated close to the old Soviet border, was seized as early as June 27, whereas Novogrudek to the west was not overrun until nine days later, on July 6. This situation, coupled with the paralysis of the rail and road network, created confusion and despair among many of those who had planned to escape eastward.

The suddenness and strength of the German attack resulted in inordinately heavy losses for the Soviets and sowed chaos in every sphere of life. The following is an eyewitness account of the scene in bombarded Riga on June 27, 1941, the sixth day of the war:

While the radio was broadcasting victory announcements, we saw Red Army soldiers coming down the street. . . . They walked without order, their uniforms soiled and tattered, their heads bowed. They trudged along in dust-covered boots. . . . They could barely drag themselves forward. Once in a while they would sit down on the sidewalk, stretch their feet on the pavement, and rearrange their foot wrappings, or just lean against a wall, sitting there lifelessly without saying a word to anyone.[1]

If this is how the army looked, one can easily imagine the situation at all levels of the civilian administration. In many localities, for example, persons responded to the mobilization decree issued on the first day of the war (affecting those born between 1905 and 1918) and reported to enlistment centers, but the authorities were unable to process them.[2] On June 23, the second day of the war, the conscription office in Vilna was "completely abandoned; there was no one to talk to."[3] In a few localities where reservists were mobilized, they were soon released and sent home.

Enemy paratroopers and secret agents who were dropped behind the Red Army lines posed a considerable danger to the civilian authorities. In addition to the divisions of the regular Romanian army, which operated against the Soviet forces on the southern front, the Wehrmacht was assisted (particularly in the Baltic countries and the western Ukraine) by local irregular forces set up by Lithuanian, Latvian, Estonian, and Ukrainian nationalist underground organizations. As they pursued the retreating Soviet units and seized strategic facilities and urban centers, they began to take repressive measures against the Jewish population, whom they regarded as having sympathized and collaborated with the hated Soviet rulers. As time passed, these measures became increasingly severe. Soon these forces were joined by local municipal officials, police, fire brigades, post office and railway workers, and soldiers and officers who had deserted the Red Army. They took over whole city sections,[4] murdering Soviet officials and looting Soviet institutions. Needless to say, terrorizing the local Jewish inhabitants was high on their list of priorities. Even where the Red Army remained in control, at least officially, there were growing signs of estrangement and hostility toward the Jews on the part of their neighbors, who had feared to display these sentiments until then.

As the enemy continued to advance in almost all sectors of the frontier, the Soviet authorities ordered the mobilization of volunteers for civil defense. Brief first-aid courses were given, attended mostly by women. In various localities the authorities announced the establishment of "engineering battalions," in which thousands of people were mobilized to build fortifications and barriers and dig trenches. Another initiative was the formation of "storm battalions," composed mostly of Soviet loyalists and party activists, to protect state and party buildings. Vigorous oral and written propaganda campaigns were waged here and there; many Jews took an active part in them.

Wasting no time, Moscow issued directives concerning practical preparations for partisan warfare and the evacuation of thousands of families of Soviet officials and the military to the east. On June 27, 1941, only five days after the war broke out, the Soviet Government and the Central Committee of the Communist Party took an official decision on "evacuation of the population and objects of industrial, material, and state value." This resolution affected eight Soviet republics, including all the annexed areas.[5]

The evacuation decision meant nothing to most residents of the annexed areas, including the Jews, mainly because it came too late; the enemy had already overrun large parts of these territories. The proclamation stated that civilians would be evacuated on the basis of an order of priorities. The first to go were specialists and the engineering and technical staff of strategically important enterprises, as well as women, children, the disabled, and men over the age of 50. In fact, the families of Communist Party members and government officials, the so-called "party and Soviet aktiv" (officials and activists), were favored similarly.

The civilian authorities and Party agencies were supposed to reach an agreement with local army commands about evacuation routes and the allocation of transport vehicles for people and equipment. However, owing to setbacks on the front and the pressure of logistical imperatives, the army was given priority in food supplies, materials, and means of transportation. This seriously disrupted the logistics of the civilian evacuation. Evacuation routes, too, were problematic, since the Germans had either captured or encircled the main junctions. Thus the evacuation proceeded mainly along secondary roads and twisting and badly maintained byways. In Estonia, it also took place by sea.

By June, 1941, a majority of Jews in the annexed territories had become full-fledged Soviet citizens. As such, they considered themselves relatively safe from the ravages of the war that had swept almost all of Europe. This feeling was grounded largely in their trust in the might of the Soviet Union and, particularly, the "great Red Army," which the media glorified day in and day out as "invincible." Although they had witnessed the collapse of the Polish state and its army within a few days in September, 1939, hardly anyone imagined that terms like "military collapse" could be applied to the USSR. Within a short time, however, all the rosy assessments had been disproved, and the horrors of Nazi occupation suddenly loomed on the horizon as a tangible and imminent prospect.

The period of Soviet occupation had desensitized the Jews in the annexed areas to the Nazi menace, chiefly because the Soviet media went to great lengths to whitewash events across the border. Consequently, the frantic retreat of the Red Army in the first days of the invasion sowed confusion and helplessness that soon gave way to despair.

The first to face the realities of the war and the difficult decisions it foisted on them were the inhabitants of small towns in the western frontier areas on the east banks of the Nemen, Bug, San, and Prut rivers, where the German advance had been particularly rapid. The following is an eyewitness account of the first hours of the war in the Bessarabian frontier settlement of Lipkany:

We are awakened by sudden gunfire. A military drill? The fusillade grows stronger. One shell, then another, fell between the houses and shook the whole town. People leave their houses in panic. We've got to run away! But where to? To "there," the banks of the Prut? Sounds of weeping and wailing. Bareheaded, leaving their belts behind, Soviet officers flee their barracks. They ignore our pleas. . . . But the people comforted themselves by expressing hopes that the Germans would soon take to their heels, naked and barefoot. Once the Soviet "pieces" start singing, the German, shoeless, will flee for his life.[6]

The hopes of the Lipkany Jews were soon dashed; on the following day, June 23, they were evacuated with other civilians to the town of Rishen, where "six or seven families squeezed into one room [or were housed] in hallways and attics, while a great many of them camped under the open sky."

Moreover, due to the speedy advance and outflanking movements of the invading forces, the area was shortly cut off from other parts of Bessarabia, and avenues of retreat and escape for troops and civilians alike were blocked. Jews elsewhere found themselves in a similar predicament.

The Jews were alarmed at the sight of the humiliating retreat of the Red Army and the collapse of civilian authorities, one after another, in disregard of the fate of the local population. Even as the horror approached from the west, nationalist gangs threatened the Jews with massacres. Their plight was grave indeed, and their options were limited and uncertain. The first was to follow the Red Army columns as they retreated to areas still under Soviet control. The second was to disperse and seek temporary shelter in the forests and villages, while trying to elude both the regular army units and the nationalist gangs. The third option was to wait and see. Before long, the second option proved unfeasible; nationalists had already posted guards blocking exit from numerous localities, and these sentries missed no opportunity to attack any Jews who happened their way. Furthermore, no effective steps were taken to commence guerrilla warfare in the areas occupied by the invading forces. A few special units were hastily established, but they were used to guard the rear and flanks of the retreating army columns, sporadically engaging enemy troops in rear-guard operations. The hasty flight of senior officials and Party functionaries liquidated the only force capable of spearheading an effective partisan movement, into which at least some local Jews could be absorbed.

Thus the Jews' practical alternatives were two: stay or flee. Those who preferred the latter faced additional quandaries: where to go? how? and with whom? As the evacuation of state enterprises and party institutions proceeded, and as the civilian population, including the Jews, was left to its own devices, the need to take fateful decisions became increasingly urgent. "Although we had little idea what could be expected if we remained and came under German rule," wrote a witness who escaped and subsequently joined and fought in the ranks of the Red Army, "many decided to leave with the retreating army units, no matter what." Another factor that induced large numbers of Jews to depart immediately was their great fear of their non-Jewish neighbors; many sensed the terrible hatred that had been mounting during the previous years. Explicit threats reinforced profound apprehensions of another "Kishinev-style" pogrom. A Jew from Riga who managed a nationalized factory during Soviet rule recounted the following:

On June 27, upon arrival at the Maraudom factory, I saw that two gallows had been erected. A woman worker informed me with tears in her eyes that one was for me and the other for Ozin (a Communist Latvian manager). I went and mentioned what I had been told. I was advised quietly to run away "without making any noise." I took a horse and a cart from the plant, fetched my wife and children, and off we went. On the way, shots were fired at us from the windows. At kilometer 18 we met Dr. Dubinski, who, as a chief physician, had a bus at his disposal. He agreed to take my wife and children, and for many months I had no idea where they were.[7]

Although the future seemed uncertain, the Jews sensed that the Nazi occupation would bring a change for the worse. In fact, the imminent arrival of the Wehrmacht terrified the Jewish community, which was already trembling at the prospect of anti-Jewish riots and reprisals by local elements. The only questions were how long the unrest would continue, how many victims it would claim, and so on. Jewish communities throughout the annexed areas hummed with speculations and assessments.

Some Jews knew full well that escape was their only option. These individuals belonged to three main groups:

1. Members of the Communist Party and the Komsomol, senior officials in the party apparatus, trade unions, Interior Ministry (especially the police services including the secret police), NKVD, and militias.

2. Administrators responsible for the implementation of sovietization policies, especially in economic contexts such as nationalization of enterprises and land (this group included Jews whose integration into the Soviet state apparatus coincided with the ouster of non-Jews).

3. Persons who, while not affiliated with official Soviet agencies, were regarded as sympathizers with the regime and who confirmed this publicly in workplaces or at mass assemblies.

To these groups we should add the numerous refugees from western Poland who had already experienced Nazi policies toward the Jewish population. Many people in this category were among the first to decide to flee, for the second time, and they urged the local Jews to do the same.

Jewish youth unburdened with families were especially inclined to join the stream of refugees heading for the Soviet interior. On the whole, however, broad and diverse sections of the Jewish population, including entire families, were swept up by the movement eastward. There were also persons suspected of hostility toward the Soviet regime, some facing arrest or exile: property owners; members of the Bund, the Revisionists, and the Betar youth movement; veterans of the anti-Bolshevik campaigns of 1918–1920; and others.

The considerations and arguments described above were not always sufficient to sway individuals faced with the dilemma of "fight or flight." In some places, vacillators were won over by the prevailing public mood: "The Jews were confused and did not know what to do. The leaders were in jail and there was no one to consult. . . . The decision was taken on the spur of the moment: to flee!"[8]

In a few cases, entire Jewish communities fled en masse. In the small Bessarabian town of Orgeyev, for example, an announcement was made on July 7 that all residents should leave temporarily for the Soviet interior. Thus, "people began fleeing toward the border on foot or in horse- and ox-driven carts."[9] Some of the escapees headed for two border towns, Criuleni and Rozan. Within two days, all of the Jewish residents, except those without any means of escape, had fled the town.

Among those who favored escape were people who regarded this move as temporary, since "the Germans will be defeated within a few days" and they would be able to return. For this reason they did not take sufficient provisions. Others believed that "the old people and women have nothing to fear. Only young men face danger."

Some counseled against escape, as the following account makes clear:

It was as if someone were whispering in my ear: "Run away, buddy, get away from Aleksandria fast. Take your parents, leave everything behind, and run for your lives. Something tragic is going to happen here. The worst of all: the murder of Jews!" But this voice issuing from the heart was countered by another, the voice of reason, which spoke with cold logic: "What foolishness, Shalom. What does this mean, murder? Are people going to be murdered just like that? Sure, there will be restrictions and decrees, just as in Poland when the Germans occupied it. But murder? Suddenly I realized that it wasn't the voice of my reason at all. It was the voice of my parents talking to me at the same time. They were firmly against leaving everything and setting off into the unknown. They kept delaying me, too. Neighbors came in and began comforting one another, saying that the devil is not as black as he's painted. God will help. Maybe the town commandant will be a good-natured or greedy type, with whom we can get along. Besides, where shall we run in these crazy days, at our age? Become vagabonds in the Russian winter? They also say that the Russians don't let anyone cross the old Korets-Novogorod-Volynsk border. Some of the town people have just come back from there. One of them is our neighbor, and he confirms the rumor. After all, that's why he came back.[10]

In several cases Jewish youths managed to climb onto army trucks heading east but changed their minds after their mothers begged them to get off and stay. "The boys yielded to their mothers' entreaties and in so doing sealed their own fate." Some young people succeeded in persuading their parents to join them on their way east. By and large, however, they remained in their native towns and villages together with their parents and younger siblings. Family solidarity was the dominant factor in delaying Jewish attempts to flee. Tens of thousands of teenagers and breadwinners who had considered escaping, and who had an opportunity to do so, rejected the idea outright for this reason alone. This tragic rationale was re-used in the ghettos and death camps.

Those opposed to escape included both optimists and pessimists. The former clung to the belief that the war between two giants would finally put an end to the Nazi nightmare threatening the Jews. They were reluctant to leave their homes and flee to the east because they thought the war would be short and fought on the enemy's soil. Hadn't Soviet *politruks* (propaganda officers) promised as much on countless occasions? Even some who considered the possibility of German victory argued that staying put was preferable to setting out toward an uncertain future. In addition, many hesitated to risk the consequences of disobeying official orders against the abandoning of workplaces and unauthorized travel out of town.

Although the German mistreatment of Jews was widely known, hardly anyone considered systematic mass murder. Some Jews were exultant about the Soviet withdrawal. They were convinced that the Germans would defeat the Soviets and refused to believe the atrocity tales brought by refugees from the west. They dismissed these accounts as the dissembling of Soviet propagandists and countered them by citing the conduct of the Germans in World War I. German Jews, or those acculturated as Germans (e.g., in Courland, Estonia, and Eastern Galicia), actually believed that the Germans would not harm them.[11]

Astonishingly, some Jews actually looked forward to the Germans' arrival. Most of these individuals had been interned by the Soviet authorities and had anticipated years of exile in the Russian interior. Some of them were liberated by nationalist gangs and even by German soldiers during the panicky retreat of the Red Army.

Some Jews in the western Ukraine and western Belorussia may have learned a lesson from the fate of the refugees who had previously arrived from western Poland and remained homeless and jobless. The Soviet authorities eventually came to regard them as unreliable elements and exiled some to the Russian interior. Jews of Polesie, Wolhynia, and Eastern Galicia feared that they might find themselves in similar straits should they decide to abandon their homes and join the retreating Red Army. Still, the stories of German atrocities had their effect. Thus Jewish refugees from western Poland were found on both sides in the debate about whether to flee or stay put.

Ultimately, no mass flight of Jews occurred. Without reliable information about conditions in the German-occupied areas, and unable to make a balanced assessment of the future course of events, the Jews could not reach a collective decision to abandon their homes and embark on wanderings within the USSR. Had they been able to organize in some way, many of them might have found a way to survive. However, the invasion left them stunned and immobile.

In Bessarabia, some Jews hoped that the occupation would be administered not by the Germans but by the Romanians, with whom, so the argument went, one could get along by greasing palms. "We'll pay them ransom and do whatever we can." The rabbi of the Bessarabian town of Yedinsty recalls the state of mind in his community: "Although you can expect a pogrom, at least the lucky ones will survive."[12] Arguments of this kind caused many Jews to change their minds at the last moment about escaping, as happened, for instance, in the town of Romanovka.[13]

In some cases, the Jews' reasoning was influenced by Soviet arrests and deportations only a few days before the invasion: "It's better to die with the Star of David sewn on one's back than to stand in line under Russian rule, even for the toilet."[14]

The review of arguments against escape would not be complete without mention of the reluctance to abandon property. For some, this attachment was so deeply ingrained that they simply could not understand "how someone can leave his home and all his possessions and begin the life of a nomad." This was especially true of those who owned real estate. The Jewish landowners in particular were determined "not to abandon their inheritance and their homes."[15]

Testimonies indicate that the attitude of the authorities toward the Jews who joined the organized evacuation generally conformed to instructions, whereas the treatment of those who left of their own accord differed from place to place.[16]

The success or failure of attempts to escape to the Russian interior by Jews shortly after the outbreak of the war was determined directly by many factors, discussed below.

During the few days when it was still possible to run away, many local authorities appealed for calm and warned the population not to escape, while they themselves plunged into feverish preparations to leave and evacuate their offices together with their staff and equipment. According to Mendel Liberman, a resident of Yedinsty:

The residents themselves did not know what the real situation was, because even radio announcements did not coincide with the facts. Consequently, we fed on rumors. At the same time, we sensed that the state institutions were preparing to leave for the Russian interior. All senior officials, including Jews, were told to get ready for evacuation. We also heard that a special permit was needed; otherwise a person would not be allowed to cross the Dniester on the Russian-Bessarabian border. Anxiety mounted. . . . Jews began burying some of their possessions and valuables in the ground. As all this was going on, the enemy began to bombard the town.[17]

When local residents, including teachers, went to the local Party building to ask for permits to cross the Dniester, they were reprimanded: "What does this mean? Do you really have no trust in the might of the Red Army? You are sowing panic." A Soviet attaché informed all employees of the local State Bank that "no enemy will dare to set foot on the soil of the Soviet homeland, and there is no reason to fear German-Romanian occupiers." Only a few hours after this announcement, news spread through the town that he and other senior officials, including a Jewish manager by the name of Steinbortz, had already left and were on their way to Russia.[18]

In most places the civilian authorities departed in haste, if not in panic. Nor did they flinch from commandeering the few available transport vehicles for themselves and their families, thereby precluding the possibility of escape by ordinary folk.[19]

The authorities often imposed news blackouts and withheld the truth from the frightened populace. Such was the case in the towns of Slonim in western Belorussia and Sarny in Polesie. Having learned that "the last [state] institutions are leaving town and the rear-guard of the army is beating a panicky retreat," some Jewish residents of Sarny began "leaving on foot, carrying babies in their arms and small bundles on their backs."[20]

The authorities in many localities issued decrees forbidding residents to quit their work posts; violators were to be treated as deserters. By the time the locals realized that the officials had left, as in the western Belorussian town of Kremenets, it was too late. After the Soviet authorities had fled Slonim, the telephone operators remained on the job and responded to all calls. The telephone exchange employed many young Jewish women; with the outbreak of the war they were given strict orders not to leave their posts even for one moment. In their frantic departure, the authorities did not give any thought to this vital communications center and felt no need to tell the operators to quit working and, perhaps, join them in their flight. The women stayed on until the Germans arrived and captured the post office.[21]

In the Estonian town of Pärnu a local resident named Ferman, who had been drafted into the civil defense because he was a fireman, was ordered to remain at his post until the last moment, even after his own family was evacuated. Shmuel Ribak of Tallinn was mobilized in the first days of the war as a driver for a minister in the Estonian Government. He drove his boss to the border, only to be turned back so that the minister might continue performing his duties in the capital. In the last days of the evacuation, the minister boarded one of the ships due to sail to a Soviet harbor. Ribak described what happened next:

I was left alone with the car and didn't know what to do. . . . I wanted to drive home because my parents were in Tallinn. . . . I had hardly started to return when Soviet sailors approached me and warned me that the Germans were already in the city. Together with them I boarded a small warship, a minesweeper of some kind, and arrived at Kronstadt.[22]

Jews conscripted into the Latvian Workers' Guard and similar organizations established to defend public facilities and institutions faced special problems. The very existence of these units boosted Jewish morale, but many of their members had to remain with them on call and for guard duty. Thus many families were broken up in the most difficult of times.

In localities close to the old Soviet border, the escapees fleeing eastward went by horse-drawn carts or on foot. In all other areas, however, more effective means of transportation, such as trains (if they still operated) or motor vehicles, were needed. Since even in peacetime these were under the strict control of the state authorities and Party Councils, escape plans hinged on obtaining permission to board an eastbound train or other vehicle. Testimonies indicate that state officials, their families, and families of Red Army officers were usually given preferential treatment; only occasionally were rank-and-file citizens, usually women, allowed to board trains or other vehicles. Events in the Latvian town of Liepaja, which the Germans captured after a week of heavy fighting, illustrate this order of priorities:

Families of soldiers and Soviet officials gathered at the harbor on the second day of the war, June 23, and were put on a train. Many Jewish residents of the town also streamed to the railway station. which was soon packed with people. Men were not allowed to board the train; only women with children could squeeze in. By the next day it was too late: the escape routes had already been cut off.[23]

Citizens flocked to the railway station in Kolomyja in hopes of fleeing eastward; they were turned back and told that there was no room for ordinary people. Jewish students from this town, who had attended the University of Lvov, managed to catch an evacuation train only to be told by security men that only women were allowed on board. The students continued on foot, many dying en route.[24] In Lvov, special trains were reserved for the families of Soviet officials and Red Army officers. However, as these trains were still being used to transport exiled convicts and their families, no space was available even for Party members and sympathizers, let alone families of ordinary citizens.[25]

Many Jews who finally reached the old Soviet border, by train or on foot, found an unexpected obstacle there: the restrictions on the entry of inhabitants of the annexed areas were still in force in most sectors of the frontier. The preferential treatment applied earlier in access to transportation and evacuation permits recurred at the border-crossing points. Soviet officials and their families came first. Officials of the local administration and employees of industrial and other enterprises that had previously been evacuated in an organized fashion, as well as card-carrying Party members and others with special permits issued by the security services, also had reason to hope for admission to the USSR. Tens of thousands of "ordinary citizens" (including many Jews) were detained at the border and barred from traveling east. Jewish escapees from the town of Olshany (western Belorussia) who arrived on carts, bicycles, and foot in the town of Radoskovichi on the old Polish-Soviet border, were greeted by large signs in Russian: "Persons crossing the border without a permit will be shot." Border guards told the crowds that assembled at the border crossings to return to their homes, because "at night we will not hesitate to shoot anyone in the vicinity of the border."[26] On the fourth day of the war, Jewish youths from Nesvizh who arrived at the old border, some 10 kilometers from their town, were ordered to turn back so as "not to create panic at a time when the Germans are being repelled." When the youngsters refused, the sentries threatened them at gunpoint. Only a handful managed to slip across the border.[27]

Thousands of evacuees and escapees from the Baltic countries, including Communist Party members and state officials, were detained for several days at the old Soviet-Latvian border near Sebezh, under heavy aerial bombardment, "until instructions arrive from Moscow."[28] A Red Army general actually asserted that "if there really are one or two spies among the thousands of people waiting at the border, it's better to let the German aircraft destroy everyone seeking to enter Russia than to let two spies infiltrate the country."[29] For the Jews, the delay in crossing the border spelled disaster. Many of them returned to their homes, straight into the hands of the Germans and their collaborators—Latvians, Ukrainians, Lithuanians, and others. In some cases, Soviet border guards forced the escapees to board trains heading back to their places of origin.[30]

In due course, the points of entry were opened wide (either on instructions from higher echelons or because the sentries had abandoned their posts out of fear of the approaching Germans). By then, it was too late. Those waiting had already dispersed; they fell into the clutches of the Germans or the nationalist gangs that collaborated with them.

Not everywhere did the Soviet authorities harass and obstruct the Jewish escapees. Testimonies and memoirs attest to manifestations of sympathy and assistance. This usually happened in places where the military situation was relatively propitious and where the distance to the front and the border, coupled with the availability of transport vehicles, facilitated assistance efforts. Such favorable circumstances prevailed, for example, in the Wolhynian town of Rokitno, situated near the old Soviet border, which was evacuated at a relatively late stage (July 10, 1941):

Rumors spread that the NKVD would hand out permits allowing people to cross into Soviet Russia. At dawn a long, sinuous line of people, mostly Jews, had already formed, waiting impatiently for the piece of paper that would offer them a glimmer of hope. The rumor proved to be true; the permits were distributed and Jewish residents began seeking transportation, mainly by horses and carts. One could only dream of traveling by train, but thanks to the efforts of the district Communist Party Committee a freight car was found. . . . We arrived at the crossing point on the old border between the Soviet Union and Poland. . . . Our documents were inspected and we were allowed to continue on our journey.[31]

A refugee from western Poland who, at the end of 1939, had slipped across the Soviet-Lithuanian border on his way to Vilna, where he remained until the war broke out in June, 1941, wrote in his memoirs that the Russians behaved very humanely at that time:

Families of Russian officers were given automobiles to drive them east, and the women wanted to take all their household belongings with them. However, officers in charge of the evacuation arrived and threw everything out of the cars, saying that people and not goods must be rescued. Thanks to their intervention, we managed to squeeze a few more women into the cars.[32]

In Estonia, the military and geographical circumstances permitted the evacuation of everyone "who so desired." Although certain documents, including an evacuation permit were necessary, they were relatively easy to obtain until early August, 1941, six weeks after the war began.[33] The authorities in Bessarabia, too, did nothing to hinder evacuees who applied for special permits to cross the Dniester, which formed the Romanian-Soviet border. Testimonies indicate that most of the refugees were Jews. Furthermore, once the authorities decided to carry out a general evacuation of the area, they rapidly built several provisional bridges and crossings over the Dniester, since the large numbers of escapees had overwhelmed the available facilities. In some cases Red Army soldiers were specially dispatched to ferry groups of Jews who had reached the right bank of the Dniester "at the last moment," in places where there was no other way to cross.[34]

A Hebrew teacher from the village of Marculesti, who reached one of the villages on the Dniester during his flight to the east, provided a typical account of the assistance offered the Jewish refugees by the Soviet authorities:

The residents were running in all directions, making preparations to cross the Dniester, to save their lives and rescue their meager possessions. For their part, the Soviet authorities too made last-minute efforts to prepare for total evacuation. Everyone waited for the Red Army to build a temporary bridge over the river which would allow everyone to escape. However, due the shortage of proper tools and materials, the work proceeded at a slow pace. We were terribly pressed for time. Many Red Army units had arrived at the Dniester, and in their wake came the hated Nazis with their Romanian helpers. . . . As we stood and listened to the bad tidings, a Jew approached us and revealed that a soldier, probably from the Border Police, was sitting under a tree in a nearby alley and handing out papers to all refugees seeking to cross the Dniester to the Ukraine. . . .

Half an hour later I was in possession of a document stating that I was a refugee from Marculesti in Bessarabia, a teacher by profession, accompanied by a family of three. Later on, this provisional document extricated me from tight spots on several occasions and, more importantly, several times it enabled me to obtain some food. . . . The document specified neither my national origin, nor the subject I had taught in the past, nor my social and ideological affiliation. . . .

In the meantime, more units of the retreating Red Army arrived. Expectations in the village mounted as the enemy troops drew near. This difficult situation forced the authorities to finish building the bridge. Late Saturday afternoon the army got moving and began crossing the Dniester. Our turn came at midnight; we crossed the river on a cart that brought us to the nearest village, Kamionka.[35]

The testimonies also express appreciation to the Red Army and the Soviet authorities for their sympathy and assistance to Jewish escapees, from the moment permission to flee was granted until the actual crossing of the Dniester. Since most of the localities were relatively close to the eastern border, it was easy to reach the river by horse- or ox-driven carts. After crossing to the east bank, the escapees were allowed to board eastbound trains at no charge. So powerful was the outflux that Jews who stayed behind in some communities wondered how they would assemble a quorum for public prayer.[36]

Jewish escapees in other localities were helped and treated humanely. A Soviet official in charge of transportation in the town of Swierzen Nowy (western Belorussia) went to great lengths to help one such escapee. He knew that this Jew had been a political prisoner under Polish rule and "might be counted among the first victims once the Germans arrive."

The secretary of the Communist Party in the town of David-Gorodek (Polesie) intervened on behalf of some 20 local young men and women, securing transit permits for them after border guards had turned them back.

In the Estonian town of Fellin (Vilyandy) the local authorities made great efforts to convince the Jews to take part in the organized evacuation; Alfreda Pik, a veteran Communist who chaired the municipal council, personally visited all the Jewish residents.[37] Consequently, at least half the Jewish population of the town left for the Soviet Union. Authorities in other places made similar efforts.

Nevertheless, cases in which Jews were accorded special treatment were few. Elsewhere, the Soviet authorities treated Jewish escapees and evacuees pragmatically if not cynically. To some extent, this attitude was informed by guidelines from "on high"; sometimes, too, it stemmed from the personal considerations of local functionaries. Thus the difficulties that the fleeing Jews faced cannot be regarded as the outcome of hostile policies or deliberate discrimination. Still, the prevailing view in pro-Soviet circles at the time—that the Soviet authorities had planned the rescue of the country's Jewish citizens during World War II—is untenable. Although much of the Jewish population in the annexed areas (both those evacuated in an organized fashion and those who escaped on their own) could not have survived without official assistance, this aid, in nearly every case, was tendered as part of a general policy and pattern of action that showed no preference for the Jews.

In summary, we may state that the Soviet authorities' behavior saved many thousands of Jews from Auschwitz, Treblinka, and Ponar, albeit sometimes in strange ways (including exile to Siberia!). Although their rescue was dependent on these authorities, it stemmed from considerations that had very little to do with humanitarian motives, let alone a desire to save Jews.

The first Jews to abandon their homes and flee eastward were residents of towns and villages situated near the German-Soviet frontier.[38] Jewish residents of towns and villages further from the frontier welcomed the refugees warmly and hosted them in their homes. After a day or two, however, the Germans drew close to these localities too, and the erstwhile hosts joined the masses of refugees streaming eastward.

Employees of internal security agencies, senior state and public functionaries, and factory managers were allowed to take their families with them; sometimes they made room in their vehicles for other relatives and friends. On several occasions senior Jewish officials, together with their families, were allowed to board trains meant to transport families of Soviet officers. Jewish drivers were in special demand, since non-Jews often refused to drive for personal or national reasons. Those who were forced to do so at gunpoint would drive away during bombardments, encounters with nationalist gangs, and so on.[39] Physicians were urged to join the evacuation in order to accompany wounded soldiers or tender medical services en route; several were allowed to take their families along.

Members of the Writers' Association in Bialystok (most of whom were local Jews or refugees from western Poland) were given a special car in one of the last trains bound for Russia.[40] In a number of places, evacuation was offered to young Jews who belonged to the Komsomol or other organizations, such as the Workers' Guard or the Shock Battalions, that were set up at the time. They had evidently enlisted in these frameworks in order to participate in the struggle against the Nazi enemy, who had reached the gates of their towns. In fact, the Jewish fighters in these units, mostly aged 17–25, represented a wide range of social and ideological affiliations.[41] In Estonia, where protracted rear-guard battles were taking place, the proportion of Jews was three times greater in the fighting units than in the population as a whole.[42]

Jewish inhabitants of the Baltic countries who were willing to fight the Nazis in the first days of the invasion had the additional option of joining these countries' territorial corps in the Red Army. Hundreds of Jewish sol-diers performed their regular service within these formations, although they were usually victimized by the anti-Soviet attitudes of their fellow soldiers. Their plight worsened during the German invasion, since they sometimes had to fear their non-Jewish comrades in arms. After the fact, these forces were an instrument through which individuals among the Jewish soldiers who survived were able to move into Russia proper.

Elsewhere along the front, Red Army units helped young Jews reach or cross the border.[43] In the course of long peregrinations, under enemy bom-bardments and when manning ambushes, young Jews and soldiers estab-lished friendly relations that lasted throughout the Jews' wanderings in the vast expanses of the USSR; some Jews were even allowed to join army units.

Prominent among these young Jews were members of youth movements who, under Soviet rule, had continued to maintain close ties and participate in local underground activity. Confronted with the possibility of sudden ex-ile, they had readied themselves before the war to depart at a moment's no-tice. In fact, the first reports of the Nazi invasion set off alarms within various youth movements, which immediately girded for flight to the east in the wake of the retreating Red Army. Usually they were well equipped and their morale was high:

On June 22, the day the war broke out, our secretariat gathered for an urgent meeting. We decided that the entire kibbutz would move eastward. We broke up into four groups and agreed to meet at the Russian border. Any group that reached one of the agreed-upon places was to wait for the next group. Once the latter arrived the first group was to set off, and so forth. We adhered to this arrangement all the way. Provisions were secured jointly. The Soviets were evacuating their people and we sneaked aboard one of the railroad cars. One group was missing. Some time later we found their knapsacks contain-ing photographs of our comrades. Their train had been bombed and all were killed.[44]

Those who managed somehow to cling to army units gained some pro-tection against German paratroopers and local nationalists. Against Luft-waffe attacks, however, there was no defense; now and then the passengers would disembark and hide alongside the train until the worst was over; oc-casionally they even helped repair the tracks.

On the whole, these escapees fared incomparably better than those flee-ing on foot, bicycles, or carts, who—unprotected by the army—were easy prey for nationalist gangs that waylaid them on the roads leading to the border. A few were offered transport in Red Army vehicles.[45] Some of the escapees attempted to reach official border crossings by roundabout routes; many succeeded in evading sentries who could have forced them to return. However, not everyone intercepted by border guards was driven back. Men, women, and children would wait for hours, even days, standing in the fields under the blistering July sun, until the guards received new, more accommodating instructions or simply abandoned their posts without warning.

Tenacity and perseverance were often decisive in effecting a successful escape.[46] Because the Wehrmacht was using flanking tactics, would-be escapees had to plan their routes very carefully and reconnoiter constantly for movements of the invading army. They often had to change direction and even double back at length in order to avoid an encounter with the German rear-guard.[47] Homesick and beset with guilt feelings about those who had stayed behind, some turned around. Others perished in flight; their numbers cannot be estimated.

Having left their homes haphazardly and without any means of transportation, they began to straggle. Before long, the Gentiles whom they had hired to carry their bundles rose up against them, killed them, and looted the baggage loaded on the carts. The ground was truly burning under the escapees' feet. They couldn't even bring themselves to look back. Enemy aircraft strafed the roads relentlessly in order to hinder the retreat of the Soviet army. The shells formed craters in the Bessarabian dirt roads and claimed many victims. Trains, too, were bombed from the air and many passengers perished. After each raid, the refugees would get off the train and dig a mass grave alongside the tracks to bury their loved ones. In some cases they barely covered the graves with soil; they weren't deep enough to ensure that dogs would not reach the bodies, but every fresh attack from the air forced everyone to stop digging and resume his flight. . . . The soil of Bessarabia and the Ukraine was sown with Jewish corpses.[48]

The chaos brought on by the invasion prevented any supervision of organized evacuation, let alone spontaneous mass flight. In the few places where the enemy advance was relatively sluggish, such as Estonia and Bessarabia, the authorities were able to exercise some measure of control over organized evacuation thanks to the registration system introduced for all persons seeking to cross into the USSR via the Gulf of Finland (in Estonia) or the Dniester (in Bessarabia).

Many years after the war, the Soviets published estimates of the number of evacuees. Most of these estimates, however, included those who had fled on their own, and are incomplete and fragmentary in any case. Furthermore, few of them include information on the ethnic composition of the evacuees.[49]

Notwithstanding this, there is no doubt that the Jews were overrepresented among the evacuees. One reason for this was their high representation in the government and public sectors and miscellaneous enterprises. Another was their strong motivation to avoid Nazi occupation. In addition, Jewish officials who participated in the organized evacuation took their families with them, whereas their non-Jewish colleagues were not as committed to family solidarity, and they did not fear that their relatives would be persecuted under Nazi rule.

The scope of escape and evacuation of Jews from the annexed territories was determined by a combination of factors. The principal ones were high motivation; official ability and willingness to offer assistance and encouragement; the distance to the old Soviet-Polish border;[50] the time interval between the outbreak of the war and the capture of a locality by German forces; the proportion and status of Jews in the state apparatus, the economy, and the Communist Party; the available transportation; and finally and decisively, the invading forces' decision to outflank a given locality or to overrun it at the first opportunity.

The total number of Jewish escapees and evacuees from western Poland and the annexed areas may be estimated at 140,000-170,000.[51] Between 75,000 and 100,000 of them reached the unoccupied territories of the Soviet Union. Half fled from the Baltic countries and former Romanian territories; the others came from former areas of Poland. This estimate includes thousands of Jews who just happened to be in the Soviet Union proper—serving in the military, on business trips, attending university, recuperating in rest homes, and so on—when the war broke out. It appears that the share of Jews who managed to elude the advancing German armies did not exceed 7 percent of the overall Jewish population.

14

Conclusion

For roughly 20 years, the Soviet Union had strived consistently to reannex areas to its west that had been part of the Russian Empire. These efforts paid off on the eve of World War II, August 23, 1939, when the Ribbentrop-Molotov pact was signed. The annexed territories, stretching 1,000 kilometers from the Gulf of Finland to the Black Sea, contained two million Jews—a substantial minority (10 percent on average) of the multinational population. Even though their economic, national, and civil rights had eroded steadily during the preceding 20 years, the Jews had been allowed to maintain an impressive and nearly autonomous system of Jewish and secular education in Hebrew and Yiddish. They also had their own welfare and cultural institutions, successful newspapers, and all types of ideological and political frameworks, with the exception of the banned Communist Party.

The sudden Red Army invasion of these territories, followed by Soviet annexation, coincided with the Nazi expansion in Europe. This had obvious implications for the Jewish population. The first reaction of most Jews in the annexed territories was satisfaction—or at least relief—at having been spared a Nazi takeover. Quite a few, however, feared that, although the imminent Nazi invasion had been averted, the Soviet regime was merely the lesser of two evils. In other words, as one contemporary Jewish observer rued, the Soviet incursion had commuted the Jews' death sentence to life imprisonment. A small minority of Jews with Communist affiliations reacted with extreme enthusiasm and a sense of vindication. After all, their ideological and political vision, for which they had struggled for years and even served prison terms, had finally come true. Many of them embraced the new regime and accepted important administrative, defense, and economic positions in its service.

Those who were satisfied or elated would not be so for long. After a brief honeymoon, the new regime introduced a package of harsh measures collectively termed "sovietization." Although this policy was imposed on the entire population of the annexed territories, the Jews were more affected than the majority national groups because of their unique economic, cultural, and religious circumstances and characteristics.

The sudden change of regime and the imposed sovietization of most areas of life triggered fundamental changes among the Jews. First of all, their socioeconomic condition suffered, since their role in commerce, industry, and other aspects of the economy had been far more significant than that of other population groups. Many Jews, particularly those who had been well off, were immediately deprived of their economic status. Those who were able to adjust accepted wage-paying jobs in production, administration, and sales. Their standards of living declined, unless they belonged to the poorest classes that had little to lose. This was especially so in the former Polish and Romanian areas (and, to a lesser extent, in the Baltic republics). In this context, measures forcing Jews to work on the Sabbath were particularly painful, especially because such labor was often a prerequisite for survival.

Jewish education suffered grievously under sovietization. Schools that had taught in the Hebrew language and inculcated Jewish national and religious values were now replaced by a new system characterized primarily by instruction in Yiddish. These schools became the predominant (if not the only) Jewish institutions in the community, serving as centers of cultural and community life for the entire Jewish population. In due course, evidence accumulated of an official intent to scale down Jewish education, as had been done in the USSR proper, or to eliminate it altogether, as was done there after World War II.

Cultural institutions, effective vehicles for inculcating Soviet Communist ideology, underwent similar trends. The Jewish press played a highly visible role in this transformation. During the period reviewed, however, the number of Jewish journals declined until all that remained were one daily newspaper, one weekly, and two biweeklies. The Jewish theater, in contrast, enjoyed fairly good conditions and underwent something of a rebirth. Although the expectations of the Yiddish-speaking patrons were only partially fulfilled, at least 52 plays were performed in more than 100 localities; most of them were original Jewish works.

Literature fared badly in some respects; for example, during the period of Soviet rule, no more than 14 books were published by Jewish authors and poets from the previously Polish areas. However, local writers and poets, refugees from western Poland, and visitors from the USSR took part in a large number of literary and cultural events. Two developments in Jewish academic studies were particularly noteworthy: the establishment of the Institute for Jewish Culture (founded by YIVO) in Vilna, officially integrated into the Lithuanian Academy of Sciences, and the inauguration of a chair in Yiddish studies at the University of Vilna. In general, the Jewish population belittled the quality and significance of these institutions and feared for their future under Soviet rule.

The Jewish minority had several characteristics that made it a convenient group for the new leaders to deal with. It was a loyal community, able to adjust and integrate into the new system. This reflected the Jews' relatively strong Communist affiliations, command of languages, and occupational diversity. Furthermore, the Jews were largely free of tendencies to political isolationism, unlike other minorities such as Poles and Lithuanians. Many Jews were appointed to Party and government positions, including posts with the security services, in total contrast to previous regimes in the annexed territories, which had excluded Jews from their administrative echelons. Subsequently, for various reasons—including Ukrainization and Belorussification policies and the desire to play down the Jews' role in government in order to keep opponents of the regime from labeling it "Jewish"—Jews in high-ranking government and Party positions were ousted. Despite this, most members of the majority peoples, who were strongly nationalistic and rampantly antisemitic to begin with, continued to regard the Jewish minority as a primary instrument of the hated Soviet regime. As time passed, they began to threaten the Jews with pogroms, sometimes explicitly.

As the Soviet regime established itself in the annexed territories, it acted with growing vigor to undermine the Jews' traditional values. The Jewish public began to show signs of sober, critical rethinking. However, the constant threat of Nazi Germany and the awareness that their non-Jewish neighbors might retaliate against them at the first opportunity reinforced the Jews' consciousness that, despite everything, Soviet rule was the lesser of two evils. Thus, most of the Jews reconciled themselves to the situation (at least until the danger passed). In any event, it was clear that they had to avoid outright conflict with the authorities and restrain their urge to resist, except in issues that were perceived as matters of life and death.

A salient case of this type was the continuation of underground activities by the Zionist youth movements. In this respect, there was little difference between Ha-shomer ha-Tsa'ir, which chose to "disperse without disbanding" (as the slogan went) while eschewing anti-Soviet activities, and Betar and the IZL, which attempted at first to continue target practice as if nothing had changed. Even the boldest undertakings of these movements, such as illegal escape to Vilna and Romania and semi-legal flight to other countries, were not anti-Soviet per se.

While the authorities cracked down on non-Jewish underground activity, they usually countered such operations by Jewish groups (almost all of which were Zionist youth movements) with propaganda only. Arrests, trials, and deportations were ordinarily invoked only when centers of activity were exposed by chance or by informers.

However, the new regime singled out large groups of Jews—former Bundists, Zionist political activists, and employer and merchant classes—as "enemies of the people." These were not as fortunate. Because of the socioeconomic structure of the Jewish population, the Jews were harder hit than their non-Jewish neighbors. The proportion of Jews among the hundreds of thousands of refugees from western Poland deported to the Soviet interior was especially high, since most of the refugees were Jewish.

Testimonies and memoirs indicate that the investigations and deportations often were accompanied by antisemitic abuse and violence. Nevertheless, no evidence was found of intentional discrimination against Jews during the rapid sovietization and the crackdown on enemies of the people.

Although the basic principles of sovietization were the same throughout the annexed areas, administrative, political, and ethnic factors created regional variations. In general, the more dependent an area was on governmental and Party institutions of the indigenous Soviet republics, the more severe and rapid the sovietization. The regions in the Ukrainian SSR sphere of influence (Eastern Galicia, Wolhynia, Northern Bukovina, and Bessarabia) provide extreme and vivid examples of such a situation. The Jewish population in these areas, which exceeded one million, was not allowed to publish a local newspaper during most of this period; it had to settle for a Jewish newspaper from faraway Kiev. In addition to the difficulties of sovietization, the Ukrainization policy applied in some of these areas was fairly stringent. It also appears that antisemitic persecution and incidents were more prevalent in these areas than elsewhere.

An extreme example of an "independent" area was Lithuania, with a Jewish population of 250,000. Of the seven Jewish state theaters established in the annexed territories, three were located there. Of 535 Jewish state schools, 170 were in Lithuania. Lithuania was also the only annexed territory with a regular Jewish daily newspaper. The Jews of Lithuania, unlike those in the other annexed territories, held high positions in the government and Party apparatus. Moreover, Lithuania became the gateway through which thousands of Jewish refugees left the Soviet Union, mainly for Palestine. This was largely owing to the refugees' own initiative and unflagging activity, coupled with impressive assistance from institutions such as the American Jewish Joint Distribution Committee (AJJDC) and individuals such as the Japanese consul in Kovno.

Nevertheless, the central Soviet authorities clearly played a major role in the emigration of Jewish refugees. It is reasonable to assume that one of the Soviet Union's considerations in taking this surprising step was long-term political interest (dislodging the British from the Middle East); another had to do with defense and intelligence-gathering (e.g., the Soblen affair). In all, 4,000–5,000 Jews from the annexed areas left the Soviet Union legally in 1940–41. This controlled emigration reflected similar Soviet political thinking articulated several years later by Gromyko in his support of the establishment of the Jewish State; thinking of this type surfaced again in the 1970s, when mass immigration of Soviet Jews to Israel (primarily from the Baltic republics) was allowed.

The annexation of the western border territories boosted the Jewish population of the Soviet Union to five million, restoring its magnitude during the Czarist period. Despite the reunification, however, the two parts of the nation were interrelated only in certain areas of life. Jews who had lived under Soviet rule for 20 years had learned to be very cautious and reserved in their contacts. Nevertheless, many of them were eager to help the Jews from the annexed territories, especially in the fields of culture and education. Sometimes the central authorities encouraged this activity; in other cases the initiative was their own. So far as the government and Party establishment was concerned, these efforts were unilateral and technical/political in nature. In retrospect, this contact with fellow Jews in the western areas was a profoundly emotional experience for Soviet Jews, and it manifested itself in an awakening of Jewish national consciousness.

Just as the Jews in the annexed territories were moved by the discovery of important Soviet generals, artists, and functionaries who spoke the *mama loshn* (the Jews' "mother tongue"; i.e., Yiddish), so were the Soviet Jews excited and jealous when they beheld the vibrancy of Jewish life in the annexed areas, and they derived encouragement and strength by dealing with the specific problems of the Jewish population in their assimilationist countries. Hence, on several occasions, representatives of the Soviet establishment identified more strongly with their brethren in the west than with the institutions that had sent them there. The cultural and national revival among Soviet Jews was certainly inconsistent with government policy, as these aspects of Jewish life had previously been in decline as a result of government attitudes. One may assume that the revival was temporary and that its end was visible at the very outset, just as the cultural and educational activity of Jews in the annexed territories was short-lived. However, the significance of these developments in the critical period following the Nazi invasion of June 22, 1941, transcended the direct impact of routine Jewish life in the annexed territories.

IMPLICATIONS OF SOVIETIZATION ON JEWS LIVING IN THE ANNEXED AREAS DURING THE NAZI INVASION

Several characteristics of the brief term of Soviet rule in the areas, and several events that occurred during this time, directly affected the Jews' lives after the Nazi invasion.

Economic Aspects

The Soviet nationalization of business, industry, and immobiliers, coupled with the confiscation of real estate, currency, and valuables, did much to help the Nazi forces complete their dispossession of the entire Jewish population. The Soviets had deprived formerly affluent Jews of the jewelry, money, and valuables with which they might have averted death or harsh measures, at least temporarily. However, the Jews had been able to hoard food during the Soviet period, even though the regime regarded this as illegal commerce; they had also managed to obtain needed items of clothing such as fur and leather coats and high boots. Thus, quite a few Jewish families forestalled the risk of an encounter with the enemy while attempting to procure vital necessities.

Soviet productivization and proletarization policies induced many Jews to accept jobs that required physical labor; this prepared them physically and mentally to withstand forced labor under Nazi occupation. More fortunate still were those who had managed to acquire a sought-after trade (e.g., carpenters, locksmiths, glaziers, and tinsmiths) or at least some practical experience under the Soviet rule.

The Jews' efforts to attain social and economic equality during the sovietization period induced many groups to effect a rapprochement or, at least, interact openly. This upturn in Jewish solidarity and mutual assistance became especially important in the ghettos, labor camps, and partisan units of the Nazi era.

Social Aspects

Sovietization accelerated the disintegration of Jewish society and the family unit. As an unexpected benefit, this made it easier for young members of the community to leave their parents and escape eastward from the Nazis and their allies in the summer of 1941. In this fashion they avoided the dangers of German *aktionnen,* "selections," liquidation of ghettos, and extermination camps.

The persecution, internment, and deportation of local Jewish leaders strengthened the public importance of Jews imprisoned by the Soviets subsequently and liberated by the Nazis. Some of these individuals headed *Judenrate* (Jewish councils established by order of the Nazis in the Jewish communities of occupied Europe). Few members of these councils had previously been active or influential in the local community; some had been unknown; a few were refugees. Needless to say, the composition of the Judenrate and the origin of their members often had a decisive effect on the actions of these councils.

After the Soviets admitted Jews to the ranks of official and public administrators in defense, industry, and education, Jews and non-Jews increasingly interrelated and formed friendships. The character of these relationships became critical during the subsequent Nazi period. In their adjustment to Soviet life, these Jews adopted Soviet social habits such as drinking vodka and "proletarian" dress; Jewish youth resorted to such behavior when bitter circumstances under Nazi occupation forced them to flee from place to place and disguise their identity.

During the sovietization period, some residents of the annexed territories were allowed to visit the Soviet interior as government representatives or on "fact-finding" tours, vacation, or family visits. Those who happened to be in the interior in June, 1941, were spared the immediate encounter with the Nazi invaders. Having a family in the Soviet Union proper was presumably one of the factors that motivated Jews in the annexed territories to flee when the war spread eastward in the summer of 1941, in hope of obtaining advice and guidance, if not refuge, in the homes of relatives.

Because the USSR and Germany were on friendly terms following the Ribbentrop-Molotov pact, the controlled Soviet media reported little about the persecution of Jews in Germany and the occupied countries, including western Poland. This encouraged many Jews not to escape from the Germans when they invaded in the summer of 1941.

Certain groups (the upper and middle classes, Zionist activists, and Bundists) had a more concrete reason to refrain from fleeing into the Soviet Union: the Soviets had conducted mass imprisonments and deportations among their ranks in 1940 and again, with greater vigor, in June, 1941, just before the Germans invaded. These operations were carried out cruelly; thousands of their victims perished in and en route to the Soviet *gulag*. It is worth emphasizing, however, that these deportations had the effect of sparing hundreds of thousands of Jews originally from Poland, Romania, and the Baltic countries from the Nazi extermination machine.

Political Aspects

The participation of many Jews in the government and Party mechanisms, particularly in the military and defense services (including Jews who had been conscripted into the Red Army and transferred with their units to the USSR proper before the Nazi invasion) made it easier for them to escape to the east, often with their families, when Germany went to war against the USSR. Local authorities sometimes provided them with transportation, and they were able to cross the old Soviet border without any problem. Obviously, these Jews and their families were more highly motivated to escape German occupation than Jews who were not identified as active Communists or recognized as Bolshevik agents and supporters of the Soviet regime.

The impressive political integration of Jews was displeasing to non-Jewish nationalist groups that rejected Soviet rule in their countries. They construed the appointment of young Jews as officers in the militia as an act of ingratitude and betrayal on the Jews' part, especially when such officers arrested and deported individuals who had been prominent or considered patriots under previous regimes. In this fashion, the Soviets hastened the deterioration of relations between the Jews and much of the non-Jewish population. The tragic consequences became evident with the Nazi invasion, when resident non-Jews launched pogroms and joined the Nazi murder machine enthusiastically. To this day, many residents of and emigrés from the former annexed territories excuse their countrymen's participation in the Nazi genocide on the grounds of thirst for revenge against Jews who had collaborated with the Soviets and treated their non-Jewish neighbors high-handedly.

Service in defense formations such as Workers' Guards and auxiliary militia made many Jews familiar with military life and experience in the use of arms. A large number of Jews were able to participate in the armed struggle against the Nazis; some of them displayed proficiency in defending Jewish lives including their own. In time, these included Jewish paratroopers who were dropped into occupied territory from Tallinn in the north to Kishinev in the south. Some of them entered the ghettos and bolstered the morale and strength of the fighters there. On several occasions, previous acquaintance with officers under the Soviet regime helped the Jews integrate into anti-Nazi partisan units or regular units of the Red Army.

Another aspect of the sovietization period that had considerable consequences during the Nazi occupation was the matter of refugees. By the time many of them reached the Soviet-controlled zone, their ordeal had included border-running—sometimes in both directions—outwitting of sentries, presentation of false documents, bribery, and similar ruses. Needless to say, such experience may have been literally life-saving during the Holocaust.

Cultural Aspects

In addition to the older generation in the Soviet-occupied territories (excluding Galicia and Northern Bukovina, which formerly were part of the Austro-Hungarian Empire), who had learned some Russian under the czars, the younger generation, during the sovietization period, had an opportunity to study the Russian language in the regular schools, night schools, and special courses. Russophone refugees from the annexed territories found it easier to get along and, especially, to integrate into the military and the economy. Some served as interpreters for the military command and for non-Jewish comrades from their native regions.

Religious Aspects

Soviet rule accelerated the decline of religious observance among the Jews in the annexed areas, as a result of systematic propaganda and the objective difficulty of following Jewish law under the new regime. Many Jews were forced to work on the Sabbath and eat non-kosher foods. When the ghettos and detention camps were ravaged with famine, only a few Jews categorically rejected food that was obviously not kosher; nearly all accepted the yoke of Sabbath labor. One may therefore regard the substantial erosion of religious observance during the Soviet period as a factor that eased the crisis of breaking clear taboos in order to survive the Holocaust.

Ideological Aspects

One of the most important factors of the Soviet period that affected the Jews' behavior during the Holocaust was the continuous underground activity. Such activity took various forms among the Jewish population. When the Soviets ordered the Jewish organizations and youth movements to dissolve, many went underground and focused on ideological activities and reinforcement of values (e.g., continued use of the Hebrew language, discussion and study of Zionism, Eretz Yisrael, and the Bible). Their operations included preservation of archives, preparation and circulation of illegal publications, and aid to friends in danger who sought to escape to Vilna and continue on from there.

As previously discussed, Vilna became a major center for thousands of party activists, yeshiva students, halutsim, and members and leaders of Zionist movements. From time to time the activists were imprisoned and some were deported; nevertheless, underground activity continued in many communities until the Nazi invasion in June, 1941.

Most of the underground groups were established by young activists who sought to replace previous leaders, some of whom had been arrested and others of whom had discontinued their activity. Activists of the underground movements and parties—especially those connected with movements that coalesced in the underground (such as Irgun Berit Tsiyon and Herut in Lithuania, and Deror in Poland)—adhered to their former Zionist routine as best they could; they also accused the shattered Zionist leadership of not having come through at critical moments.

These young leaders eventually became the heads of the underground organizations, commanders of partisan units, and ghetto fighters. The fact that most of them came from similar backgrounds and that some even knew each other personally, either before the war or as a result of collaboration in the Vilna rikkuz, contributed to their solidarity in various situations under Nazi occupation. It is no coincidence that some of them became well-known underground leaders in the ghettos of Poland and Lithuania. Examples are

Abba Kovner, Yitzhak Zuckerman, Chaika Grossman, Mordechai Aniele-wicz, Mordechai Tenenbaum, and Josef Glazman. Three particularly note-worthy individuals who later led the struggle against the British in Palestine—Dr. Moshe Kleinboim (Sneh), head of the Hagana command; Menachem Begin, commander of the IZL; and Dr. Israel Scheib (Eldad), a leader of Lohamei Herut Yisrael (Lehi, or the "Stern Group")—had all spent some time in Soviet Vilna.

Local Communists flourished under the Soviets, and after having oper-ated in the underground for several years, many of them became prominent public figures. After the Nazi invasion, when these activists extended their operations to the ghettos and detention camps, they had to be exceedingly wary. Their enemies included some Jews, who had ample motive to turn them in or take revenge on them for actions they had committed while in power (although such incidents were rare). Moreover, unlike the Zionists and members of other movements, whose underground activities during the Nazi occupation were a direct continuation of their operations under the So-viets, the Communists took a relatively long time to recover and had to start almost from scratch.

Activists of the Zionist organizations were especially prominent in the mass exodus from the annexed territories that ensued with the Nazi invasion in June, 1941. They were known for mutual aid, high morale, and an ability to find their bearings in this volatile environment. Together they endured the hardship of travel and made their way to the "receiving areas" that the So-viets had created for refugees, such as kolkhozes, work brigades, and com-munes in Central Asia. Many of these activists remained in touch with comrades who had been drafted into the armed forces. Eventually they be-came the vanguard of the *beriha* (postwar escape) and the *ha'apala* (illegal immigration to Palestine). In this they were joined by other members of the underground who, after their activity under Soviet rule, participated in the anti-German armed resistance in the ghettos and forests and were fortunate enough to survive the inferno of the Holocaust.

Notes

For works frequently cited in the notes, the following abbreviations are used; they are cited in full in the chapter (ch.) note (n.) listed after each entry.

'Al hurvot Besarabiya: ch. 2, n. 25
'Aliti mi-spetzya: ch. 5, n. 32.
'Al masu'ot Polin: ch. 5, n. 4.
Azoy iz es geshen in Lite: ch. 4, n. 5.
Butkute-Rameliene: ch. 4, n. 5.
Baranowicze: ch. 2, n. 6.
Brichen: ch. 12, n. 26.
"Chernovits ha-yehudit": ch. 2., n. 19.
Dina Porat: ch. 9, n. 62.
Dos banayte folk: ch. 1, n. 4
Dos Sovetishe idntum: ch. 1, n. 4.
Dovid Lederman: ch. 8, n. 20.
Doyres Bundistn: ch. 12, n. 16.
Entsiqlopediya shel galuyot: ch. 5, n. 6.
Gebrente trit: ch. 9, n. 37.
"Ha-hayim ha-yehudi'im": ch. 5, n. 3.
"Hatsalat talmidey yeshivot Polin": ch. 7, n. 40.
Hayalim almonim: ch. 9, n. 48.
Hekhal she-shaqa': ch. 2, n. 12
History of MSSR: ch. 3., n. 2.
In rod fun tsorn: ch. 1, n. 2.
In shayn fun morgenshtern: ch. 8, n. 27.
'Ir ve-ya'ar be-matsor: ch. 13, n. 3.
J.T.A. [Jewish Telegraphic Agency] Bulletin: ch. 2, n. 21.
Kaminska: ch. 6, n. 62.
Ka-haya ha-nirdefet: ch. 8, n. 29.
Kovno ha-yehudit be-hurbana: ch. 3, n. 54.
Khrushchev Remembers: ch. 3, n. 42.
Khurbn Braynsk: ch. 4, n. 15.

Khurbn un retung: ch. 9, n. 9.
Knekht zaynen mir geven: ch. 4, n. 33
Lithuanian Archives: ch. 4, n. 5.
Ma'aser rishon: ch. 9, n. 8.
Markuleshti: ch. 12, n. 21.
Matatias Carp: ch. 1, n. 10.
Megiles Rusland: ch. 6, n. 29.
Mit zikh un mit andere: ch. 3, n. 32.
Moldavskaya SSR: ch. 3, n. 48.
Mosedot tora: ch. 5, n. 27.
Moshe Grosman: ch. 6, n. 23.
Niv ha-midrashiya: ch. 7, n. 41.
OHD [Oral History Department]: ch. 2, n. 2.
Orhayuv be-vinyana u-ve-hurbana: ch. 4, n. 10
Pinkas Bricheva: ch. 6, n. 58.
Pinkes Slonim: ch. 2, n. 8.
Pomerantz: ch. 13, n. 10.
Qehillat Bendery: ch. 7, n. 10.
"Sefarim mi-ta'am": ch. 5, n. 17.
Rabban shel yisrael: ch. 7, n. 31.
Rokitno ve-ha-seviva: ch. 5, n. 28.
Sawicki: ch. 9, n. 4.
Sefer ha-shomer ha-tsa'ir: ch. 9, n. 2.
Sefer Kalarash: ch. 12, n. 12.
Sefer Kowel: ch. 2, n. 4.
Sefer Nesvizh: ch. 7, n. 23.
Sefer qehillat Khutin: ch. 4, n. 1.
Sefer Stolyn: ch. 5, n. 30.
Sefer zikaron li-qedoshey Sokoli: ch. 4, n. 27.
Sefer Zholkiev: ch. 3, n. 8.
"Sho'at yehudey Polin": ch. 2, n. 10.
Soviet Bukovina: ch. 2, n. 20.
Soviet Lithuanian Encyclopaedia: ch. 3, n. 36.
Struggles of a Generation: ch. 2, n. 18.
Struggles of the Workers of Bukovina: ch. 2, n. 20.
Tania Fuks: ch. 3, n. 33.
The Holocaust of Volhynian Jews: ch. 4, n. 16.
Tsanin: ch. 9, n. 25.
"Tsvishn hamer un serp": ch. 5, n. 41.
Warhaftig: ch. 9, n. 5.
Weinryb: ch. 7, n. 21.
Yad le-Yedinits: ch. 5, n. 14.
Yahadut Lita: ch. 5, n. 33.
"Yamim tragi'im": ch. 12, n. 26.
"Yerushalayim de-Lita," ch. 8, n. 6.
Yiddish Publications: ch. 5, n. 15.
YVA [Yad Vashem Archives]: ch. 3, n. 35.
Ziman (Zimanas): ch. 3, n. 37.

CHAPTER 1

1. *Oktyabr* (Minsk), September 21, 1939.
2. Shlomo Shtokfish, *In rod fun tsorn* [In a Circle of Rage] (Tel Aviv: 1976), 1, 2, 21 (Hereafter cited as *In rod fun tsorn*).

3. From a speech by Molotov in the Supreme Soviet on October 31, 1939, as published in *Pravda* (Moscow), November 1, 1939.
4. Solomon Schwartz, "Der khurbn fun di yidn in Sovetn-farband" [Destruction of Soviet Jewry] *Algemeyne entsiklopedye* [General Encyclopedia], vol. "Yidn" (New York: 1963), 6:246–247. Cf. Jacob Lestschinsky, *Dos sovetishe idntum, zayn fargangenhayt un kegnvart* [Soviet Jewry: Its Past and Present] (New York: 1941), 366 (hereafter cited as *Dos Sovetishe idntum*). According to this source, another 200,000 Jewish refugees reached the Soviet-controlled area of Poland from the German-held area, bringing the total to 1,500,000, or 11 percent of the population. Dr. Philip Friedman, a well-known researcher of Polish Jewry, reaches the same conclusion. For details see *Biuletyn głównej komisji badania zbrodni niemieckich w Polsce* 1 [Bulletin of the Supreme Commission of Inquiry into the Crimes of the Germans in Poland] (Warsaw: 1946), 156. In all, there were more than 2,000,000 Jews in the Soviet-annexed areas; this figure is corroborated by the well-known Soviet Jewish demographer L. Zinger, *Dos banayte folk* [The Renewed People] (Moscow: 1941), 121.
5. Concerning the transfer of Germans from the western Ukraine and Belorussia, and the return of Ukrainians, Belorussians, and Russians from the German-occupied areas.
6. According to Polish sources, more than 1,000,000 persons (i.e., 7–8 percent of the population of western Belorussia and the western Ukraine) were exiled from these areas during World War II. About 50 percent of them were Poles, itemized as follows: more than 300,000 from the Bialystok, Lida, Grodno, and Vilna districts; more than 200,000 from the Polesia and Novogrudek districts; about 150,000 from Wolhynia; and about 400,000 from southeastern Poland (Eastern Galicia) (*Documents on Polish-Soviet Relations 1939–1945* [London-Melbourne-Toronto: General Sikorski Historical Institute, 21]). In August, 1943, the Polish embassy in Kuybyshev estimated that roughly 30 percent of persons deported and arrested in eastern Poland were Jewish, including refugees who wished to return to the German-occupied zone.
7. Only four of the 33 women political prisoners interned in Kovno at the time were Lithuanian; the rest were Jewish.
8. Lithuanian nationalists' relations with the Nazi counterespionage services, and their willingness to join the German side in the war against the Soviets, are described in the Ambassador's memorandum of June 19, 1941 to the Soviet Ministry of Foreign Affairs. See *Documents on German Foreign Policy, 1918–1945, Series D* (Washington, D.C.: Department of State, 1964), XII, no. 650, 1054–1055.
9. Including a representative of the Romanian Communist Party Central Committee, a Jew named S. Siegelbaum, who spent a protracted period behind bars.
10. According to Soviet sources, about 150,000 persons returned to Bessarabia by the end of July, 1940. A delegation representing 14,000 Jews born in Bessarabia and Bukovina asked the Soviet consul in Bucharest to help them remove their possessions, and came away empty-handed. In other cases, Romanian gendarmes forced returnees to cross the border in places not meant for this. These areas were mined, and many would-be returnees were killed. Others were shot to death by Soviet border guards or Romanians when they were ordered to turn back. See Matatias Carp, *Cartea Neagra [Black Book]* (Bucharest: 1947), 3:439 (hereafter cited as Matatias Carp).

CHAPTER 2

1. Dov Levin, "Yerushalayim de-Lita—shisha shavu'ot be-sograyim" [Jerusalem of Lithuania (Vilna)—six weeks in parentheses], *Gal-ed* (Tel Aviv), 3:1978, 78–81.
2. Testimony of M. Rakovchik, Institute for Contemporary Jewry, the Hebrew University of Jerusalem, Oral History Department (hereafter cited as OHD), 1, 3(20).
3. Gershon Adiv (Adelson), diary, September 18, 1939, 24. Adiv, a member of Kibbutz Ruhama (formerly 'Amal), reached his home town of Vilna as part of a delegation and spent approximately half a year there until he succeeded in returning to Palestine.
4. *Kowel, sefer 'edut ve-zikaron* [Kowel, Testimonial and Memorial Book] (Tel Aviv: 1957), 391 (hereafter cited as *Sefer Kowel*). The Hebrew expression used for "celebrating"—

tsahala ve-sameha—is used in the Scroll of Esther to describe the Jews' response to their delivery from Haman.

5. Testimony of Shalom Hamiel, OHD, 5.
6. *Baranowicze* [Baranovichi, Memorial Book] (Tel Aviv: 1954), 208 (hereafter cited as *Baranowicze*).
7. *Sefer Kobryn—megilat hayim ve-hurban* [Kobryn Book—An Account of Life and Destruction] (Tel Aviv: 1951), 299.
8. *Rozhinoy, sefer zikaron li-qehilat Rozhinoy ve-ha-seviva* [Rozhinoy, Memorial Book for the Rozana Community and Vicinity] (Tel Aviv: 1957), 150; *Pinkes Slonim* [subtitled Ruin of the Community—In Memoriam] (Tel Aviv: 1962) 2:3–10 (hereafter cited as *Pinkes Slonim*). Cf. *Sefer zikaron Czyzewo* [Tshizew Memorial Book] (Tel Aviv: 1961), 857.
9. *Pinkes Slonim,* 18.
10. Report by Dr. Moshe Kleinboim (Sneh), "Sho'at yehudey Polin" [Destruction of Polish Jewry] (Jerusalem: 1940), 34 (hereafter cited as "Sho'at yehudey Polin").
11. This rumor is described in detail by P. Lit, "Shisha hodashim be-Lita ha-Sovietit" [Six Months in Soviet Lithuania], *Ha-mashqif* (Tel Aviv), February 4, 1940.
12. R. Berkman-Shif, "Ha-yeshiva ha-aharona shel ha-mo'atza ha-pedagogit" [The last meeting of the pedagogical council], *Hekhal* [A Sanctuary Asunder] (Tel Aviv: 1962), 191.
13. Testimonies of E. Golan, OHD, 2–3, and A. Melamed, OHD, 9–10.
14. Testimony of Y. Zlotokrilov, OHD, 2; see also testimony of D. Elkind, OHD, 1.
15. See testimonies of M. Heltzer, OHD, 2; "Ben-Yosef," OHD, 2. S. Ribak (OHD, 18) testifies that Gutkin was subsequently shot by Estonian nationalists.
16. This phenomenon in Ha-shomer ha-Tsa'ir is described in the testimonies of A. Turchin, OHD, 4–5; "Adami," OHD, 2; A. Libling, OHD, 2–3; M. Kimhi, OHD, 4. As for the Betar cell in Sekureni, "a majority of [which] went over to the Communist movement overnight," see Ze'ev Igeret, "Bein milhama le-milhama" [Between two wars], *Sekuren be-vinyana u-ve-hurbana* [The Existence and Destruction of Sekureni] (Tel Aviv: 1954), 70. An attempt by Jewish Communists to persuade the Gordoniya Society to switch allegiances (including the use of threats) is described in the testimony of Hemda Ish-Shalom, Diaspora Research Institute, Tel Aviv University, 20. Members of Ha-shomer ha-Tsa'ir debated whether Socialism could be imported into an area "by means of the Red Army tanks" (testimony of S. Ronen, OHD, 3).
17. "Anyone who's ready for the underground," asserted an emissary from Palestine, Aharon Cohen, addressing members of Ha-shomer ha-Tsa'ir, "should also be ready for Siberia" (testimony of M. Kimhi, OHD, 5).
18. The frantic but "pointless" all-night deliberations in the Zionist Center at Kishinev are described by M. Fridman, "From the Banks of the Prut to Angara," in Benjamin West, Ed., *Struggles of a Generation—The Jews Under Soviet Rule* (Tel Aviv: 1959), 2:91 (hereafter cited as *Struggles of a Generation*).
19. Several testimonies support this allegation. For example: "Agitated Jews tore off the epaulettes of fleeing Romanian officers" (Zvi Yavetz, "Chernovits ha-yehudit lifnei ha-sho'a" [Jewish Czernowitz before the Holocaust], *Shvut* (Tel Aviv), 2:1974, 174 (hereafter cited as "Chernovits ha-yehudit"). See also testimony of Gershon Sobelman, OHD, 2.
20. A Soviet source identifies the young man as Moshe Shayer. (N. M. Kunilo, Ed., *Radyanska Bukovina 1940–1945* [Kiev: 1967], Document 214, 324 (hereafter cited as *Soviet Bukovina*). Some time later the Soviet authorities granted the parents of the deceased a monthly pension (*Borotba trudyashchikh Bukoviny za sotialne i za natsionalne vizvoleniya i rozednana z Ukrainskoyu RSR* [Chernovtsy: 1958], 401 (hereafter cited as *Struggle of the Workers of Bukovina*). Cf. testimony of Gershon Sobelman, OHD, 2.
21. Large-scale riots took place in Moldavia at the time. In Dorohoi, dozens of Jews were killed or wounded when fired upon by Romanian troops. For details, see *Jewish Telegraphic Agency Bulletin* (hereafter cited as *J.T.A. Bulletin*), July 8–10, 1940.
22. Testimony of M. Kimhi, OHD, 10, 30. There is reason to believe that this is the leaflet mentioned in *Soviet Bukovina*, Document 3, 13.
23. I. Antonescu's letter to Dr. V. Filderman (October 16, 1942), contains the following report: "Even before the Soviet units came into sight, Jews in Bessarabia and Bukovina attacked

our officers, spat in their faces, ripped off their epaulettes, and, whenever they could, murdered our soldiers" (Matatias Carp, 3, 184–185; see also n. 19).

Testimonies of Jews partially corroborate these facts, with the exception of the commission of murder. A Jewish officer says that he was attacked by young Jews, who tore off his epaulettes (testimony of Y. Weisbrod, OHD, 6); a Jew from Beltsy admits: "I knocked a Romanian soldier off his horse" (testimony of "Adami," OHD, 5). Berl Lvovsky, age 14, "lunged at the commander of a Romanian unit and tried to tear off his epaulettes. The commander fired his weapon and the youngster fell" (Itzik Fefer, "Iber Besarabie" [Around Bessarabia], *Hayntike Nays* [Kovno], July 2, 1940).

24. Testimony of Zvi (Hirsh) Shwarzman, OHD, 2.
25. Y. Shildkraut, *'Al hurvot Besarabiya* [On the Ruins of Bessarabia] (Tel Aviv: 1954), 245.
26. Ibid., 246. In Vilna, this newspaper, edited by the Zionist Dr. Jacob Vigodsky, published the following headline: "Congratulations upon your liberation, oppressed Jewish masses in Bessarabia and Bukovina" (*Vilner Togblat* [Vilna], June 28, 1940).
27. Poet Itzik Fefer describes the pogrom that was to precede the arrival of the Red Army in "In Sovetishn Kishinev" [In Soviet Kishinev], *Der Shtern* (the Kiev newspaper), July 9, 1940, 3.

CHAPTER 3

1. *Folksblat* (Kovno), July 4, 1940.
2. Testimony of M. Epstein, OHD, 6; cf. S. Tamir, "Ha-'amim ha-Balti'im nilhamim 'al herutam" [The Baltic Peoples Fight for Their Freedom], *Ha-mashqif,* June 20, 1940.
3. *Unzer Vort* (Riga), June 28, 1940.
4. "Chernovits ha-yehudit," 174.
5. According to Soviet sources, about 150,000 persons reached Bessarabia from Romania by July 26, 1940 (*Istoriya Moldavskoy SSR* [History of the Moldavian SSR] [Kishinev: 1955], 2:354) (hereafter cited as *History of MSSR*). According to official sources in Bucharest, 9,500 Jews left Romania by July 3, 1940, with intent to return to Bessarabia (*J.T.A. Bulletin,* July 4, 1940, 2). About two years later, Jewish sources reported that "in the first few months of the Russian occupation of Bessarabia, tens of thousands of Bessarabian Jews, who had been dispersed all over Romania, went [to Bessarabia]" (letter of the Rescue Committee for Bessarabian Jews, Tel Aviv, November, 1942, 1–2). As for Bukovina, a report dated August 18, 1940, asserted that 10,000 Jews had fled this area (*American Jewish Yearbook,* 1940: 435).
6. A delegation representing 14,000 Jews who had been born in Bessarabia and Bukovina asked the Soviet consul in Bucharest to help them get their personal property out, but his reply was not encouraging (*Der Amerikaner* [New York], October 25, 1940, 5); cf. *Matatias Carp,* 436. The repatriates' plight and the sufferings inflicted on them by both the Romanians and the Soviets are described in the *J.T.A. Bulletin,* July 10, 1940.
7. *In rod fun tsorn,* 11.
8. Benzion Ben-Shalom, "Zholkiew bi-mei ha-kibush ha-sovieti" [Zolkiew During the Soviet Occupation], *Sefer Zholkiew* [Zolkiew Memorial Book) (Jerusalem: 1969), 7.
9. Dine Godiner, "21 September 1939," *Telekhan* (Los Angeles), 62, 45, 91.
10. From a report by Engineer Anshel Reiss, in "Sho'at yehudey Polin", 27.
11. *Pinqas Pruzhene, Berez, Kartuska, Malets, Shereshev, Selets* [Memorial Book of Pruzana, Bereza, Kartuska, Malecz, Szereszow, Sielce] (Buenos Aires: 1958), 459–460.
12. For an excellent example of this, see M. Sakzier, "Ha-yoshevet-rosh shel mo'etzet ha-'ir" [Chairwoman of the municipal council], *Shvut,* 5:1977, 113–116.
13. "Easterners" was the pejorative given to people sent from the USSR to oversee various aspects of sovietization.
14. *Pinqas Klezk* (A Memorial to the Jewish Community of Klezk/Kletsk [Poland]) (Tel Aviv: 1960), 88, 321–322.
15. *Bialystoker Shtern,* February 18, 1940.

16. *Sefer Rokitno ve-ha-seviva* [Testimonial and Memorial Book for Rokitno and Vicinity] (Tel Aviv: 1966), 253–254.
17. Report by Dr. Moshe Kleinboim (Sneh), in "Sho'at yehudey Polin", 38.
18. The figures are quoted from *Belaruskaya sovetskaya entsiklapediya* (Encyclopedia of Soviet Belorussia) (Minsk: 1939), 422; cf. *Jewish Chronicle* (London), November 24, 1939; Nicolas P. Vakar, *Byelorussia* (Cambridge: 1956), 858. The individuals in question were evidently Bracha Gutalevitz and Israel Nadler. Cf. "Mentshlekhe virde" [Human Dignity], *Oktyabr,* November 20, 1939.
19. As stated in *Ukrainska radianska entsiklopediya* (Encyclopedia of the Soviet Ukraine) (Kiev: 1962), 17:152; "Sho'at yehudey Polin", Appendix B, 56; *J.T.A. Bulletin,* February 25, 1940; cf. Shmuel Spector, *The Holocaust of Volhynian Jews 1941–1944* (Jerusalem: 1990), 25.
20. "Der historisher tog" [The historic day] [Editorial], *Di Idishe Shtime* (Kovno), July 14, 1940.
21. For details see "Linke grupe fun poaley tsiyon tret arayn in LDJS" [A leftist group from Po'aley Tsiyon joins the organization of working youth of Latvia] *Kamf* (Riga), July 2, 1940.
22. It was reported, for example, that of 32 candidates for the Belorussian Supreme Soviet from the Brest district, 24 were Belorussians, 4 were Russians, 2 were Ukrainians, one was Jewish, and one was Polish (*Oktyabr,* January 12, 1940).
23. *Der Shtern,* September 11, 1940. The twelve Jewish deputies included Rivka Gawze from the Baranowicze area, a former member of Ha-shomer ha-Tsa'ir. Her election and activity in this function are described in her testimony, (Giv'at Haviva: Moreshet Archives), A12, 2–4.
24. Jacob Lestchinsky, *Dos sovetishe idntum,* 378.
25. Yehoshua Frankfurt, "Mi-hayey yehudey Kovel tahat ha-shilton ha-sovieti" [How the Jews of Kowel lived under Soviet rule], *Sefer Kowel,* 384.
26. *Jewish Chronicle,* December 27, 1940; cf. "Sho'at yehudey Polin", 56; Abraham Wein, "Di yidn in Lemberger shtotrat" [The Jews in the Lemberg (Lvov) municipal council], *Yorbukh* (Tel Aviv: World Federation of Polish Jews, 1970) 3:315.
27. *Der Shtern,* December 8, 1940.
28. *Oktyabr,* December 11, November 28, and December 5, 1940; *Der Emes* (Kovno), December 12, 1940; *Ufboi* (Riga), April, 1941.
29. *Der Shtern,* November 24, 1940; cf. "A virdiker kandidat" [A respectable candidate], ibid., September 24, 1940. Former residents of Borislav testified that Dr. Deutschmeister had been close to Left Po'aley Tsiyon before the war.
30. *Oktyabr,* December 17, 1940.
31. *In rod fun tsorn,* 26.
32. Dovid Sfard, *Mit zikh un mit andere* [With Myself and With Others] (Jerusalem: 1984), 104–105 (hereafter cited as *Mit zikh un mit andere*).
33. Tania Fuks, *A vanderung iber okupirte gebitn* [Wanderings in the Occupied Areas] (Buenos Aires: 1947), 68–69 (hereafter cited as Tania Fuks).
34. Rabbi David Kahana testified (OHD, 10) that many Jewish Communists had been dismissed from their posts in Lvov in early 1940.
35. Testimony of Gustav Samuel Ostler, Yad Vashem Archives (hereafter cited as YVA) 03/1644, 14.
36. The members were Itzik Meskup ("Adomas"), Alter Kleiner, Berl Fridman ("Latvis"), Yankl Vinitzki, and Hayim Aizen; Aizen also served as director of the Cadres Department of the Party. One of the seven members of the Politburo of the Communist Party of Lithuania was Jewish: namely, Itzik Meskup, who was also chosen as second secretary of the district committee. The following played important roles in the Party Central Committee: Shmerl Maymin (director of the commercial section); Genrik Ziman (secretary of the minorities bureau); I. Sher (instructor in Shavli); Boris Shneider, and Deborah Berzak (*Mazioji lietuviskoji tarybine enciklopedija,* "Vilnius," 2:382 (hereafter cited as *Soviet Lithuanian Encyclopedia*).

37. Joseph Gar, *Viderklangen* [Echoes] (Tel Aviv: 1961), 24. Cf. Dov Levin, "Ziman (Zimanas), derekh hayim shel manhig qomunisti yehudi be-Lita" [Ziman (Zimanas): Life of a Jewish Communist Leader in Lithuania], *Shvut,* 1:1973, 95–100 (hereafter cited as "Ziman [Zimanas]").

38. These figures were estimated on the basis of the family and first names of polling-committee members, as listed by the press (*Vilner Emes* [Vilna], December 31, 1941, 2–6).

39. I.V., "A shvere yerushe" [A grim legacy], *Unzer Vort* (Riga), July 5, 1940.

40. "Der protses fun die grodner pogromshchikes" [Trial of the perpetrators of the pogrom in Grodno], *Bialystoker Shtern* (Bialystok), July 2, 1940.

41. *J.T.A. Bulletin,* September 21, 1940.

42. *Khrushchev Remembers, with an Introduction, Commentary and Notes by Edward Crankshaw,* Transl. and Ed., Strobe Talbott (Boston: 1971), 144–145 (hereafter cited as *Khrushchev Remembers*). In his memoirs, Khrushchev describes an episode connected with this epithet:

> I remember that once we invited Ukrainians, Jews, and Poles—mostly workers but some intellectuals, too—to a meeting in the Lvov opera house. It struck me as very strange to hear the Jewish speakers at this meeting refer to themselves as "yids." They said things like, "We yids hereby declare ourselves in favor of such-and-such."
> Out in the lobby after the meeting I stopped some of these men and demanded, "How dare you use the word 'yid'? Don't you know it's a very offensive term, an insult to the Jewish nation?"
> "Here in the western Ukraine it's just the opposite," they explained. "We call ourselves yids and consider the word 'Jew' an insult."
> Apparently what they said was true. If you go back to Ukrainian literature—take Gogol for instance—you'll see that "yid" isn't used derisively or insultingly. But even after this custom was explained to us, it continued to grate on our sensibilities until we got used to it.

> Journalist P. Schwartz describes an incident that he experienced in Tarnopol when he went out to buy a Jewish newspaper. The vendor recoiled at the pejorative *zhid* and insisted that it must never be used (P. Schwartz, *Dos iz geven der onhoyb* (This Was the Beginning) (New York: 1943), 309–310. Concerning the ban on the use of *zhid,* see also *Sho'at yehudei Polin,* 25.

43. *Bialystoker Shtern,* February 4 and February 12, 1940.

44. *Oktyabr,* December 15, 1940.

45. Testimony of A. Kovenski, YVA, Q-1253/105; *Volkovisk be-milhemet ha-'olam ha-sheniya 1939–1945* [Wolkowisk in World War II] (Tel Aviv: 1946), 62.

46. *Shtraln* (Kovno), 11 (46), July 17, 1940.

47. Based on a letter written to the author by a lieutenant-colonel in the Lithuanian army, A. Aliskauskas of Chicago, dated January 21, 1977. See also Shimon Kants, Ed., *Rozhishch 'ayarati* [Rozyszcze: My Town] (Tel Aviv: 1976), 197–198; Rafael Yaffe, *Sventsian tsvishn tsvey velt milkhomes* [Svinzian Between Two World Wars: Svinzian Region—Yizkor Book in Memory of Twenty-Three Jewish Communities] (Tel Aviv: 1965), 1520–1521; testimony, YVA, 3218/109–110, 3.

48. According to Soviet sources, the national composition of the 266 deputies of the Supreme Soviet of the Moldavian SSR was the following: Moldavians 56 percent, Ukrainians 22 percent, Russians 17 percent, and "others" 5 percent (i.e., Jews along with Gagus and Bulgarians). The Jews accounted for 7 percent of the population (Moldavian SSR in the Great Patriotic War (*Moldavskaya SSR v velikoy otchestvennoy voine* [Kishinev: 1970], 38, hereafter cited as *Moldavskaya SSR*).

49. K. Shabtai, "Fun shavl biz Akir" [From Shavli (Siauliai) to Akir], *Idisher Kemfer* [Jewish Fighter] (New York), October 13, 1950, 5–6.

50. The participation of a young Jew from Vilna in appropriation of a Polish estate owners' lounge is described by D. L., "Mir nemen iber dem klub shlakhetski" [We Appropriate the Noblemen's Lounge] *Shtraln,* 9 (44), August 2, 1940.

51. *Sefer Zholkiew,* 547; *Volozhin* (Tel Aviv: 1970), 533; Testimony, YVA, 369/8–3, 6.

52. *Der Shtern,* June 11, 1940; testimonies of A. Strazh, OHD, 17; Malka Smoli, OHD, 5–6; A. Ulstein, OHD, 13–14; Jacob Sapirstein, OHD, 2.
53. The leaflet is reproduced in B. Baranauskas, Ed., *Masines zudynes Lietuvoje* [Mass Murders in Lithuania] (Vilnius: 1965), 1: 50–51. For an English translation of the entire leaflet, see E. Razauskas, Ed., *Documents Accuse* (Vilnius: 1970), 124–125.
54. L. Garfunkel, *Kovno ha-yehudit be-hurbana* [Destruction of Jewish Kovno] (Jerusalem: 1959), 28–36.

CHAPTER 4

1. Michael Shor—son of an estate owner, member of the Romanian parliament representing the People's Party in the Khutin district—was sentenced to death for allegedly exploiting and beating workers (*Sefer qehillat Khutin* [Khutin Community Book] [Tel Aviv: 1974], 32). According to testimony of Dr. Lipa Zaydman (YVA, 03/1920, 5), the verdict was not carried out, but Shor died in prison. (See also ch. 12, n. 10.)
2. *Pinkes Slonim,* 8–10.
3. Testimony, YVA, B-3467/3–14, 6–7.
4. Z. Segalowitz, *Be-netiv ha-lehavot* [In the Path of the Flames] (Jerusalem: 1946), 165.
5. The figure is as cited in *Lietuviu archyvas—bolsevizmo metai* [Lithuanian Archives—The Year of Bolshevism] (Kaunas-Vilnius: 1943), 2:162 (hereafter cited as *Lithuanian Archives*); in later Soviet sources the figure is slightly, different: 1,597 businesses (A. Butkute-Rameliene, *Lietuvos komunistu partijos kova už Tarybų Lietuvos isitvirtimą* [The Struggle of the Lithuanian Communist Party for the Consolidation of Soviet Lithuania] [Vilnius: 1958], 79 (hereafter cited as Butkute-Rameliene).
6. Joseph Gar, *Azoy iz es geshen in Lite* [So It Happened in Lithuania] (Tel Aviv: 1965), 112.
7. "Chernovits ha-yehudit," 109.
8. For example, three of the 16 farms in the Vilkomir (Ukmerge) district of Lithuania that were nationalized by the authorized district committee in its meeting on May 6, 1941, were owned by Jews. See V. Kančevicius, Ed., *Tarybų valdžios atkurimas Lietuvoje 1940–1941* [Establishment of Soviet Rule in Lithuania, 1940–1941] (Vilnius: 1965), Doc. 182, 254–255.
9. S. Volfson, "Fun shtetl hendler tsu a nayvirt" [From village shopkeeper to farmowner], *Der Emes,* June 11, 1941, 5.
10. See Benzion Haimovitz, "Yameha ha-aharonim shel qehilatenu," *Orhayuv be-vinyana u-ve-hurbana* [The last days of our community, Orhayuv [Orhei] as it was and as it fell] (Tel Aviv: 1959, 159); *Jewish Chronicle* (London), September 20, 1940, 6.
11. See Dov Levin, "Yehudei Lita ha-sovietit ba-mishor ha-kalkali-sotsiali (1940–1941)" [The Socioeconomic Condition of the Jews of Soviet Lithuania], *Reva'on le-mehqar hevrati* [Social Research Quarterly], 5:1984, 20:171–191.
12. *Lithuanian Archives,* 4:194.
13. *Lubtch ve-Delatich* [Lubcz and Delatycze Memorial Book] (Tel Aviv: 1971), 35–36.
14. For example, Menahem Reznik of Lida, formerly a well-known Po'aley Tsiyon functionary and an owner of two shops in the town, was appointed assistant to the director of the economic section of the local NKVD because the latter was a relative of his. Leizer Malbim, formerly an affluent merchant, a leader of Berit ha-Hayyal (Union of Jewish Veterans) in Novogrudek, and the son of the chairman of the local kehilla, managed the timber and forests trust for some time. The former commander of the Betar cell in the town of Pren (Prienai in Lithuanian), Abraham Shtukarevich, was not only admitted to an artel but rose in the ranks rather quickly, ultimately becoming the director of the artel's planning department.
15. *Khurbn Braynsk* [Bransk Book of Memories] (New York: 1948), 248.
16. This was the situation in Tuchin (Tuczin), Korets (Korec), Rozhishch (Rozyszcze), Mezhirichi (Miedzyrzecz), Radzivilov (Radziwillow), and other localities (parentheses denote the present Russian spellings; others follow the previous Polish usage). For further details on the sovietization of Wolhynia, see Shmuel Spector, *The Holocaust of*

Volhynian Jews 1941–1944 (Jerusalem: 1990), 29–33, (hereafter cited as *Holocaust of Volhynian Jews*).

17. *Baranowicze,* 208.
18. *Der Emes,* January 30, 1941. For details about an invention by a worker at the Maistas meat plant, for which he was awarded 300 rubles, see *Der Emes,* April 27, 1941.
19. Concerning reports on Bessarabian radio that Jews were being recruited in that area for travel to Birobidzhan, with travel expenses paid by the government, see *Der Amerikaner,* September 15, 1940. According to this source, the first group, including 360 people, had already set out from Kishinev. However, this report is not corroborated by any other source. The same is true of a report in the *Jewish Chronicle,* September 27, 1939, about an official appeal to the Jews of Galicia in this regard.
20. This problem evidently lasted many months; shortly before Passover of 1941, industrial workers were still required to work on Jewish festivals ("Fabrikn bashlisn tsu arbetn in di teg fun die religieze yoym-toyvim" [Factories decide to work on religious festival days], *Der Emes,* April 13, 1941).
21. *Der Emes,* March 7, 1941.
22. This letter, dated February 27, 1941, is one of many written by the Getz family of the western Belorussian town of Brestowice to their son Itzhak (Irving) in Chicago.
23. "Di nit-natsionalizirte fabriklekh vern arayngetsoygn in der sotsialistisher produktsie" [Small factories that were not nationalized are merged into socialist production], *Vilner Emes,* October 16, 1940.
24. A member of the Lithuanian Communist Party Central Committee, Berl Latvis-Fridman, addressed the Jewish middle class with solicitous statements of this type. See "Der mitlshtand darf zen in undz di beste fraynt" [The middle class should regard us as best friends] *Di Idishe Shtime,* July 14, 1940.
25. "A gerotener onhoyb velkher darf nit blaybn keyn onhoyb" [A good beginning that should not remain a beginning], *Der Emes,* April 18, 1941.
26. Such people received money from overseas by striking a deal with someone interested in sending money overseas. In his Hebrew-language correspondence with his two daughters in Palestine, H. A. Israelov, owner of a winery in Keydan (Kedainiai in Lithuanian), makes at least 13 allusions to transactions of this kind. For example: "You're allowed to take the money to Aunt Ester-Feige; here I give Mina money every month" (August 24, 1940); "You'll be able to get as much money as you'll need from her. We'll settle the account with her" (March 4, 1941).
27. *Sefer zikaron li-qedoshei Sokoli* [Sokoli Memorial Book] (Tel Aviv: 1962), 45; *Oktyabr,* January 1, 1940. Another Soviet newspaper of the time cites 400–500 rubles as the monthly income of artel members in Wolhynia ("In loytsker geverbn arteln" [The vocational cooperatives of Luck], *Der Shtern,* January 22, 1940).
28. Aharon Weiss, "The Economic and Social Problems of East Galician Jewry under Soviet Rule 1939–1941," *Shvut,* 11:71–86. These figures are based on conversations with Abraham Wein, Meir Weiss, and Dr. Z. Radai of Eastern Galicia.
29. Getz family correspondence (see n. 22).
30. For information on the wages (in rubles) earned by 14 Jews in Vilna and the vicinity in 1940–1941, see Dov Levin, *Fighting Back—Lithuanian Jewry's Armed Resistance to the Nazis 1941–1945* (New York, London: 1985), 213 and Fig. B3.
31. *Vilner Emes,* November 29, 1940. Members of the *Der Emes* board earned 1,000 rubles, whereas printing workers at the same newspaper earned only 200 (testimony of Hirsh Osherowich, OHD, 22–23).
32. In this context, it was reported overseas that "the Jews of Lithuania haven't met with the clothing problem yet. They have always been well-equipped in this regard and can still wait another four or five years until they'll have to go down to the Soviet standard" (S. Dorfson, "Litvishe idn untern sovetishn rezshim" [Lithuanian Jewry under Soviet rule], *Der Amerikaner,* January 31, 1941, 12).
33. Abraham Zak, *Knekht zaynen mir geven* I [We Were Slaves] (Buenos Aires: 1956), 163–164.

34. Testimony of M. Milstein, OHD, 9.
35. See letter by Golde Poliansky, *Der Emes,* June 1, 1941.

CHAPTER 5

1. As early as 1919, the Commissariat for Higher Education of Soviet Russia, inspired by Jewish Communist activists, ruled that "Hebrew is not the vernacular of the Jewish masses; accordingly it is not considered the language of [one of] the national minorities. In the pedagogical sense, its status is that of a foreign language which is not the vernacular of the masses in the RSFSR (*Kultur un bildung,* 9–10, November 12, 1919, 1). On December 22, 1923, the teaching of religion was banned "for groups of more than three children," even in private settings (Arye Yodfat, "Ha-dat ha-yehudit be-misgeret ha-ma'amad ha-huqi shel ha-dat bi-verit ha-mo'etsot" [Jewish religion in the context of the legal status of religion in the Soviet Union], *Behinot* [Jerusalem], 1:1970, 136).
2. Zvi Lipset, "Batei ha-sefer ha-yehudi'im bi-verit ha-mo'etsot u-sheqi'atam" [Jewish schools in the Soviet Union and their decline], *Behinot,* 1:1970, 62.
3. Hersh Smolar, "Ha-hayim ha-yehudi'im be-ma'arav Belorusiya ha-sovietit—1939–1941, periha u-sheqi'a" [Jewish life in Soviet Western Belorussia—1939–1941, efflorescence and decline], *Shvut* 4:1976, 132 (hereafter cited as "Ha-hayim ha-yehudi'im"). An undated report on Jewish education in the Bialystok district in 1939–1941 (Polish, Ringelblum collection, 73/4/217) confirms the existence of this trend of thought.
4. *Oktyabr,* March 20, 1940; cf. Yitzhak Ganoz, *Be-ma'glei ha-duba ha-gedola* [In the Embrace of the Great Bear] (Tel Aviv: 1971), 25–28; *'Al masu'ot Polin* [On the Ruins of Poland] (Merhavia: 1940), 132 *Encyclopaedia of the Jewish Diaspora* (Jerusalem: 1973), s.v. *Grodna* (Grodno).
5. This figure, like many others for Wolhynia, is cited by S. Spector, *The Holocaust of Volhynian Jews,* 20, 33–35.
6. Abraham Oks, "Tarnopol be-eys der tzveyter velt milkhome" [Tarnopol during World War II], *Sefer yizkor Tarnopol* [Tarnopol Memorial Book], *Entsiqlopediya shel galuyot* [Diaspora Encyclopaedia] (Jerusalem–Tel Aviv: 1955), 347.
7. According to *Der Shtern* of September 30, 1940, 3.9 percent of pupils in Ukrainian schools were Jewish. Assuming that this rate had not changed by January, 1940, when the total enrollment was 1,150,000, the number of Jewish pupils in the western Ukraine was 44,850. It is estimated that there were 37,000 Jewish pupils in Eastern Galicia alone. See Aharon Weiss, "Temurot ba-hinukh shel yehudei Galicia ha-mizrahit bi-tequfat ha-shilton ha-sovieti" [Changes in the education of Jews of Eastern Galicia during the period of Soviet rule], *Gal-ed* (Tel Aviv), 4–5: 1978, 443.
8. Table 4–2 is based on reports in *Oktyabr* (Minsk), February 14, May 5, September 14, and December 15, 1940; and *Der Emes* ("Kultur Khronik"), May 23, 1941.
9. Yankl Yud, "Kovner hebreishe gimnazie bashlosn aribertsugeyn af idish" [the Hebrew high school in Kovno decides to go over to Yiddish], *Di Idishe Shtime,* July 18, 1940.
10. The above figures were culled from scattered reports in the Soviet-Jewish press of the time, chiefly in Lithuania. For further details see Dov Levin, "Ma'arakhot ha-hinukh ha-yehudi be-lita ha-sovietit 1940–1941" [Jewish education systems in Soviet Lithuania 1940–1941], *Shvut,* 6, 1978: 68–91; cf. *Bialystoker Shtern,* February 9, 1941.
11. *History of MSSR,* 36; cf. *Moldavskaya SSR,* (Kishinev: 1970), 67.
12. David Vinitsky, *Besarabiya ha-yehudit be-ma'arkhoteha* [Jewish Bessarabia in Its Struggles] (Jerusalem–Tel Aviv: 1973), 610–611, 681.
13. In 1941, the government book publisher in Minsk, under the auspices of the Belorussian Commissariat for Higher Education, published a 41-page pamphlet called *I. L. Peretz far der shul* [I. L. Peretz for Use in Schools] by Gershon Yevrov, containing methodological instructions and explanatory notes for teachers in Jewish schools.
14. M. Reicher, "Di martirielogie fun di yedinitser yidn" [Martyrology of the Yedinitz Jews], *Yad le-Yedinits* [Yedintsy Memorial Book] (Tel Aviv: 1973), 739 J. Kermish, *Sho'at yehudei*

Kolomea bi-ferots milhemet ha-'olam ha-sheniya [Community Memoir of Kolomyja and Vicinity], 1972; File of the United Polish Jewry Relief Committee, Jerusalem, June, 1940 (851/121/12/12), 5.

15. Cf. Ch. Szmeruk, *Yiddish Publications in the USSR (from the Late Thirties up to 1948)*, Yad Vashem Studies, 4:1960, 106–107 (hereafter cited as *Yiddish Publications*).

16. Hugo Gold, ed., *Geschichte der Juden in der Bukowina* [History of the Jews in Bukowina] (Tel Aviv: 1962), I:82; cf. *Der Shtern*, October 5, 1940.

17. Yankl Yud, "In fabrik fun idishen lernbukh" [In the Jewish Textbook Factory], *Folksblat*, October 16, 1940; Dov Levin, "Sefarim mi-ta'am: sifrei limud u-qeriya be-yiddish be-Lita ha-sovietit (1940–1941)" [Sponsored books: Yiddish-language textbooks and reading matter in Soviet Lithuania, 1940–1941], *Yad la-Kore–The Reader's Aid*, 16, 2–3:1977, 112–113, n. 8 (hereafter cited as "Sefarim mi-ta'am").

18. A. Ayzen, "Di 12-te mitl'shul in Vilne" [High School No. 12 in Vilna], *Vilner Emes*, November 4, 1940.

19. "Akhtung farvalters fun yidishe folkshuln" (For the information of principals of public [elementary] schools), *Folksblat*, October 15, 1940.

20. *Der Emes*, May 22, 1941.

21. *Folksblat*, October 30, 1940. These institutions are described in detail at the end of this chapter.

22. *Oktyabr*, February 15, 1940.

23. Testimony of Ita Bell, OHD, 3. Cf. testimonies of Shoshana Simon and Haviva Burstein, recorded in Hebrew in 1943/44. These testimonies are included in the memoirs of members of the *ma'apilim* (illegal immigrants) group affiliated with Irgun Berit Tsiyon in the Kovno ghetto; the memoirs were incorporated verbatim into a collection kept inter alia at YVA, B/12–15, pp. 22–25, 32–37.

24. P. Hofner, "In di yidishe shuln fun Lvover gegnt" [In the Jewish schools in the Lvov area], *Der Emes*, March 4, 1941.

25. The principal of an ORT (Obshchestvo Rasprostraneniya Truda sredi Yevreyev [Society for Manual Work among Jews]) school alleged that the Komsomol actually controlled the institution (testimony of J. Oleiski, OHD, p. 3); cf. S. Levin, "Di rol fun komyug organizatsie" [Function of the Komsomol organization], *Shtraln*, April 20, 1941.

26. *Folksblat*, October 15, 1940.

27. Rabbi Mordechai Gifter, "Yeshivat Telz" [Telz yeshiva], in Shmuel K. Mirsky, Ed., *Mosedot tora be-eiropa be-vinyanam u-ve-hurbanam* [European Religious Institutions As They Were and As They Fell] (New York: 1956), 184 (hereafter cited as *Mosedot tora*).

28. *Rokitno ve-ha-seviva* [Rokitno and the Vicinity], Israel: 1967, 107.

29. From a letter by Abraham Jashpan, Rio de Janeiro, January 6, 1975. Liba Brik-Barak, a former teacher at this school, corroborates this.

30. Incidents of these kinds in eastern Poland are described in *Sefer 'edut ve-zikaron li-qehilat Pinsk-Karlin* [Pinsk-Karlin Testimonial and Memorial Book] (Tel Aviv: 1967), 2:128; *Sefer Lida* [Lida Book] (Tel Aviv: 1970), 261; "Sho'at yehudey Polin", 25; *Sefer zikaron li-qehilat Stolyn ve-ha-seviva* [Memorial Book for the Community of Stolyn and Vicinity] (Tel Aviv: 1952), 110 (hereafter cited as *Sefer Stolyn*).

31. Mordechai Bilroi, "Mi-tokh pirqei yoman" [From diary entries], *'Al masu'ot Polin* [On the Ruins of Poland] (Merhavia: 1940), 129. A former Betar activist in Shavli, Berke Ekdesh was so persevering as "to speak nothing but Hebrew, refuse to answer in other languages, and refer to himself only as Moshe Akravi" (testimony of Dov Shilansky, OHD, 62–63).

32. See also *Sefer Stolyn*, 110; *Sefer zikaron li-qehilat Ludwipol* [Ludwipol Community Memorial Book] (Tel Aviv: 1965), 36–37; *Rishonim la-mered—Lahwa* [The First to Rebel: Lawha], (Jerusalem–Tel Aviv: 1957), 37–38; Shalom Cholawski, *'Ir ve-ya'ar be-matsor* [Town and Forest Under Siege] (Tel Aviv: 1973), 36–37; Yitzhak Levin, *'Aliti mi-spetzya* [I reached Eretz Yisrael from La Spezia [Italy] (Tel Aviv: 1947), 41; E. Ben-Shimon, "Sof pasuq" [The end], *Hekhal she-shaqa'*, [The Palace Asunder] (Tel Aviv: 1962), 203; testimonies of David Pur, Yitzhak Tsur, and Yona Rosenfeld, OHD; testimony of S. Shushan, OHD, 2.

33. Eliezer Yerushalmi, "Ha-gimnasiya ha-'ivrit be-Shavli" [The Hebrew high school in Shavli], *Yahadut Lita* [Lithuanian Jewry] (Tel Aviv: 1972), 2:146. The rumor concerning Ben-Gurion's hostile remarks about the Hebrew teachers in Lithuania recurs, with variations, in several testimonies and reminiscences of former teachers of the time.
34. *Rokitno ve-ha-seviva,* 107. The case of an Orthodox teacher who publicly renounced his beliefs in is described in *Oktyabr,* January 22, 1940.
35. Testimony of Yankl Yakir, OHD 2:21.
36. The official name of this institute was "Institut far Yidisher Proleterisher Kultur ba der Alukrainisher Visenshaftlekher Akademie" [Institute for Jewish Proletarian Culture at the Ukrainian Academy of the Sciences]; it had previously operated in a smaller format as "Kateder far Yidisher Kultur ba der Alukraynisher Visenshaftlekher Akademie" [Chair for Jewish Culture at the Ukrainian Academy of the Sciences].
37. As reported in the memoirs of an Institute employee, Ester Rosental-Shneiderman. *Naftulei derakhim* [Twisting Paths] (Tel Aviv: 1974), 2:329.
38. See E. Volobrinsky, who strongly criticizes the report of the 1929 YIVO conference. "Fashizirter yidishizm" [Yiddishism-cum-Fascism], *Fashizirter yidishizm un zayn visnshaft* [Yiddishism-cum-Fascism and Its Scholarship] (Minsk: 1930).
39. Testimony of Eliahu Yonas, OHD, 12–13.
40. *Vilner Togblat,* August 16, 1940, 1; as cited by Leiser Ran, *Ash fun Yerusholayim de-Lite* [Ashes from Jerusalem of Lithuania] (New York: 1959), 176.
41. "Der idisher visnshaftlekher institut in Vilne zevakst zikh" [The Jewish scholarly institute in Vilna grows], *Idishe Kultur* 4, New York, April, 1941, 57. For further details, see Dov Levin, "YIVO bein ha-patish ve-ha-magal" [YIVO between the hammer and the sickle], *Ha-Universita* (Jerusalem), 22:18–28. See also Dov Levin, "Tsvishn hamer un serp" [Between hammer and sickle: YIVO in Vilna under the Soviets], *YIVO Bleter* (New York), Jubilee Volume XLVI, in Honor of YIVO's Fiftieth Anniversary, 1925–1975 (New York: 1980), 78–97).

CHAPTER 6

1. S. Kaczerginsky, *Tsuvishn hamer un serp* [Between Hammer and Sickle] (Paris: 1949), 15–16. Cf. Haya Lazar, "Kitvei 'et ve-'itonim yomi'im yehudi'im be-Vilna" [Jewish journals and daily newspapers in Vilna], in Yehuda Gothelf, Ed., *'Itonut yehudit she-hayeta* [A Jewish Press That Was] (Tel Aviv: 1973), 251.
2. Hersh Smolar, "Ha-hayim ha-yehudi'im," 128.
3. Ibid., 129.
4. Until February 22, 1940, the newspaper appeared three or four times per week; from then until July 6, 1940, it came out twice a week. From this time until the German invasion, it was published as a weekly, usually appearing on Sundays.
5. Hersh Smolar, *Hekhan ata haver Sidorov?* [Where are you, comrade Sidorov?] (Tel Aviv: 1975), 117.
6. Hersh Smolar, "Ha-hayim ha-yehudi'im," 129.
7. The memoirs of a Jewish journalist allude to the existence of a news sheet or bulletin in Brest, western Belorussia (L. Leneman, "Peretz Markish und der NKVD redaktor Rabinovich" [Peretz Markish and the NKVD editor Rabinovich], *Di goldene keyt* [The Golden Chain] [Tel Aviv], 43, 1962: 132]; cf. "Sho'at yehudey Polin", 30–61. An additional source, Soviet-Jewish author Dovid Hofstein, remarked during his encounter with Jewish authors and journalists in Lvov that "since Lvov is going to be a Ukrainian city, there's no reason to have a Yiddish newspaper here" (David Grodner, "In Soviet Poland and Lithuania," *Contemporary Jewish Record,* 1943, 144). According to a report from Kishinev, "a Communist newspaper called *Besaraber Shtern*" began to appear in Lvov about a month after the Red Army came in; on August 1, the report continued, a radio station would open in Kishinev "with Yiddish broadcasts each and every day" (*Der Amerikaner,* July 26, 1940, 5). This uncorroborated report was preceded by an item originating in Jewish circles in London, based on reports from Radio Moscow: "The Russian authorities in the occupied

territories of Bessarabia and Northern Bukovina have recognized the Jews as a national minority; therefore they have given permission to start up a Jewish newspaper in this area. Jewish newspapers will now appear in Czernowitz, Kishinev, and Cetatea-Alba. More than 150 Jewish journalists who had lost their jobs about two years ago, when the Romanian authorities shut down the Jewish papers, will now have work" (*J.T.A. Bulletin*, July 11, 1940). See also n. 22.

8. According to Jewish sources overseas, a journal named *Der Arbeter*, edited by Dovid Kenigsberg, appeared briefly and intermittently in Lvov in late 1939 (*Der Amerikaner*, September 15, 1939; *Jewish Chronicle*, December 22, 1939); see also n. 22.

9. A. Kantchin, "A naye yidishe teglekhe tsaytung" [A new Jewish daily newspaper], *Oktyabr*, June 20, 1941. According to this source, the newspaper appeared under the auspices of the district committee of the Communist Party. Brief items about the advent of the new publication had appeared previously (*Der Emes*, May 30, 1941, *Ufboi* 10 (May, 1941, 16). *Ufboi* 11 (June, 1941, 16) reported that a Yiddish-language almanac on matters of literature and art in Lvov had made its debut in May. Another source reports that the name of the Lvov publication was *Lemberger Shtern* (Tania Fuks, 106).

10. This matter is discussed at great length and detail by Dov Levin, "Ha-'emes' ha-aharon ve-sofo—ha-'itonut ha-yehudit be-Lita ha-Sovietit, 1940–1941" [The last *Emes* and its demise—the Jewish press in Soviet Lithuania, 1940–1941], *Shvut*, 5:1977, 38–48.

11. Concerning the takeover by the Jewish Communists, led by G. Ziman, E. Kolodny, and others, see A. Gar, "Di Kovner togtsaytung *Folksblat*" [The Daily *Folksblat* of Kovno], *Lite* [Lithuania] (Tel Aviv: 1965), 2:433–442. As for Ziman himself, see Dov Levin, "Ziman (Zimanas)," *Shvut*, 1: 1973, 95–100.

12. Dr. Jacob Wigodsky, "Der kegnzaytiker banemen zich fun Ratnfarband, Lite, un yidn" (The attitudes of the Soviet Union, Lithuania, and the Jews toward each other), *Vilner Togblat*, July 2, 1940.

13. S. Kaczerginsky, *Tsuvishn hamer un serp* [Between Hammer and Sickle], Paris: 1949: 24–25.

14. In a letter to the editor, a proofreader at Government Printing House No. 4 complained about "spelling troubles," citing several Hebrew words for which no final decision on Yiddish spelling had been made: "יאמטעוו or יאמטעוו, אנמעוו or בנארים or בצגארים, and so on." (A. Volpe, "A vikhtiker inyen" [An important matter], *Der Emes*, March 28, 1941).

15. By April, 1941, the newspaper had been reduced from eight pages to six. On June 20 and 21, 1941 (the last days before the Soviet-German war), the newspaper was only four pages in length, and even these were downsized.

16. Testimony of Hirsh Osherovitz, OHD, 1:15–16.

17. In a conversation between community leaders in Riga and the senior Soviet representative in Latvia, A. Vishinsky, the latter promised that the Jews would, at some future time, be allowed to publish a weekly journal (testimony of A. Godin, OHD, 2). For ten years Godin had been the secretary of the chairman of the kehilla (Rabbi M. Dubin) and an editor of *Haynt*.

18. In all, the evening edition (*Ovnt Oysgabe*) of *Kamf* came out 38 times; the last issue appeared on August 12, 1940, about three days after the official Soviet annexation of Latvia.

19. Op. cit., July 4, 1940. One article on this theme, published the previous day in the local Russian newspaper *Proletarskaya Pravda*, appeared in *Kamf* (Riga) on July 2, 1940; see also an article about an antisemitic incident in the army, ibid., July 10, 1940.

20. In a five-part series published under the title *"Di yidishe gezelshaftlekhkeyt un der nayer velt krizis"* [Jewish public life and the new world crisis], *Kamf* listed the solutions prescribed by the major Jewish "bourgeois" movements or parties: assimilation, Orthodoxy, Zionism, Territorialism, Folkism, and Bundism. The five articles appeared in this order between July 5 and July 11, 1940.

21. Originally *Politish literarisher khoydesh-zhurnal* [Political-Literary Monthly Journal], as of November, 1940, it was subtitled *Zhurnal far politik, visenshaft un kunst* [Journal for Politics, Scholarship, and the Arts].

22. On August 14, 1940, *Arbeter* referred obliquely to anew a Yiddish-language newspaper in Czernowitz named *Der Arbeter*. Testimonies by several readers in Czernowitz affiliated

with Ha-shomer ha-Tsa'ir suggest that a publication of this name was indeed published in Czernowitz, but not systematically or for long. According to one testimony, Soviet-Jewish author Itzik Fefer asked Jewish authors and purveyors of culture in Czernowitz: "Why do you need another Yiddish newspaper? In the meantime, take *Shtern* [from Kiev], and as for the future—we'll see" (testimony of M. Kimhi, OHD, 14). See also n. 8.

With respect to Bessarabia, there was a spate of articles and reports connected with the appearance of a local Yiddish-language newspaper. In Kishinev, it even had a name: *Besaraber Emes* (testimony of K. A. Bartini, OHD, 1:16); according to *Der Amerikaner* (July 26, 1940), the newspaper was called *Besaraber Shtern,* and it had, for all practical purposes, already begun to appear in Kishinev (cf. *J.T.A. Bulletin,* July 11, 1940). However, according to a different conjecture, the plans to publish a Jewish newspaper in Bessarabia never materialized because some of the writers objected to its choice of editor, Yehiel Shrayzman (testimony of Y. Yakir, OHD, 5:34); see also end of n. 7.

23. Moshe Grosman, *In farkhishuften Land fun legendarn Dzugashvili* [In the Enchanted Land of the Legendary Dzugashvili (Stalin)], (Paris: 1949), 29 (hereafter cited as Moshe Grosman).

24. Many of these refugee authors are known by name: Baruch Olitsky, Mordechai Elay, Joseph Akrutny, Zisha Bagish, Mikhael Burstein, Pesach Binecki, Moshe Broderzon, Moshe Grosman, Shmuel Drayer, Perl Halter, Meir Halpern, Samuel Hoffer, Bunim Heller, Moses Waldman, S. Wolman, Leizer Wolf, I. M. Weissenberg, Moses Zalberg, Abraham Zak, Sholem Zhirman, Dovid Zukelik, Samuel Zaromb, Melech Chomny, Israel Trunk, Isaac Yonasewitz, Pinchas Katz, Berl Mark, Leib Morgentau, Dovid Mitzmacher, Hersh Smolar, Chaim Semyaticki, Dovid Sfard, Benjamin Ellis, Israel Emiot, Perl Pomerantz, C. L. Fuks, Leo Finkelstein, Shmerl Kaczerginsky, Efraim Kaganovsky, B. Kutcher, Nachman Rapp, Marek Rakowsky, Shmuel Drayer, Joseph Rubinstein, and Solomon Sheinberg. (Burstein, Drayer, Zhirman, Semyaticki, and Kaczerginsky moved to Vilna in 1941.) In Bialystok, quite a few local writers were present at the time, including Solomon Burstein and Jacob Gordon. According to one version of this account, 200 Jewish writers congregated in Bialystok at first. Forty of them remained, but only a few of them were admitted to the Writers' Association (Isaac Yonesawitz, *Tsvishn tsvey fayeren* [Between Two Fires] (Buenos Aires: 1971), 273.

25. Sheine-Miriam Broderzon, *Mayn laydns-veg mit Moshe Broderzon* [My Via Dolorosa with Moshe Broderzon] (Buenos Aires: 1960), 18.

26. Abraham Zak, *Knekht zaynen mir geven* [We Were Slaves], 21–22.

27. *Mit zikh un mit andere* [With Ourselves and with Others], 110–111. For further details on the subsequent lectures and discussions, see "Sheferishe shrayber konferents in Minsk" [Conference of Creative Writers in Minsk], *Ufboi* (Riga) 8:1941, 13.

28. Abraham Zak, *op. cit.,* 63.

29. Reverberations and descriptions of this incident appear in the writings and remembrances of many participants in the assembly. See, for example, Joseph Rubinstein, *Megiles Rusland* [A Story of Russia] (Tel Aviv: 1971), 23; *Mit zikh un mit andere,* 84.

30. For details on the writers who reached Lvov, see Solomon Schweitzer, "Dos yidish kultur leben in Poyln" [Jewish cultural life in Poland], *Yorbuch fun der velt federatsie fun Poylishe yidn* [Yearbook of the World Federation of Polish Jews] (Tel Aviv: 1967), 2:157–159; *Encyclopedia of the Diaspora* (Tel Aviv–Jerusalem: 1956), s.v. "Lvov," 753, 765–767; T. Fuks, 38–106; A. Lvovski, "Ufbli fun yidisher kultur in mayrev-ukraine" [Efflorescence of Jewish Culture in the Western Ukraine], *Ufboi* 7, April, 1941, 17. Additional details on Eastern Galicia in this chapter are culled from Aharon Weiss, "Teatron ve-sifrut yiddish be-Galitsya ha-mizrahit ba-shanim 1939–1941" [Yiddish theater and literature in Eastern Galicia, 1939–1941], *Behinot* 8–9, 1980: 118–128.

31. *Bialystoker Shtern,* February 6, 1941.

32. Tania Fuks, 55.

33. *Sovetish Literatur,* 3:1941, 39.

34. M. Grosman, 64.

35. For details see Ch. Szmeruk, "Yiddish Publications," *Yad Vashem Studies,* 4:1960, 11.

36. An example is a poem by B. Heller, "Mayn mame in geto" [My Mother in the Ghetto], written in 1940 but published only after the war in his collection, *Durkh shotn un shayn* [Through Shadow and Light] (Warsaw: 1948), 86–87. For details see Ch. Szmeruk, "Yiddish Publications," *Yad Vashem Studies* 4:1960, 116–117.
37. *Ufboi* 3; January, 1941: 111.
38. "Oyfname fun di Moskver idishe shrayber in tse-ka KP(B) fun Vaysrusland" [A reception for Jewish writers from Moscow in the central committee of the Communist Party of Belorussia], *Bialystoker Shtern,* February 18, 1940; cf. "Brigade fun moskver yidishe shrayber in Bialystok" [A brigade of Jewish writers from Moscow in Bialystok], ibid. (Hersh Smolar, "Ha-hayim ha-yehudi'im" [Jewish Life], *Shvut* 4:1976, 133).
39. "Der ovnt lekhoved dem 15-yorikn yubiley funem zhurnal Shtern" [An Evening in Honor of the 15th Anniversary of *Der Shtern*], *Bialystoker Shtern,* August 26, 1940.
40. Golde Frades, "Sheferisher tsuzamenkum fun die Moskver un Lvover shrayber" [A creative encounter between writers from Moscow and Lvov], *Der Emes,* March 12, 1941.
41. "This is how all the plays of the governmental Jewish theater were broadcast. It was a special pleasure to listen to Jewish songs . . . from the outdoor loudspeakers in Lvov—the same outdoors where, not long ago, people made sure not to utter a word of Yiddish" (Tania Fuks, 61).
42. For example, Wenglowa Street in Vilna was renamed for Sholem Aleichem, Arkliu Street for Abraham Goldfaden, Shveicarija Street for Julius Shimelevich (a Jewish revolutionary), Finn Street for I. L. Peretz, and Hagaon Street for Mark Antokolski. (*Der Emes,* May 21, 1941).
43. *Bleter 1940, Zamlbuch far literatur und kunst, aroysgegeben fun farband fun di yidishe shrayber und kinstler-plastiker in Lite,* [Journal for Literature and the Arts, published by the Alliance of Writers and Plastic Artists], Kovno, 1940, 214 (2). (The cover was designed by the painter Sliosberg.)
44. For the names of the participants, their works, and further details about the Yiddish-language writers in Lithuania, see Dov Levin, Etnahta qetsara shel tiqvot [A Brief Pause of Hope], *Qiryat Sefer* (Jerusalem: 1978), 53:238–249.
45. A copy of this book, perhaps the only one in existence—actually a coverless, unbound collection of numbered pages—is in the possession of its author, who resides in Tel Aviv.
46. Testimony of K. A. Bartini, OHD, 17.
47. Thus, for example, the story "Di fon" [The Flag] by Yehiel Shraybman, one of the few Yiddish-language authors whom the authorities viewed favorably, was published in the Riga journal *Ufboi* (No. 9, May, 1941). The first Yiddish work to be printed in a Soviet forum was the poem "Mir zaynen fray" [We Are Free] by Hersh Kholodenko, a folk poet from Bendery, in the daily newspaper *Der Shtern* on July 6, 1940.
48. According to one version, the broadcasts were to begin on August 5, 1940 (*Der Amerikaner,* July 26, 1940, 5).
49. Testimony of Y. Yakir, OHD, 5:3.
50. The Jewish authors who found themselves in Baranowicze at the time included Hersh-Leib Koshber (Vainstein), Meshulam Surkis, Shmuel-Abba Soifer, Yankl Fridman, Isaac Fanner, Yosef Burg, Hersh Segal, Haim Ginigar, Leizer Podriachik, Isaac Schwartz, and Joseph Lerner (the last five served as teachers also).
51. One of these, Silberman, was an editor of the local newspaper *Radianska Bukovina.*
52. Klara Blum, "Di yidishe dichtern fun Chernovtsy" [The Jewish poetess from Czernowitz], *Der Emes* (Kovno), February 4, 1941, 3.
53. L. Strongin, "Der vuks fun der Sovetisher yidisher literatur" [Growth of Soviet Jewish literature], *Vilner Emes,* November 20, 1940.
54. L. Strongin, "Di aktuele oyfgabn in der yidish farlag arbet" [The current tasks of Jewish publishing activity], *Der Emes,* January 15, 1941.
55. For additional details on this matter see Dov Levin, "Sifrut mi-ta'am" [Literature in Service of the Regime], *Yad la-Kore,* 2–3:1977, 224–237.
56. M. Grosman, 63.
57. *Der Amerikaner,* January 2, 1941; cf. *Jewish Chronicle,* December 27, 1940.

58. All private libraries, newspapers and journals, and games were kept together in a public club established in Aharon Tsinman's home in Briceva; various entertainment programs, such as movies, plays, and parties, were offered in the yard. M. and L. Parnas, *Pinkas Bricheva* [Briceva Memorial Book] (Tel Aviv: 1970), 477.

59. Testimonies of Z. Goldstein, OHD, 11; Rabbi Yeshayahu Elkis, OHD, 6; Ze'ev Gitelman, OHD, 15.

60. Testimonies of Z. Goldstein, OHD, 11; "Adami," OHD, 112; Y. Yakir, OHD, 4:17; K. A. Bartini, OHD, 1:20.

61. Alter Kacyzne, for example, tried to escape to the east but was murdered by local Ukrainians in the vicinity of Tarnopol. Dovid Kenigsberg was killed by Ukrainians in a pogrom within the first few days of the German presence in Lvov. Leibush Dreykurs and Yerahmiel Green perished at the Yanovska camp. Moshe Shimel died in a labor camp near Zloczow. Jacob Shudrich helped organize the resistance movement in the Lvov ghetto and was murdered when, together with a group of young Jews, he tried to reach the forests to fight the Nazis. Rachel Korn and Nachum Bomza succeeded in reaching the USSR.

62. Ida Kaminska, *My Life—My Theater* (New York: 1973), 112–114; see also testimony of Ida Kaminska, OHD, 5.

63. *Der Shtern,* June 11, 1940.

64. Isaac Turkow-Grodberg, *Oyf Mayn Veg* [On My Way], Tel Aviv, 1971: 121; and Turkow-Grodberg, *Sovetishe Dramaturgie* (Warsaw: 1955), 229; Tania Fuks, 96.

65. *Ufboi,* April, 1941, 7:7.

66. "Der kolektiv bay 'yiteg' badint Kovne un Provints," [The Yiteg collective troupe performs in Kovno and Province], *Folksblat,* August 17, 1940.

67. Testimony of A. Jofe, OHD, p. 4.

68. For additional details on these two theaters and Yiddish theatrical activity in the outlying towns of Lithuania, see Dov Levin, "Shenat periha ve-shirat ha-barbur" [A year of flowering and the swan song], *Bamah* (Jerusalem), 72, 1977:250–261; 73–74, 1977:262–279.

69. "In Chernovitser yidishn melukhe-teater" [In the Czernowitz Jewish governmental theater], *Ufboi,* June, 1941, 12:25.

CHAPTER 7

1. Rabbis and Orthodox Jews were known to have taken part in receptions for the Red Army. The rabbi of the Bessarabian town of Perlitz, for example, greeted the soldiers clutching a Torah scroll and was treated sympathetically (testimony of Y. Yakir, OHD, 2:3–4). However, religious Jews were given hints in the very first days that hard times awaited them. Thus a Jewish soldier in the Red Army told a group of Jews wreathed in beards and forelocks from the Yedinitz (Yedintsy) area: "You're happy the Russians have come, but you'll still cry about it plenty, especially you, with your beards and forelocks! Go home and celebrate less!" (testimony of Rabbi Y. Elkis, OHD, p. 5).

2. See B. Shulman, "Di harbstike idishe religieze yontoyvim" [The Autumn Religious Festivals of the Jews], *Bialystoker Shtern,* October 6, 1940.

3. A. V., "Groyse anti-religieze farzamlung in Vilkomir" [Large anti-religious assembly in Vilkomir], *Folksblat,* October 17, 1940.

4. *Oktyabr,* May 10, 1941.

5. *J.T.A. Bulletin,* October 4, 1939.

6. "Derklerung fun der kompartey oyf dem folksmiting lekhoved di politarestirte dem 19-te yuni" [Communist Party announcement of a people's assembly in honor of the political prisoners], *Folksblat,* July 1, 1940.

7. Testimony of Rabbi David Kahana, OHD, 11.

8. "Chernovits ha-yehudit, *Shvut,* 5, 1977:110; cf. "Dikui ha-yehudim tahat ha-shilton ha-sovieti be-Bukovina" [Repression of the Jews under Soviet Rule in Bukovina], *Ha-mashqif,* November 20, 1940.

9. Testimony of Lippa Zaydman, YVA, Z-03/1920–1798/56.

10. "Mi-yomano shel na' va-nad" [From the diary of a nomad, readied for press by Rabbi Shimon Efrati], *Qehillat Bendery* [Bendery Memorial Book] (Tel Aviv: 1975), 147.
11. Ibid., 151.
12. Testimonies of Rabbi David Kahana, OHD, p. 19; Jacob Sapirstein, OHD, p. 3.
13. Testimony of A. Godin, OHD, 7.
14. Letter dated October 21, 1940, part of a collection of letters written in 1940–1941 by the Getz family of Brestowice to their son in Chicago. Astonishingly, these grave remarks were not deleted by the censor, as had been the practice in other cases.
15. S. I. Dorfson, "Di Litvishe idn unter dem Sovetishn rezhim" [Lithuanian Jewry under Soviet rule], *Der Amerikaner,* January 31, 1941, 12; testimony of A. Ben-Efraim, OHD, 11.
16. A. Petchenik, *Tsiyonizm un idishkayt in Sovet Rusland* [Zionism and Jewishness in Soviet Russia] (New York: 1943), 56–57.
17. "Entfers af briv" [Replies to letters], *Der Emes,* March 1, 1941; for reverberations of this episode, see *J.T.A. Bulletin,* June 19, 1941.
18. Testimony of Rabbi David Kahana, OHD, 13.
19. *Der Amerikaner,* May 15, 1941; cf. "Ha-hayim ha-dati'im shel ha-yehudim be-Galitsia ha-mizrahit" [Religious life of the Jews in Eastern Galicia], *Hatsofe* (Tel Aviv), January 15, 1941.
20. Testimony of Isaac Levin, OHD, 58; testimony of Rabbi David Kahana, OHD, 13.
21. Bernard D. Weinryb, "Polish Jews under Soviet Rule," *The Jews in the Soviet Satellites,* Ed. Peter Meyer, Eugen Dushinsky, and Nicolas Sylvian (Syracuse University Press: 1953), Part III. The article is based on Testimony 10,579 in the YIVO archives. Concerning religious life in Lithuania in 1940–1941, see Dov Levin, "Hofesh dati mugbal ve-'al tenai" [Religious freedom under restrictions and conditions], *Sinai* (Jerusalem), 1976, 79: 183–199.
22. "Mi-yomano shel na' va-nad" [From the Diary of a Nomad], *Qehillat Bendery,* 149.
23. *Sefer Nesvizh* [Nesvizh Memorial Book] (Tel Aviv: 1976), 125.
24. *Sefer zikaron li-qehilat Vileyka ve-ha-mahozot* [Memorial Book for the Community of Wilejka and the Surrounding Districts] (Tel Aviv: 1972), 84.
25. *Sefer zi Karon le-gedoshey Sokoli* [Sokoli Martyr's Book], 48–49.
26. Testimony of Rabbi David Kahana, OHD, 17.
27. *Jewish Chronicle,* March 28, 1941.
28. Testimonies of A. Ulstein, OHD, 44; E. Golan, OHD, 77; I. Schmidt, OHD, 21.
29. A. Petchenik, 44–45.
30. Testimony of A. Godin, OHD, 48.
31. Dov Levin, "Mikhtav me-et S. Dubnow zal me-ha-shana ha-aharona le-hayav" [Letter by the late S. Dubnow from the last year of his life], prepared for publication by Yosef Meisel, *Qiryat Sefer* [Jerusalem: 1944], 2:178). A calendar in Bessarabia was prepared surreptitiously by the local rabbi and handed out to 40–50 families (testimony of Rabbi Y. Elkis, OHD, 17–18). Rabbi Hayyim Ozer Grodzinski, chairman of the Va'ad Hayeshivos in Vilna, "made sure to publish a ten-year Jewish 'calendar' before it was too late, printing many thousands of copies and disseminating it wherever possible" (*Rabban shel yisrael,* Bnei Brak, 1971:157). Concerning a calendar written "at a price affordable by all" by Rabbi Zaydel Waytzl of Slonim, see *Pinkes Slonim,* 2:162.
32. "After the kehilla in Vilna was liquidated, they did not know what to do with the cemetery. The municipality, which had taken over all the kehilla property, did not want it. . . . The mayor appointed a 'committee of religious Jews' composed of five synagogue and burial-society administrators. This committee was given responsibility for the cemetery, the Great Synagogue, and the community bathhouse. A minimum fee of 115 rubles was set for burial; the committee was entitled to collect it from any person who wanted a burial plot. For those who wanted a special plot, the committee was entitled to charge up to 20,000 rubles" (I.P., "Shisha hodashim be-Lita ha-sovietit" [Six months in Soviet Lithuania], *Davar* [Tel Aviv], February 14, 1941).
33. *Rabban shel yisrael,* 163–168.
34. Testimony of Yeshayahu Szrek, recorded by Dr. Aharon Weiss.
35. *Kehillat Bendery,* 153; cf. testimony of Rabbi David Kahana, OHD, 13.

36. I. Shildkraut.
37. Such were the conditions in the western Belorussian town of Brestowice (Brestovitsa, Belorussian) (letter from the Getz family, October 21, 1940).
38. *Khurbn Braynsk,* 249–250.
39. Testimony of Rabbi David Kahana, OHD, 18; see also "Farshtarkn di anti religieze propagande" [Step up the anti-religious propaganda] (Editorial), *Bialystoker Shtern,* March 23, 1941.
40. Details are provided in Chapter 7; cf. Efraim Zuroff, "Hatsalat talmidey yeshivot Polin derekh ha-mizrah ha-rahoq bi-tequfat ha-sho'a" [Rescue of students of Polish yeshivas via the Far East during the Holocaust period], *Mi-Dor Dor,* Jerusalem, Summer, 1979, 67–69 (hereafter cited as "Hatsalat talmidey yeshivot Polin").
41. *Niv ha-midrashiya* [Voice of the College] (Tel Aviv: 1964), 7.
42. "Yeshivot Lita qor'ot le-'ezra," [Lithuanian yeshivas call out for help], *Hatsofe,* February 20, 1940.
43. Mark Vizhnitzer, "Homer le-toldot ha-yeshivot be-eiropa ha-mizrahit" [Material for the history of the Eastern European yeshivas], *Mosedot tora,* 163; cf. "Ketsad hayim ha-yehudim be-Lita ha-sovietit" [How the Jews in Soviet Lithuania live], *Hatsofe,* September 29, 1940.
44. After reaching Palestine in September, 1940, the rabbi of Polangen (Palanga) reported that "Slobodka, Telz, Ponovezh, and Kelm are migrating from town to town, and the students continue to study God's word." "Mi-Polangen ve-'ad Tel Aviv" [From Polangen to Tel Aviv], *Hatsofe,* September 30, 1940. The yeshiva of Telz was shut down after its spacious academy building was padlocked; the students dispersed to the towns of Trishik (Tryškiai), Shidlove (Šiluva), Yelok (Ylakiai), and Popilan (Papilė). In each of these localities, matters were administered by a committee of students, with supervision still exercised in various ways from Telz. Isaac Alperowitz, Ed., *Sefer Telz* [Telšiai Book] (Tel Aviv: 1984), 65, 86–87, 116–117, 128, 153).

CHAPTER 8

1. "In Luck there was hardly a home without a Jewish tenant" (YVA, 2131/191-S); cf. *Sefer yizkor li-qehillat Luboml* [Luboml Community Memorial Book] (Tel Aviv: 1975), 237. According to reports by the AJJDC representative, who reached Vilna in late 1939 after crossing Soviet-occupied eastern Poland, there were about 500,000 Jewish refugees in the region: 60,000 in Bialystok, about 60,000 in Grodno, 40,000 in Luck and Kowel, 20,000 in the peripheral towns of the western Ukraine, and approximately 300,000 (!) in Lvov (*J.T.A. Bulletin,* November 2, 1939, 6). It is worth noting that according to Dr. Philip Friedman, some 70,000 Jewish refugees had congregated in Lvov ("Hurban yehudei Lvov bi-tequfat 1941–1944" [Destruction of Lvov Jewry in the 1941–1944 period], in Natan Gelber, Ed., *Entsiqlopedya shel galuyot* s.v. "Poland," 4:590).
2. A. Petchenik, visiting the area when the war broke out, estimates the number of Jewish refugees at one million (A. Petchenik, 59–60). The same number is cited in *J.T.A. Bulletin,* September 28, 1939, 1. About one month later, the same publication (October 31, 1939, 4) presented a more modest estimate of 500,000–1,000,000. In 1941, a different Jewish source (*Jewish Affairs* [New York], August, 1941) estimated their number at 150,000. A report in the Hebrew-language daily newspaper *Davar* of Tel Aviv (October 27, 1939) mentions information based on a report by the Warsaw correspondent of the newspaper *Politiken,* to the effect that there were about 400,000 Jewish refugees in the Soviet-occupied areas of Poland. Similarly, the Polish ambassador to the USSR, in a report to the Polish government-in-exile in London, asserted that the Soviets estimated the number of Jews who had fled from the German-occupied zone into the areas under their control at 400,000 (Stanislaw Kot, *Conversations with the Kremlin and Dispatches from Russia* [New York: 1963], XII).
3. A. Tartakower and K. R. Grossman, *The Jewish Refugee* (New York: 1944), 43. Reitlinger cites the same figure, based on a report by a postwar investigative committee in Poland

(Gerald Reitlinger, *The Final Solution* [New York: 1953], 52; cf. Weinryb, 342; S. Schwarz, *Evrei v Sovetskom Soyuze (1939–1965)* [Jews in the Soviet Union 1939–1965] (New York: 1966), 33. The Polish Committee for Investigation of Nazi War Crimes arrived at the same estimate (*Biuletin głównej komisji badania zbrodni niemeckich w Polsce,* 1:127).

4. *Sefer yizkor li-qehillat Sarnaki* [Sarnaki Community Memorial Book] (Haifa: 1968), 201; cf. testimony, YVA P-3155/302:2.

5. "Shreklikhe lage fun idishe pleytim in Vilne" [The terrible plight of Jewish refugees in Vilna], *Di Idishe Shtime,* October 31, 1939; "Sovet militer noch alts in Vilne" [Soviet troops still in Vilna] *Forverts,* November 1, 1939, 1.

6. For details see Dov Levin, "Yerushalayim de-Lita: shisha shavu'ot be-sograyim" [Jerusalem of Lithuania: Six Weeks in Parentheses], *Gal-Ed,* 1976:3, 81–82.

7. The Vilna residents trapped in the town of Dukshty (Dukstas) at the time included Itzik Wittenberg, a leftist trade union activist and subsequently the commander of the *Fareynigte Partizaner Organizatsye* (United Partisan Organization [UPO]) in the Vilna ghetto.

8. According to a report by the chairman of the Palestine Office in Warsaw, the Romanian border was opened to the vestiges of the Polish army on September 17–20. "In this fashion," he stated, "about 1,200–1,300 Jewish refugees entered Romania; some 10,000–12,000 Jewish soldiers, officers, and doctors entered together with the army" ("Sho'at yehudey Polin", 26); cf. *J.T.A. Bulletin,* September 28, 1939.

9. Testimonies of Moses Hoffman and Zvi Farber (testimony, YVA 0–59) in Erich Kulka, "Goral ha-pleitim ha-yehudim m-Czechoslovakia be-verit ha-mo'etsot" [Fate of the Jewish Refugees from Czechoslovakia in the Soviet Union], *Yad Vashem Studies* (Jerusalem: 1976), 11:305–307. This article also cites the testimony of a Jewish Communist (see ibid. for the testimony of David Elefant (YVA 0–59), who fled from the advancing Wehrmacht with a group of 80 Jewish refugees (a majority of whom were left-leaning and pro-Soviet) and found refuge in Rowne. Several weeks later they were transported to Kamenets-Podolsk, where they were kept under surveillance to some extent (ibid., 238–239).

10. *In rod fun tsorn,* 26.

11. Testimony of Felix Davidson, YVA 03/1365; cf. Tania Fuks, 42–43.

12. Yosef Litvak, "Ha-shilton ha-sovieti ve-hatsalat yehudim 'Polani'im' ve-'ma'aravi'im' " [Soviet rule and the rescue of "Polish" and "Western" Jews], *Behinot,* 1972:2–3, 60, based on the testimony in YVA 1283/91.

13. *Sefer Ruzhyn* [Ruzhyn Book] (Tel Aviv: 1957), 231; cf. the testimony of Zvi Pachter in the trial of Adolf Eichmann in Jerusalem, *Ha-yo'ets ha-mishpati la-memshala neged Adolf Eichmann* [The Attorney-general vs. Adolf Eichmann], Testimonies (Jerusalem: 1963), 1:150–157.

14. Some of those who reached Bessarabia and Northern Bukovina at this time were young adults born in Transylvania and other parts of central and western Romania, who had political and ideological affinities for the Soviet Communist regime.

15. See Y. Artzi, "Ha-tenua' be-Romania bi-mey milhama ve-sho'a" [The movement in Romania in days of war and Holocaust], *Masu'ah* (Tel Aviv), 1973, 1:106–107.

16. A Jewish source reports that a delegation representing 14,000 Jews born in Bessarabia and Northern Bukovina applied to the Soviet consul in Bucharest to help them take out personal property—in vain (*Der Amerikaner,* October 5, 1940, 5). On August 6, 1940, in contrast, the Romanian Ministry of the Interior publicly denied having hindered the Jews or anyone else who wished to leave the Soviet-occupied areas. "Anyone born or domiciled in Bessarabia or Northern Bukovina," the Romanian press release stated, "is free to go there." Furthermore, "Anyone who cannot afford the travel expenses will be provided with train fare at no charge" (*J.T.A. Bulletin,* August 7, 1940, 1).

17. There were also instances in which Romanian gendarmes forced Jews to cross the Soviet frontier. The areas were mined and many perished in the explosions. Other Jews were shot to death by Soviet border guards, and others were killed by Romanian gunfire when they tried to turn back (Matatias Carp, 436); cf. testimony of Julius Weisbrod, OHD, 10–13.

18. The arrival of a large group from Lithuania, Estonia, the western Ukraine, and western Belorussia, most members of which were interned in quarantine camps, is described in "In Moskve iz ongekumen a grupe sovetishe birger fun Frankraykh" [Group of Soviet citizens

reaches Moscow from France], *Der Emes,* March 20, 1941. See also "Tsurikgekert zikh naye grupe politishe emigrantn" [New group of political emigrants returns], *Kamf,* July 3, 1940, 1.

19. B. Volk, "Fun frantsoyzishe koncentratsie lagers in Sovetishe Lite" [From French concentration camps to Soviet Lithuania], *Der Emes,* May 25, 1941, 5.
20. One of the memoir writers (himself a refugee from Warsaw) estimated, on the basis of his impressions, that about 90 percent of the refugees left their wives and children behind in the German-occupied zone (Dovid Lederman, *Fun yener zayt forhang* [From the Other Side of the Curtain] [Buenos Aires: 1960], 83). (Hereafter cited as Dovid Lederman).
21. "Sho'at yehudey Polin", 43; *Qehillat Rohatyn ve-ha-seviva* [The Community of Rohatyn and Vicinity] (Tel Aviv: 1962), 222.
22. Testimony of Eliezer Skali, 2 (recorded by Dr. Aharon Weiss).
23. *Volkovisker yizkor bukh* [Wolkowisk Memorial Book] (New York: 1949), 2:660–661.
24. Joshua Stengel, *Problemen bay yidn in Poyln* [Problems of Polish Jewry] (Tel Aviv: 1977), 201–202.
25. Dovid Lederman, 75; cf. Moshe Grosman, 22.
26. Abraham Zak, *Knekht zaynen mir geven,* 65, 132; cf. Moshe Grosman, 22.
27. Joel Perel, *In shayn fun morgenshtern* [In Light of the Morning Star] (Tel Aviv: 1968), 47.
28. Zerubavel, Frida, *Hayiti plita* [I Was a Refugee] (Tel Aviv: 1941), 49.
29. Schneider, Leon, *Ka-haya ha-nirdefet* [Like a Beast of Prey] (Tel Aviv: 1977), 16; P. Schwartz, *Dos iz geven der onhoyb,* 210.
30. Yoel Perel, 48, *Pinqas Ludmir* [Polish: *Wlodzimierz Wolynski,* Memorial Book for the Ludmir Community] (Tel Aviv: 1962), 338. See also Israel Kravietz, *Der gehenem baym lebn* [Living Hell] (undated), 33–35; cf. testimony of Friedman, YVA, F-1483/143, 2.
31. Hersh Smolar, "Ha-hayim ha-yehudi'im," *Shvut,* 4:1976, 130.
32. The term *gorkombezh* is used in the *Bialystoker Shtern;* the memoirs (M. Grosman, 93; Abraham Zak, 134) use the term *kompombezh.*
33. The reference is evidently to refugees who volunteered for mining work in the Donbas area of the Ukraine and other Soviet localities. See also n. 39.
34. *Bialystoker Shtern,* February 10, 1940, 1.
35. "Ha-hayim ha-yehudi'im," 130.
36. Thus, for example, M. D., an attorney from Warsaw, was appointed as assistant principal of the Jewish school in Tuczyn (testimony of Martin Danzig, YVA D-2964/89, 3).
37. In Dombrovits (Dabrowica, in Wolhynia), for example, Jewish refugees from Lodz opened a small textile factory (*Sefer Dombrovits* [Dabrowica Book] [Tel Aviv: 1965], 680).
38. Young Itche Fuks, a printing worker who reached Bialystok as a refugee from western Poland, was elected by his comrades to the municipal council in his new place of residence. This occupational success story is described in *Oktyabr,* December 15, 1940. Paula Shmukler, a laborer in a Warsaw clothing factory, was appointed supervisor of a factory department in Rowne, Wolhynia, and was suggested as a member of the regional price committee; see *Der Shtern,* February 10, 1940.
39. Moshe Aizenbud, *Gelebt hinter kratn* [Behind Bars] (Buenos Aires: 1956), 62.
40. Contemporary publications made several references to the number of labor volunteers who set out for the USSR. See *Oktyabr,* November 4, 1939, concerning 7,000 persons who left for Mogilev, Belorussia, on October 31, 1939. See *J.T.A. Bulletin,* November 20, 1939, and January 4, 1940, concerning 10,000 refugees who were transferred to the Donbas area. *Bialystoker Shtern,* on February 10, 1940, reported on the departure of 1,500 refugees from Bialystok, Grodno, and Volkovisk for work in coal mines. Concerning "30,000 refugees who have already gone out."
41. *In rod fun tsorn,* 42–49.
42. Hersh Smolar, "Ha-hayim ha-yehudi'im," *Shvut,* 4:1976, 130. According to another source, women and children prostrated themselves on the streetcar rails in Minsk, generated public commotion, and insisted at the top of their lungs that they wished to return to Bialystok, Lvov, Kowel, and Luck (Moshe Grosman, 67).
43. Hershl Waynroych, *Blut oyf der zun* [Blood on the sun] (New York: 1950), 162.

44. Moshe Grosman, 17. Cf. a statement attributed to one Nussbaum, a Bund Party leader who returned to the German zone with his wife at the time: "It's better to die in a Nazi camp as a revolutionary than in a Soviet camp as a counter-revolutionary" (written testimonial by a former Communist activist in Lublin, David Shtokfish, OHD, 8).

45. Shlomo Shtokfish, *In rod fun tsorn,* 56–58, 72.

46. See testimony of Selina and Israel Shumacher, OHD; Abraham Lederman, 132; Moshe Grosman, 94; *Mit zikh un mit andere,* 113; *In rod fun tsorn,* 48.

47. *Khrushchev Remembers,* 141.

48. Abraham Zak, *Knekht zaynen mir geven,* 136.

49. Testimony of Shlomo Levin, OHD (20) 2.

50. Following are three typical examples of the rationales offered by the refugees: "We refused to accept passports, believing that this would make us Soviet citizens who, for this reason, would not be allowed to leave the Soviet Union" (Shmelke Shpiegelman, "Zayt mir moykhl libe eltern" [Forgive me, dear parents], *Sefer Kozhenits* [Kozienice Memorial Book] [Tel Aviv: 1969], 353). "My brother-in-law and I were willing to become citizens of the USSR, but my sister kept stopping us, arguing that this would sever the strand of hope that connects our parents with us" (*Pinkes Slonim,* 39). "Deciding to accept Soviet citizenship means remaining here forever! Parting forever with home and close relatives" (Moshe Grosman, 84).

51. Moshe Grosman, 76, 93.

52. Moshe Grosman (101) estimates it at 75–90 percent.

53. Dovid Lederman, 126–127.

54. Tania Fuks, 81; *Sefer Stryj,* 162.

55. Testimony of Henryk Niger, YVA 03/1178,8.

56. Testimonies of "Ben-Ha'Am" (Grauzalts), OHD, 4; Henryk Dorsky, YVA 03/1680,5; Hershko Barzel, YVA 03/1680, 6. In Bialystok, attempts were made to remove Jewish writers and artists from the transports, usually in vain.

57. According to Polish sources, more than one million persons were exiled from eastern Poland throughout the war, of whom 50 percent were Poles (see ch. 1, n. 6). An August, 1943, report from the Polish embassy in Kuybyshev estimates that 30 percent of those interned and exiled (including refugees) were Jews; see *Report of the Relief Accorded to Polish Citizens by the Polish Embassy in the USSR,* September 1941–April 1943, p. 3.

58. Researcher Shlomo Schwartz estimates the number of Jews deported at about 500,000. Others concur (e.g., A. Petchenik, 60–61). However, some place the figure at roughly 250,000 (Weinryb, *The Jews in the Soviet Satellites* [Syracuse University Press: 1953], 348) or 200,000 (Kalman Nussbaum, *Ve-hafakh lahem le-ro'ets—ha-yehudim ba-tsava ha-'amami bi-verit ha-mo'etsot* [Betrayal—The Jews in the Polish People's Army in the USSR, "Story of an Illusion"] [Tel Aviv: 1984], 26). Some of the estimates evidently included local Jewish residents who were interned and exiled. Tania Fuks (82) estimates that 70,000 Jews were deported from Lvov alone at this time. Whatever the number, one may adduce from all these sources that 75–80 percent of all Polish refugees deported to the Soviet Union were Jews who had refused to accept Soviet citizenship.

59. Yosef Litvak, "Ha-shilton ha-sovieti ve-hatsalat yehudim 'Polani'im' ve-'ma'aravi'im'" [Soviet rule and the rescue of "Polish" and "Western" Jews], *Behinot,* 1972: 2–3, 58.

CHAPTER 9

1. Benzion Benshalom, *Be-sa'ar bi-yom sufa* [In a Storm on a Stormy Day] (Tel Aviv: 1944), 100.

2. Author Abba Kovner, a man immersed in Jewish Vilna of the time, captured the magnetism of this city in poetry: "Wherefore did fate destine you, Vilna, for such great salvation, ingathering thousands of miserable souls like salvaged embers; to the pride of the Jewish city?" (*Sefer ha-shomer ha-tsa'ir,* 2nd Ed. [Merhavia: 1956], 1:464).

3. Concerning the *halutsim,* see "Tseror mikhtavim" [Bundle of letters], 'Ein Harod, March 8, 1940. Concerning the yeshiva students, see "Shvere ekonomishe lage fun di Vilner idn" [The grave economic condition of the Jews of Vilna], *Di Idishe Shtime,* October 30, 1940.

4. The figures are cited from A. Sawicki, "Yidish-Poylishe pleytim in Vilne" [Jewish-Polish Refugees in Vilna], *YIVO Bleter* (New York), XVIII, 1941: 281 (Hereafter cited as Sawicki).

5. Zorach Warhaftig, *Refugee and Survivor—Rescue Efforts During the Holocaust* (Yad Vashem, World Zionist Organization: 1988), 41; cf. Zvi Barak, "Plitey Polin be-Lita bashanim 1939–1941" [Polish refugees in Lithuania, 1939–1941], *Yahadut Lita*, 2:353–355.

6. Of the many estimates that appeared in print at the time, the most reasonable seems to be that of the secretary-general of the relief organization for Polish Jews in London, A. Kaizer. Kaizer estimates that there were 11,000 refugees and another 2,500 yeshiva students in Vilna in February, 1940, not to mention roughly 3,000 Jewish refugees from the Suwalki area who had taken up residence in the towns of southern Lithuania (*J.T.A. Bulletin*, February 24, 1940, 6). An AJJDC report dated September 18, 1940, corroborates this estimate. Cf. the report of the Palestine Committee in Vilna (Histadrut Executive Committee Archives, File 372/1); "Be'ayat ha-plitim she-bi-gevulot Lita" [Problem of the refugees within the borders of Lithuania], *Ha-'olam*, 26, March 16, 1940, 676.

7. Based on summarizing documents and reports in the AJJDC archives, as cited by Yehuda Bauer, "Rescue Operations through Vilna," *Yad Vashem Studies*, 9:1973, 215 and n. 1.

8. *Ha-medina* [The State], Collection Marking the 20th Anniversary of Betar (Tel Aviv: 1944), 21. A different contemporary source estimates the number of Revisionist affiliates in Vilna as approximately 1,400 (*J.T.A. Bulletin*, November 10, 1939, 2). See also Israel Scheib, *Ma'aser rishon* [First Tithe] (Tel Aviv: 1953), 40. The commissioner of Betar in Poland, Menachem Begin, cites a similar number in his letter of June 6, 1940, to Betar headquarters in London (Jabotinsky Archives, Tel Aviv).

9. A. Sawicki; cf. the detailed report of all the refugee yeshivas in Lithuania, in *Khurbn un retung—di geshichte fun vaad hatsolo in Amerika* [Destruction and Rescue—The Story of the va'ad hatsala in America] (New York: 1957), 147–148 (hereafter cited as *Khurbn un retung*).

10. Moses W. Beckelman, "Polish Refugees Eastward Bound," *Jewish Social Service Quarterly* (New York), September, 1941, 52. Barak cites the following figures: "Halutsim—2,500, plus about 800 Zionist functionaries (including 250 veterans)" (*Yahadut Lita*, 2: 358).

11. A. Sawicki, 281.

12. For further details, see Dov Levin, "Yerushalyim de-Lita ke-miqlat ara'i li-feleitim yehudim be-milhemet ha-'olam ha-sheniya" ["Jerusalem of Lithuania" (Vilna) as a temporary asylum for Jewish refugees during World War II], *Uma ve-lashon: Nation and Language—Studies in Memory of Prof. Aryeh Tartakower* (Jerusalem: 1985), 95–114.

13. A. Sawicki, 281.

14. S. R., "Ha-yeshivot be-Lita tahat ha-shilton ha-sovieti" [The yeshivas in Lithuania under Soviet rule], *Hatsofe*, January 30, 1941. See also *Rabban shel yisrael*, 152.

15. Concerning its operating principles, see the minutes of its inaugural meeting, December 23, 1939, YIVO Archives, New York.

16. The AJJDC alone transferred $742,000 between September, 1939, and June, 1940 (Yehuda Bauer, "Rescue Operations through Vilna," *Yad Vashem Studies*, 9:1973, 216).

17. *Khurbn un retung*, 171.

18. See excerpt from a letter by the AJJDC representative, M. Beckelman, dated February 18, 1940: Zvi Barak, *Yahadut Lita*, 2:358. The original letter is kept in the AJJDC archives, *General and Emergency, Lithuania 1937–1941*, 41.

19. The Mir Yeshiva, including its students and rabbis (284 individuals) settled in Keydan (Kedainiai); the Hafetz Hayyim Yeshiva of Radun (202 persons) in Utyan (Utena); the Ohel Torah Yeshiva of Baranowicze (167) in Trakai (Troki); the Knesset Beit Yitzhak Yeshiva of Kamenets (203) in Rasein (Raseiniai); the Beit Yosef Yeshiva of Pinsk (174) in Vilkomir (Ukmerge); the Torat Hesed Yeshiva of Baranowicze (30) in Tavrig (Taurage); the Etz Haim Yeshiva of Kletsk (44) in Yaneve (Jonava), and so on. (This information is based on a Va'ad Hayeshivos list reproduced in *Khurbn un retung*, 147. See also ibid., 151, and *Rabban shel yisrael*, 154–155.

20. Members of the Ha-po'el ha-Mizrachi training collective congregated at the Kalinova farms and the village of Azholu Buda; members of the Ha-shomer ha-Tsa'ir collective at the Mikhalina farm; the Dror–He-haluts ha-Tsa'ir members at a farm near Valakumpiai;

the Ha-manof collective in Keydan; the Ba-hazit group in Panevežys (Ponevezh); and Ba-minhara in Vilkomir (Ukmerge) ("Ha-rikuz ha-shomeri be-Vilna" [The Ha-shomer congregation in Vilna], *Sefer ha-shomer ha-tsa'ir,* 1:447).

21. By an official order issued on August 5, 1940, the Mir Yeshiva was dissolved into "groups" in four locations: Krakinova (Krekinava), Ramigola, Shat (Šeta), and Krok (Krakes). The dean of spiritual affairs, Rabbi Yeheẓkiel Levenstein, "migrated from one group to the next" (I. Epstein, "Mir," *Mosedot tora,* 120).

22. *Yahadut Lita,* 2:367; cf. Yehuda Bauer, *Yad Vashem Studies,* 9:1973, 219.

23. "Ketsad hayim yehudey Vilna ve-Lita" [How the Jews of Vilna and Lithuania live], *Davar,* January 21, 1941.

24. As late as November 29, 1940, the *Vilner Emes* mentioned the existence (under the Lithuanian Red Cross) of the Jewish Refugees' Committee in Vilna as a place where refugees with medical, technical, or agricultural training might register.

25. M. Tsanin, *Grenetsn biz tsum himl* [Borders up to Heaven] (Tel Aviv: 1970), 140.

26. The office reopened in Lithuania in late 1939 with a political composition identical to that in Warsaw. It was housed in the local Palestine Office in Kovno; its director, Zvi Brik (Barak) had an advisory member of the Warsaw office (Warhaftig, 60–65; cf. *Yahadut Lita,* 2:358).

27. Testimony of Zorach Warhaftig, OHD, 21.

28. "Dr. E. Elkes (Pozdnyakov's personal physician) told me Pozdnyakov had informed him that night that the answer was 'yes.' He did not know any details. . . . The moment the Palestine Office opened, I ran to Glovackas. I came, and he told me: Yes, there's a favorable answer. Transit visas have come in" (testimony of Z. Warhaftig, OHD, 2: 22); cf. Z. Warhaftig, 121). See also the second section of n. 62.

29. Rabbi Jacob Goldman, "Rabbi Herzog's First Rescue Journey," *Niv ha-midrashiya,* 8. A telegram to him affirmed that the British Embassy in Moscow would make the practical arrangements and that the refugee groups would be no larger than 100 persons.

30. A borderline case in this sense was the Palestine emigration permit given to Mordechai and Yehudit Leshem, who had previously lived in Memel (and for this reason may have been regarded as refugees) (testimony of Yehudit Leshem, YVA L-3234/202, 12–20). A truly exceptional case was the emigration permit given to Rabbi S. Menachem Halevi Katz of Polangen (Palanga). His trip via Odessa, Istanbul, and Beirut to Haifa in September, 1940, took about three weeks. ("Ketsad hayim ha-yehudim be-Lita ha-sovietit," *Hatsofe,* September 29, 1940). The exit visas given to a group of about 20 local Jews led by the Sobolevitz-Soblen brothers are discussed at the end of this chapter.

31. They continued from Japan to Shanghai, Singapore, and Bombay, and thence by ship to Palestine ("Mahalakh ha-'aliya ba-hodashim ha-aharonim" [Jewish immigration to Palestine in the past few months], *Davar,* March 30, 1940).

32. Testimony of Shimon Bergman, YVA, 03/3041, 4; cf. *J.T.A. Bulletin,* December 5, 1940, and n. 54.

33. K. Brodsky, "Di vanderungen fun Poylishn 'he-haluts' un zayn arbet in Lite unter der Sovetn okupatsye" [Migrations of the Polish He-haluts and its activity under Soviet occupation], *Khalutsim in Poyln* [Halutsim in Poland] (New York: 1961), 2:51.

34. Testimony of Azriel Rosen, OHD, 13.

35. For remarks and summaries in this matter see Dov Levin, "Yerushalyim de-Lita," *Uma ve-Lashon,* 113–114.

36. Partial and hypothetical answers to the riddle of this turnabout appeared in print at that time. See, for example, "Ketsad hayim yehudey Vilna ve-Lita" [How the Jews of Vilna and Lithuania are living], *Davar,* January 21, 1941. The director of the Palestine Office in Kovno expressed the mystery tellingly: "Just as we didn't know before why they suddenly began to allow it, so don't we know today why it has stopped" (testimony of Zvi Barak, OHD, 25).

37. Z. Segalowich, *Gebrente trit* [Burning Steps] (Buenos Aires: 1947), 168.

38. Testimony of Isaac Levin and his wife, OHD, 2–3. A slightly different version of the Curacao visa affair appears in Z. Warhaftig, (102–108). The Levins urged the refugee public to obtain this strange document, the importance of which became apparent only later.

39. The deputy dean of the Mir yeshiva and his wife stated that the yeshiva had authorized only three people to make the formal arrangements: "Everyone else was and still may be igno-

rant of the organizational details of the operation" (testimony of Rabbi Hayim Shmulewitz and his wife, YVA D-2625/235:2.

40. Z. Warhaftig, 142; cf. E. Zuroff, "Hatsalat talmidey yeshivot Polin," 68–69.

41. From the diary of Zvi Rosen, "He-haluts ha-Dati," [The Religious Pioneer] August 6–7, 1940.

42. Testimony of Shimon Bergman, YVA 03/3043, 3. The Dutch consul initially wrote out the visas longhand, and "the pace was rather slow." Subsequently a rubber stamp bearing the visa was ordered. Zorach Warhaftig (testimony, OHD, 2–15) describes similar actions connected with documents issued by the British consulate in Kovno.

43. Testimony of A. Rosen, OHD, 5. The emissary from Kovno was Yaakov Raanan. See also the letter by Dov Kalfus to the author, October 1, 1975, and testimony of Z. Warhaftig, OHD, 2:18.

44. Natan Yellin-Mor, "Ha-kremlin hitsi'a mahteret yehudit" [The Kremlin Offers (to set up) a Jewish underground], *Etgar* (Tel Aviv), May 18, 1961, 6. A. Pasilikus, the daughter of an industrialist named Hochenberg, who, with his family, emigrated from Kovno to the United States in February, 1941, with the help of a forged Polish passport, testifies about this affair in a letter to the author dated June 22, 1973. See also n. 30.

45. Dozens of memoirs and testimonies mention this man appreciatively. See, for example, *Yahadut Lita,* 2:370; Z. Segalowich, *Gebrente trit,* 189, 205; Tsanin [Wonders up to Heaven], 160.

46. The *Times* of London interviewed Rabbi Herzog on this matter on December 19, 1939. See also *Hatsofe,* August 2, 1940, and Rabbi Jacob Goldman in *Niv ha-midrashiya,* n. 29.

47. The original versions of Barlas's letters (in English), one dated November 22, 1940, to an agent of the Soviet shipping company Sovturtflot, and the other dated December 28, 1940, to Intourist in Kovno, are reproduced in Haim Barlas, *Hatsala bi-mey ha-sho'a* [Rescue During the Holocaust] (Lohamei Hagetta'ot: 1975), 224–225.

48. Testimony of A. Rosen, OHD, 13, 14; Y. Banai, *Hayalim almonim* [Anonymous Soldiers] (Tel Aviv: 1958), 54–55; I. Scheib, *Ma'aser rishon,* 54; *Hatsofe,* September 30, 1940; and Rabbi Isaac Edelstein, "Bi-mey sufa" [In the days of the tempest], *Gal-Ed,* 3:1976, 355.

49. As for fund-raising, see *J.T.A. Bulletin,* July 30, 1940. One action taken by this organization was to contact Breckinridge Long, a senior official in the U.S. Department of State, by means of Senator Robert A. Taft and James MacDonald. Long showed sensitivity to the refugee issue and sent appropriate instructions to the United States consuls in Lithuania and Latvia (*Khurbn un retung,* 166–174, 200–202). According to one estimate, 400 yeshiva rabbis and students among the Polish refugees in Lithuania were given entrance visas for the United States. Hundreds of additional visas were sent out in response to the mass appeals, but most reached Berlin because of technical mishaps (ibid., 203, 205).

50. *J.T.A. Bulletin,* August 19, 1940.

51. Sporadic efforts were made to coordinate activities or at least stay in contact. Thus, for example, Agudath Israel in London corresponded with Rabbi Herzog and Jewish institutions in the United States (*J.T.A. Bulletin,* July 30, 1940).

52. These letters virtually confirmed that an entrance permit to Palestine, valid until October 26, 1940, was being kept for them and their relatives at the British consulate (H. Barlas, *Dapim le-heqer ha-sho'a ve-ha-mered* [Documents for study of the Holocaust and the uprising], 255; for a reproduction of the communique, see Warhaftig, 144).

53. Testimony of A. M. De Jong, YVA D-2303/67. This file also contains one of De Jong's original visas.

54. Testimony of Shimon Bergman, YVA 03/3043,3; cf. Warhaftig, 107–111.

55. Reminiscences of Sempo Sugihara, YVA, Righteous Gentiles file, 1054; see also *Mosedot tora,* 122 and n. 21.

56. Z. Segalowich, *Gebrente trit,* 168; I. Scheib, *Ma'aser rishon,* 50.

57. J. M. Tsanin, *Grenetsn biz tsum himl,* 152; testimony of Rabbi Yitzhak Levin, OHD, 10.

58. Y. Banai, *Hayalim almonim,* 48–51. Zorach Warhaftig, whose conversation with the deputy prime minister of Lithuania was evidently quite helpful in securing the authorities' willingness to let the refugees leave, received an exit permit but was "wanted" by the security services at the time (testimony of Z. Warhaftig, OHD, C:14). Even after they had set out, the refugees were not safe from arrest (ibid., 13).

59. Testimony of Rabbi Hayim Shmulewitz, YVA 03/3034, 2.

60. Testimony of A. Rosen, OHD, 9. Travel fare to Istanbul (via Odessa) was initially $25 but rose to $40, $80, and finally to as much as $100. Travel fare to Vladivostok increased from $200 to $300 ("Ketsad hayim yehudei Vilna ve-Lita," *Davar*, January 21, 1941; Z. Segalowich, *Gebrente trit*, 204; *Khurbn un retung*, 230.)

61. Z. Segalowich, *Gebrente trit*, 182.

62. Dina Porat, "Nesibot ve-sibot le-matan vizot ma'avar sovietiot li-felitey Polin ha-yehudit be-Vilna ba-shanim 1940–1941 [Circumstances and reasons for granting Polish Jewish refugees in Vilna Soviet transit visas in 1940–41], *Shvut*, 6:1978, 66. See also Baruch Oren, "Mi-Vilna derekh Yapan la-'olam ha-hofshi" [From Vilna across Japan to the free world], *Yalqut Moreshet*, 11:1969, 44.

   Abraham Klodawski, a refugee from Poland who waited in Kovno for an exit permit, wrote the following in his diary on December 12, 1940: "There has been a perceptible change for the better for those heading to Palestine. According to information I received from Dr. Elhanan Elkes, it seems that Pozdnyakov's secretary had told him that they, the Soviets, want to rid themselves of the Zionists as quickly as possible ('We don't need them underfoot')" ("'Im ha-no'ar ha-tsioni mi-Polin ba-derekh le-Erets Yisrael" [With Zionist youth from Poland en route to Palestine], *Masu'ah*, 12, 1984, 179).

63. Leopold Trepper, head of the "Red Orchestra"—the Soviet intelligence unit in Western Europe during World War II—was evidently not convinced by this line of reasoning. "The Soviets," he asserted, "do not need a flow of refugees in order to send spies overseas, and it hardly stands to reason that they would contact Polish refugees in Vilna, of all people, for this purpose, since they are well aware of these people's views and their desire to break ranks with the Soviet regime." However, Trepper adds, "One cannot totally rule out the hypothesis that once the outflux of refugees began, the Soviets used the opportunity to smuggle out spies" (Dina Porat, 65).

64. One of the refugees, a well-known author and pundit from Warsaw, was offered an exit permit in return for joining the Polish army, upon reaching Western Europe, in order to gather appropriate information (Herman Kruk, *Togbukh fun Vilner geto* [Vilna Ghetto Diary] [New York: 1961], 33); cf. R. K. (Z. Rimon), "Mi-saviv le-kadur ha-arets—le-Erets Yisrael" [Around the World to Palestine], *Mi-bifnim*, September, 1941:114. Another source mentioned three individuals (Leizer, Kleinboim, and Brandshtater) who were forced to promise in writing to work for the Soviets in Palestine; see J. M. Tsanin, *Grenetsn biz tsum himl*, 154; cf. OHD, testimony of Tsanin, 11–13.

65. This deal is described in greater detail in Natan Yellin-Mor, "Ha-kremlin hitsi'a mahteret yehudit," *Etgar*, 5, May 16, 1961, 6–7; Yellin-Mor, "Mahteret tsiyonit be-hasut ha-sovietim" [A Zionist underground under Soviet patronage], *Ha'aretz* Friday Supplement, January 8, 1970, 10–12; testimony of Abraham Shtukarevich, Diaspora Research Institute, Tel Aviv University, 8–10.

   Yehezkel Pularevich, Glazman's close friend and deputy in the underground period—the last commander of the Betar cell in Kovno—does not endorse Yellin-Mor's version of events because, among other things, Glazman had not apprised him of it at the time. Furthermore, when he applied for an exit permit in the conventional fashion, he was told that if he agreed to engage in espionage work overseas, he and his comrades (including Joseph Glazman and Menachem Begin) would be allowed to leave. Polarevich's account is corroborated by Abraham Shtukarevich, Testimony, Diaspora Research Institute, Tel Aviv University, 8–10, and by Shtukarevich's comments in a workshop on Zionist underground activity in the Soviet-occupied areas between 1939 and 1940, held at Bar-Ilan University (Ramat Gan, Israel) on March 2, 1982.

66. *J.T.A. Bulletin*, March 3, 1940.

67. "Ha-metsi'ut be-'gan ha-'eden' ha-sovieti" [Realities in the Soviet paradise], *Ha-mashqif*, January 13, 1941.

68. *New York Times*, January 2, 1960, and August 14, 1961. Jacob Oleiski, a comrade of his in Left Po'aley Tsiyon in Vilkaviskis, indicated in his oral testimony that Robert's activity in this party had been a smoke screen for his Communist Party connections.

69. Letter to Dov Levin, dated June 7, 1975, by Meir Rothstein of Haifa, a brother-in-law of the Soblens.

70. According to various sources, there were 15–20 people in the group that left (Meir Roth-stein, *op. cit.;* letter by Attorney A. Ankorion to Dov Levin, January 17, 1975; letter by Dr. B. Bludz to Dov Levin, February 27, 1975; *New York Times,* November 30, 1960).
71. Zvi Brik-Barak, director of the Palestine Office in Kovno, described this to the author on the basis of his impression from a visit to the local Intourist office. Dr. H. Rachkovsky of Vilkaviskis, had inadvertently encountered the group in a Moscow hotel and asserted that the trip had indeed been organized by the NKVD. Dr. Bludz's (see n. 70) letter retells the following joke that circulated among the Jews of Kovno: Sobolevitz the senior told the So-viets in Lithuania: "I was in Russia and left lots of belongings there, and you took it. Now I'm leaving you lots of belongings that I gathered in Lithuania. If you let me go to Amer-ica, you'll find the belongings that I'll gather there after you get there."
72. This is the account retold by Sarah Vishkov (née Sobolevich), a cousin of the Soblen broth-ers, who lived in Palestine at the time. Cf. letter of Dr. A. Ankorion (see n. 70), a friend of the Sobolevitz family who, as a lawyer and member of Knesset (the Israeli parliament), dealt with the Soblen affair when Robert Soblen sought asylum in Israel in 1962. See also Natan Ro'i, "Parashat Soblen—rikushetim" [Ricochets of the Soblen affair], *Davar ha-shavua'* (Tel Aviv), September 12, 1986, 14–15. Another Jewish refugee, one Reines, had promised upon his departure from Lithuania to spy for the Soviets. When he reached the United States, however, he immediately described his undertaking to the American secu-rity services. See the testimony of Samuel Tkatch (former director of the Intourist office in Kovno), OHD, 16.

CHAPTER 10

1. *Janow 'al yad Pinsk* [Janow near Pinsk] (Jerusalem: 1969), 312; Tania Fuks, 43.
2. Testimony of Zvi Hirsh Shvartzman, OHD, 3–5.
3. Diary of G. Adiv, October 20–21, 1939, 30–33.
4. "Kovner yidisher meydl a kolvirtnitze in Ukraine" [A Jewess from Kovno—a member of a *kolkhoz* in the Ukraine], *Der Emes,* March 9, 1941.
5. Zalman Kvars, *Folksblat,* October 22, 1940; Levi Shalit, "Rakishker andershdikayt in der yidisher Lite" [The peculiarity of Rakishok in Jewish Lithuania], in M. Bakalczuk-Felin, Ed., *Yizkor bukh fun Rakishok un umgegent* [Memorial Book of Rakishok and Environs] (Johannesburg: 1952), 47–48.
6. *In rod fun tsorn,* 40–41.
7. "Sovetishe literatur in Yidish" [Soviet Literature in Yiddish], *Der Shtern,* September 28, 1939. About two days later, the same daily newspaper reported that the Cinema Studio in Leningrad had invited poet Peretz Markish to make a short film on Jewish life in the Soviet Union "for the Jewish population in the western Ukraine and western Belorussia."
8. "A bagegenish fun Moskver shrayber aktiv mit di redaktsies fun Minsker Oktyabr un Shtern" [An encounter between Moscow activist writers and the Minsk editorial boards of (the periodicals) *Oktyabr* and *Shtern*], *Ufboi,* May 9, 1941.
9. Golde Frades, "Lern bicher a shlog oyfgabe" [Textbooks as the most urgent task], *Der Emes,* March 26, 1941.
10. Testimony of Eliahu Ginsburg, OHD, 2–4; cf. L. Strongin, "Di aktuele oyfgabn in der yidisher farlag arbet" [The current tasks of Jewish publishing activity], *Der Emes,* January 15, 1941.
11. Kaminska, 118–120.
12. Testimony of Israel Beker, Israel Goor Museum of the Theater, Jerusalem, Tape No. 2.
13. L. Vaysman, "Bafrayung" [Liberation], *Der Shtern,* September 23, 1939; cf. poem by S. Shkarovsky, "Es is gekumen di oysleyzung" (Redemption Has Arrived), ibid., Septem-ber 24, 1939: "Redemption has now arrived for the masses of enslaved Jews, too."
14. Y. Erengros, O. Finkel, and Z. Tsirlin, Eds., *Di bafrayte brider* [The Liberated Brethren], Literary Journal (Governmental Publishing House of Belorussia, Minsk: 1939). Apart from works by Jews, this publication included three Belorussian works in translation, a speech by Molotov, and congratulations and poems in praise of Stalin.

15. Joseph Rubinstein, *Megiles Rusland,* 22, 26.
16. Based on the figures on children's books published by author and poet Leib Kvitko, one can assume that other veteran Jewish authors in the Soviet Union underwent a similar process. Kvitko published seven works in 1935, five in 1936, one in 1938, one in 1939, and six in 1940–1941 (18 months).
17. K. (Ch.) Shmeruk, "Ha-pirsumim be-yidish bi-verit ha-mo'etsot ba-shanim 1917–1960," in K. (Ch.) Shmeruk, Ed., *Jewish Publications in the Soviet Union, 1917–1960* (Jerusalem: 1961), 91.
18. See, for example, Moshe Grosman, 60.
19. See Moshe Grosman, 60.
20. Joseph Rubinstein, *Megiles Rusland,* 25.
21. Moshe Grosman, 60.
22. Moshe Grosman, 41.
23. *Mit zikh un mit andere,* 111.
24. Tania Fuks, 94.
25. *Mit zikh un mit andere,* 111–112.
26. H. Smolar, "Ha-hayim ha-yehudi'im," *Shvut,* 4:1976, 126–136.
27. Ch. Szmeruk, "Yiddish Publications," 110–111; see also Yud, *A shmues mit khaveirim shrayber fun Minsk"* [A conversation with comrade writers from Minsk], *Der Emes,* February 22, 1941.
28. *Ufboi,* 7, April, 1941; cf. Golde Frades, "Sheferishe tsuzamenbund fun di Moskver un Lvover shrayber" [A creative encounter between writers from Moscow and Lvov], *Der Emes,* March 12, 1942.

CHAPTER 11

1. Yudke, "'Im ahim ba-mahteret" [With brothers in the underground], *Bi-mey sho'a* [Reported by He-haluts Couriers] (Ein-Harod: 1940), 240.
2. Shlomo Kles, *Ma'asef,* 5:1973, 122; cf. *Mi-ma'amaqim,* nos. 1 and 3; *Sefer ha-shomer ha-tsa'ir,* 2:208, 212, 221.
3. *'Al masu'ot polin,* 119.
4. Levi Dror, "Shomerey ha-gahelet" [Keepers of the ember], *Sefer ha-shomer ha-tsa'ir,* 2:211; Shlomo Kles, *Ma'asef,* 5:117.
5. *Tseror yedi'ot* (Collection of news items, typescript) Palestine, Hakibbutz Hameuhad, February 12, 1940.
6. *Ka-haya ha-nirdefet,* 22.
7. Minutes of Leah Epstein's remarks at Jewish National Fund headquarters, Tevet 16, 5701 (January 15, 1941). A copy of this document is kept in Moshe Kol's collection at the Masu'ah archives in Tel Yitzhak.
8. Ben-tsiyon Shroster, "Tenu'at Herzliya be-Latvia bi-mei milhemet ha-'olam ha-sheniya" [The Herzliya movement in Latvia during World War II], *Masu'ah,* 3:1975, 198–199.
9. Yeshayahu (Shayke) Weiner, "Pizur ve-lo hisul" [Dispersion, not liquidation], *Sefer ha-shomer ha-tsa'ir,* 1:471; cf. Levi Deror, op. cit., 2:227.
10. Sarah Nashmit, *Hayu halutsim be-Lita, sipura shel tenua'1916–1941* [There Were Pioneers in Lithuania: The Story of a Movement, 1916–1941] (Lohamei Hagetta'ot: 1983), 277.
11. Anshel Spilman, *Ha-ish she-qiyem et ha-neder* [The Man Who Kept His Vow] (Tel Aviv: 1974), 112.
12. Testimony of Abba Kovner, YVA 3176:1.
13. From a letter by Teddy Pik of Kibbutz Netser Sereni to Yitzhak Porath in Afiqim, August 19, 1958. (A copy of the letter is kept at the Institute for Contemporary Jewry as an appendix to T. Pik's testimony.)
14. "Selma Mirbaum-Eisenberg ve-shirata" [Selma Mirbaum-Eisenberg and her poetry], *Yalqut moreshet,* 23:1977, 10; testimony of M. Kimhi, OHD, 23.
15. "Derekh ha-yisurim ve-ha-gevura shel Betar Czernowitz" [The path of afflictions and valor of Betar in Czernowitz], *Pirsumey muze'on ha-lohamim ve-ha-partizanim,* May, 1969, 6:2.

16. "Chernowitz ha-yehudit," *Shvut,* 2:1974, 176.
17. A Gordoniya activist in Czernowitz described this: "We tried even not to dress as athleti-
cally as the halutsim did. We went to places where we had never gone as movement members: cafés and places like that" (testimony of Hemda Ish-Shalom, Diaspora Research
Institute, 27–28; cf. Levi Deror, *Sefer ha-shomer ha-tsa'ir,* 2:213; Ida Kaminska-Miron,
"Mi-Piotrkow 'ad ha-qolhoz ha-Turqmeni be-Vukhara" [From Piotrkow to the Turkmen
kolkhoz in Bukhara], *Yalqut moreshet,* 24:1977, 182.
18. *Sefer zikaron li-qehilat Nesvizh,* 123–124.
19. Other examples of this "lexicon": "Mr. 'Labor Camp' visited us" meant deportation to a
labor camp. The absence of "Zuzinka" alluded to material deprivation. (The *zuz* was a coin
used by the Jews during the Bar-Kokhba period.) "Attending university" referred to activity in an underground movement. Yitzhak Zuckerman's nom de guerre in Deror was
Zaddik or Yeffim. Scheindl Schwartz, also of Deror, was code-named "Tamara Shahor"
(the Hebrew *shahor,* like the Yiddish *shvarts (shwartz),* means "black") or Ludmila. Zviya
Lubetkin was simply "Z." David Kozhibrodsky was "Kozha." Yitzhak Zalmanson of
Ha-shomer ha-Tsa'ir was "Itzik Zalman."
20. A copy of this letter, in Hebrew, meant for dissemination among major activists in the
halutsic movements, is kept in Aharon Cohen's private archives at Kibbutz Sha'ar
ha-'Amaqim.
21. The typewritten memorandum was signed by Y. Dzhibejsky (Ha-No'ar ha-Tsiyoni),
A. Cohen and D. Goberman (Ha-shomer ha-Tsair), B. Heshroni (Gordoniya), A. Greenberg (Ha-Kibbutz ha-Meuhad). It bears the handwritten date February 17, 1940. It, too, is
kept in Aharon Cohen's private archives.
22. M. Fridman, "From the Banks of the Prut to Angara," *Struggles of a Generation,*
2:113–114.
23. Anshel Spilman, *Ha-ish she-kiyem et ha-neder,* 95–96.
24. In one of the last letters to arrive from Riga (June 1, 1941), Misha Lifschitz, a member of
the local leadership, wrote: "The younger members of the family are holding on strong
and repaying the old debt to Menachem Mendel [i.e., the Jewish National Fund]. In the
summer they'll surely go for a trip [*moshava* (scouting camp), denoting a return to the
old scouting routine] as they had in the past when we went to Troki. We would really like
to get together and fulfill the old hope. How is cousin Nissan [Reznik] and his brother
Salomon?" (from Moshe Kol's collection at the Massu'a archives in Tel Yitzhak).
25. Jehoshua A. Gilboa, *Lishmor la-netsah—pirqey asir bi-verit ha-mo'etsot* [To Safeguard
unto Eternity—Episodes of a Prisoner in the Soviet Union], Tel Aviv, 1963.

CHAPTER 12

1. Testimony of Shamai Tokel, YVA 03/3668, 2–3.
2. *Pinkes Slonim,* 2:19, 21–23.
3. See, for example, *Shchuchin unter der Sovetisher makht* [Szczuczyn under Soviet domi-
nation], *Khurbn kehiles Shchuchin* [Destruction of the Szczuczyn Community] (Tel Aviv:
1954), 76.
4. "Vilner aktualitetn" [Vilna current events], *Di Idishe Shtime,* November 5, 1939. Former
Communists, too, were arrested at this time for "Trotskyite deviations."
5. Partial information about the arrests first appeared in *Forverts,* October 19, 1939, in prominent front-page article. Over the next few weeks, this paper presented more detailed reports
in a tone of rage and bitterness. The wives of Reizen and Tschernikhov, terrified for the
fate of their husbands, pounded the doors of the NKVD every day but were not honored
with an answer (S. Kaczerginsky, *Tsvishn hamer un serp,* 18). Finally, Mrs. Tschernikhov
herself was arrested. According to reliable reports, Tschernikhov was shot by an escort
guard between Minsk and Borisov on June 24, 1941, while being evacuated to Russia on
foot along with other internees from the prison in Wilejka. He was 59 years old. (Mikhal
Astor, *Geshikhte fun Frayland lige* [Story of Freeland League] [Buenos Aires–New York:
1967], 1:451).

Joseph Herman, a political prisoner in Chervin (formerly the Igumen Monastery) reports that his cellmates had been Bund activists Zheleznikov, Aharonovich, and Teitl; nearby, in a tiny cell, was Anna Rosental. They were taken away on April 28, 1941, and did not return. For a more complete account see *Unzer tsayt* (New York), 2: 1975, 28–29.

6. *Struggles of a Generation,* 2:70–71.

7. Ibid., 83.

8. One of the overseas reports about the conditions of internment imposed on Zionists, especially Revisionists, stated that "not even one man in all of Lithuania, not even one lawyer, had the courage to concern himself with the reason for their arrest" ("Ha-metsi'ut be-gan ha-'eden ha-sovieti" [Realities in the Soviet paradise], *Ha-mashqif,* January 13, 1941); cf. *Der Amerikaner,* December 27, 1940.

9. Elhanan Halperin, party chairman; David Karstadt, secretary-general, and A. Syrkin, co-ordinator (testimony of "Amitai," OHD, 2); cf. *Yahadut Latvia* [Latvian Jewry, Memorial Book] (Tel Aviv: 1953), 316.

10. Testimony of K. A. Bartini, OHD, 1:8; cf. testimony of M. Ososkin, OHD, 4, 16; M. Fridman, "From the Banks of the Prut to Angara," *Struggles of a Generation,* 2:92.

11. In Kishinev, three members of the central committee of the united Tse'irey Tsiyon–Po'aley Tsiyon party were interned, as were the editor of *Unzer tsayt,* the director of the Palestine Office, the secretary of Tarbut, two Mizrachi leaders, and a member of the General Zionist Central Committee. Several of these individuals were tried in absentia and sentenced to five to ten years' confinement in labor camps; in January, 1941, they were sent to the Arkhangelsk area of the northern USSR. Only a few survived (I. Shildkraut, *'Al hurvot Besarabiya,* 203; M. Fridman, "From the Banks of the Prut to Angara," 2:92–93, 97–98.

12. In Kalarash, for example, former mayors were arrested (*Sefer Kalarash* [Kalarash book] [Tel Aviv]: 1966], 395–396). One of those arrested in Khutin was Michael Shor, a former member of parliament with Marshal Abrescu's People's Party (testimony of Dr. Lippa Zaydman, YVA 03/1920, 5). See also ch. 3, n. 1.

13. *Sefer Qehillat Khutin,* (Tel Aviv: 1974), 92.

14. According to reports that reached London, the former head of the Cracow kehilla, Dr. Rafael Landau, and the president of the NZO (the Revisionists' New Zionist Organization) in Eastern Galicia, Dr. Jacob Shechter, were arrested at this time and exiled to the Soviet interior (*J.T.A. Bulletin,* February 25, 1940). In Lvov, the family of a police inspector named Fridman was arrested and exiled to Kazakhstan (testimony of Fridman, YVA 03/2128, 2).

15. In February, 1940, the wife and two sons of a reserve captain named Shneidsher were arrested and exiled to the Narim area in the Ural Mountains. Shneidsher had been arrested and exiled to the Soviet Union in December, 1939; he may have been murdered in the forests of Katyn (oral testimony by his son, June 17, 1977). The murder of 1,000 Jewish officers in the Katyn forests is described by Salomon W. Slowes, *Katyn 1940* (Tel Aviv: 1986); cf. testimonies of M. Levin, OHD, 15–21; "Yoram," OHD, 6–8; and A. Libo, OHD, 22.

16. The names of hundreds of Jews who had been interned and exiled from dozens of localities in that period are cited in the following sources: *Entsiqlopedya shel galuyot,* "Lvov," 4:753–760, 763; "Sho'at yehudey Polin"; testimony of Dr. B. V., circular of the Committee for Polish Jewry, 851/121/12/13, December, 1940, 4; testimony of Dr. S. Langnus, OHD, 5–10; J. S. Hertz, Ed., *Doyres Bundistn* [Generations of Bundists] (New York: 1956), Vol. 2:189, 193, 205; *J.T.A. Bulletin,* May 7, 1940.

17. In Luck, for example, Krindel Jozman was arrested for Communist activity and taken to the Kartuz-Bereza prison, where he languished for many years (Joel Perel, *In shayn fun morgenshtern,* 83).

18. "The Jewish rabbis were treated less strictly than the Catholic priests" (Z. H., "Di bolshevikes in mizrokh Galitsye" [The Bolsheviks in Eastern Galicia], circular of the Committee for Polish Jewry, December, 1940). Concerning the arrest of Rabbi Levi Bielcki in Semyatich (Polish: Siemiatycze), see Leah Bielcki, "Fun Semyatich biz Kazakhstan" [From Semyatich to Kazakhstan], *Qehillat Semyatich* [Semyatich community] (Tel Aviv: 1964), 379–381.

19. Two of the persons arrested in this operation were liberated by Lithuanian prisoners who broke out of the prison when the Nazis invaded; they subsequently served as members of

the Judenrat in the Kovno ghetto. For details on their internment and liberation, see the testimonies of Leib Garfunkel, OHD, 8–12, and Zvi Levin, OHD, 13–14.

20. Testimony of Rachel Katz, OHD, 13–14, 34–36; cf. testimonies of Gitta Kaplan, OHD, 32; Ben-Haim, OHD, 29–30; Ze'ev Uzhvansky, OHD, 20–21; Baruch Brashinsky, OHD, 8; Samuel Ribak, OHD, 6; and Michael Heltzer, OHD, 3.

21. A list of names of 21 families (more than 60 people altogether) from the Bessarabian town of Marculesti, who were deported on June 11, 1941, appears in M. Ben-Brit, "Gerush mishpahot le-Sibir" [Deportation of families to Siberia], *Markuleshti—yad lemoshava yehudit be-Besarabiya* [Markuleshti—Memorial to a Jewish Town in Bessarabia] (Tel Aviv: 1977), 378.

22. *Azoy iz es geshen in Lite,* 143–146.

23. Testimony of David Elkind, OHD, 9. In the Latvian town of Libau (Liepaja), an indigent Jew whose name was identical with that of a "bourgeois" individual was swept up for deportation; in the end, they sent him back home (testimony of Meir Kron, OHD, 5; cf. testimony of Zvi Glazer, OHD, 8). Instances of informing by non-Jews are described in *Sefer Burshtyn* [Bursztyn book] (Jerusalem–Tel Aviv: 1960), 165–166, 317–318.

24. A photocopy of the original text is kept in *Lithuanian Archives,* 1:37–51. For an abbreviated English translation, see W. B. Walsh, *Readings in Russian History* (Syracuse University Press: 1959), 634–638.

25. For additional information on the fate of those deported from the Baltic countries, see Dov Levin, "Yehudei Estonia ba-shana ha-rishona la-shilton ha-sovieti 1940–1941" [Estonian Jewry in the first year of Soviet rule 1940–1941], *Behinot,* 7:1977, 98–101; and Dov Levin, "Estonian Jews in the U.S.S.R. 1941–1945), *Yad Vashem Studies,* 11:1976, 408–409. Concerning those deported from Latvia, see Dov Levin, "Milhemet qiyum be-galut Sibir" [Struggle for survival in Siberian exile], *'Iyunim be-yahadut zemanenu* [Studies in Contemporary Jewry in Honor of Moshe Davis] (Jerusalem: 1984), 125–145. For deportees from Lithuania, see Dov Levin, "Arrests and Deportations of Lithuanian Jews to Remote Areas of the Soviet Union, 1940–1941, *Crossroads,* 11:1984, 67–108.

26. *Pinqas Bricheva,* 393; S. Kandler, "Yamim tragi'im" [Tragic days], *Sefer Kalarash* [Kalarash Book], 397; Shalom Weisberg, "Yemey tahapukhot" [Days of Upheaval], in *Brichen.* (Tel Aviv: 1964), 129.

27. Monia Zisman, a leader in the Gordoniya movement, was interned and exiled to Irkutsk five days after the war broke out. Journalist J. Veinstein of Tse'irei Tsiyon was arrested at a later date (M. Fridman, "From the Prut to Angara," *Struggles of a Generation,* 2:125). Hebrew author and educator K. A. Bartini of Kishinev was arrested and deported with his family on July 2, a few days before the Red Army retreated (testimony of K. A. Bartini, OHD, 2:11).

28. For further information on the deportees and their fate see Dov Levin, "Yehudey Besarabiya ba-shilton ha-sovieti," [Bessarabian Jewry under Soviet Rule] *Shvut,* 4:1976, 110–118.

29. Manfred Reifer, "Das Jahr Sowjetokkupation (1940–1941) [The year of Soviet Occupation, 1940–1941], in Hugo Gold, Ed., *Geschichte der Juden in der Bukowina, 1919–1944* [History of the Jews in Bukovina] (Tel Aviv: 1962), 2:11–13, 236.

30. Tania Fuks, 112; the figure is taken from *Pinqas Qehillot Romania* [Annals of the Romanian Jewish Communities] (Jerusalem: 1980), 2:487; see also Avraham Ben-Yonah, "The Story of Zionist Prisoners," *Struggles of a Generation,* 2:135. See also *Encyclopaedia Judaica,* s.v. "Bukovina."

31. Testimony of Leib Garfunkel, OHD, 5–10; see also testimony of Miron Sheskin, OHD, 3; and *Pinsk,* 2:318.

32. S. Weisberg, *Brichen,* 123, 130; see also Avraham Ben-Yonah, *Struggles of a Generation,* 2:133.

33. "The Storm Breaks over Lithuania—in Prison and Concentration Camp," *Struggles of a Generation,* 2:67–68. See also Roman Prister, " 'Im magen david be-Sibir" [With a Star of David in Siberia], *Ha'aretz* Friday Supplement (Tel Aviv), November 17, 1970.

34. Remarks by Rabbi Mordechai Nurock in a meeting of the Knesset (Israel Parliament) on January 19, 1959, *Divrei ha-Kneset* [Proceedings of the Knesset], 13:488.

35. Rafael Federman, "Yosef Aronovich," *Doyres Bundistn* [Generations of Bundists], ed. J. S. Hertz, 1969, 3:122.

36. *Pinsk,* 2:313–314.

37. Tsanin, 16.
38. Dov Tayts, "Mayn heym" [My home], *Sefer zikaron qehillat Wilejka ha-mahozit* (Memorial Book for the Community of Wilejka District), 215; cf. *Yizkor qehillot Luninets/ Kozhanhorod* [Memorial Book for the Luniniec-Kozh'horodok Communities], Tel Aviv, 1952:70; *Sefer Lida* [Lida Book] (Tel Aviv: 1970), 276.
39. *Pinsk*, 2:318; cf. Dovid Abramovich, "Biten in di teg fun September khoydesh 1939" [Biten on September 1, 1939], *Pinqas Biten* [Biten Memorial Book], 205; *Rokitno ve-haseviva*, 238.
40. Letter in the author's possession.
41. *J.T.A. Bulletin*, October 9, 1940; cf. Eliahu Mote Bokshtein, "Kartuz-Bereze 1939–1941," *Pinqas Pruzhene, Bereze, Malch, Shershev, Siets*, Buenos Aires, 1958, 460–461; testimony of Devora Nashkes, YVA 03/3081, 2; *Volozhyn*, 529–556.
42. Testimony of Y. Asir, YVA A-415/28, 1–2; cf. *Rozhishitz 'ayarati*, 201.
43. Moshe Aizenbud, *Gelebt hinter kratn*, 55.
44. Concerning the victims of the anti-speculation campaign, see Dov Levin, "Yehudei Lita ha-sovietit ba-mishor ha-kalkali-sotsyali," *Reva'on le-mehqar hevrati*, 20:1984, 226–231.
45. *Documents on Polish-Soviet Relations 1939–1945*, Vol. I, 1939–1941, 573–574. See also Introduction, n. 6.

CHAPTER 13

1. Testimony of Shmuel Shushan, OHD, 5.
2. The 1919–1920 age groups (i.e., those aged 21–22), were drafted for regular service in the western areas of the USSR as far back as April, 1941. See G. Geler, "Mit freyd in di reyen fun der royter armey" [With joy to the ranks of the Red Army], *Der Emes*, April 20, 1941.
3. Testimony of Yitzhak Shapira, OHD, 1; cf. Shalom Cholawski, *'Ir ve-ya'ar be-matsor*, 47.
4. In Lvov the Ukrainians seized church steeples and began shooting from them in all directions. Yitzhak Levin, *'Aliti mi-spetzya*, 52. Concerning similar events in Riga, see the testimonies of Bela Mendelevich, OHD, 9; B. Gerchik, OHD, 2.
5. The Ukraine, Belorussia, Moldavia, Lithuania, Latvia, Estonia, the Karelo-Finnish republic, and several districts of the RSFSR. An Evacuation Council was set up on June 24. U. A. Polyakov, *Esheloni idut na vostok* [The Trains are Moving Eastward] [Moscow: 1966], 10.
6. Israel Rushko, "'Al hurvotayikh Lipkan" [Upon your ruins, Lipkan], *Qehillat Lipkani* [Lipkan Memorial Book] (Tel Aviv: 1963), 304.
7. Testimony of Yaakov Shkolnik, OHD, 1–2.
8. See, for example, S. Kandel, "Yamim tragi'im" [Tragic days], *Sefer Kalarash*, 398. Most of the escapees from Kalarash managed to cross the Dniester. S. Waisman, "Hurban ve-ye'ush" [Destruction and despair], op. cit., 402; cf. Rabbi Avraham Shlapid, "Megilat ha-dema'ot" [The scroll of tears], *Pinkas Brichevă*, 396; Sh. Yevkovski, "Ba-shvi ha-sovieti u-verihati mi-Tsekhanivits" [In Soviet captivity and my escape from Ciechanowice], *Tsekhanivits mehoz Bialystok* (Ciechanowice, Bialystok District) (Tel Aviv: 1964), 585.
9. Haya Mundrian, "'Im ha-sho'a" [As the Holocaust came], *Orhayuv be-vinyana u-ve-hurbana*, [Oregeyev as It Was and in Its Destruction] (Tel Aviv: 1949), 149–150.
10. Shalom Golani, "Aleksandria—yoman ha-sho'a [Aleksandria—a Holocaust diary], *Pinkas qehillat aleksandria* [Aleksandria Memorial Book] (Tel Aviv: 1972), 202; cf. Eliezer Pomerantz, *Bi-redifa aharei ha-emet* [In Pursuit of the Truth] (Haifa: 1966), 83.
11. Ben-Zion Shroster, "Pegishot 'im yehudim bi-shenot ha-milhama u-le-ahareha bi-verit ha-mo'etsot" [Meetings with Jews during and after the war], *Masu'ah*, 5:1977, 200.
12. Testimony of Rabbi Y. Elkis, OHD; cf. testimonies of K. A. Bertini, OHD, 2:13; Avraham Turchin, OHD, 2:10–11. See also Kandel, *Sefer Kalarash*, 398.
13. *'Al hurvot Besarabiya*, 250–251.
14. Testimony of Yaakov Shkolnik, OHD, 1; see also testimonies of Yaakov Brashinski, OHD, 2; M. Eidelberg, OHD, 7, S. Ribak, OHD, 47; D. Elkind, OHD, 25; Y. Zlotokrilov, OHD, 3; and A. Godin, OHD, 4. Cf. M. Ben-Berith, "Ha-milhama partsa" [The war has broken out], *Markuleshti—yad le-moshava yehudit be-versarabia*, 379–380.

15. M. Ben-Berith, "Ba-derekh le-ukraina" [On the way to the Ukraine], op. cit., 382; cf. Yeta Shapiro Rosenzweig, "Gam be-ponar hayinu" [We were in Ponar, too] (Lohamei Hagetta'ot: 1979), 14–15.
16. On the question of whether Jews were given preferential treatment in the evacuation, see Dov Levin, "The Attitude of the Soviet Union to the Rescue of the Jews," *Rescue Attempts and Efforts during the Holocaust* (Jerusalem: 1977), 183–193.
17. M. Reicher, "Di martirielogie fun di yedintser yidn," 714, 756–758; cf. testimony of Rabbi Y. Elkis, OHD, 25.
18. Ibid.
19. "Bi-shenot ha-shilton ha-sovieti" [In the years of Soviet rule], *Pinqas Zhetl* [Zhetl Memorial Book] (Tel Aviv: 1958), 314.
20. Shlomo Zandweis, "Sarni—iz oyfkum, ekzistentents un untergant" (Sarny—its formation, existence, and destruction], *Sefer yizkor li-qehilat sarni* [Sarny Community Memorial Book] (Tel Aviv: 1961), 80–81.
21. Noah Kaplinski, *"Kakh hufqarnu 'al yedei ha-sovietim"* [This is how we were abandoned by the Soviets], *Pinkes Slonim.*
22. Testimonies of S. Ribak, OHD, 38; Zvi Glazer, OHD, 10–11.
23. Testimony of Yehudith Himmelfarb, YVA 03/2597, 6; cf. testimony of "Ira," OHD 24.
24. Yosef Kermish, "Sho'at yehudei Kolomiya be-ferots milhemet ha-'olam ha-sheniya" [The Holocaust of Kolomyja Jewry at the outbreak of World War II], *Sefer zikaron li-qehilat Kolomiya ve-ha-seviva* [Memorial Book for Kolomyja and Its Environs], Tel Aviv, 1972: 272–273.
25. Tania Fuks, 112; cf. testimony of Adolf Arb, YVA 03/1795, 3.
26. Pesah Gershonowitz, *Lebn un umkum fun Olshan* [Under German Rule: The Life and Destruction of Olshan] (Tel Aviv: 1961), 195.
27. S. Cholawski, *'Ir ve-ya'ar be-matsor,* 47; cf. M. Geffen, C. Grossman, S. Cholawski, *et al., Sefer ha-partizanim ha-yehudim* [The Book of Jewish Partisans], 1:545; *Sefer Nesvizh,* 121.
28. Yankel Piker, *Azoy iz geven* [This is How It Was] (Tel Aviv: 1979), 77; cf. Hana Leah Kravchuk, "Mir antloyfn fun der heym" [Running away from home], in Shimeon Noy, Ed., *Yanova 'al gedot ha-Viliya* [Yizkor Book in Memory of the Jewish Community of Yanova] (Tel Aviv: 1973), 393; cf. testimonies of Hava Zimzon, YVA 2129/1909, 2–3; H. Borkanas, op. cit., 11–12.
29. Testimony of Shaul Beilinson, OHD, 5.
30. Testimony, YVA A-2243/7152; E. Pomerantz, *Bi-redifa aharei ha-emet,* 83–84.
31. Yaakov Schwartz, "Yetsiyat Rokitno" [Leaving Rokitno], *Rokitno ve-ha-seviva,* 251–252.
32. Testimony of Shlomo Geizler, YVA C-3462/314, 8.
33. Testimonies of S. Ribak, OHD, 42–44; Gitta Kaplan, OHD, 33; M. Heltzer, OHD, 8–9; Zvi Glazer, OHD, 10–11; and Riva Tzimbalov, OHD, 7–8.
34. Testimony of "Adami," OHD, 23.
35. Ben-Berith, *Ba-derekh le-Ukraina,* 384.
36. Mundrian, "'Im ha-sho'a," 149; cf.Shildkraut, *'Al hurvot besarabiya,* 249.
37. Testimony of M. Eidelberg, OHD, 8.
38. See n. 49.
39. Piker, *Azoy iz geven,* 76; cf. testimonies of Asher Leitman, OHD, 10; Rafael Golan, OHD, 11; and Meir Kron, OHD, 5.
40. An orderly evacuation of writers became possible after a delegation of leading members of the Association (the Belorussian chairman and Maxim Tank, Dovid Sfard, and Ber Mark) appealed to the District Committee of the Communist Party. The secretary gave them a permit to board the train. Dovid Sfard, *Mit zikh un mit andere,* 121; cf. Scheine-Miriam Broderson, *Mayn laydens-veg mit Moshe Broderson* [My Via Dolorosa with Moshe Broderson], 31–32.
41. In Bialystok, for example, several former political prisoners decided to remain in the city to help maintain public order (since the local militia had scattered) and to defend the city if necessary. This action was contrary to the instructions of the local Communist Party, which had advised them to join the evacuees. Only a handful survived by finding a way to

join the partisans. One of them was the author Hersh Smolar; see *Mit zikh un mit andere,* 121; cf. Hersh Smolar, "Ha-hayim ha-yehudi'im," *Shvut,* 4:1976, 135–136.

42. In a letter dated March 5, 1976, M. Sher, a former community leader in Tallinn, informed the author that he possessed a list of 120 Jewish fighters in the "battalions" in Estonia at the time. Another list, compiled in Israel on the basis of testimonies by former residents of Estonia, especially Yaakov Kaplan of Tel Aviv (formerly of Tartu, Estonia), contains 80 names and some biographical details. At least 60 of the 80 died in combat. For details, see Dov Levin, "Estonian Jews in the Soviet Union, 1941–1954," *Yad Vashem Studies,* 11:1971, 212–214.

43. Alexander Kantorovski, "Sokolka Under Occupation," in *Sokolka Memorial Book* (Jerusalem: 1968), 343; testimony of Israel Friedman, OHD, 1–2.

44. Levi Dror, "Shomrey ha-gahelet" [Keepers of the ember], *Sefer ha-shomer ha-tsa'ir,* 2:227.

45. One of those who made this hazardous journey under the hot July sun was a blind Communist leader from Latvia, Max Shatz-Anin. He managed to reach the USSR, where he spent the war years. See M. Shatz-Anin, "Oyf mayn lebens-veg" [On my way of life], *Sovetish Heymland,* 11:1970, 148–149.

46. Pomerantz, 83–84.

47. Because direct rail connections to the USSR had been cut off, the escape route of many Jews from central Latvia passed through eastern Estonia, whereas Jews from Lithuania fled in the direction of Pskow, through eastern Latvia. Many of them found themselves stuck at the old Soviet-Latvian border near the town of Zilupe. See testimony of Arieh Shabbath, YVA 2987/258, 2.

48. Kandel, "Yamim tragi'im," *Sefer Kalarash,* 398.

49. The ledger of evacuees from Lithuania, which took place in the Soviet Union on May 25, 1943, lists 19,592 persons, of whom 8,500 were Jews. Of these, about 5,500 were civilians; others were draftees attached to the Lithuanian Division. (S. Varasinskas, *Karo sukuriuose* [The Events of War] [Vilnius: 1970], 38–39).

50. The number of Jews who fled from Wolhynia clearly underscores the significance of this factor. The share of Jews who succeeded in fleeing from five communities located near the old Soviet border was as follows: Rokitno 25 percent, Korzec (Korets) 20 percent, Mizocz (Mizoch) 15 percent, Ostrog (Ostra) 10.5 percent, and Dabrowica (Dombrovits) 7.8 percent. By contrast, the proportion of escapees from the five communities that were most distant from the old border was Turzysk (Trysk) 3 percent, Maciejow (Macheyuv) 2.5 percent, Kowel 1.6 percent, Luck 1.5 percent, and Uscilug (Ustilug) 0.3 percent. (S. Spector, *The Holocaust of Volhynian Jews,* 52–53.)

51. This estimate is itemized as follows:

Eastern Galicia	26,000–35,000
Western Belorussia	22,000–30,000
Wolhynia	12,000–13,000
Total, former Polish territories	60,000–78,000[a]
Northern Bukovia	5,000–10,000
Bessarabia	45,000–50,000
Total, former Romanian territories	50,000–60,000[b]
Lithuania	14,000–15,000[c]
Latvia	14,000–15,000[d]
Estonia	2,000– 2,500[e]
Total, Baltic countries	30,000–32,500

It should be noted that although both Wolhynia and Bessarabia were overrun within a month, only 5 percent of Jews succeeded in fleeing Wolhynia, whereas 25 percent escaped from Bessarabia; 6 percent fled from Lithuania, which was overrun in less than a week. The last figure reflects the fact that the proportion of Lithuanian Jews in the state, public, economic, and Party sectors was incomparably higher than in Wolhynia and other districts of the western Ukraine and western Belorussia. Consequently, relatively large numbers of Jews belonged to the groups given high priority in organized evacuations.

[a]Figures for Wolhynia are found in S. Spector, *The Holocaust of Volhynian Jews,* 55. Bernard Weinryb estimates the total number of Jews who fled from the former Polish territories at 120,000–180,000, (B. Weinryb, P. Meyer, *et al., The Jews in the Soviet Satellites* [Syracuse University Press: 1953], 353).

[b]Dov Levin, "Yehudey Besarabiya ba-shilton ha-sovieti," *Shvut,* 4:1976, 101–118, 152–153. G. Reitlinger mentions a figure twice as high for these areas; see G. Reitlinger, *Die Endlösung* (Berlin: 1956), 457, 467.

[c]——————— *Fighting Back,* 28–32.

[d]——————— *'Im ha-gav el ha-qir* [With Their Backs to the Wall–The Armed Struggle of Latvian Jewry Against the Nazis, 1941–1945] (Tel Aviv: 1978), 57–59.

[e]——————— "Estonian Jews in the USSR, 1941–1945," *Yad Vashem Studies,* 11:1971, 273–297.

For figures for Bessarabia and Northern Bukovina, see also Jan Ancel, "The Romanian Way of Solving the 'Jewish Problem' in Bessarabia and Bukovina, June–July 1941," *Yad Vashem Studies* (Jerusalem: 1988), 19:230–231.

Index

The following abreviations are used in the index: Ukr. = Ukraine, jnl. = journal, org. = organization, newsp. = newspaper, Lat. = Latvia, mov. = movement, child. = children's

effect on Jews during Nazi invasion, 298–
303
Russification of schools, 10
teachers role in, 109, 224
Spektor, Shlomo, 99
standard and quality of living, 83–88, 294
Sternberg, Jacob, 149
streets, named for Jewish authors, 137, 139
Strongin, Leib, 141, 224–25
Sugihara, S., 212–13
Sukkot, etrogim for, 160
Sutzkever, Abraham, 122, 137
synagogues, 156–59, 184–85
expropriations of, 70, 157

Tallinn, 12
Tarbut education system, 28, 29, 30, 90,
91, 95
Tarnopol, 33
taxes, 67, 70, 83
on synagogues, 156
Tchernichowsky, Saul, 108
teachers, 77, 138, 201
brought from Ukraine or Belorussia, 17,
98, 224
Hebrew, 108–109
students and, 106, 109–110
Tellesin, Ziama, 223, 227
Tenenbaum, Mordechai, 239, 253, 303
textbooks, for Jewish schools, 140, 224
theaters, Jewish, xviii, 136, 143–150, 201,
202, 225–26, 294
Timoshenko, Semyon, 16
Tolstoy, Leo, 149
Torah Dissemination Committee (Telz), 106
trade unions and professional associations,
67, 69
Jewish, 28
Jews in, 23
trains, as means of escape, 284–85, 290
"trustees," 71–72
"trusts," 67, 74
Tshernikov, Joseph, 112, 259
Tsintsinatus, Aaron, 259
TSISHO (Tsentral Idishe Shul Organizatsie),
schools, 29–30, 90, 91, 95
Tsisser, Y., 148

Ufboi (jnl.), 126, 134, 138
Ukraine, 16, 79, 80
Donbas area, 7, 79, 190, 222
Ukrainian (language), 10, 93, 102, 231
Ukrainians (non-Jewish), 6, 17, 44, 47,
56, 275
mass murder of Jews, 64
Ukrainization, 47, 57, 63, 95

ultra-Orthodox Jews, 25, 166
Umru, Dovid, 122, 147
unemployment, 78, 79. *See also* labor market
Union of Soviet Socialist Republics (USSR),
3, 14
annexation to, 7, 12, 16.
See also citizenship; Soviet . . .
University of Vilna, chair in Yiddish studies
in, 103, 113, 295
Unzer Vort (newsp., Lat.), 41, 60, 125
urban dwellers, Jewish, 19–20

Va'ad ha-Hatsala (American), 211
Va'ad Hayeshivos (Poland), 30, 201, 202
Vilna (Vilnius), 10, 33, 59, 69, 82, 111–112,
116, 126, 136, 246–47, 302
Jewish population, 18
Jewish refugees in, 180, 199–202
Jewish newspapers in, 30
Jewish schools, 98
Vilner Emes (newsp.), 53, 122, 233
Vilner Tog (newsp.), 117
Vilner Togblat (newsp.), 121, 122–23
Vilnius. *See* Vilna
Vinchevsky, Morris, 99
Vinitski, Yankl, 45, 50
Vishinsky, Andrei, 11
vostochniks, 48, 52

wages, 84, 272
Warhaftig, David, 261
Warhaftig, Zorach, 206
Weber, Hirsh, 136, 233
Weinreich, Max, 112
Weiss, Samuel, 258
Wolf, Leizer, 122, 181
Wolhynia, Jewish population, 18
women, working, 87–88
Workers' Guard (Latvia), 45, 265, 284, 301
writers' association, 130–31, 136
Jews in general, 137
Wygodsky, Jacob, 121–122

Yavetz, Zvi, 41, 245
Yavneh organization, schools of, 28, 29, 90
yeshivot, 28, 30, 152–57, 164, 184, 249
expropriations of, 70, 157, 165
student refugees, 200, 206, 211
Yevsektsia, 92, 224
Yiddish (language), xii, 19, 40, 46, 60, 105,
141, 148
authors, writers, poets, 126–43, 201, 202,
223, 226–34
cultural institutions, 111–114
education institutions, 28–30, 90, 91, 92,
93, 95, 96, 98, 99, 188, 294